WILLIAM CARLOS WILLIAMS: THE CRITICAL HERITAGE

THE CRITICAL HERITAGE SERIES

General Editor: B. C. Southam

The Critical Heritage series collects together a large body of criticism on major figures in literature. Each volume presents the contemporary responses to a particular writer, enabling the student to follow the formation of critical attitudes to the writer's work and its place within a literary tradition.

The carefully selected sources range from landmark essays in the history of criticism to fragments of contemporary opinion and little published documentary material, such as letters and diaries.

Significant pieces of criticism from later periods are also included in order to demonstrate fluctuations in reputation following the writer's death.

WILLIAM CARLOS WILLIAMS

THE CRITICAL HERITAGE

Edited by

CHARLES DOYLE

London and New York

First published in 1980
Reprinted in 1997 by Routledge

2 Park Square, Milton Park,
Abingdon, Oxon, OX14 4RN
&
711 Third Avenue, New York, NY 10017

Transferred to Digital Printing 2007

Routledge is an imprint of the Taylor & Francis Group, an informa business

First issued in paperback 2013

Compilation, introduction, notes and index © 1980 Charles Doyle

All rights reserved. No part of this book may be reprinted or reproduced or utilized in any form or by any electronic, mechanical, or other means, now known or hereafter invented, including photocopying and recording or in any information storage or retrieval system, without permission in writing from the publishers.

British Library Cataloguing in Publication Data

ISBN13: 978-0-415-15944-9 (hbk)
ISBN13: 978-0-415-85212-8 (pbk)

Publisher's Note
The publisher has gone to great lengths to ensure the quality of this reprint but points out that some imperfections in the original may be apparent

General Editor's Preface

The reception given to a writer by his contemporaries and near-contemporaries is evidence of considerable value to the student of literature. On one side we learn a great deal about the state of criticism at large and in particular about the development of critical attitudes towards a single writer; at the same time, through private comments in letters, journals or marginalia, we gain an insight upon the tastes and literary thought of individual readers of the period. Evidence of this kind helps us to understand the writer's historical situation, the nature of his immediate reading-public, and his response to these pressures.

The separate volumes in the *Critical Heritage Series* present a record of this early criticism. Clearly, for many of the highly productive and lengthily reviewed nineteenth- and twentieth-century writers, there exists an enormous body of material; and in these cases the volume editors have made a selection of the most important views, significant for their intrinsic critical worth or for their representative quality—perhaps even registering incomprehension!

For earlier writers, notably pre-eighteenth century, the materials are much scarcer and the historical period has been extended, sometimes far beyond the writer's lifetime, in order to show the inception and growth of critical views which were initially slow to appear.

In each volume the documents are headed by an Introduction, discussing the material assembled and relating the early stages of the author's reception to what we have come to identify as the critical tradition. The volumes will make available much material which would otherwise be difficult of access and it is hoped that the modern reader will be thereby helped towards an informed understanding of the ways in which literature has been read and judged.

B.C.S.

To Colin Partridge

CONTENTS

	ACKNOWLEDGMENTS	xv
	ABBREVIATIONS	xviii
	INTRODUCTION	1

'Poems' (May 1909)
1. Unsigned review, 'Rutherford American', May 1909   49
2. EZRA POUND, letter to Williams, May 1909   50

'The Tempers' (September 1913)
3. EZRA POUND, review, 'New Freewoman', December 1913   52

'Al Que Quiere!' (December 1917)
4. DOROTHY DUDLEY, review, 'Poetry', April 1918   54
5. CONRAD AIKEN, from 'Scepticisms: Notes on Contemporary Poetry', 1919   57

'Kora in Hell: Improvisations' (September 1920)
6. EZRA POUND, letter, November 1917   59
7. MARIANNE MOORE, review, 'Contact', 1921   62
8. HELEN BIRCH-BARTLETT, review, 'Poetry', March 1921   67
9. W. C. BLUM, from American Letter, 'Dial', May 1921   68

'Sour Grapes' (December 1921)
10. KENNETH BURKE, review, 'Dial', February 1922   70
11. HART CRANE, from a letter to Gorham Munson, October 1922   73

'Spring and All' (Autumn 1923)
12. MARION STROBEL, review, 'Poetry', November 1923   75
13. PAUL ROSENFELD, from 'Port of New York', 1924   76
14. ALFRED KREYMBORG, from 'Troubadour: An Autobiography', 1925   82

'In the American Grain' (November 1925)
15. HENRY SEIDEL CANBY, review, 'Saturday Review of Literature', December 1925   84

16	KENNETH BURKE, review, 'New York Herald Tribune Books', March 1926	86
17	D. H. LAWRENCE, review, 'Nation', April 1926	89
18	HART CRANE, from a letter to Waldo Frank, November 1926	92
19	GORHAM MUNSON, from 'Destinations: A Canvass of American Literature Since 1900', 1928	93

'A Voyage to Pagany' (September 1928)

20	LOUIS ZUKOFSKY, from 'Prepositions' (1967), dated 1928	109
21	MORLEY CALLAGHAN, review, 'New York Herald Tribune Books', October 1928	112
22	Unsigned review, 'Times Literary Supplement', November 1928	114
23	Unsigned review, 'Saturday Review of Literature', March 1929	116

'The Knife of the Times' (March 1932)

24	Unsigned review, 'New York Herald Tribune Books', June 1932	118
25	GERTRUDE DIAMANT, review, 'New York Post', June 1932	119

'Contact' (February, April and October 1932)

26	AUSTIN WARREN, review, 'New English Weekly', October 1932	121

'Collected Poems 1921–1931' (January 1934)

27	WALLACE STEVENS, Preface, January 1934	124
28	PHILIP BLAIR RICE, review, 'Nation', March 1934	127
29	BABETTE DEUTSCH, review, 'New York Herald Tribune Books', April 1934	130
30	MARIANNE MOORE, review, 'Poetry', May 1934	131
31	WILLIAM CARLOS WILLIAMS, letter to Marianne Moore, May 1934	133
32	BASIL BUNTING, Carlos Williams's Recent Poetry, 'Westminster Magazine', Summer 1934	134
33	RAYMOND LARSSON, review, 'Commonweal', January 1935	138

'White Mule' (June 1937)

34	ALFRED KAZIN, review, 'New York Times Book Review', June 1937	140

35	N. L. ROTHMAN, review, 'Saturday Review of Literature', June 1937	142
36	PHILIP RAHV, review, 'Nation', June 1937	143
37	FORD MADOX FORD, from The Fate of the Semiclassic, 'Forum', September 1937	145
38	FORD MADOX FORD, from a letter to Stanley Unwin, January 1939	148

'Life Along the Passaic River' (February 1938)

39	EDA LOU WALTON, review, 'Nation', March 1938	150
40	N. L. ROTHMAN, review, 'Saturday Review', March 1938	152
41	FRED R. MILLER, review, 'New Republic', April 1938	153
42	ROBERT MCALMON, from 'Being Geniuses Together', 1938	154

'The Complete Collected Poems 1906-1938' (November 1938)

43	PHILIP HORTON, review, 'New Republic', December 1938	156
44	YVOR WINTERS, Poetry of Feeling, 'Kenyon Review', Winter 1939	158
45	PAUL ROSENFELD, review, 'Saturday Review', February 1939	162
46	R. P. BLACKMUR, review, 'Partisan Review', Winter 1939	163

'In the Money' (October 1940)

47	F. W. DUPEE, review, 'New Republic', November 1940	165
48	PAUL ROSENFELD, review, 'Nation', November 1940	166

'The Wedge' (September 1944)

49	RANDALL JARRELL, review, 'Partisan Review', 1945	169
50	R. P. BLACKMUR, review, from 'Language as Gesture', dated 1945	170

'Paterson (Book One)' (June 1946)

51	ISAAC ROSENFELD, review, 'Nation', August 1946	173
52	RANDALL JARRELL, review, 'Partisan Review', September–October 1946	174
53	PARKER TYLER, from The Poet of Paterson Book One, 'Briarcliff Quarterly', October 1946	178
54	EDWIN HONIG, review, 'Poetry', February 1947	180
55	ROBERT LOWELL, review, 'Sewanee Review', Summer 1947	184

'Paterson (Book Two)' (April 1948)

56 ROBERT LOWELL, review, 'Nation', June 1948 — 188
57 LESLIE FIEDLER, review, 'Partisan Review', August 1948 — 191
58 LOUIS L. MARTZ, review, 'Yale Review', Autumn 1948 — 195

'A Dream of Love' (September 1948)

59 MAURICE H. IRVINE, review, 'New York Times Book Review', February 1949 — 199
60 R. W. FLINT, review, 'Kenyon Review', Summer 1950 — 200

'Selected Poems' (March 1949)

61 ROBERT FITZGERALD, review, 'New Republic', April 1949 — 202
62 ROLFE HUMPHRIES, review, 'Nation', July 1949 — 206
63 RICHARD WILBUR, review, 'Sewanee Review', Winter 1950 — 207

'Paterson (Book Three)' (December 1949)

64 VIVIAN MERCIER, review, 'Commonweal', March 1950 — 210
65 RICHARD ELLMANN, review, 'Yale Review', Spring 1950 — 211
66 MONROE K. SPEARS, review, 'Poetry', April 1950 — 213
67 HAYDEN CARRUTH, review, 'Nation', April 1950 — 218

'The Collected Later Poems' (November 1950)

68 JOHN FREDERICK NIMS, review, 'Chicago Sunday Tribune', December 1950 — 222
69 Unsigned review, 'Times Literary Supplement', March 1951 — 223
70 DAVID DAICHES, review, 'Yale Review', Autumn 1951 — 224

'Make Light of It' (November 1950)

71 BABETTE DEUTSCH, review, 'New York Herald Tribune Books', December 1950 — 227
72 ROBERT HALSBAND, review, 'Saturday Review', December 1950 — 228
73 ROBERT GORHAM DAVIS, review, 'New York Times Book Review', December 1950 — 230

'Paterson (Book Four)' (June 1951)

74 RICHARD EBERHART, review, 'New York Times Book Review', June 1951 — 232
75 DUDLEY FITTS, review, 'Saturday Review', July 1951 — 233
76 HAYDEN CARRUTH, review, 'Nation', August 1951 — 234

77	M. L. ROSENTHAL, review, 'New Republic', August 1951	236
78	RANDALL JARRELL, review, 'Partisan Review', November–December 1951	238
79	Unsigned review, 'Times Literary Supplement', February 1952	241

'Autobiography' (September 1951)

80	HARVEY BREIT, review, 'Atlantic Monthly', October 1951	246
81	LAWRENCE FERLINGHETTI, review, 'San Francisco Chronicle', October 1951	248
82	MATTHEW JOSEPHSON, review, 'Saturday Review', October 1951	250
83	MAXWELL GEISMAR, review, 'New Republic', December 1951	253
84	RICHARD ELLMANN, review, 'Kenyon Review', Winter 1952	255

'The Collected Earlier Poems' (December 1951)

85	I. L. SALOMON, review, 'Saturday Review', March 1952	258
86	G. S. FRASER, review, 'New Statesman', April 1952	259
87	JOSEPH BENNETT, The Lyre and the Sledgehammer, 'Hudson Review', Summer 1952	261

'The Build-Up' (October 1952)

88	WINFIELD TOWNLEY SCOTT, review, 'New York Herald Tribune Books', November 1952	272
89	ERNEST JONES, review, 'Nation', November 1952	274

'The Desert Music' (March 1954)

90	KENNETH REXROTH, review, 'New York Times Book Review', March 1954	275
91	JOHN CIARDI, review, 'Nation', April 1954	277
92	WILLIAM CARLOS WILLIAMS, letter to Richard Eberhart, May 1954	279
93	LOUIS L. MARTZ, review, 'Yale Review', Winter 1955	281

'Selected Essays' (November 1954)

94	NICHOLAS JOOST, review, 'Commonweal', December 1954	283
95	JOHN R. WILLINGHAM, review, 'Nation', January 1955	286
96	THOMAS H. CARTER, review, 'Shenandoah', Spring 1955	288

'Journey to Love' (October 1955)

97 WALLACE FOWLIE, review, 'New York Times Book Review', December 1955 — 294
98 RICHARD EBERHART, review, 'Saturday Review', February 1956 — 295
99 PAUL GOODMAN, review, 'Poetry', March 1956 — 296

'The Selected Letters' (August 1957)

100 WINFIELD TOWNLEY SCOTT, review, 'Saturday Review', September 1957 — 301
101 KATHERINE HOSKINS, review, 'Nation', October 1957 — 303
102 REED WHITTEMORE, review, 'Yale Review', December 1957 — 305
103 HUGH KENNER, review, 'Poetry', June 1958 — 306

'I Wanted to Write a Poem' (April 1958)

104 WINFIELD TOWNLEY SCOTT, review, 'New York Times Book Review', December 1958 — 311
105 HUGH KENNER, review, 'Poetry', May 1959 — 312

'Paterson (Book Five)' (September 1958)

106 M. L. ROSENTHAL, review, 'Nation', May 1958 — 316
107 W. D. SNODGRASS, review, 'Hudson Review', Spring 1959 — 318
108 CHARLES OLSON, review, 'Evergreen Review', Summer 1959 — 319
109 JOHN BERRYMAN, review, 'American Scholar', Summer 1959 — 322

'Yes, Mrs Williams' (June 1959)

110 JOHN C. THIRLWALL, review, 'New York Times Book Review', June 1959 — 323
111 THOMAS PARKINSON, review, 'San Francisco Chronicle', July 1959 — 325

'The Farmers' Daughters' (September 1961)

112 IRVING HOWE, review, 'New Republic', November 1961 — 327
113 ARTHUR M. KAY, review, 'Arizona Quarterly', Winter 1962 — 330

'Many Loves and Other Plays' (September 1961)

114 KENNETH REXROTH, review, 'New Leader', December 1961 — 333

115	NORMAN HOLMES PEARSON, review, 'Yale Review', December 1961	335
116	BENJAMIN T. SPENCER, review, 'Modern Drama', May 1963	336

'Pictures from Brueghel' (June 1962)

117	STANLEY KUNITZ, review, 'Harper's Magazine', October 1962	340
118	ROBERT CREELEY, review, 'Nation', October 1962	341
119	ALAN STEPHENS, review, 'Poetry', January 1963	343
120	KEITH HARRISON, review, 'Spectator', May 1964	345
121	DONALD DAVIE, review, 'Review', December 1964	346
122	THOM GUNN, review, 'Encounter', July 1965	350

Valedictories

123	DENISE LEVERTOV, 'Nation', March 1963	353
124	HAYDEN CARRUTH, 'New Republic', April 1963	355
125	KENNETH BURKE, 'New York Review of Books', Spring–Summer 1963	359
126	PETER WHIGHAM, 'Agenda', October–November 1963	369
127	EDWARD DAHLBERG, from 'Alms for Oblivion', 1964	377

'The Collected Later Poems' (new edition, May 1963)

128	JAMES DICKEY, review, 'Poetry', February 1964	384
129	THOMAS CLARK, review, 'New Statesman', July 1965	385

'The William Carlos Williams Reader'
(September 1966)

130	PHILIP TOYNBEE, review, 'Observer', March 1967	388
131	Unsigned review, 'Times Literary Supplement', April 1967	391
132	CHARLES TOMLINSON, review, 'Encounter', November 1967	392

BIBLIOGRAPHY	398
APPENDIX: THE PRINTING OF WILLIAMS' WORKS 1909–67	408
INDEX	417

Acknowledgments

I am grateful to the University of Victoria for a sabbatical leave during which much of the work for this book was undertaken, and to the Canada Council for a Leave Fellowship; also to the Reference and Inter-Library Loan Divisions, MacPherson Library, University of Victoria, and, by no means least, to Mrs Betty Grillowitzer for typing the manuscript.

Every effort has been made to locate copyright holders, but the editor and publishers regret that it has proved impossible to trace some of them. We wish to thank the following for permission to reprint copyright material: 'Agenda' for No. 126; The Atlantic Monthly Company for No. 80, Copyright © 1951; Basil Bunting for No. 32; 'Chicago Tribune' for No. 68; 'Commonweal' for Nos 33, 64 and 94; André Deutsch Ltd for No. 20 (published by Rapp & Whiting); Farrar, Straus & Giroux, Inc., for No. 109, from 'Freedom of the Poet' by John Berryman, Copyright © 1959 by John Berryman, Copyright © 1976 by Kate Berryman; Leslie Fiedler for No. 57; Thom Gunn for No. 122; Harcourt, Brace, Jovanovich, Inc., and George Allen & Unwin Ltd for No. 50, copyright, 1945, by Richard P. Blackmur; Harcourt, Brace, Jovanovich, Inc., and the 'Partisan Review' for No. 46, copyright October 1939 by 'Partisan Review'; 'Harper's Magazine' and Stanley Kunitz for No. 117, copyright 1962, 1975 by Stanley Kunitz; David Higham Associates Limited as representatives of the Estate of Ford Madox Ford for No. 37, reprinted from 'Forum', September 1937; 'Hudson Review' for Nos 87 and 107, copyright © 1952 and 1959 by The Hudson Review, Inc.; IHT Corporation for Nos 21, 24, 29, 71, 88; Mrs Randall Jarrell and the 'Partisan Review' for Nos 49, 52, copyright September 1946 by 'Partisan Review', and 78, copyright November-December 1951 by 'Partisan Review'; Arthur Kay and 'Arizona Quarterly' for No. 113, copyright

xvi Acknowledgments

'Arizona Quarterly'; 'The Kenyon Review' and Richard
Ellmann for No. 84, Copyright 1952 by 'The Kenyon
Review'; 'The Kenyon Review' and the Estate of Yvor
Winters for No. 44, Copyright, 1938, by Kenyon College;
Alfred A. Knopf, Inc., and Faber & Faber Ltd for No. 27;
Professor Norman Macleod for No. 53; 'Modern Drama' for
No. 116; 'Nation' for Nos 28, 36, 39, 48, 51, 56, 62, 67,
76, 89, 91, 95, 101, 106, 118; New Directions Publishing
Corporation for Nos 31 and 92, Copyright © 1957 by William
Carlos Williams, reprinted by permission of New Directions
Publishing Corporation, agents for Mrs William Carlos
Williams, No. 108, Copyright 1966 by Charles Olson, and
No. 123, Copyright © 1963 by Denise Levertov Goodman;
New Directions Publishing Corporation and Faber & Faber
Ltd for Nos 2 and 6, from 'The Selected Letters of Ezra
Pound 1907-1941', edited by D. D. Paige, Copyright 1950
by Ezra Pound, and No. 3, reprinted by permission of New
Directions Publishing Corporation, agents for the Trustees
of the Ezra Pound Literary Property Trust; 'New Leader'
for No. 114, reprinted with permission from 'New Leader',
11 December 1961. Copyright © The American Labor Confer-
ence on International Affairs, Inc.; 'New Republic' for
Nos 61, 77, 83, 112 and 124; 'New Statesman' for Nos 86
and 129; 'New York Post' for No. 25; 'New York Review of
Books' and University of California Press for No. 125;
'New York Times' for Nos 34, 59, 73, 74, 90, 97, 104, 110,
© 1937, 1949, 1950, 1951, 1954, 1955, 1958 and 1959 by the
New York Times Company; the 'Observer' for No. 130; the
Administrator of the Estate of Charles Olson for No. 108,
Copyright the Estate of Charles Olson; Oxford University
Press, New York, for No. 5; 'Poetry' for Nos 4, 8, 12 and
30, Copyright 1918, 1921, 1923 and 1934 The Modern Poetry
Association; 'Poetry' and James Dickey for No. 128, Copy-
right 1964 The Modern Poetry Association; 'Poetry' and
Mrs Paul Goodman for No. 99, Copyright 1956 The Modern
Poetry Association; 'Poetry' and Edwin Honig for No. 54,
Copyright 1947 The Modern Poetry Association; 'Poetry' and
Hugh Kenner for Nos 103 and 105, Copyright 1958, 1959 The
Modern Poetry Association; 'Poetry' and Monroe K. Spears
for No. 66, Copyright 1950 The Modern Poetry Association;
'Poetry' and Alan Stephens for No. 119, Copyright 1963
The Modern Poetry Association; Laurence Pollinger Ltd for
No. 42, from Kay Boyle and Robert McAlmon, 'Being Geniuses
Together'; Laurence Pollinger Ltd and the Estate of the
late Mrs Frieda Lawrence Ravagli for No. 17; Princeton
University Press for No. 38, Copyright © 1965 by Princeton
University Press; 'Review' for No. 121; 'San Francisco
Chronicle' for Nos 81 and 111; 'Saturday Review/World' for
Nos 15, 23, 35, 40, 45, 72, 75, 82, 85, 98, 100; 'Sewanee
Review' for Nos 55 and 63, Copyright by the University of
the South; 'Shenandoah' (The Washington and Lee University

Review) for No. 96, Copyright 1955 by 'Shenandoah'; 'Spectator' for No. 120; Times Newspapers Ltd for Nos 22, 69, 79 and 131; Charles Tomlinson for No. 132; University of Illinois Press for No. 13; University of Minnesota Press, Minneapolis, for No. 127, © 1964 by the University of Minnesota; 'Yale Review' for Nos 58, 65, 70, 93, 102 and 115, Copyright Yale University Press.

Abbreviations

AQQ	'Al Que Quiere!' (Boston, 1917)
'Autobiography'	'The Autobiography of William Carlos Williams' (New York, 1951)
'Bibliography'	Emily Mitchell Wallace, 'A Bibliography of William Carlos Williams' (Middletown, Conn., 1968)
BU	'The Build-Up' (New York, 1952)
Buffalo Collection	Williams' papers and manuscripts in the Poetry Room, Lockwood Memorial Library, State University of New York at Buffalo
CCP 1906-38	'The Complete Collected Poems of William Carlos Williams 1906-1938' (Norfolk, Conn., 1938)
CEP	'The Collected Earlier Poems of William Carlos Williams' (Norfolk, Conn., 1951)
CLP	'The Collected Later Poems of William Carlos Williams' (Norfolk, Conn., 1950; revised 1963)
CP 1921-31	'Collected Poems 1921-1931', with a preface by Wallace Stevens (New York, 1934)
DM	'The Desert Music and Other Poems' (New York, 1954)

Abbreviations

FD	'The Farmers' Daughters' (Norfolk, Conn., 1961)
GAN	'The Great American Novel' (Paris, 1923), included in 'Imaginations' edited by Webster Schott (New York, 1970)
IAG	'In the American Grain' (New York, 1925; revised 1966)
IM	'In the Money' (Norfolk, Conn., 1940)
IWWP	'I Wanted to Write a Poem', edited by Edith Heal (Boston, 1958)
JL	'Journey to Love' (New York, 1955)
'Kora'	'Kora in Hell: Improvisations' (Boston, 1920), included in 'Imaginations', edited by Webster Schott (New York, 1970)
ML	'Many Loves and Other Plays' (Norfolk, Conn., 1961)
P	'Paterson [Collected]' (Norfolk, Conn., 1963) and the separate Books of the poem, published respectively in 1946, 1948, 1949, 1951 and 1958
PB	'Pictures from Brueghel and Other Poems' (Norfolk, Conn., 1962)
SA	'Spring and All' (Dijon, France, 1923), included in 'Imaginations', edited by Webster Schott (New York, 1970)
SE	'Selected Essays' (New York, 1954)
SL	'The Selected Letters of William Carlos Williams', edited by John C. Thirlwall (New York, 1957)
VP	'A Voyage to Pagany' (New York, 1928)
WM	'White Mule' (Norfolk, Conn., 1937)
Yale Collection	Williams' papers and manuscripts in the American Literature Collection, the Beinecke Library, Yale University

Introduction

'Before meeting Ezra Pound is like B.C. and A.D.'
William Carlos Williams' often-quoted remark in 'I Wanted
to Write a Poem' (1) locates precisely the beginning of
intelligent critical response to his poetry. During the
academic year 1902-3 Pound and he, both students at the
University of Pennsylvania, were introduced to each other
by a common acquaintance who felt that Pound would like
to meet Williams because each was writing verse. (2)
When Williams showed his work, Pound was not impressed.
Williams recalled that 'He was impressed with his own
poetry; but then, I was impressed with my own poetry,
too, so we got along all right' (IWWP, 5). At that time
Williams was reading Shakespeare, Palgrave's 'Golden
Treasury' and the romantic poets, particularly Keats.
Among the more contemporary versifiers he expressed
approval of James Whitcomb Riley, sentimental Hoosier
dialect poet, and the influential Canadian poet of 'Vaga-
bondia', Bliss Carman. To earn pocket-money from his
father, he read Darwin's 'The Origin of Species' and 'The
Descent of Man', but in the three-volume illustrated
family set of Dante's 'Divine Comedy' he got no further
than Gustave Doré's engravings, admitting later that 'The
text escaped me'. (3) Characterizing his verse-writing
of these early years, Williams recalled two very different kinds, the first - 'More Whitmanesque than Keats' -
being 'My quick spontaneous poems, as opposed to my
studied Keatsian sonnets!' (IWWP, 5).

In 1954 Williams wrote to Pound that he had 'deeply
influenced my formative years', (4) but to Edith Heal
somewhat later he observed that 'I always kept myself
free from anything that Pound said' (IWWP, 6). As a
young man Williams was very versatile. He began training
in dentistry but settled on medicine as a working profession, and his long career as a general practitioner in
his home town of Rutherford, N.J., had considerable

influence on his writing and became an important part of the Williams 'myth'. Settling upon an avocation proved more difficult, since he possessed (or believed himself to possess) some measure of talent in music, painting and acting. Before he met Pound, however, he had already decided to concentrate on writing. What Pound did for him, Williams sums up in 'Letter to an Australian Editor', more than forty years later, when he says, 'I am deeply indebted to him for much of my early knowledge of the problems faced by a writer.' (5) Where Williams read Carman and Richard Hovey, Pound then and thereafter attacked his reading, pressing upon him in the early years such works as 'Longinus on the Sublime'; at a later period, he was responsible for Williams finding a key book such as Brooks Adams' 'The Law of Civilisation and Decay'. At first Williams found Pound's verse anarchic in substance and did not wish to be influenced by it, but within a few years Pound's sense of 'the problems faced by a writer' had begun to shape the work of his fellow-poet, both in theory and practice.

Reception of Williams' books by reviewers over the years is both a contrast and a complement to the reception of Pound. Pound's early work was reviewed in England by such writers as Edward Thomas, Rupert Brooke, F. S. Flint and Ford Madox Ford (first in 1915, when he was still Hueffer), whereas Williams was virtually unknown, although his earliest magazine-published poems, apart from those in 'Poetry' (Chicago), appeared in 'Poetry Review' and the 'Egoist', both based in London. As far as public reputation is concerned, Williams was long a-borning, never genuinely secure until the last fifteen years of his life. Pound's reputation, on the other hand, tended to undulate: greeted with early enthusiasm, his stock in London had declined by the middle of the First World War and thereafter, much complicated by his political involvements, it was in both Europe and the United States to suffer from alternating neglect and notoriety before the renown of his last years.

The present collection of reviews and comments on William Carlos Williams' work and career has been culled from a much larger body of material, but one aim kept clearly in mind has been that the selection should represent adequately the actual trends of critical response. In a surprising number of cases nuances and suggestions are provided by ephemeral reviews, which add to the standard critical materials. Few excerpts or essays have been taken from books, which are generally quite widely available, but in some instances such items have been included as crucial either for filling a gap or for summing up

Williams' reputation at a given stage. A small number of
the selected reviews may appear superficial, or downright
foolish, but they have been included as part of the pattern of significant response to the successive volumes of
Williams' work.

WILLIAMS AND POUND

Williams and Pound each had his first book printed at his
own expense, but by the time Pound's 'A Lume Spento' was
published in Venice in 1908 he was already in Europe, and
had become an instance of 'the permanent expatriate
type'. (6) Williams settled into his lifelong home town
of Rutherford, N.J., and from there launched his official
career as poet with 'Poems' (1909). Pound's response to
Williams' book was devastatingly blunt (No. 2) and
includes copious advice as to what 'Dear Billy' should
read. Williams apparently had been equally frank in
commenting on 'A Lume Spento'; Pound had thanked him for
giving the work 'long enough consideration to know what
he really thinks' (7) and had proffered a list of objec-
tives for the poet, which included 'To paint the thing'
as he sees it and 'Freedom from didacticism'. Candid
criticism remained one of the good features of the
writers' lifelong friendship.
    On holiday from Leipzig where he was furthering his
studies in medicine, Williams visited Pound briefly in
London in 1910. This was the milieu described by Richard
Aldington in chapter VII of 'Life for Life's Sake', where
'to get in at all you had to know the passwords – Omar,
"Vita Nuova", "Aucassin"', (8) requirements very likely
sponsored by Pound himself. Williams, in his 'Autobiography', suggests that he had already discovered 'Aucassin
and Nicolette' (which was to have formal effects on his
own work) in Philadelphia student days through his friendship with Hilda Doolittle (H.D.) ('Autobiography', 52) and
had also read 'Vita Nuova' (probably at Pound's suggestion, 'Autobiography', 66).
    These years between 'Poems' and 'The Tempers' (1913)
are probably the period when Pound's influence on Williams
was most formative. He was obviously impressed with Pound
in the poet's role as is suggested by Orrick Johns'
account of one of Williams' visits to Grantwood: (9)

> He described Pound's appearance to us, his silky beard,
> long flowing hair, and unconventional clothes, and his
> contagious, crusading earnestness. There were books on
> Pound's bed, and floor everywhere, in five languages,

as another friend reported to me, and Ezra could really read them all.

Pound was back in the United States in the latter part of 1910 and Williams saw a great deal of him. Through Pound's personal influence Williams' poems were published in 'Poetry Review' (London) in 1912; that same year, in October, Pound became overseas correspondent for the new Chicago magazine, 'Poetry', and through his suggestion the June 1913 number of the magazine included a group of Williams' poems. Pound arranged with Elkin Mathews of London for publication of Williams' 'The Tempers', wrote the introduction and then reviewed the book in the 'New Freewoman' (No. 3). The poems themselves show Pound's influence, candidly acknowledged by Williams, although he adds with a touch of irony that they were influenced 'even more by Palgrave's "Golden Treasury"' (IWWP, 16).

Harriet Monroe, in 'A Poet's Life', provides a glimpse of Williams' positive response to criticism in those days. Writing to accept the group of poems which were to appear in the June 1913 issue of 'Poetry' she offered detailed technical suggestions, for revising one poem and modifying another, and she chided him: (10)

> In Proof of Immortality you are using a fixed iambic measure to which the fourth and sixth lines do not seem to me to conform. They are both a syllable short. Will you please consider this point? I do not care much either for the title of this poem. Wouldn't The Immortal be better, or something else which you may think of?

Williams replied: 'I am startled to see that you are fast gravitating to the usual editorial position'; however, he followed most of her suggestions, but demurred on a point of metrics:

> Your suggestion The Immortal is permissible in the place of Proof of Immortality, but not so amusing. As to the meter in this piece, if you wish to judge it as a fixed iambic measure you are dogmatically right as to the disturbing fourth and sixth lines; but why not call it some other kind of measure?

Proof of Immortality appeared in 'Poetry', but in 'The Collected Earlier Poems' (1951) it is titled Immortal.

5 Introduction

KREYMBORG, STIEGLITZ AND THE VISUAL ARTS

While the young Williams had seen Whitman as a model, Pound as early as 1909, from the vantage-point of his 'world'citizenship', said of Whitman, 'His crudity is an exceeding great stench, but it *is* America.' (11) To this America Williams had committed himself, and that commitment included a continuing consciousness of Whitman's importance as may be attested by the blurb of 'Al Que Quiere!' (1917) advertised (in Williams' tone) as 'a book in which, we venture to predict, the poets of the future will dig for material as the poets of today dig in Whitman's "Leaves of Grass"'' ('Bibliography', 12). Pound, a year or two earlier, had seen signs of an artistic and cultural awakening in the United States and, in his essay The Renaissance, in 'Poetry', 1914, had laid down prescriptions for fostering this awakening. Again he was in the position of advising from afar, but none the less his reaction to Williams' developing localism (contained in a letter included almost in its entirety in 'Kora in Hell' (1920)) firmly reminds Williams, whose father had brought the family to Rutherford from the West Indies in 1881, of his background: 'And America! What the hell do you a bloomin' foreigner know about the place? Your pere only penetrated the edge ...' (No. 6). (See also Williams' letter to Pound of 23 March 1933, at which point in time their squabble about 'murika' still continued. SL, 139-40.) By 1917 Williams indeed knew and felt a great deal about 'the place'. Although Pound continued to help get Williams' work published, in magazines such as the 'Egoist', and in the Pound-edited anthologies 'Des Imagistes' (1914) and 'Catholic Anthology' (1915), Pound's direct literary influence on Williams from that time on was replaced by that of such poets as Alfred Kreymborg, Maxwell Bodenheim and Mina Loy. Other artistic forces were also at work upon him.

As he mentions in the 'Autobiography', Williams was one of the many American artists to feel the impact of the 1913 Armory Show, the International Exhibition of Modern Art, which provoked an uproar of citizen outrage and artistic exhilaration in New York City, and which revealed to the American public masterpieces of Cubism, Futurism and other modernist painting styles. Reminiscing fifty years later Williams still felt the excitement of the time: (12)

> In Paris, painters from Cézanne to Pissarro had been painting their revolutionary canvases for fifty or more years but it was not until I clapped my eyes on Marcel Duchamp's 'Nude Descending a Staircase' that I burst out laughing from the relief it brought me! I

felt as if an enormous weight had been lifted from my
spirit for which I was infinitely grateful.

By late 1915 Williams had become much involved with Kreymborg's 'Others', and the group which was centred on the artists' colony at Grantwood, N.J.; besides Kreymborg and Mina Loy it included, among others, Marianne Moore, Duchamp and the young photographer Man Ray. Many of these artists found a creative focus in '291', the New York gallery of the photographer and editor Alfred Stieglitz, who like Williams was a first-generation American and intensely Americanist, and who had an extensive and sophisticated knowledge of contemporary European art and had been instrumental in setting up the Armory Show. From the pages of Stieglitz's magazine 'Camera Work' and, later, '291', Williams could discover in the theoretical pronouncements of artists such as Gleizes, Picabia and Kandinsky, attitudes and perspectives which undoubtedly affected his own work. (13) Through Kreymborg, also, Williams met Walter Arensberg, the financial backer of 'Others', and joined the crowd at his New York studio; it was a group which consisted mostly of painters and writers influenced by Stieglitz and which gave access not only to Duchamp and Gleizes themselves, but to paintings, drawings and sculpture by Picasso, Duchamp, Gleizes and Brancusi. Stieglitz's awareness of European art was made to serve American purposes. Williams' view, first extensively presented in 'In the American Grain', that the American's failure to sustain contact with his immediate environment would need to be overcome by the American artist's attention to the objects near at hand, was in fact Stieglitz's view and its implications were developed by members of the Stieglitz group such as Waldo Frank, Paul Rosenfeld and the painter Marsden Hartley.

From 'Personae' onwards, Pound's work attracted considerable notice. Williams had to wait until publication of 'In the American Grain' (1925) before he gained any extensive critical recognition, but during the 1920s he earned the attention of several perceptive critics, particularly Marianne Moore and Kenneth Burke, both of whom became lifelong associates and commentators on his work. D. H. Lawrence provided a penetrating review of 'In the American Grain' (No. 17) and Gorham Munson's William Carlos Williams, a United States Poet (No. 19), a chapter of Munson's 'Destinations: a Canvass of American Literature Since 1900' (1928), was the ablest overview to appear in the first long phase of Williams' career, although Paul Rosenfeld's 'Port of New York' essay (No. 13) has the special significance of placing Williams in the context of

the Stieglitz group.
  Pound had provided a potential critical term for use in considering Williams' poetry when he said 'The thing that saves your work is *opacity* ...' (No. 6); presumably this is approval of Williams' denotational use of language, whereby (to cite Pound's essay, Cavalcanti) 'a term is left meaning one particular thing'. (14) Very much apropos Williams' important phrase in the 'Kora' Prologue about 'seeing the thing itself without forethought or afterthought but with great intensity of perception' (SE, 5), Pound's term is also relevant to a much later comment of Williams' where he allies a drawing by Stuart Davis, which was included in the first edition of 'Kora', with the Improvisations themselves, suggesting that both are 'an impressionistic view of the simultaneous' (IWWP, 29). Not only Kandinsky's definition of 'Improvisation' but also his definition of 'Impression' is to the purpose here. (15) Marianne Moore seems highly sensitive to such possibilities when, after quoting from 'Kora', she says: 'Observe how, by means of his rehabilitating power of the mind, he is able to *fix* the atmosphere of a moment' (No. 7). In this convergence we have the link between two of Williams' own later dicta: 'No ideas but in things!' and 'Only the imagination is real'. Not without point does another reviewer of 'Kora' (No. 8) speak of its 'colossally nice simplicity' and guess at 'something partly eastern about it'. Considerably later, in her review of 'Collected Poems 1921-1931' (1934) (No. 30), Marianne Moore perceives Williams' 'wide-eyed resignation' and his 'abandon born of inner security', observations which Williams responds to as 'overwhelmingly important', telling her that his 'sudden resignation to existence' had occurred when he was about twenty years old. All this is the beginning of the long background to a key perception in 'Paterson' (xx, 12):

> ...an identity - it can't be
> otherwise - an
> interpenetration, both ways.

Or, as J. Hillis Miller sums it up in his fine Williams chapter in 'Poets of Reality', 'After his resignation there is always and everywhere only one realm. Consciousness permeates the world, and the world has entered into the mind.' (16)

THE 1920s

In the Preface of 'Paterson', Williams declares it his aim 'To make a start, /out of particulars'. Long before, in an extended review of 'Sour Grapes' (No. 10), Kenneth Burke had noted pithily that 'what Williams sees, he sees in a flash', and he described Williams as 'engaged in discovering the shortest route between object and subject'. Burke draws our attention to the notion which was, in effect, masthead of the first series of 'Contact' magazine (1920-3), jointly edited by Williams and Robert McAlmon. A sense of the need in life and art for 'contact' (of which Burke offers that succinct definition: 'man with nothing but the thing and the feeling for that thing') became paramount to Williams at this time. He asserts that for the artist, contact, 'intensity of perception', is essential in achieving the 'vividness' which it is his task to achieve. (17) Both his emphasis on 'immediate contact with the world' and his Americanism chime in with McAlmon's views, but they also owe much to Stieglitz and to the writings of Hartley (whose 'Adventures in the Arts' was first published in New York in 1921) and Rosenfeld.

Rosenfeld in 'Port of New York' (1924) (No. 13) provided the earliest overview of Williams' work. Despite what Lewis Mumford described as Rosenfeld's 'lyric wisdom', his airy and over-written impressionism, the Williams essay, and indeed the book as a whole, is still valuable, both as a source of the cultural texture of the early 1920s (when Rosenfeld himself was a leading critic) and in relating a number of artists to what he perceives as the central United States 'myth', the failure of man's search for the 'sacred mountain', the Earthly Paradise, a quest in which (18)

> America had interposed. America had made an end of the divine delusion. There was no Earthly Paradise. The earth was everywhere what it was in the Old World, no Hesperidean garden of luscious fruits and dreamy skies and endless summer afternoon, but a realm submitted to suffering and age and death, where men had to labour in the sweat of their brows.

Summing up Rosenfeld's sense of the outcome of Columbus' most important voyage of discovery, these words occur in his fine opening essay, on Albert Pinkham Rider, of whose artistic limitations he says: 'But Rider could not bring his whole man into contact with the object' ('Port of New York', 15). Later he judges of Marsden Hartley that 'The object is never visible to him as an integral portion of

the chain of which he himself is a link' (p. 93). Perhaps
because Rosenfeld wrote more firmly about painters and
composers his essay on Williams lacks the thrust and density of some pieces of 'Port of New York', but he rightly
sees Williams as concentrated on the reality of the American experience, and values his poems for 'the signal of
imminent habitable land they give' (p. 114). Published
in the year between Lawrence's 'Studies in Classic American Literature' and Williams' 'In the American Grain',
'Port of New York' relates to those two works as a pioneer
exploration of the 'new ground'.

Towards the end of the decade Gorham Munson offered his
own overview of the 'United States poet' (No. 19), which
even by its title shows clearly that he saw Williams' work
in a nationalistic context. Six years previously, in an
early number of his magazine 'Secession', Munson had
declared, 'The act of Ezra Pound in 1908 need not be
repeated. The young American can now function in his home
milieu.' (19) In the same essay, attacking the genteel
tradition, stultifying good taste and 'hazy vague states
of mind' then prevalent (Rosenfeld is among his targets),
he sees the necessity for replacing these with the 'stark
hard definition ... [and] ... accurate rendering of
immediate sensations' which he feels is particularly
characteristic of Williams' writing. Perhaps for this
reason, in 'Destinations' Munson undervalues 'Kora',
seeing it as 'a detour'. After an instant in which he
seems to give positive significance to Pound's term
'opacity' he proceeds to make it a synonym for 'obscurity'. Nor does he see point to Williams' cult of 'the
new', which had come to 'Kora' via Marcel Duchamp's view
of the nature of art.

Munson regards this 'United States poet' as 'unmistakably a man who has been pressed upon continuously by
American sociology', (20) suggesting that the 'Kora'
improvisations derive not so much from Rimbaud as from a
youthful phase of the exotic background of Williams'
mother, spent in Paris as a painting student under
Carolus Duran. In contrast, the one European critic
apart from D. H. Lawrence to make a significant contribution to Williams criticism at this time, tends to over-
estimate Rimbaud's influence.

'Musical' and 'verbalist' qualities, and the 'objectivized vision' promoted first in American poetry by Ezra
Pound, are related back to the French symbolist poets by
René Taupin in 'L'Influence du symbolisme français sur la
Poésie Américaine' (Paris, 1929). Seeing Williams as one
of the American group of writers influenced by symbolism
and recognizing the importance of 'Kora' in his general

development, Taupin considers that Williams has the most
clearly American sensibility among these writers, but he
concludes none the less that the American poet has not
given his country an indigenous poetic technique.
Apposite here is a much later comment made, soon after
publication of a new edition of 'Kora' by City Lights
Books in 1957, by Kenneth Rexroth: 'the only important
prose poems in America are to be found in William Carlos
Williams' "Kora in Hell", a sort of prose "Vita Nuova"
which shows a familiarity with Max Jacob and Farge'. (21)
Apart from his Leipzig period, Williams had as a child
attended a French-Swiss school and later added to his
first-hand experience of Europe by spending a six-month
'sabbatical' there in 1924, chiefly in Paris. In Europe
again in 1927, he did not follow the example of the
expatriates, who seemed to have settled there. 'Nothing
from abroad would have the reality for me that native
writing of the same quality would have,' he declared in
'Contact', IV (1922), (22) but evidence of his mind's
availability to the influences of European writing and
painting may be found, for example, in his observations
on Matisse and Juan Gris, his translations of Soupault
and, later, Yvan Goll and René Char. Nevertheless, he
was always clear about his priorities, which are central
to his long-standing quarrel with Eliot (begun on
Williams' side in the Prologue to 'Kora', shortly thereafter to be explicitly supported in Rosenfeld's 'Port of
New York'). Eliot himself had virtually nothing to say
directly about the quarrel, but Hugh Sykes Davies in the
July 1932 'Criterion' greeted Williams' new series of
'Contact' with somewhat heavy irony: 'nearly every contributor succeeds in being unlike his idea of a European
writer'. Long engaged in the issue, Williams had
written for Pound a Sample Critical Statement, published
in 'Contact' in 1921, where he denied insisting that the
American writer should ignore Europe; but he did assert
that a writer's work must begin in 'the sensual accidents
of his immediate contacts'. A possible further dimension
to these considerations is added by a comment in Bryher's
recent autobiography, 'The Heart to Artemis'. Of
Williams' 1924 Paris sojourn she says 'his apparent hatred
of his native land startled even us'. (23)

Apart from Taupin's essay, there was virtually no
response to Williams' work in Europe before the Second
World War, although the 'Times Literary Supplement'
reviewer found 'A Voyage to Pagany' 'an interesting
curiosity' (No. 22). F. R. Leavis, in 'Scrutiny',
reviewing Pound's 'Active Anthology', remarked casually
that Williams' work had already become outdated and

irrelevant. (24) Only Pound's friend and disciple Basil
Bunting, among British commentators at that time, responded to Williams' poetry positively and with understanding, in the American 'Westminster Magazine' (summer 1934)
(No. 32). Such neglect was not suffered by Williams
alone, however; of the major American poets only Eliot and
Pound, the expatriates, received substantial attention.
Conversely, the 'Dial', which during the 1920s became the
most influential magazine of the arts in the English-
speaking world, published the earliest English translation
of Rilke and featured cultural reports from such figures
as Hofmannsthal, Eliot and Thomas Mann. Writing to Gilbert Seldes, the 'Dial's' managing editor, in 1922,
Williams felt constrained to admit that the contents which
most interested him 'are usually by some Europeans'. (25)
Particularly in the early 1920s the 'Dial', and its
publisher-editor Scofield Thayer, was pro-Eliot and
against that 'localism' which Thayer believed inevitably
made American art provincial. Thayer's co-publisher
James Sibley Watson was, on the other hand, a great
admirer of Williams and even wrote editorials under a
pseudonym, W. C. Blum, intended to suggest his particular
respect for Williams.

From 'In the American Grain' onwards Williams' books
(with a few exceptions, such as the small editions published by the Alcestis Press in the mid-1930s) were seriously and substantially reviewed. Almost inevitably, the
most penetrating comment on 'In the American Grain' is
D. H. Lawrence's brilliant piece in the 'Nation' (No. 17),
wherein Lawrence takes hold of Williams' central conception of the 'local' (brought into focus, as is well
known, by Dewey's 1920 'Dial' essay, Americanism and
Localism) and relates it to 'contact'. Lawrence perceives why Poe's distinction between nationalism and
localism is important to Williams, and why he can take the
(what may have seemed surprising) view that 'it is a *new
locality* that is in Poe assertive' and that 'it is a
beginning he has in mind, a juvenescent *local* literature'
(IAG, 216, 217). Lawrence sees clearly, as does Zukofsky
a year or two later on reading 'A Voyage to Pagany' (No.
20), that Williams' own concern is with how to '*begin* to
be American' and that he feels the only positive way to do
it (in contrast with the fearful, puritanical attempt
hitherto) is, in Lawrence's phrase, to 'touch America as
she is', to make contact with the hidden genius of the
continent.

For Williams all economic aspects of the vocation of
American poet were considerably straitened. He largely
paid for publication of his first five books himself.

The next two were limited editions printed in France: 'The Great American Novel' (1923) issued from William Bird's Three Mountains Press, one in a series edited by Pound, and 'Spring and All' (also 1923), as one of the Contact Editions, collaborative fruit of Bird and McAlmon (who had met through Hemingway in 1922). Then, sixteen years after Williams paid Reid Howell of Rutherford $50 to print 'Poems', Albert and Charles Boni published 'In the American Grain' in New York. 'It was my first book by a commercial publisher', Williams wrote later, 'and I was dancing on air' ('Autobiography', 236). The Bonis produced what he described as 'a beautiful book', but he felt that they made virtually no attempt to sell it. Williams was now considered worthy of critical notice, but more than a decade was still to elapse before he achieved any kind of publishing security.

Almost at the moment 'In the American Grain' was published, Williams became friendly with John Riordan, a young engineer who was a member of A. R. Orage's writing class in New York. (26) Riordan proved to be a useful critic of Williams' poetry. They shared the desire to be 'scientific' (i.e. objective) and their correspondence of this period deals centrally with the relationship between 'fact' and 'experience'. Riordan brought to Williams' notice C. P. Steinmetz's 'Four Lectures on Relativity and Space' (New York and London, 1923) and A. N. Whitehead's 'Science and the Modern World' (New York, 1925) (Williams wrote in his copy of the latter, when he finished reading it at sea in September 1927, 'A milestone surely in my career ...'). Suggesting to him that 'when anyone begins to know anything about what we call "emotions" and "nerve adjustments" it will be found that the structure of your poems (written intuitively) is as rigid as any mathematical solution' (27) Riordan is in effect saying that poet and poem are part of a process. 'Behind this idea', Weaver notes, 'were both the Gurdjieffian discipline of observation without analysis or intellectuality in which Orage had trained his students, and the mathematician's delight in the theory of relativity.' One can see why such an approach to the nature of poetry would appeal to Williams, although temperamentally and intellectually Riordan was very different from him. Riordan's remark about emotions almost seems to address itself directly to Williams' statement eight years earlier: 'The world of the sense lies unintelligible on all sides. It only exists when its emotion is fastened to it. This is artistic creation.' (28) Here the 'fastening' of emotion to action is virtually identical with transforming it imaginatively (by 'invention', Williams would later say). Equally important, even a great scientific discovery (such as the Curies' isolating of radium - a 'fact' which was to provide, in 'Paterson', a counterpart to Pound's 'radiant nodes', the 'radiant gist') is 'stale, useless' once it has been achieved. Only the very act of discovery engenders a live emotion. Adapting from Pound, Williams holds that 'a truth twenty years old is a lie because the emotion has gone out of it'. In contrast he introduces an idea which was to become central for the Objectivist group of poets: 'To each thing its special quality, its special value that will enable it to stand alone. When each poem has achieved its particular form unlike any other, when it shall stand alone - then we have achieved our language.' Most remarkable in Notes from a Talk on Poetry is the phrase, 'when its emotion is fastened to it', and the whole range of thinking implied by that phrase. No wonder, then, that Williams proposed to Riordan that they should collaborate in writing a 'Modern Prosody'. Riordan had suggested to him that one's emotions could be measured objectively, and that the world of phenomena has *a priori* existence but is nevertheless part of a system of relativity (as Weaver shows, this is background to Williams' gradually evolved theories of measure, particularly 'the variable foot'). Finally, Whitehead's book, a copy of which Riordan had given to Williams in December 1926, contains this statement on the relation between subject and object: 'So far as there is dependence, the *things* pave the way for the *cognition*, rather than *vice versa*. But the point is that the actual things experienced enter a common world which transcends knowledge, though it includes knowledge.' (29) For Williams, of course, the 'things' too are in some sense 'transcended'. From early in his career he felt that the imagination intensified pre-existent reality, and that from this intensification comes the 'eternal moment' when we are truly alive - hence his view of the importance of the fact, and the process, of moment-to-moment experience. The capturing of the 'eternal moment' in poetry (*as* poetry) he apprehends as realizing 'vividness', declaring that 'poetry should strive for nothing else, [but] this vividness alone, *per se*' (SE, 68) (November 1928). The capture depends therefore on language, and we may relate this to Williams' sense of history - as much a matter of language and imagination as of data - and the consequent texture of 'In the American Grain'.

Another commentator on Williams' work at this period was Louis Zukofsky, whose notational and sometimes sketchy published observations form only part of his critical response to Williams. Meeting Zukofsky (through Pound's

introduction, early in 1928) re-focused Williams' work and
his thinking about it in a specific way. He admired
Zukofsky's early poetry for its quality of being based on
words, language, rather than 'thoughts', and may himself
have invented the name of the Objectivist group when he
noted, 'Your early poems, even when the thought has enough
force or freshness, have not been objectivized in new or
fresh observations' (SL, 101). Zukofsky had found in
Williams (twenty years his senior) the kind of poet he was
looking for. Responding to 'Spring and All', he said of
Williams that 'his exclusions of sentimentalities, extra-
neous comparisons, similes, overweening autobiographies of
the heart, of all which permits factitious "reflections
about," of sequence, of all but the full sight of the
immediate' manifest a 'living' aesthetic. (30) At another
point in his somewhat rambling critique Zukofsky antici-
pates ideas of Edward Dahlberg and Charles Olson, when he
defines the concept of Williams' 'reiterated improvisations': ' ... it is a definite metaphysical concept: the
thought is the thing which, in turn, produces the thought'
('Symposium', 69). Of American modernist poets, including
Williams, Zukofsky points out the characteristic importance of 'devices emphasizing cadence by arrangement of
line and typography' and he further stresses the importance of the visual in Williams by making a parallel: 'In
Williams, the advance in the use of image has been from a
word structure parallelling French painting (Cézanne) to
the same structure in movement - "Della Primavera Tra[n]s-
portata Alla Morale"' ('Symposium', 73). Later, in his
introductory material to 'An "Objectivists" Anthology'
(1932), Zukofsky included 'Spring and All' on his list of
essential reading, singling out poems in which 'objectification is to be found' and including among his selection
his rewritten version of Williams' March (in the closing
section of the anthology - poems by various people, all
'revised' in some way by the editor. Many years earlier
March had also been drastically revised by H.D.). (31)
'I admire Louis', Williams wrote to Norman Holmes Pearson
in 1938, 'but his work is either the end, the collapse or
the final justification of the objective method' (SL,
175). Yet from the beginning he had sent Zukofsky typescripts for comment and we find him in late 1929, for
example, responding: 'Your notes have been of great
assistance to me in revising the Stein thing.' (32) Well
after 1938 Williams continued to send Zukofsky his writings, a prime example being the typescript of 'The Wedge'
(1944), now in the Buffalo Collection, which is extensively annotated in Zukofsky's hand.
    Pound continued his championing of Williams in

contributing to the 'Dial' in November 1928 a piece
occasioned by 'A Voyage to Pagany', Dr Williams' Position.
Reprinted a number of times since, it is not one of
Pound's more incisive essays, its discursiveness conveying
a sense that he (as he says is typical of Williams) 'has
meditated in full and at leisure' on his friend's position
after nearly two decades of public literary activity.
Noting Williams' integrity and objectivity, he says: 'One
might accuse him of being, blessedly, the observant
foreigner, perceiving American vegetation and landscape
quite directly, as something put there for him to look at;
and his contemplative habit extends, also blessedly, to
the fauna.' Following this Jamesian pronouncement he
contrasts Williams (whom, he asserts, is analytical) with
the average American writer, the provincial sedulous ape
who offers pale imitations of what happens elsewhere.
Such writers are 'porous types', easily penetrated, as
compared with the resistant, opaque Williams. And if
Williams is not strong on form neither are the 'Iliad' or
Aeschylus' 'Prometheus': 'The component of these great
works and *the* indispensable component is texture; which
Dr Williams has in the best, and in increasingly frequent,
passages of his writing.' Pound sees Williams, in contrast to the run-of-the-mill genteel novelist of the time,
as 'hurling himself at an indomitable chaos, and yanking
and hauling as much of it as possible into some sort of
order (or beauty), aware of it both as chaos and as potential'. (33) He concludes by suggesting, but not exploring, a possible contrast in method between 'A Voyage to
Pagany' and W. H. Hudson's 'A Traveller in Little Things'.
Respecting both men's work, he was to remark a decade
later that 'Most of Williams' "Life Along the Passaic
[River]" is as good as W. H. Hudson at his best'. (34)

THE 1930s

Reviewers of Williams' first collection of short stories,
'The Knife of the Times' (1932), tended to see his fiction
as technically derived from his Imagist/Objectivist poetic
practice, combined with his supposed clinical objectivity
as a medical practitioner; but Wallace Stevens went a
stage further. Introducing Williams' 'Collected Poems
1921-1931' (1934) (No. 27) Stevens offered the dictum that
Williams' 'passion for the anti-poetic is a blood passion', a remark which was to plague and irritate Williams
because (as he had made clear at the end of his essay on
Marianne Moore in 1931) for him no subject or material is
anti-poetic and no 'special things and special places are

reserved for art' (SE, 130). Stevens' point lodged itself and, despite Williams' demurrers, was to be repeated by one critic after another over the years, much as the little poem This is Just to Say, from this volume, was to become the paradigmatic Williams poem for many critics on either side of the question - for some seeming not to be poetry at all, for others to be a celebration of the physical life, rendered with strict economy but with a high degree of essential 'vividness'. As Williams wrote to Marianne Moore in response to her review of the book (No. 31), 'I feel as much a part of things as trees and stones' (SL, 147).

By the mid-1930s Williams had been publishing for a quarter of a century. Known in *avant-garde* circles in Europe and the United States, recognized among his fellows as a writer of stature, he still had not achieved regular book publication under the colophon of an established house. Published by a group of like-minded fellow-poets, 'Collected Poems 1921-1931' was followed in 1935 and 1936 by two collections issued under the Alcestis Press imprint. 'An Early Martyr and Other Poems', bearing the title-page legend 'BY WILLIAM CARLOS WILLIAMS/aetate suae/ 52 (September)', was issued from a Fifth Avenue, New York, address. 'Adam & Eve & The City' was published from Peru, Vermont. Each was printed in an edition of under 200 copies. Williams described the publisher, Ronald Lane Latimer (or James G. Leippert), who may have instigated the writing of his autobiography (SL, 149-51), as 'a strange person'. An interesting glimpse into the question of Williams publication at this time is provided by contrasting two of his remarks, more than twenty years apart. Of 'An Early Martyr' he grumbled to Edith Heal in 1958, 'None of them - the poems - had been seen; the magazines wouldn't publish me' (IWWP, 55). Miss Heal reminded him of the claim on the blurb: 'Many of these poems have been published in the magazines - almost all of them.' Williams had written in February 1935, answering a request for contributions to Latimer's periodical, 'Alcestis', 'I haven't a damned thing to send you for #3 - not a line of a poem. Everything has been snatched out of my hands the moment it's written' (SL, 152). (Two of his poems had appeared a month earlier in 'Alcestis' no. 2. He made twenty other magazine appearances that year.)

Alcestis Press books did not sell and Latimer apparently soon went out of publishing. Nor were the books reviewed (although T. C. Wilson contributed a rather generalized piece on 'An Early Martyr' to 'Poetry' in May 1936), so there is little critical notice of Williams in the mid-1930s. Right then he was adopting a more overtly political role. As early as 1920 he had contributed a defence of a young radical to the 'Freeman' ('Bibliography', Item C50), and throughout his life his general tendency was towards a socialistic point of view, but he rarely wrote with direct political intention until this period (35), when he agreed to become advisory editor of 'Blast', a magazine of proletarian fiction started by his new-found friend Fred R. Miller, and when he took to contributing to such periodicals as 'New Democracy', 'New Republic' and 'New Masses'. His rather earnest, though cautious, assessments of books of verse by the proletarian Sol Funaroff and the 'Missouri dirt farmer' H. H. Lewis appeared in 'New Masses' and he answered one of the frequent questionnaires of the period in an ironic two-liner:

> What's wrong with American literature?
> You ask me? How much do I get?

As early as 1936, however, he had written to the editors of 'Partisan Review and Anvil' of a 'democracy of feeling which will defeat Marxism in America' (SL, 157). Proletarian writers such as Funaroff, Herman Spector and Joseph Vogel (editors of 'Dynamo') criticized his writing for its lack of social commitment. Looking perhaps from a somewhat different angle, and interested in 'the objectivist method' of Williams' prose, the 'New York Herald Tribune' reviewer of 'White Mule', Willard Maas, says (11 July 1937, Books, 4):

> One gathers that Williams has definite social consciousness, and that he feels rather intensely about labour problems, but that does not prevent him from making Joe Stecher, ex-labour organiser, a strike breaker and a sympathetic character. Williams' ideas are powerful because there is no attitudinizing or false underscoring.

Deep disillusionment, Linda Wagner suggests, (36) pervaded Williams' sense of life then, and certainly his letters are sprinkled with observations such as his acidulous remark to Pearson that, 'It's a world unfit for literature' (SL, 175).

In the meantime he had made contact with James Laughlin, who was to found New Directions publishing house in 1937. As a Harvard student, Laughlin had edited for Munson's 'New Democracy' a poetry section called New Directions. Admiration for Pound's work led Laughlin to Williams, to whom he wrote in the autumn of 1936. At first sceptical of any possible liaison, we find Williams shortly writing to Laughlin: 'Dear God: You mention, casually, that you are willing to publish my "White Mule", that you will pay for it and that we shall then share ...' (SL, 161). How different this Williams sounds from the man H. L. Mencken had written to Alfred Knopf about, presumably scotching a rare chance to break in with a New York publisher: (37)

> Williams' poems in the main fatigue me severely. Nevertheless he undoubtedly has a large following, and inasmuch as most of his existing books are inaccessible, I believe that a comprehensive collection of his work will have a chance. He would certainly do a lot of loud whooping for it himself, and he might get some effective aid from the other writers of advanced verse.

Laughlin brought out 'White Mule' in mid-1937, followed it in a few months with Williams' second book of short stories, 'Life Along the Passaic River' (1938) and, within the year, 'The Complete Collected Poems 1906-1938'. 'White Mule' was, Williams recalled, 'a hit of a day' with the New York critics ('Autobiography', 301). To Richard Johns, editor of 'Pagany', he wrote that the book 'has received a very good break from the reviewers, so much so that it looks like a winner'. (38) His 'first real success' was somewhat circumscribed by the fact that Laughlin, on a ski-ing holiday in New Zealand, could not be reached to authorize extending the printing run (1,100 copies were printed) when it seemed, to Williams at least, that the book might take on. Ford Madox Ford, who had chatted favourably in 'Forum' (No. 37) about 'White Mule' and Laughlin's approach to publishing, attempted to persuade Stanley Unwin to bring out an English edition (No. 38) but nothing came of it.

Williams now got himself involved in a political squabble which was to affect his status and reputation more than a decade later. The new 'Partisan Review', socialist but anti-Communist in outlook, announced that he would be among its contributors. As part of a 'campaign to discourage pro-Communist authors from printing' (39) in the resuscitated quarterly, 'New Masses' repudiated this claim, saying that Williams had actually refused to appear in 'Partisan Review'. Professing to have no special interest in either magazine, Williams yet chose in favour of 'New Masses' and, by letter, withdrew an earlier offer to submit a poem to 'Partisan Review'. Within a week 'New Masses' published Williams' assessment of four pamphlets by H. H. Lewis, which he had reviewed in 'Poetry' nearly two years earlier. Declaring himself in favour of 'labour' Williams offers schemes for cheap publication and distribution of printed matter. Conceding Lewis nothing as an inventor of new forms (and therefore a truly central poet), he admires the 'revolutionary', seeing in such individuals men comparable with the best of the Puritan colonists. For once he acknowledges that, in Lewis' case, it is the poems' content that counts, though their exhortation to political action strictly limits them as poems. (40) Williams made his pro-'New Masses' move just at the moment when American intellectuals generally were becoming disillusioned with Communism. His only further contribution is a review of Funaroff's 'The Spider and the Clock', which appeared in August 1938; but the social circumstances of the time had caused him, at least temporarily, to shift his aesthetic base. His social concern shows most directly in the stories of 'Life Along the Passaic River' (1938), which again attracted a plethora of reviews in New York periodicals, particularly those with a socio-political focus. Paul Rosenfeld, for example, praised these stories as 'a true, sympathetic comprehension ... of the ways and qualities of the poor Poles, Italians and Jews of the North Jersey industrial area' ('New York Herald Tribune', 27 February, 1938, Books, 6).

Social consciousness is seen as a characteristic also of Williams' poetry by Horace Gregory, who compares him with D. H. Lawrence. In the poems of each are 'the same flashes of insight into the essential nature of humanity as it exists in the modern world', hence the social component in their work. Gregory, perhaps more convincingly, approves of Williams' poems 'because they seem to be written from the very centre of a spoken language, many ... seem to possess a classic purity of utterance'. Read aloud, 'there would be an almost kinaesthetic brilliance radiating from each poem' ('New York Herald Tribune', 5 February 1939, Books, 10). But if the note sounded by critics of Williams' fiction was positive, commentators on the poetry were generally less wholehearted. Philip Horton, for example, reviewing 'The Complete Collected Poems 1906-1938' (No. 43) turned Stevens' 'anti-poetic' and 'sentimental' against Williams, seeing Williams' 'objectivisim' as a 'deliberate stylization of the anti-poetic state of mind', but claiming that, while 'overtly' objective, Williams was really sentimental and was attempting to solve his own inner conflict by substituting the impersonal for the personal. Yvor Winters, like Horton an exponent of Hart Crane, dealt in antithetical terms with Crane and Williams in 'Primitivism and Decadence: a Study of American Experimental Poetry' (1937). Eventually to become one of Williams' most ambivalent critics, Winters in this book treats him as a major figure, several times lauding his widely-praised poem By the Road to the Contagious Hospital, naming it one of the 'handful of best poems of the Imagist movement'; (41) yet elsewhere in the same work he upbraids Williams as one who 'encourages in his juniors a profound conviction of their natural rightness, a sentimental debauchery of self-indulgence' (Winters, op cit., 55). At one point extravagant in his praise of Williams' The Destruction of Tenochtitlan, seeing it as 'superior in all likelihood to nearly any other prose of our time' (Winters, op. cit., 63), he suggests at another that Williams is insensitive to the history of language. He includes Williams in a list of the modern masters of free verse, but at the same time points out that free verse is a limited medium. Setting up a contrast between Williams and Hart Crane, in terms of his central motif - primitivism and decadence, Winters says that 'Dr Williams is more consistently excellent than Crane, and at his best is possibly better' (Winters, op. cit., 95), but his whole response to Williams is a qualified one, in the following tone (p. 84):

> Dr W. C. Williams, an experimental poet by virtue of his meter, is in other qualities of his language one of the most richly traditional poets of the past hundred and fifty years; in fact, making allowances for his somewhat narrow intellectual scope, one would be tempted to compare him, in this respect, to such poets as Hardy and Bridges.

Just after Williams' death, and near the end of his own life, Winters' judgment of Williams' intellectual capacities had resolved itself into the acerb observation that he was 'a foolish and ignorant man, but at moments a fine stylist' (No. 44, headnote).

New Directions published several more Williams titles in the years immediately before the United States entered the Second World War in 1941, but these did not appreciably alter the critical reception of his work. Ruth Lechlitner's extended overview of the poems, in 'Poetry', September 1939, provided a contrast to the condescending 'Time' magazine paragraph in late December 1938, which describes Williams as 'predominantly a poetaster' with 'a new-fangled code to express a primitive notion of beauty'. Lechlitner's essay, the first comprehensive assessment of Williams' work to appear in over a decade, sums up rather than provides fresh insights. Observing that Williams had not joined the expatriates she believes that his sustained contact with America has resulted in deepening social perceptions. Echoing Stevens' points about Williams' supposed balancing of the sentimental with the anti-poetic, she lists also his use of broken forms and contemporary speech, his 'clean' use of words. Condemning the 'opacity' of 'Kora in Hell', she perceives elsewhere in Williams' *oeuvre* the influence of D. H. Lawrence (and equates Lawrence's sense of 'godhead' with Williams' 'seeing the whole thing at once'). Feeling that Williams' poems of the later 1930s had taken a wrong direction, into psychology, she judges that 'Williams' treatment of subjects with social import is best when there is no analysis that is not implicit in the aspects of the object viewed. He stops just short of implications...'. Her rather obscure sketch of Objectivist aesthetics seems to reduce itself ultimately to repeating Williams' own dictum, 'No ideas but in things'. Concluding that isolated perceptions are of little value, she sees in the major work-in-progress, 'Paterson', possibilities of 'fusion or cohesion' of 'separately represented facets of the American social scene into something completely observed' (and thus seems to subscribe to Williams' own aesthetic observation – 'without forethought or afterthought, but with great intensity or perception').

Generally sympathetic, Louis Untermeyer in a notice in the 'Yale Review' (spring 1939) suggests that praise for the steadfastness of Williams' 'anti-poetic' attitude has probably done him a disservice because his range is much greater than that. Nervous of Williams' 'explorations of the limbo between poetry and prose', Untermeyer adds (P, 613)

> But most of his experiments in stripped utterance are as powerful as they are native, and some of his longer poems make a new verse out of broken and syncopated rhythms. Like his prose, this poetry is the very opposite of fine writing....

Williams, however, was stuck with the label 'anti-poetic'. R. P. Blackmur, somewhat akin to Winters in his approach, sees Williams as 'attention-caller' to 'the unrelenting significance of the banal' (No. 46), and his attitude is generally shared by reviewers of 'In the Money' (1940), who looked upon the novel as part of Williams' 'rehabilitation' of the commonplace, though few accounts were as urbane as Clifton Fadiman's ('New Yorker', 2 November 1940, 85), to whom it was 'a kind of radio serial rewritten by a serious artist: a succession of domestic trials, triumphs, and tribulations forming the content, but transfigured by Dr Williams' patient and almost surgically

dexterous feeling for the essence of the minutiae of
American middle-class life'. Blackmur's description of
Williams' verse technique as 'unexpanded notation' has
proved fruitful, but his judgment that 'Dr Williams has no
perception of the normal' (Blackmur seems to oppose
'normal' to 'average') should be balanced against the tone
of comments such as Fadiman's or, more seriously, Horace
Gregory's Introduction to the New Directions reissue of
'In the American Grain' (1939). Siding with Williams on
the somewhat thorny question of localism, Gregory perceives him as having a very firmly-rooted sense of the
normal:

> Anyone who has read all of Dr. Williams' prose and
> verse becomes aware of its great ability to grow at
> its own pace. And if anyone is looking for the secret
> of its good health and the freedom it exerts within
> an individual speech and manner, it may be found in its
> determination to 'stay at home', to accept the roots of
> its being and to grow slowly to its full maturity.
> This radical willingness to accept the limitations of
> normal growth has given Dr Williams' work a quality
> that resembles an aspect of life itself....

As the 1940s began, Williams' critical reputation was
about equally divided between those who felt that he was
a poet of 'pure' language, restricted by too close an
attention fo the 'anti-poetic' (the 'banal', the 'commonplace'), and those who saw his work, in Paul Rosenfeld's
phrase, as 'a sort of spiritual prolongation of the voyages of Columbus' (No. 48).

An otherwise unremarkable review of 'In the Money' in
'Time' magazine (2 December 1940, 83) links Williams'
fictional technique to Zola's 'Naturalism' and suggests
that 'Williams makes clear "social significances" which
the authors of "Middletown" can only bumble over'. No
critic has so far explored a possible connection between
Williams' work and the sociological studies of 'Middletown' carried out by R. S. Lynd in the 1920s and 1930s.
Lynd's 'Middletown in Transition' (1937) was drawn to
Williams' attention by David Lyle, the engineer who had
moved to Paterson, N.J., in 1938 and almost at once
begun a copious correspondence with Williams which was
itself to have a direct and crucial effect on both the
structure and texture of 'Paterson'. Detailed parallels
may be made between the poem's method and Lynd's procedures and observations, starting with an obscure reference to 'good Muncie' (P, 18) and the knowledge that the
'Middletown' studies were based, at least partially, on

the small mid-west town of Muncie, Ind. Such, however, is not our present concern. (42)

Another reviewer of 'In the Money', Ruth Lechlitner ('New York Herald Tribune', 17 November 1940, Books 18), perceiving this 'sociological' approach of Williams' as an extension of his 'objectivism' into fiction, saw it as a limitation and suggested that 'the complete social and economic background of the Stecher family' could not be presented by a detached observer with the same impact as 'when he steps in as an interpreter and lets loose his own feelings regarding his characters'. Typical comments on the fictional style are 'authentic America ... firm and uncluttered, sharp and vivid' and 'direct, unassuming ... fresh and individual' but ironically 'objectification' proves to have unexpected pitfalls. Direct and unassuming he may be, but in the words of the same reviewer ('Canadian Forum', December 1940, 290), 'it takes a little getting used to. It is not unlikely that this manner has kept him from the wide public he deserves'.

THE REDEEMING (LANG)WEDGE

Objectivist aesthetics were much akin to those expressed in two 'Little Review' essays by Fernand Léger. (43) Léger clearly saw the distinction between 'plastic' beauty and 'sentimental, descriptive or imitative values'; holding that every object has its own independent value, he felt that the creative act is a mysterious struggle between objective and subjective. The artist's task is to attempt to see objects '*in isolation* - their value enhanced by every known means', thus enabling them to take on a degree of 'personality' never before realized.

An obvious offshoot of Objectivist theory, Williams' well-known definition of the poem as a machine resembles Léger's formulations. A full decade before Cummington Press published 'The Wedge', (44) Williams had written, reviewing George Oppen's 'Discrete Series': (45)

> It is the acceptable fact of the poem as a mechanism that is the proof of its meaning and this is as technical a matter as in the case of any other machine. Without the poem being a workable mechanism in its own right, while at the same time it constitutes the meaning of, the poem as a whole, it will remain ineffective.

He had decided, in the years leading up to 'The Wedge',

that the artist must be both 'objective' and 'sensual', needing the latter quality to 'produce' vital experience and the former to prevent ego or thought from predetermining its structure. Both qualities depend on *where* he is, simply because he *happens* to be there, and on his local idiom, whatever it happens to be - in Williams' case, the American idiom. One Buffalo Collection typescript has alternative titles, 'The Language' and 'The (Lang)WEDGE' (associated with the metaphor of the flower that splits the rock). Zukofsky, in his detailed criticism, recommended that some Joycean prose passages be recast into poems, and thereby emphasized his sense of the poet as technician. The titles proposed for the book were, he felt, over-explicit.

Some years before his involvement with Fred R. Miller, 'Blast' and 'New Masses', Williams had written to Kay Boyle that poetry is not involved in causes, ('socialism, communism') but 'deals with reality, the actuality of every day, by virtue of its use of language' (SL, 131). By contrast, his Introduction to 'The Wedge' contains his best-known statement that man is *used by* language, the poem having a more objective quality and presence than man himself. The Freudian view of poem-making as self-therapy (which he subscribes to elsewhere) is dismissed and a metamorphic view of man offered. Again he rejects sentimentality, particularly the sentimentality of the rhetorical. The poet's constructing of his machine is anti-rhetorical, he makes it from 'words as he finds them interrelated about him' (CLP, 5) and in the resulting composition, 'the intimate form', is to be discerned 'the exact meaning' of any work of art. Promoting as they do Whitehead's 'common world which transcends knowledge' and bodied forth in poems vaunting nature's process (volcanic eruptions, flowers forcing growth through rock), these views in some sense anticipate the methods of 'Paterson', towards which Williams had been building for many years.

Unlike Williams' small press books of the 1930s, 'The Wedge' got a fair number of reviews. F. O. Matthiessen, in a 'New Republic' notice afterwards incorporated into 'The Responsibilities of the Critic', (46) writes of Williams' reaffirmation of 'the belief shared by Whitman and Thoreau that a poem must grow organically out of physical life'. Williams, Matthiessen says, 'can become so happily absorbed in the immediate concrete details that he mistakes their life for the structure of his poem'. Obviously employing the term in a way different from Williams, he suggests that no poem in 'The Wedge' 'shows the formal invention that made The Yachts or The Catholic Bells into sustained wholes'. Since many

25 Introduction

critics (Randall Jarrell among them) have praised The
Yachts for its formal perfection (and some for its marxist
symbolism!) Williams' own 1961 comment on this anthology-
piece is worthy of note: (47)

> This is the one consciously imitative poem I ever
> wrote ... I felt ashamed to have forgotten the American
> idiom so completely. As yet I was not sufficiently
> grounded in the variable foot, though I was consciously
> enough grounded to make me feel that something had gone
> amiss. I was unhappy at the result. I felt ashamed of
> myself. I have never forgotten it.

To return to 'The Wedge', Blackmur expresses much the same
view as Matthiessen, though perhaps more succinctly, since
he does so observing that each Williams poem takes its own
form, with the poet letting 'the modes do as far as possible all the work' (No. 50).

Writing to Norman Macleod in 1945, responding to a pro-
posal for a Williams number of 'Briarcliff Quarterly',
Williams fulminated against critics whom he saw as insisting that he should fit into 'some neo-classic *recognizable*
context'. He declared that the first part of 'Paterson'
'begins my detailed reply ... but I have already been informed that "Paterson" will not be accepted because of
its formlessness' (SL, 239). His anger is understandable.
Since early in the century when he had discovered 'the
wonders of "Aucassin and Nicolette", prose and verse
alternating' ('Autobiography', 52), he had been preparing
the way for his long poem. Signs of its central method
are available throughout his career, in 'Spring and All',
'Kora in Hell', The Descent of Winter, and elsewhere.
The 'Dial' had featured Paterson in February 1927, of
which fourteen lines survive in 'Paterson', containing
several important elements of the long poem: the figure of
Mr/Dr Paterson, the dictum 'No ideas but in things', and
the macrocosm/microcosm ('Inside the bus one sees/his
thoughts sitting and standing' - P 18). (48) After this
date references to a projected long poem and scraps which
have direct bearing on 'Paterson' occur from time to time,
and in a postscript to a letter to Zukofsky as early as
June 1932 (Yale Collection) Williams notes, 'Paterson untouched', as if the work were then in progress. On the
other hand, he told the critic Henry Wells in 1955 that
'I conceived the whole of "Paterson" in one stroke'
(SL, 333).

Some of the critical debate about 'Paterson' is contained within the poem itself and in associated manuscript material. One note in the Yale Collection sets

out the central, juxtapositional or montage method:

> There are to be completely worked up parts in *each* section – as completely formal as possible: in each part well displayed.
> **BUT** – juxtaposed to them are unfinished pieces – put in without fuss – for their very immediacy of expression – as they have been written under stress, under **LACK** of a satisfactory form – or for their need to be just there, the information.

Williams' sense of 'the poem' (a term he preferred to 'poetry') had been much the same when he asserted in 1913 to Harriet Monroe that 'life is above all things else at any moment subversive of life as it was the moment before' (SL, 23-4). 'Words form a new city', Zukofsky had written in 1930. (49) As Dr Paterson and the city of Paterson are one, the man-city, so the creating of the word-city is the poet's 'primary effort' to make himself. Through the word, the *logos*, 'Paterson' is a conflict between Williams and his own experience of chaotic, pluralist America, resulting, as many critics have pointed out, in a number of polarizations: marriage/divorce, man/woman, convention/instinct, ideas and things, art and nature. Not a narrative, but 'a dispersal and a metamorphosis' (P, 10), the poem coheres in a juxtaposition of motifs which invite participation and include debate on the uses of poetry and *ad hoc* musings on the viability of this very poem.

Containing such phrases as 'a local pride ... a reply to Greek and Latin with the bare hands...', the complete poem's opening headnote is a manifesto incorporating a critical attitude to poetry, and to 'Paterson'. Launching the work, Williams states his rejection of expatriatism, parodies Eliot and alludes to 'the craft/subverted by thought' and consequent 'writing of stale poems'. The remaining element in this Preface to what Dudley Fitts called 'an Ars Poetica for contemporary America' (No. 75) rests in the phrase 'from mathematics to particulars'. Behind it is Williams' continued pragmatism and 'objectivity', but also since the Preface begins 'To make a start,/out of particulars/and make them general', there is his notion of 'interpenetration', process. Mathematics was a subject of correspondence between Williams and David Lyle. Lyle's aim became the synthesizing of all areas of knowledge through the discovery of a common language, and this led him to mathematics. We find him quoting to Williams Havelock Ellis' saying that 'thinking is counting', and citing along with Walter Lippman's view of the Good Society, Alfred Korzybski's supposed correlating of

mathematical symbols and the central nervous system as
'awaiting the issuance of a new language from somewhere
out beyond the more recondite Math...' (50) Lyle's epistolary method, juxtapositional and notational, is a chief
source for Williams' formal invention in 'Paterson'.
Williams, in fact, at one point thought of naming Lyle
('Faitoute' in 'Paterson') co-author of the poem, but
eventually ceased even to open Lyle's letters.

Criticism from other writers that Williams dealt in
'literature as something disconnected from life' is incorporated into the poem, specifically through letters from
Edward Dahlberg (P, 40) and from Williams' 'discovery',
the poetess Marcia Nardi (long quotations from whose
letters usurp large stretches of 'Paterson (Book Two)').
Parody of Pound ('IN/venshun./O. KAY/In venshun' - p, 218)
suggests mockery of the medium as well as self-question-
ing. Book Four, section ii, includes the parenthesis
'(What I miss, said your mother, is the poetry, the pure
poem of the first parts .)' (P, 202) and throughout, both
in the 'completely worked up parts' and 'unfinished
pieces' ('Only one answer: write carelessly so that nothing that is not green will survive' - P, 155), the poet's
role is questioned, particularly his role as a mere
writer, for 'to write, nine tenths of the problem/is to
live' (P, 138). Yet the ultimate conclusion is that 'La
Vertue/est toute dans l'effort' (P, 221), or

> We know nothing and can know nothing
>   but
> the dance, to dance a measure
> contrapuntally,
>   Satyrically, the tragic foot.

Dancing a measure seems to be Williams' final justification for 'the poem,' which, as he had said years earlier,
'creates a new object, a play, a dance which is not a
mirror up to nature' (SA, 91).

Undoubtedly, he was of small interest to the critics
in the early 1940s, but publication of 'Paterson (Book
One)' to a degree changed this, although Robert Lowell
could still observe in 1947 (No. 55)

> 'Paterson' has made no stir either in the little maga-
> zines or the commercial press; and yet I can think of
> no book published in 1946 that is as important, or of
> any living English or American poet who has written
> anything better or more ambitious.

Most reviewers reserved judgment on the poem as a whole,

the method of which Isaac Rosenfeld (No. 51) saw as 'a generalizing lyricism with an *ars poetica* as its motive', and Ruth Lechlitner ('New York Herald Tribune', 22 September 1946, Books, 3) as 'a synthesis through the sensual texture of word and phrase, figure and image, in which meaning becomes implicit in the sound'. Randall Jarrell's review (No. 52) is, as Lowell pointed out, a classic instance of the 'shock of recognition'. It is hardly too strong to suggest that this may have been the most important review, in his lifetime, of any of Williams' books. Certainly, despite something of a reaction which set in with the reception of 'Paterson (Book Two)' only two years later, and despite Jarrell's growing disillusionment with each successive book of 'Paterson', this is the moment when Williams' literary fortunes began to take a decisive upturn. In less than 1,500 words Jarrell has provided an assessment of 'Paterson (Book One)' which is both generous and importantly perceptive. Its amplitude is the more remarkable since Williams believed that, up to this point, Jarrell had not been particularly sympathetic to the aesthetics of his kind of poetry. Not merely an *ars poetica*, the poem's motive as Jarrell sees it is to ask and answer: 'How can you find a language so close to the world that the world can be understood in it?' Favourable judgment was accompanied by high expectations. 'Paterson (Book One)' demonstrated more clearly than ever before that Williams was a poet to be reckoned with. If he could sustain this level for the whole poem, said Jarrell, he would create 'far and away the best long poem any American has written'; in fact, adds Lowell, 'the most successful really long poem since "The Prelude"'.

Lowell's view continued favourable when he reviewed 'Paterson (Book Two)' for the 'Nation' (No. 56), but for others the wonder and delight occasioned by Book One began to dissipate and doubts were raised about the whole venture. Williams was by then accepted, in Leslie Fiedler's words (No. 57), as 'a Grand Old Man, a survivor, who saw the young Ezra plain, who dates back to the almost unimaginable heyday of Imagism'. Fiedler goes on to complain, respectfully enough, of Williams' sentimentality, his confinement to the visual sense, his catchall attitude to material, and his flatness; William Van O'Connor ('Saturday Review', 25 September 1948) charged Williams with lack of 'historical and philosophical perspective on contemporary America', while Edwin Honig ('Poetry', April 1949, 37-41) felt that an 'unobtrusive autobiographic turn' (particularly the poetess's correspondence) had begun to disrupt the poem. Williams had, in fact, had difficulty in moving from Book One to Book Two, once stopping work on the poem for many months. Yale drafts show him asserting that 'The Whole Poem is/ONE/ ... ', yet noting elsewhere that it is 'a somewhat long episodic poem'. Presumably unaware of Williams' contradictory views of his own work, Honig, for one, felt 'on the one hand, ... the structural limitation of the poem's method, and, on the other, ... the theoretical uncertainty of its conception', both of which accounted for the disruption of 'the objective symbolic relationships set up in Book One', a disruption caused by the 'depressive weight' of documentary material. Marcia Nardi's correspondence, first intended for use as an 'interlude' between Books, was finally given the position late in Book Two which so many critics have found impedes the poem's process. Only Ruth Lechlitner ('New York Herald Tribune' 27 June 1948 Books) saw distinctive value in the material: 'It is probably the most naked revelation of the modern woman whose creative capacities are either blocked or exiled by her need for love as a woman....'

Another branch of Williams' talent was displayed at this time. Both as actor and writer he had been interested in the drama since student days. His opera libretto 'The First President' had been published in 'New Caravan' in 1936. Now, in 1948, New Directions brought out his play 'A Dream of Love'. Reviews were few and sketchy and it could not have pleased Williams if he read R.W. Flint's remarks in 'Kenyon Review' (No. 60), finding in the play 'a fatal incoherence at the centre' and describing the writer as 'a poet of the anti-poetic'. The following summer an off-Broadway group performed 'A Dream of Love', but for a short run during a July heatwave in a theatre without air-conditioning. Even so, J. C. Thirlwall notes, the production received a highly favourable review from William Saroyan. (51)

As a result of his enthusiasm for 'Paterson (Book One)' Randall Jarrell contributed an able and urbane Introduction to Williams' 'Selected Poems' (1949), but thereafter Jarrell's enthusiasm for Williams' long poem diminished, his notice for Book Four containing the damning remark that '"Paterson" has been getting rather steadily worse' (No. 78); but he was still able to say of Williams: 'he is one of the best poets alive' and to judge 'Journey to Love' (1955), in a brief 1956 'Yale Review' note, as 'a warm, thoughtful sympathetic book'. On the other hand, from Williams' point of view few things can have been more damaging than Jarrell's making public his feeling that, 'in his long one-sided war with Eliot Dr Williams seems to have come off surprisingly badly', and offering the opinion that the 'Four Quartets', compared with 'Paterson', is a poem of great range and elevation. Because of his pleasure at Jarrell's 'Paterson (Book One)' review, Williams had invited the Jarrells to supper, but, as he told Babette Deutsch in 1947, he felt that Jarrell had already 'reverted to his old instinctive antagonism' (SL, 259). None the less, he later wrote enthusiastically about Jarrell's poetry to John Crowe Ransom and others.

A large measure of public recognition now came to Williams, just as his health was beginning to fade and the final, long semi-invalid stage of his life had begun. For the first two books of 'Paterson' and for 'Selected Poems' he received the National Book Award in 1950. Two years earlier he had been offered the post of Poetry Consultant at the Library of Congress, but was unable to accept because of the demands of his medical practice. When opportunity came again in 1952, he was assailed both by ill-health and the prevailing reactionary political climate. From the late 1940s onwards he suffered a series of heart attacks and strokes, fearful from 1947 of the onset of paralysis in his right arm. A month before he was to take up the Poetry Consultancy he was victim of a severe stroke. Two months later, in October 1952, he suffered another, losing the power of speech and use of his right arm. An organization called the Foundation for Traditional Poetry (established in 1949, seemingly for the purpose of attacking American modernist poets) printed in its magazine, the 'Lyric', an open letter against Williams' appointment as Poetry Consultant, listing seven points which seemed to indicate that since the late 1930s he had been a Communist fellow-traveller. (52) Together with his friendship with Pound, then incarcerated in St Elizabeth's in Washington, D.C., this led to an F.B.I. investigation and his being indexed as a Communist by the House Committee on Un-American Activities.

At this very moment his last novel, 'The Build-Up', concluding the Stecher trilogy, was published to few and lukewarm reviews, although Robert Gorham Davis ('New York Times Book Review', 19 October 1952) placed him in considerable company, first by finding 'A Voyage to Pagany' 'remotely Jamesian', and concluding of the book under consideration:

> Gertrude Stein's 'Three Lives' derived from Flaubert's A Simple Heart, but went even further in the respectful objectivity with which it expressed the inner lives of simple people. But for Mr Williams, the repetitions, the understatements, the careful eliminations used by Stein and her pupil Hemingway are still too artful.

Davis found 'The Build-Up' 'too low-keyed and too underwrought'; but it may be said that Williams' portrayal of American society in the early twentieth century, particularly of the individualist striving of the Stechers, forms its own ironic comment on his 'Communism'.

WILLIAMS AS 'GRAND OLD MAN' OF LETTERS: 1951-63

By mid-1951 publication of 'Paterson' according to its original plan was complete. Apart from Richard Ellmann's remark that 'Paterson' 'is the most pro-poetic of poems', reception of Book Three was by no means wholehearted, that of Book Four noticeably more positive (in part because it was then seen as completing the poem). When Book Four appeared in June 1951, 'The Collected Later Poems' and 'Make Light of It' (collected stories) had come out half a year earlier and 'Autobiography' and 'The Collected Earlier Poems' were to follow before the end of the year. None was then published in an English edition, that was still more than a decade away; but in the later 1950s a handful of British little magazines reflected Williams' influence and a new generation of poets on both sides of the Atlantic took him as their master. In England these included the editors of 'Migrant', Michael Shayer and Gael Turnbull (Turnbull later published a moving diary account of a visit to Williams' Rutherford home in September 1958), (53) and in the United States such poets as Robert Creeley, Paul Blackburn, Cid Corman and Denise Levertov. As the text of 'Paterson' shows, Allen Ginsberg had been in touch with Williams at least as early as 1949. (54) A lifelong supporter of little magazines and obscure literary ventures, Williams was gratified and excited by the response of younger writers to his work. Contemporaneously his attitude to some older writers began to mellow. Robert Lowell, who had first been turned on to 'Paterson' by Jarrell's review, received a letter of thanks from Williams (SL, 259) for his own piece in 'Sewanee Review' (No. 55) and this led to a plan for a joint reading in Washington, D.C. Later, when Jarrell was disenchanted Lowell was not and Williams wrote to him, 'it is cheering to me to hear that you enjoyed the fourth book of "Paterson" and that you didn't think I had let the reader down' (SL, 301). Responding to a Lowell letter in March 1952 Williams wrote, 'Thank you for it, it has changed my attitude toward Eliot more than anything I have ever read of him' (SL, 311-13). He expresses on this occasion a sense of affinity with both Pound and Eliot, and takes the opportunity to suggest to Lowell that there may, after all, be a fifth book of 'Paterson', 'embodying everything I've learned of "the line" to date'.

Besides 'Selected Essays' (1954) and 'The Selected Letters' (1957) and a fourth impression of 'In the American Grain' (1956), among the other works published during the last decade of Williams' life were three important volumes of poems: 'The Desert Music' (1954), 'Journey to Love' (1955) and 'Pictures from Brueghel' (1962) for which he was posthumously awarded a Pulitzer Prize, and the Gold Medal for Poetry of the National Institute of Arts and Letters. From London in March 1963 MacGibbon & Kee wrote to Williams that they planned to bring out a volume of his poems. The letter reached Rutherford two days after Williams' death, but before the end of that year the English 'Pictures from Brueghel' (which includes both 'The Desert Music' and 'Journey to Love') had been published. A decade earlier, in 1953, the year Williams received the Bollingen Award for Poetry, Peter Owen brought out a London edition of 'Paterson Books 1 and 2' (an offprint from the 1949 New Directions 'New Classics' edition), but Williams' work had then made little or no impression. The breakthrough for 'Paterson' came with the 1964 MacGibbon & Kee edition (which included 'Paterson (Book Five)', added in 1958). In the meantime in the U.S.A. Williams' collected plays and an updated volume of collected stories were both published in 1961.

The first major step in the building of Williams' reputation appears to have been the systematic publication of his work in the late 1930s by James Laughlin. When the war period brought a lull, another individual, in a somewhat different way, became involved in the process. Charles Abbott, on becoming Librarian at the Lockwood Memorial Library of what is now the State University of New York at Buffalo, planned a resource collection of modern poetry materials. From mid-1942 Williams sent Abbott papers, and eventually the Poetry Room of the Lockwood Library built up one of the two main Williams archives. As early as 1946 we find Williams writing to Abbott about the university's offer of an honorary degree (SL, 244; it was awarded in 1948). A volume called 'Poets at Work' (1948) resulted from Abbott's early collecting activities (55) and includes the text of Williams' Philomena Andronico with a discussion of the poem by Karl Shapiro, who later wrote a long, sympathetic essay on Williams' work which is particularly sensitive in discussing the artistic relationship between Williams and Eliot. Shapiro, even so, could refer to 'Paterson' as Williams' 'large bad poem', while finding his effort to create the 'Great American Epic' excusable because: (56)

he saw the challenge from the beginning and saw it
whole: to create American poetry out of nothing, out
of that which had never lent itself to poetry before.
To do this without betraying the present to the past
(like Eliot) and without exploiting the present (like
Sandburg) and without trying to force the future (like
Pound).

The first monograph on Williams' work, Vivienne Koch's
'William Carlos Williams' (1950), was itself quite widely
reviewed. Richard Eberhart noted that its 'method is
principally that of running commentary or paraphrase, with
more facts than evaluation'. (57) A useful, pioneering
exposition, Koch's book cannot seriously be faulted for
its limitations as a critique, but Eberhart's cavil draws
attention to a peculiarity of much of the commentary since
Williams became a recognized 'master'. Particularly in
the United States, there is all too often, as Charles
Tomlinson puts it, 'inert critical approval'. (58) Perhaps best known of the handful of British poets who have
closely studied Pound and Williams, Tomlinson has reason
to be familiar with the very different attitude of other
British critics. Of the few who have noticed Williams'
work, most have been unable to comprehend, or comfortably
accept, either his 'line' or his language.
Merely passing mention is accorded Williams in two numbers of the 'Times Literary Supplement' devoted in the
1950s to American writing: American Writing Today: Its
Independence and Vigour (17 September 1954) and The American Imagination: Its Strength and Scope (6 November 1959).
Inclusion of Williams' work in British periodicals contrasts somewhat with French (appearances at intervals
from the mid-1920s), Italian (from 1944) and German (from
1951). Idiom, a language and tone of voice related but
not fully shared, has been the chief impediment. The
reviewer of 'The Collected Later Poems' in the 'Times
Literary Supplement' in March 1951 (No. 69) is aware of
the problem. 'Between us and our appreciation of American
poetry there is often the difficulty that we are unresponsive to the subtlest effects of the American language',
he says; but he bases his conclusion, that Williams has
achieved perfection in only one or two poems ('But what
[more] after all does the effort of lyric poetry aim at
... ?'), on the observation that Williams' apparent
detachment and 'almost unstyled manner' convey a feeling
of lack of interest and make it 'hard to say exactly what
his style is'. Quite obviously, in retrospect, the
1950s were the period when it was established (and herein

lies some measure of Williams' particular importance) that American poetry is different *in kind* from English poetry. Part of the difference is attributed, in a long and sensitive 'Times Literary Supplement' review the following year (No. 79), to a continuance of the condition which had beset James and Hawthorne generations earlier, a lack of tradition. Williams is praised, in this consideration of four of his central books, for accepting the burden and taking the view, 'be reconciled, poet, with your world'. 'And yet, for some reason', says the reviewer, 'the serious critic withholds the final cachet.'

'The war is the first and only thing in the world today', Williams had written in his Introduction to 'The Wedge' in 1944. He saw art, poetry, as a sector of that war, and implicitly suggests that poetry struggles to sustain the language of its own age and place (not 'to purify the dialect of the tribe', but to prevent 'bastardization of words'). In a British anthology shortly after the war James Laughlin said of him: 'He is so American in sensibility that the English simply cannot understand what he is saying.' (59) The timing of B. Rajan's 'Focus Five: Modern American Poetry' (1950) is suggestive, one followup of the large-scale incursion of Americanism into Europe brought about by the Second World War. It also happened to be a crucial moment for Williams' reputation in the United States. Rajan claims in his Foreword that 'Focus' (1945-50) had early planned a volume devoted to American poetry, points out that this is 'the first book on its subject to be published in England', and refers to the 'scarcity of American poetry in England'. Five poets - Tate, Ransom, Warren, Stevens and Cummings - are the subjects of a symposium of essays. 'The sixth should be William Carlos Williams', says Rajan, 'and we are very sorry indeed to be unable to include a study of his work here' (presumably because they could not get one). Rajan's own essay, Imagism: A Reconsideration, does not mention Williams, and neither does a 'clean-up' piece by David Daiches, Some Notes on Contemporary American Poetry, which allots considerable space to the early verse of John Malcolm Brinnin. Daiches in the following year (1951) reviewed 'The Collected Later Poems' for the 'Yale Review' (No. 70), pointing at the difficulties, for British readers, of Williams' poetic 'inscape'. Williams, however, is represented in 'Focus Five' by four poems and provides by far the longest answer of the seven poets who responded to the questionnaire. Aggressive and characteristic, his replies vaunt the 'local', snipe at Eliot, assert that 'Our language is our own, it has no relation, except an accidental one, to English' and declare that 'We need a

new prosody as much as we need a new understanding'. By
1950 these had become typical, fully clarified, Williams
positions. In the context of the interrelationship of
English and American poetry, the four-part questionnaire
is itself revealing:

> 1. Is it nonsense to talk of a typical American
> poem? ... 2. Do you consider that the language of
> American poetry ... differs notably from that of
> English poetry? 3. Has American poetry been affected
> by those trends in English poetry in the thirties
> typified by the work of Auden, Spender, Day Lewis and
> MacNeice? 4. Has American poetry been affected by the
> romanticism now prevalent in English poetry ... ?

As Wallace Stevens noted in his answer to the questionnaire, 'At bottom this question is whether there is such a thing as an American.' The tone of the questions, at any rate, seems to assume a dependency rather than merely a difference.

By 1958, Dennis Donoghue could write of Williams, with sympathetic approval: (60)

> I often think that Williams is best understood as a
> grammarian; skilled in reading the signs. He had no
> interest in the kind of thing that interested Stevens:
> philosophy, ontology, epistemology, gorgeous nonsense
> of the mind; but he was engrossed in history, because
> he thought of history as signs, footprints, tracks in
> the mud, proof that someone has lived there.... When
> he saw a footprint he had no interest in the meaning
> of the experience as knowledge, perception, vision or
> even truth: he just wanted to find the foot. If he
> saw a blackbird, he had no interest in the thirteen
> ways in which Stevens saw it: one way was enough,
> given reasonable lucidity. This is to say that Williams was a moralist, not a philosophic poet.

Donoghue's finely detailed essay, while it does not add anything actually new to Williams commentary, is the first full-scale consideration by a serious British critic. A year later, it was followed by Donald Davie's review of 'In the American Grain' (coupled with Janet Lewis's 'Invasion') in 'Essays in Criticism'. (61) Davie expresses admiration for Williams' book, although he appears a shade anxious about its apparent debt to D. H. Lawrence ('I don't know that it has ever been acknowledged'). In 'Ezra Pound: Poet as Sculptor', published the year after Williams' death, Davie describes 'In the

American Grain' as 'Williams' prose masterpiece'. (62) Exegetically discriminating, Davie's book is often negative in its view of Pound, and one surprising and interesting element in it is the number of times he quotes Williams in order to attack Pound. His attitude to Williams' own work seems largely favourable, although in the same year (1964) he began another review, 'The case of William Carlos Williams remains the rock on which Anglo-American literary opinion splits'.

Meanwhile, the British poet Thom Gunn, then in the United States, described Williams as 'one of the most distinguished poets of the century' ('Yale Review', December 1958) but said of 'Paterson (Book Five)', 'I doubt that he would have dreamed of publishing it if his public hadn't acclaimed his recent work so uncritically.' Gunn's central objection to 'Paterson' is comparable with Davie's sense of the lack of decorum in 'the lawless world of the "Cantos"'; Gunn says, 'The real trouble is the organisation of the poem, which is completely random.'

The eight issues of 'Migrant', a small mimeographed magazine published in Worcester in 1959-60, show the pervasive influence of Williams and Charles Olson, and include contributions from Cid Corman, Robert Creeley and Denise Levertov; but their most explicit connection with American modernism is displayed in Hugh Kenner's short essay on Williams, The Drama of Utterance ('Migrant' no. 7, July 1960, 2-6):

> Williams will have no special vocabulary, around which common speech has learned to tiptoe; he will not suffer attention to be lulled by a metric or recurrences; there are not even privileged subjects to which the poem addresses itself, or approved planes of consciousness on which it functions. The Williams poem at the first word takes its life in its hands and launches itself from a precipice, submitting itself to accelerations it does not seek to control, and trusting its own capacity for intimate torsions to guide it into the water unharmed.

In the early 1960s British magazines such as 'Agenda' and 'Cambridge Opinion' published special Williams numbers. He came to be recognized, with Pound, as chief forebear of the Black Mountain movement, to which a special issue of the 'Review' was devoted in January 1964. A British scholar, Mike Weaver, has written in 'William Carlos Williams: the American Background' (1971) the most penetrating study of Williams' intellectual roots so far to appear.

Introduction

A common critical attitude to Williams is that his poetic practice is much superior to his poetics or theorizings about the nature of poetry and language ('The play of ideas ... was not familiar ground to him', says Matthew Josephson, reviewing the 'Autobiography' (No. 82)), but the reviewers of 'Selected Essays' (1954), where much of the theory is to be found, in general saw the book as a vital part of the Williams canon. Selden Rodman, for example ('New York Times Book Review', 7 November 1954), regards some of the essays as having the same intensity and importance as 'In the American Grain'. Williams' 'critical ideas are coherent, alive and brisk', says Richard Eberhart ('Saturday Review', 20 November 1954, 38), and the essays were regarded as valuable also (with the 'Autobiography', 'Selected Letters' and 'I Wanted to Write a Poem', all from the 1950s) in setting Williams in the context of his times, alongside his major contemporaries.

The great technical interest of the last fifteen years or so of his life was *measure*, eventually 'the variable foot', a concept anticipated long before in a sentence of 'Kora in Hell': 'A thing known passes out of the mind into the muscles.' Kenneth Rexroth, reviewing 'The Desert Music' (No. 90), attested to Williams' achievement in metrics: 'his poetic line is welded to American speech like muscle to bone'. Structure, not subject-matter, Williams often said, is the poet's contact with reality, the one way he can modify it. 'The only reality we can know is **MEASURE**' (SE, 283), he wrote in The Poem as a Field of Action, when he was working on 'Paterson' Books Three and Four. Nearly twenty years earlier he had said, 'Pound's line is the movement of his thought' (SE, 108). Such declarations' implied relativity and organicism are further adumbrated in the well-known 1954 letter to Eberhart giving samples of 'the variable foot' (No. 92). Like other pronouncements such as the late, long and uncollected prose piece Measure, (63) this shows the affinity between Williams' 'variable foot' and Olson's conception of a 'breath unit' or 'cadence unit', first published in Projective Verse (1950), and so impressive to Williams that he allowed it to usurp half a chapter of 'Autobiography'. (64) Both men would hold that an American poet, employing the American idiom, will have American speech rhythms. But the whole notion of measure as 'variable foot' continues to be technically elusive, as Alan Stephens shows (No. 119) in an acute discussion of 'Pictures from Brueghel' (see, also, for example, John Ciardi - No. 91). Williams' sense of the dependence of measure on the individual's psycho-physical nature (even while he may be seen as part of a larger 'process') lends some credence to Roy Harvey Pearce's finding, in 'The Continuity of American Poetry' (Princeton, 1961), that his poetry grew increasingly subjective. Eberhart, to whom Williams had taken the trouble to explain himself, takes up the question of 'measure' in reviewing 'Journey to Love', but he straddles the problem with generalizations, noting that the verse line is 'based on the natural rhythms of breathing', but adding, 'I do not mean that there is not a great deal of strategy' (No. 98).

Hugh Kenner finds special value in 'Selected Letters' for the passages on metrics (No. 103), and says: 'What Williams has been labouring to achieve since 1912, it turns out, is simply this separation of the strict musical form from the free pulse of the words'; for Williams, as he had written to Eberhart, the poem's 'music' is the continuing relation between the poet and the world. Direct connection between measure and morality is made in his On Measure - Statement for Cid Corman: 'The very grounds of our beliefs have altered. We do not live that way any more ... ' (SE, 337). Late in his career, especially as shown by 'Paterson (Book Five)' and the last three poetry collections, for him reality is centred in interaction of the human being with the world he lives in, and in a sense of reciprocity between artist and work. Such had been the view of the Stieglitz group fifty years earlier. Cid Corman, editor of 'Origin' and a Pound-Williams disciple, recognized this quality also in reviewing 'The Farmers' Daughters', Williams' last and fullest collection of short stories. Praising Williams' language as 'at once more convincing and accurate' than Hemingway's, he identifies it as 'The living speech of a time, a place, a people. All elements of society come to his feast ...' ('Massachusetts Review', winter 1962, 321-2).

When Williams died the American valedictories were overwhelmingly positive in tone, for in the last years his reputation continued the upward climb begun around 1950. An acute point made by Josephine Jacobsen ('Commonweal', 10 May 1963, 191) may show the cause. Williams' poetry, she says, 'fuses two forces often viewed as hostile: the leap of joy and the sense of moral structure'. Back in the 1930s, attempting to rebut Philip Horton's 'New Republic' review of 'The Complete Collected Poems 1906-1938', Williams had said, 'If he hadn't had Stevens to teach him how to look crookedly he wouldn't have anything at all to say.' (65) Ironically, the most important obituary piece, Kenneth Burke's long and sensitive summation first published in the 'New York Review of Books' (No. 125), is partially an essay in making Stevens' view fit. Addressing himself to the special character of Williams' 'objectivism', Burke finds it not so much objectivity as pragmatism. 'To read his books is to find him warmly there', he says, emphasizing the 'strongly personal' character of Williams' work. Part of this character, derived from Williams' profession of medicine, endows the notion of 'contact' with particular physicality. Another part is Williams' intense interest 'in the sheer survival of things' and, complementing it, his tough sense of man's self-destructiveness and feeling of 'the poignancy of what is lost'. 'Stevens meant by sentiment any personal identification with an object, as distinct from an appreciation of it in its pure singularity', Burke says, finding in Williams' poems this latter kind of sentimentality in the form of a tendency to discover 'personality' in things, 'a flash of drama'. Taking up Stevens' description of Williams as 'a kind of Diogenes of American poetry', Burke goes beyond the picture of him as a poet of beginnings, a settler on 'new ground'. Like Diogenes, he suggests, Williams wrote for an ailing culture, but as diagnostician, and perhaps physician.

Since Williams' death there has been a steady flow of books (see bibliography) and dissertations, and a spate of articles, on his work. His poetry and prose, as Wallace's 'Bibliography' records, have been translated and published in more than a dozen languages in Europe and Asia. Among the obituaries was Paul Trédant's eulogy in 'Nouvelles littéraires' (14 March 1963) and not too long delayed was the extended assessment by his Italian translator, the poet Vittorio Sereni ('Prairie Schooner', winter 1964-5). A German study of Williams' European reception, eventually published as part of a book, first appeared in two parts in the 'Jahrbuch für Amerikastudien'. Hans Galinsky's William Carlos Williams: Eine vergleichende Studie zur Aufnahme seines Werkes in Deutschland, England und Italien (1912-1965) (vol. XI, 1966, 96-175 and vol. XII, 1967, 167-205) (66) suggests that Williams' reputation had grown steadily over the years and is now secure. Critical appraisals have also been made in French, Dutch and Norwegian and several essays on Williams have appeared in the Japanese periodical 'Oberon'.

Sereni emphasizes Williams' organicism, declaring that his 'poetry is not a *poetry of ideas*, but poetry that begets ideas out of things'. Surveying critiques of modern American poetry, Kingsley Weatherhead in 'American Literary Scholarship 1968', deplores the circumstance that this very shibboleth seems to generate most Williams criticism. However, the best commentary goes fruitfully beyond it. Weaver, importantly, shows the eclecticism of

Williams' intellectual sources and provides thereby the
means to a wider range of critical approaches. Jerome
Mazzaro, in his 'William Carlos Williams: the Later Poems'
(Ithaca, N.Y., 1973), a useful counter-position to Hillis
Miller based on 'Williams' underlying view of a concinnity
of intellect and body', (67) inculcates brief synopses of
much of the related criticism. Joseph N. Riddel's recent
able (if somewhat wordy) exploration, 'The Inverted Bell'
(Baton Rouge, La, 1974), begins from the predictable point
(pp. xvi-xvii):

> Williams' 'no ideas but in things' is well on its way
> to becoming a scandal of literary criticism, if for no
> other reason than that it tempts one to scrutinize it
> extrapoetically and metaphysically as an objectivist
> response to subjectivism. Yet, the phrase radiates
> through the Williams canon.... It is an attempt,
> poetically yet rhetorically, to bring into question
> the field of ordinary logical discourse ... an attempt,
> characteristic of modern critical thought, to rescue
> poetry as a privileged language.

Riddel remarks the pitfall of accepting objectivist aesthetics as the *means* of his own investigation, and consciously seeks to test both Williams' theories and his poems in what he terms 'a philosophical (or at least, abstract) discourse' involving the thought of Nietzsche, Heidegger, Georges Bataille, Jacques Derrida and French structuralism. We are a long way from Williams' 'colossally nice simplicity' and Yvor Winters' characteristic charge that Williams 'did not know what the intellect was'! Apart from Dijkstra's 'The Hieroglyphics of a New Speech' (Princeton, N.J., 1969), an examination of the influence of Cubism and of Alfred Stieglitz and his followers on Williams' early work, most of the remaining books are either exegeses of 'Paterson' or overviews of the Williams canon, with Breslin's 'William Carlos Williams: an American Artist' (New York, 1970) as perhaps the best single-volume introduction.

Of the numerous articles since Williams' death (Linda Welshimer Wagner, for example, author of two book-length studies of Williams, has published at least fifteen articles, chiefly of explication), among those which exemplify a widening of approach to their subject may be cited Anthony Libby's 'Claritas': William Carlos Williams' Epiphanies ('Criticism', vol. XXIV, winter 1972, 22-31). Libby begins with the warning that: 'There is nothing so complex as Williams' early "imagist" simplicity, and nothing so dangerously alluring to the philosophical

critic. The poems require little interpretation, but
invite extensive theorizing....' Shifting away from the
customary explicatory methods applied, based on Imagism
and *haiku*, he interprets Williams' poems in terms of
Joycean epiphanies, to demonstrate 'a rather surprising
rigorous process of logical analysis'.

No critic has so far assumed the pre-eminence in Williams criticism which Hugh Kenner has in relation to
Pound. Perhaps more generatively than any other,
J. Hillis Miller in 'Poets of Reality', noting that
'Williams' work expresses, quietly and without fanfare,
a revolution in human sensibility' (p. 288), and seeing
his sudden resignation' as the poet's starting-point on
the journey towards the realm of his mature work, 'a space
both subjective and objective, a region of copresence in
which anywhere is everywhere' (p. 288), points a direction
for future commentary. To date, the best of that commentary includes Miller's own Williams' 'Spring and All' and
the Progress of Poetry ('Daedalus', vol. IC, no. 2, spring
1970, 405-34), which relates the book to Nietzsche's
'deconstruction of metaphysics', at the same time noting
that in it Williams (who asked, rhetorically, 'Who am I
but my own critic?' - SA, 36) contains self-interpretation
(making a similar point, Riddel applies it to Williams'
work generally). Referring to his own discussion of
Williams' theory of naming in 'Poets of Reality', Miller
suggests that for Williams creating a poem is creating a
second universe parallel to phenomenal reality and at the
same time, paradoxically, part of it.

Miller convincingly asserts that 'Spring and All' is an
integral work, its value diminished by the printing of the
poems only in 'The Collected Earlier Poems'. A complete
text is included in 'Imaginations' (New York, 1970), a
gathering by Webster Schott of Williams' short early prose
pieces. Widely and respectfully reviewed, the book's
reception seems to indicate a falling away from the high
peak of enthusiasm for Williams' work, but also that he is
widely accepted as an established major figure. No *flaneur* among the arts, Williams, as Harry Levin says in his
sensitive introduction to the new edition of 'A Voyage to
Pagany' (New York, 1970), 'was interested not in making an
impression but in registering an impact'. Plenty of evidence shows that he has done both.

During the mid-1970s, Williams' literary reputation has
settled down to more or less routine acceptance. He is a
major figure in the pantheon of American poets; those
poets following on the modernist movement owe a central
debt to him, but that mysterious excitement which attaches
to a writer when he is the immediate vital influence of

the moment appears, for the time at least, to have moved on from him. For those to whom his work is, none the less, important, such influence right now seems to be vested in the work of Pound, or the Pound-Williams followers, Olson and Zukofsky.

Reed Whittemore's 'authorized' biography, 'William Carlos Williams: Poet from Jersey', (68) has not had the impact it might have had if published ten years earlier. Whittemore's book is, of course, indispensable, but it sets up an odd barrier between reader and subject. Williams' life is 'unusually accessible', so Whittemore declares in his second paragraph, and this may be a clue to why one is uneasy about the biography. Williams' 'Autobiography' is an important revelation of the texture of his mind or, one might say, of the process of his life. Whittemore seems to have tried to emulate, or respond in kind to, his subject's style and tone. We remain in need of an objective account of Williams' life, which firmly establishes facts and dates, bodying them forth without feeling impelled to do so in some version of 'the American idiom'. Much-awaited in this sphere are Williams' collected letters, upon which Emily Mitchell Wallace has been working for a good number of years.

Two other items remain to be mentioned in a consideration of the growth of Williams' literary reputation. Paul L. Mariani, in 'William Carlos Williams: the Poet and His Critics', (69) actually summarizes and comments, item by item, on over fifty years of Williams criticism. At times over-eager and pontifical, the book is at others incisive in judgment, though it is a moot question whether such compilations are a sufficient substitute for the actual documents.

Founded in the autumn of 1975, the 'William Carlos Williams Newsletter' is published twice a year. (70) Running to an average of just over twenty pages per issue, it is appropriately modest in scope but meticulous in presentation, typically containing brief notes and commentaries on aspects of Williams' work, and generally incisive reviews and letters. Despite Williams' lack of enthusiasm for universities, he might well have seen this small publication (especially given his remarkable championing of the 'little magazine') as a fitting custodian of his literary reputation.

NOTES

1   'I Wanted to Write a Poem', edited by Edith Heal (Boston, 1958), 5.

2 Emily Mitchell Wallace, Pound and Williams at the University of Pennsylvania: Men of No Name and with a Fortune to Come, 'Pennsylvania Review', spring 1967, 41-53.
3 'The Autobiography of William Carlos Williams' (New York, 1951), 15.
4 'The Selected Letters of William Carlos Williams', edited by John C. Thirlwall (New York, 1957), 324.
5 'Briarcliff Quarterly', vol. III, no. ii, October 1946 (special Williams number), 205.
6 The phrase is from Gorham B. Munson, The Mechanics for a Literary 'Secession', 'S4N', year 4, November 1922, n.p.
7 'The Letters of Ezra Pound 1907-1941', edited by D. D. Paige (New York, 1950), 3-7; letter of 21 October 1908.
8 Richard Aldington, 'Life for Life's Sake' (New York, 1941), 100.
9 Orrick Johns, 'The Time of Our Lives' (New York, 1937), 225. Johns' remark that Williams 'had just returned from London' and that he 'surprised us by recounting the feud that had grown up between Amy Lowell and Pound' compresses time considerably, Williams' return preceded by several years the Lowell-Pound quarrel of the summer of 1914.
10 Harriet Monroe, 'A Poet's Life' (New York, 1938), 268-72. Williams' side of the correspondence is also in SL, 23-5 and 26. The two versions differ slightly in textual detail.
11 Ezra Pound, What I Feel about Walt Whitman, 'Ezra Pound: Selected Prose 1909-1965', edited by William Cookson (London, 1973), 115.
12 William Carlos Williams, Recollections, 'Art in America', vol. LI, 1 February 1963, 52, and Bram Dijkstra, 'The Hieroglyphics of a New Speech: Cubism, Stieglitz and the Early Poetry of William Carlos Williams' (Princeton, N.J., 1969).
13 Both Mike Weaver, in 'William Carlos Williams: the American Background' (London, 1971), and Dijkstra give detailed background. Each points out that excerpts from Kandinsky's 'On the Spiritual in Art' appeared in 'Camera Work' in 1912, but Weaver suggests that Williams read the key passages (those which particularly influenced the technique of 'improvisation' used in 'Kora in Hell') when they appeared in 'Blast' in June 1914. Weaver, op. cit. 38.
14 'Literary Essays of Ezra Pound', edited with an introduction by T. S. Eliot (London, 1954), 185.
15 Wassily Kandinsky, 'Concerning the Spiritual in Art',

edited by Robert Motherwell (New York, 1947), 77.
Weaver (op. cit., 39) quotes the definitions; also to
the point is Dijkstra's discussion of Robert Delaunay
and Simultaneism, 68-72.
16 J. Hillis Miller, 'Poets of Reality' (Cambridge, Mass., 1966), 287.
17 McAlmon had been a flyer on the West Coast of the United States and associate editor of an aviation magazine, the 'Ace'. Greatly exhilarated by flying, he also felt deeply each renewed contact with the earth. In addition to the usual significance given to the title of the Williams-McAlmon 'Contact' it is worth noting the command word 'Contact!', used in the early days of flight for starting the aircraft's engine, and suggesting electrical connections and, of course, flight (see, for example, 'Aviation and Space Dictionary' edited by E. J. Gentle and C. E. Chapel (Los Angeles, 4th edition, 1961), 102).
18 Paul Rosenfeld, 'Port of New York' (Urbana, Ill., 1966), 7.
19 Munson, The Mechanics for a Literary 'Secession', n.p.
20 Gorham B. Munson, 'Destinations: A Canvass of American Literature Since 1900' (New York, 1928), 107.
21 Kenneth Rexroth, The Influence of French Poetry on American, 'Assays' (New York, 1961), 153. Written in 1958, the essay introduced a selection of French translations of American poems in 'Europe' (Paris), February-March 1959. Six of Williams' poems were included.
22 'Selected Essays of William Carlos Williams' (New York, 1954), 37.
23 Bryher [Annie Winifred Ellerman], 'The Heart to Artemis: A Writer's Memoirs' (New York, 1962), 218.
24 'Scrutiny', vol. 2, 1933-4, 300.
25 William R. Wasserstrom, 'The Time of the Dial' (Syracuse, N.Y., 1963), 93. This note to Seldes was sent in November 1922. See also Wasserstrom, op. cit., 75, 100.
26 Weaver, op. cit., 46-50.
27 Letter from Riordan to Williams, 25 July 1926 (Buffalo Collection).
28 Notes from a Talk on Poetry, 'Poetry', vol. XIV, July 1919, 211-16.
29 A. N. Whitehead, 'Science and the Modern World' (New York, 1948: 1st edition 1925), 128-9. Paterson was published in the 'Dial' two months after Riordan wrote this letter to Williams.
30 Louis Zukofsky, American Poetry 1920-1930, 'Symposium', vol. II, 1931, 81. The essay is reprinted in

Introduction

Zukofsky's 'Prepositions' (London, 1967), 129-43.
31   Buffalo Collection contains a typescript of March edited by H.D. with wholesale excisions, and the poem divided by her into numbered sections. Williams followed some, but not all, of her suggestions. A note in his hand (presumably to the librarian, Charles D. Abbott) reads: 'Here's an old script (*not* original script) but corrected and "purified" by H.D. in London - perhaps in 1913 or so. W. C. Williams.'
32   Unpublished letter, Williams to Zukofsky, dated 3 November 1929 (Yale Collection). The reference is presumably to Williams' essay on Gertrude Stein, which was first published in the opening number of 'Pagany' (January-March 1930).
33   Ezra Pound, Dr Williams' Position, 'Dial', vol. LXXXV (November 1928), 395-404, reprinted in 'Literary Essays of Ezra Pound', edited with an introduction by T. S. Eliot (London, 1954), 389-98.
34   Ezra Pound, brief review-notice, 'Townsman', vol. I, no. 3, July 1938. 30.
35   An apparent exception is the Democratic Party Poem mentioned by Weaver, op. cit., 90, but not listed in 'Bibliography'.
36   Linda Welshimer Wagner, 'The Poems of William Carlos Williams' (Middletown, Conn., 1964), 26.
37   'Letters of H. L. Mencken', edited by Guy J. Forgue (New York, 1961), 369.
38   Letter of 25 June 1937, included in 'Return to Pagany: The History, Correspondence and Selections from a Little Magazine 1929-1932', edited by Stephen Halpert, with Richard Johns (Boston, 1969), 512. Williams thanks Johns for his 'critical acumen in suggesting that I leave out another element in the story'.
39   James Burkhart Gilbert, 'Writers and Partisans: A History of Literary Radicalism in America' (New York, 1968), 193, 197. Williams' two letters, dated 8 September 1937 and 16 November of the same year are in the 'Partisan Review' papers, Rutgers University, N.J.
40   An American Poet, 'New Masses', 23 November 1937, 17.
41   From the text in 'In Defense of Reason' (London, 1960), 49.
42   The Lynds' studies are briefly mentioned by Mike Weaver, op. cit., 127. A more extended mention, following Weaver, is made by Joseph N. Riddel in 'The Inverted Bell: Modernism and the Counterpoetics of William Carlos Williams' (Baton Rouge, La., 1974), 121, 122.

43 Fernand Léger, The Aesthetics of the Machine, 'Little Review', no. IX, nos 3 and 4 (1923-4), 45-9, 55-8, and A New Realism - Object, 'Little Review', vol. XI, no. 2 (winter 1926). Weaver, who does not mention these articles, notes that Williams saw Léger's film 'Ballet Mécanique' in New York in May 1926. He includes it among 'the principal plastic-mechanical analogies with which Williams was familiar' (op. cit., 69).
44 Published in an edition of 380 copies, 'The Wedge' was Williams' only book during the years of United States participation in the Second World War. Williams wrote to McAlmon in September 1943 that Laughlin 'said he'd like to do a book but that he also could not get the paper for it' (SL, 218). A number of letters of the time suggest that Williams tried the New York publishers, but without success ('Bibliography', 54-5).
45 'Poetry', vol. XLIV, May 1934, 220-5.
46 F. O. Matthiessen, 'The Responsibilities of the Critic' (New York, 1952), 129-30.
47 Letter to Thomas Edward Francis dated 4 January 1961 (Yale Collection). The Yachts was first published in 'New Republic', 8 May 1935, 364.
48 An unpublished letter dated 11 June 1914 to Williams' early friend Viola Baxter Jordan contains a passing remark about 'Handsome Mr. Towne - or any other city ... ' (Yale Collection).
49 Louis Zukofsky, 'A 1-12' (London, 1967), A 6, 30.
50 Letter from David Lyle to Williams dated 1 December 1938 (expanded 9 April 1939), 6 (Yale Collection).
51 John C. Thirlwall, Notes on William Carlos Williams as Playwright, in Williams' 'Many Loves and Other Plays' (Norfolk, Conn., 1961), 433-4.
52 'Lyric', vol. XXXII, no. 4, autumn 1952, insert.
53 First printed in 'Mica', no. 3 June 1961, and reprinted in 'Massachusetts Review', winter 1962, 297-300.
54 The second of the two Ginsberg letters cited in 'Paterson (Book Four)', undated in the text (P, 227-8), is dated 6 June 1949 (Yale Collection). The letter placed earlier (P, 204-6) is undated.
55 Rudolf Arnheim, W. H. Auden, Karl Shapiro and Donald A. Stauffer, 'Poets at Work: Essays Based on the Modern Poetry Collection at the Lockwood Memorial Library, University of Buffalo', with an introduction by Charles D. Abbott (New York, 1948).
56 Karl Shapiro, 'In Defense of Ignorance' (New York, 1952), 169.
57 Richard Eberhart, The Image of Ourselves, 'New York Times Book Review', 12 February 1950, 5.

47 Introduction

58 'William Carlos Williams: A Critical Anthology', edited by Charles Tomlinson (London, 1972), 148.
59 'Focus Five: Modern American Poetry', edited by B. Rajan (London, 1950), 186.
60 Denis Donoghue, For a Redeeming Language, 'Twentieth Century', vol. CLXIII, no. 976, June 1958, 532-42; revised after Williams' death and included in Donoghue's 'The Ordinary Universe: Soundings in Modern Literature' (London, 1968), 180-93.
61 Donald Davie, The Legacy of Fenimore Cooper, 'Essays in Criticism', vol. IX, no. 3, July 1959, 222-38.
62 Donald Davie, 'Ezra Pound: Poet as Sculptor' (London, 1964), 124.
63 Measure, edited by Hugh Kenner, 'Spectrum', vol. III, no. 3, fall 1959, 131-57; reprinted in 'Cambridge Opinion', no. 41, October 1965.
64 Charles Olson, Projective Verse, 'Poetry New York', no. 3, 1950. Republished as a booklet by Totem Press, New York, 1959.
65 Reviewer on the Spot, 'New Republic', 11 January 1939, 289.
66 See bibliography of bibliographical materials, under Galinsky.
67 Jerome Mazzaro, Williams, Kora, That Greeny Flower, 'Intrepid', no. 17, 1970, 6.
68 Reed Whittemore, William Carlos Williams: Poet from Jersey (Boston, 1975).
69 Paul L. Mariani, William Carlos Williams: The Poet and His Critics (Chicago, 1975).
70 'William Carlos Williams Newsletter', edited by Theodora R. Graham, is published at Pennsylvania State University.

'Poems'

Rutherford, N.J., May 1909

Originally intended for publication in March 1909, the book was never issued in its first printed state. Williams paid a local printer, Reid Howell, $50 to do the job, but he recalls in 'I Wanted to Write a Poem' (Boston, 1958), 10, that 'When I saw the first copy I nearly fainted. It was full of errors'.

The second, issued, state contains both corrections of misprints and alterations of wording and punctuation. All but a few copies were accidentally burned about ten years after publication. Nine copies have been traced.

---

1. UNSIGNED REVIEW, POEMS COMPOSED IN ODD MOMENTS BY ONE OF RUTHERFORD'S BRIGHT YOUNG MEN, 'RUTHERFORD AMERICAN'

Thursday, 6 May 1909, no. 977, Supplement, 4

Of small intrinsic interest this, the earliest review of Williams' work, is quoted at greater length in Emily Mitchell Wallace, 'A Bibliography of William Carlos Williams' (Middletown, Conn., 1968), 8-9.

...We are much reminded of that Dr. Williams of an older generation in Rutherford, whose graceful verse won Queen Victoria's praise.... It may well be hoped that, in his busy professional life, Dr. Williams will find more odd moments in which to record his open-eyed interest in the things of beauty, the mind and the spirit....

2. EZRA POUND, LETTER TO WILLIAMS

London, 21 May 1909

Pound (1885-1972), the most formative early influence on him, met Williams when both were students at the University of Pennsylvania. Emily Mitchell Wallace, who explores the early years of their relationship in Pound and Williams at the University of Pennsylvania, 'Pennsylvania Review', vol. I, no. 2, (spring 1967), concludes: 'The exasperated affection that marked their friendship lasted to the ënd.' Besides writing a number of articles in response to Pound's political activities, Williams gives an account in 'Autobiography' (New York, 1951). Pound's comments are fewer. Louis Zukofsky quotes him as urging, early in 1928, a meeting with Williams, 'still the best human value on my murkn visiting list' (Zukofsky, The Best Human Value, 'Nation', 31 May 1958, collected in 'Prepositions' (London, 1967), 40).

The present letter is from 'The Letters of Ezra Pound 1907-1941' edited by D. D. Paige (New York, 1950), 7-8.

I hope to God you have no feelings. If you have, burn this before reading.
Dear Billy: Thanks for your Poems. What, if anything, do you want me to do by way of criticism?
?Is it a personal, private edtn. for your friend, or??
As proof that W.C.W. has poetic instincts the book is valuable. Au contraire, if you were in London and saw the stream of current poetry, I wonder how much you would have printed? Do you want me to criticize it as if [it] were my own work?

I have sinned in nearly every possible way, even the ways I most condemn. I have printed too much. I have been praised by the greatest living poet. I am, after eight years' hammering against impenetrable adamant, become suddenly somewhat of a success.

From where do you want me to show the sharpened 'blade'? Is there anything I know about your book that you don't know?

Individual, original it is not. Great art it is not. Poetic it is, but there are innumerable poetic volumes poured out here in Gomorrah. There is no town like London to make one feel the vanity of all art except the highest. To make one disbelieve in all but the most careful and

conservative presentation of one's stuff. I have sinned
deeply against the doctrine I preach.
   Your book would not attract even passing attention
here. There are fine lines in it, but nowhere I think do
you add anything to the poets you have used as models.
   If I should publish a medical treatise explaining that
arnica was good for bruises (or cuts or whatever it is) it
would show that I had found out certain medical facts, but
it would not be of great value to the science of medicine.
You see I am getting under weigh.
   If you'll read Yeats and Browning and Francis Thompson
and Swinburne and Rossetti you'll learn something about
the progress of Eng. poetry in the last century. And if
you'll read Margaret Sackville, Rosamund Watson, Ernest
Rhys, Jim G. Fairfax, you'll learn what the people of
second rank can do, and what damn good work it is. You
are out of touch. That's all.
   Most great poetry is written in the first person (i.e.
it has been for about 2000 years). The 3rd is sometimes
usable and the 2nd nearly always wooden. (Millions of
exceptions!) What's the use of this?
   Read Aristotle's 'Poetics', Longinus' 'On the Sublime',
De Quincey, Yeats' essays.
   Lect. I. Learn your art thoroughly. If you'll study
the people in that 1st lecture and then reread your stuff
- you'll get a lot more ideas about it than you will from
any external critique I can make of the verse you have
sent me.
   Vale et me ama!
   P.S. And remember a man's real work is what *he is
going to do*, not what is behind him. Avanti e coraggio!

'The Tempers'

London, 13 September 1913

Pound arranged with Elkin Mathews, the English publisher, for publication of this volume. Again Williams paid $50 towards costs. Pound wrote an Introductory Note to the poems (which is reprinted in 'I Wanted to Write a Poem', (12-13).

---

3. EZRA POUND, REVIEW, 'NEW FREEWOMAN'

1 December 1913, vol. I, no. 12, 227

The 'New Freewoman' began publication in June 1913. By its fifth issue Pound had become a participant in the magazine. Very soon he was, in effect at least, its literary editor, and was instrumental in having its name changed to the 'Egoist', with the first issue of 1914. (See K. L. Goodwin, 'The Influence of Ezra Pound', London, 1966.)

Mr. Williams' poems are distinguished by the vigour of their emotional colouring. He makes a bold effort to express himself directly and convinces one that the emotions are veritably his own, wherever he shows traces of reading, it would seem to be a snare against which he struggles, rather than a support to lean upon. It is this that gives one hopes for his future work, and it is his directness coupled with the effect of colour - and the peculiarly vivid and rich range of colour in which his emotions seem to present themselves, 'gold against

blue' to his vision - that produces the individual quality
of his verse. His metres also are bold, heavily accented,
and built up as part of himself.

The mood of 'The Tempers' varies from that of the
splendid Postlude (which appeared in these pages some
weeks since - in a group of poems headed The Newer School),
with its

> Let there be gold of tarnished masonry,
> Temples soothed by the sun to ruin
> That sleep utterly.
> Give me hand for the dances,
> Ripples at Philae, in and out,
> And lips, my Lesbian,
> Wall flowers that once were flame.

to the macabre humour of Hic Jacet, which I quote entire.

[quotes Hic Jacet, CEP, 30]

At times he seems in danger of drifting into imaginative
reason, but the vigour of his illogicalness is nearly
always present to save him; and he is for the most part
content to present his image, or the bare speech of his
protagonist, without border or comment, as he does in the
Crude Lament;

[quotes Crude Lament, 2-6, CEP, 22]

or in the more or less unintelligible rune of The Ordeal,
where someone is evidently praying to the fire-spirit
to save a companion from witchcraft or some other magic.

One is disappointed that Mr. Williams has not given a
larger volume, and one hopes for more to come.

'Al Que Quiere!'

Boston, December 1917

4. DOROTHY DUDLEY, 'A SMALL GARDEN INDUCED TO GROW IN UNLIKELY SURROUNDINGS', 'POETRY'

Vol. XII, no. 1, April 1918, 38-43

As preface to these poems the publishers have been, I think, foolish in dealing the 'gentle reader,' as they are pleased to call him, a kind of blow over the head. They advertise the book as 'brutally powerful' and 'scornfully crude.' They intimidate one with the magnificent news that Mr. Williams 'doesn't give a damn for your opinion' and that 'his opinion of you is more important than your opinion of him.' They end by 'venturing to predict that the poets of the future will dig here for material as the poets of today dig in Whitman's "Leaves of Grass."'¹ In passing, what baseness these pretty publishers impute to the poets - the depravity of the *apache* off to the battle-field for all detachable property!

It seems a pity that Mr. Williams' indifference should have extended quite to this introduction. Just a slight remonstrative damn might have escaped him, to save a delightful volume from a foreword that hangs too oppressively over it, and deprives one of intrinsic pleasure in the poems. Unavoidably they appear for judgment in the heavy light of this challenge; which has the further fault of being misleading.

One would expect to find in 'Al Que Quiere,' despite its brief number of pages, a veritable *tour de force*, a kind of poetic Woolworth Building, massing magnificently on the horizon, but to the closer eye perhaps inexpressive, harsh, from sheer neglect of detail. One looks in vain, however, for enormous violent shapes, and finds

instead poetry of the sparer, more meticulous sort - at
its best fibrous, marvelously observant, delicate, haunt-
ing; then at moments stilted, confused, obtuse. Many of
the poems concern themselves with pure sensation; again
they seem doctrinal in character, truth in compact form,
often most deftly handled:

[quotes Riposte, CEP, 156, lines 6-11]

But at times more vulnerable, sententious even:

[quotes Pastoral, CEP, 124, lines 14-25]

Very charming, but why this feigned astonishment, when
obviously rain and wind would contribute to majesty more
than divinity schools? One should, however, let that
pass, for usually Mr. Williams is at great pains to be
authentic. He leans far out, in fact, to capture in some
snare of words those more intricate sensations that nearly
baffle expression; and often he succeeds. Trees, for
example, save for too easy an adverb in the third line,
seems a feat of accuracy.

And when he has failed in this quest for the precise
thought, the elusive difficult detail, when his verse
lacks content or suppleness, it is rarely through sem-
blance of carelessness. He appears, in fact, to have the
conscience of the great artist, only as yet to lack the
supreme ease. His very failures contradict the qualities
indicated in the foreword. Not untrammelled enough to
give any consecutive impression of power, he is too punc-
tilious to be thought of as brutal, too scrupulous to be
often crude. His concern, one feels, has been at least
to keep intact the complexion of the poem. The most un-
willing words have been brought together and touched up
with the cosmetics of style, until often they possess
that air of greater distinction which ugliness has over
prettiness. Only occasionally does he drop his devices,
as in the final section of January Morning, or seem to
relax as in Ballet Russe; when one gets the shock of a
bad nut among many more difficult to get at, perhaps, but
palatable. For the most part his reverence for tone is
unremitting, and his reward frequent. Observe the lovely
bloom of a poem like this:

[quotes A Prelude, CEP, 141]

Not many of the poems seek quite this fluid beauty.
Their virtue lies rather in the native weathered quality
of the words, like that of stones in untouched places;

and they have the same fragmentary strength. They give at
moments the effect of hardness, of fine reality; but when
the thought becomes too bold, too intricate or too emotional to manage prettily, evidently rather than mar the
surface of the poem Mr. Williams has resorted to the
obscure and the cryptic. This refuge of course has just
now the virtue or the vice, as one looks at it, of being
distinctly the fashion. Writers are 'doing it' this
season, and 'Al Que Quiere' doubtless will strengthen the
inclination. But no matter how sparse or veiled, certainly the design should never be broken or blurred; and
poems like M.B. and Keller Gegen Dom are, I think, in-
securely elliptical. Virtue, possibly by the same token,
becomes confused and ill at ease; though the first strophe
is keen beyond most of the book.

Sometimes perhaps Mr. Williams suffers from the curse
of self-consciousness. He allows one, for example, to
fall under the spell of heavy fragrant music like this:

[quotes Pastoral, CEP 161, lines 3-9]

Then as if suddenly aware of too solemn a face, he changes
brusquely to a lighter key, and the end is all too arch:

> I looked and there were little frogs
> with puffed out throats,
> singing in the slime.

Yet if these poems do not give the impression of tit-
anic power or of consistent mastery, they offer certainly
a fine assortment. There is hardly a poem that somewhere
has not edge and poignancy; and there are very few in
which certain lines, certain words, do not graze one with
the wings of reality. More than a dozen one is tempted to
quote as complete and without flaw. One of these,
Chickory (1) and Daisies seems to indicate the very task
Williams had set himself:

[quotes Chicory and Daisies, I, CEP, 122]

Whatever the intention 'Al Que Quiere' does give the
sense of a small garden induced to grow in unlikely surroundings: on the whole so deeprooted that its bloom
should last a long time, so native that very likely
meaner poets will come to pick what they can; some of the
blossoms rare and perfect, others more like those bright
hardy flowers that bloom in high places above timber-line.

One poem, To a Solitary Disciple, especially from its
twelfth line onward, has ease and elegance above the rest,

rearing itself on a tough tenuous stem to the single freedom of the last lines:

   Observe
   the jasmine lightness
   of the moon.

Note

1 This spelling was used up to and including CCP.

5. CONRAD AIKEN, MR. WILLIAMS AND HIS CAVIAR OF EXCESSIVE INDIVIDUALISM, FROM 'SCEPTICISMS: NOTES ON CONTEMPORARY POETRY'

New York, 1919, 184-5

Aiken does not mention the title of the book he is referring to, nor quote from it, but the date establishes it as 'Al Que Quiere!'. Dijkstra, in 'The Hieroglyphics of a New Speech' (Princeton, 1969), 67n., suggests this review's particular interest, comparing it with Charles Caffin's remarks in 'Camera Work', nos XXXIV-XXXV, April-July 1911, on Cezanne's theory of composition. Aiken (1889-1973) was an American poet, novelist and critic. His 'A Reviewer's ABC' includes pieces on 'Collected Poems 1921-1931' and 'Autobiography'.

Mr. Williams is a case in point. His book throughout has the savoury quality of originality. Is it poetry? That is the question. Self-portraiture it is - vivid, acridly sensuous, gnarled, by turns delicate and coarse. There is humour in it, too, which is rare enough in contemporary verse. But on the whole it is more amiable than beautiful, more entertaining than successful. The reasons for this are several. To begin with, Mr. Williams too seldom goes below the surface. He restricts his observations almost entirely to the sensory plane. His moods, so to speak, are nearly always the moods of the eye, the ear, and the nostril. We get the impression from these poems that his world is a world of plane surfaces, bizarrely

coloured, and cunningly arranged so as to give an effect
of depth and solidity; but we do not get depth itself.
When occasionally this is not true, when Mr. Williams
takes the plunge into the profounder stream of consciousness, he appears always to pick out the shallows, and to
plunge gingerly. The sensory element is kept in the fore-
ground, the tone remains whimsically colloquial, and as a
result the total effect - even when the material is
inherently emotional - is still quaintly cerebral. Is
it at bottom a sort of puritanism that keeps Mr. Williams
from letting go? There is abundant evidence here that his
personality is a rich one; but his inhibitions keep him
for ever dodging his own spotlight. He is ashamed to be
caught crying, or exulting, or adoring. On the technical
side this puritanism manifests itself in a resolute suppression of beauty. Beauty of sound he denies himself,
beauty of prosodic arrangement too; the cadences are prose
cadences, the line-lengths are more or less arbitrary, and
only seldom, in a short-winded manner, are they effective.
In brief, Mr. Williams is a realistic imagist: he has the
air of floating through experience as a sensorium and
nothing more. He denies us his emotional reactions to the
things he sees, even to the extent of excluding intensity
of personal tone from his etchings; and his readers,
therefore, have no emotional reactions, either. They see,
but do not feel. Is Mr. Williams never anything but
amused or brightly interested? The attitude has its
limits, no matter how fertile its basis of observation....

'Kora in Hell: Improvisations'

Boston, 1 September 1920

I decided that I would write something every day, without missing one day, for a year. I'd write nothing planned but take up a pencil, put the paper before me, and write anything that came into my head.... Not a word was to be changed. I didn't change any, but I did tear up some of the stuff. ('Autobiography', 158)

Some improvisations were published in the 'Little Review' from 1917 to 1919. When a new edition was published in 1957 by City Lights Books, San Francisco, the original Prologue was omitted because copyright for it was then held by Random House, who had published it in Williams' 'Selected Essays' (1954). It was replaced by a new two-page prologue.

---

6. EZRA POUND, LETTER

10 November 1917

Taken from Pound's 'Letters', 123-5, this is included almost in its entirety in the original 'Kora' Prologue. This version differs in minor details from that in 'Selected Essays'. Pound also wrote several letters of comment after the book's publication (see 'Letters', 156-61), once relating 'Kora' to Rimbaud's 'Une Saison en Enfer', but the present letter contains his most penetrating comment on the book.

My Dear William: At what date did you join the ranks of the old ladies?

Among the male portion of the community one constantly uses fragments of letters, fragments of conversation (anonymously, quite anonymously, NOT referring to the emitter by name) for the purpose of sharpening a printed argument.

I note your invitation to return to my fatherland (pencil at the top of your letter sic g.t.h.); I shall probably accept it at the end of the war.

My knowledge of the ('stet') American heart is amply indicated in L'Homme Moyen Sensuel.

I had no ulterior or hidden meaning in calling you or the imaginary correspondent an 'American' author. Still, what the hell else are you? I mean apart from being a citizen, a good fellow (in your better moments), a grouch, a slightly hypersensitized animal, etc.?? Wot bloody kind of author are you save Amurkun (same as me).

And whether, O Demosthenes, is one to be called a 'damn fool' or a 'person'?

Your sap is interrupted. Try De Gourmont's Epilogue ('95-'98). And don't expect the world to revolve about Rutherford.

If you had any confidence in America you wouldn't be so touchy about it.

I thought the - millenium that we all idiotically look for and work for was to be the day when an American artist could stay at home without being dragged into civic campaigns, dilutations of controversy, etc., when he could stay in America without growing propagandist. God knows I have to work hard enough to escape, not propagande, but getting centered in propagande.

And America! What the hell do you a bloomin' foreigner know about the place? Your père only penetrated the edge, and you've never been west of Upper Darby, or the Maunchunk switchback. Would Harriet, (1) with the swirl of the prairie wind in her underwear, or the virile Sandburg recognize you, an effete Easterner, as a **REAL** American/
INCONCEIVABLE!!!!

My dear boy, you have never felt the whoop of the **PEE**raries. You have never seen the projecting and protuberant Mts. of the Sierra Nevada. WOT can you know of the counthry?

You have the naive credulity of a Co. Claire immigrant. But I (der grosse Ich) have the virus, the bacillus of the land in my blood, for nearly three bleating centuries.

(Bloody snob. 'Eave a brick at 'im!!!!)

You (read your Freud) have a Vaterersatz, you have a paternal image at your fireside, and you call it John Bull.

Your statement about my wanting Paris to be like London is a figment of your own diseased imagination.
'I warn you that anything you say at this time may later be used against you.' The Arts vs. Williams.
Or will you carry my head on a platter? Or would you like it brought over to be punched?? A votre service, M'sieu. I am coming to inspect you.
I of course like your Old Man, and I have drunk his Goldwasser.
I was very glad to see your wholly incoherent unAmerican poems in the L.R. ['Little Review']
Of course Sandburg will tell you that you miss the 'Big drifts,' and Bodenheim will object to your not being sufficiently decadent.
(You thank your bloomin gawd you've got enough Spanish blood to muddy up your mind, and prevent the current American ideation from going through it like a blighted colländer.)
The thing that saves your work is opacity, and don't you forget it. Opacity is NOT an American quality. Fizz, swish, gabble of verbiage, these are echt Amerikanisch.
And Alas, alas, poor old Masters. Look at Oct. 'Poetry.'
But really this 'old friend' hurt feeling business is too Skipwithcannéllish; it is *peu vous*. I demand of you more robustezza. Bigod sir, you show more robustezza, or I will come over to Rutherford and have at you, *coram*, in person.
And moreover you answer my questions, p. 38, before you go on to the p.s. p. 39 which does not concern you.
Let me indulge in the American habit of quotation:
'Si le cosmopolitisme litteraire gagnait encore et qu'il réussit à éteindre ce que les différences de care ont allumé de haine de sang parmi les hommes, j'y verrais un gain pour la civilisation et pour l'humanite tout entiere....
'L'amour excessif et exclusif d'une patrie a pour immédiat corollaire l'horreur des patries étrangères. Non seulement on craint de quitter le jupe de sa maman, d'aller voir comment vivent les autres hommes, de se mêler à leurs luttes, de partager leurs travaux; non seulement on reste chez soi, mais on finit par fermer sa porte.
'Cette folie gagne certains littérateurs et la même professeur, en si tant d'expliquer le Cid ou Don Juan, rédige de gracieuse injures contre Ibsen et l'influence, hélas, trop illusoire, de son oeuvre, pourtant toute de lumiere et de beautè.' (2) Et cetera. Lie down and compose yourself.
P.S. It's also nonsense this wail that M.C.A. (3) dislikes you.

Notes

1 Harriet Monroe (1860-1936) was the editor of 'Poetry', founded in Chicago in 1912. Her autobiography 'A Poet's Life' (1938) includes a discussion of Williams with texts of some of his letters and her replies in 1913. Some of Williams' letters to her are included in SL.
2 'If literary cosmopolitanism wins again and succeeds in extinguishing the blood hatred ignited by racial differences among men, I would see in that a gain for civilization and for the whole human race....
   'Excessive and exclusive love for one's country has as immediate corollary hatred of foreign countries. Not only does one fear to leave one's mother's apron strings, to go and see how other men live, to take part in their struggles, and share their labours; not only does one stay at home, but one ends up by closing one's door.
   'This idiocy overcomes some literary men and the professor, supposedly explicating "Le Cid" or "Don Juan", writes graceful insults against Ibsen, and the influence, alas, too illusory, of his work, however full of light and beauty.' Editor's translation.
   The version of this letter given in SE differs in detail from that in 'Letters'. Paige's text includes, without comment, a number of literals, most obviously 'care' for 'race'. The closing and apparently somewhat obscure comment on Ibsen seems to be mock-Corneillian, hence the translation of 'gracieuse' as 'graceful' rather than the possible rendering, 'gratuitous'.
3 M.C.A. is Margaret Anderson, editor of the 'Little Review', which was published in Chicago from 1917 to 1929.

7. MARIANNE MOORE, REVIEW, 'CONTACT'

No. 4, 1921, 5-8

Marianne Moore (1887-1972) graduated from Bryn Mawr College in 1909. In 1921, the poet H.D. (Hilda Doolittle) and the novelist Bryher (Winifred Ellerman) published, without Miss Moore's knowledge, her first volume, 'Poems'. Besides many later volumes of verse, including 'The

Complete Poems of Marianne Moore' (New York, 1967), she
published a volume of essays, 'Predilections', and of
translations, 'The Fables of Lafontaine'. Winner of the
Pulitzer Prize, the Bollingen Prize and the National Book
Award, she was editor of the 'Dial' from 1925 to 1929.
Long interested in Williams' work she marked his receipt
of the Dial Award for 1926 with her essay, A Poet of the
Quattrocento, 'Dial', vol. 82, 1927, 213-15. Her review
of his 'Collected Poems 1921-1931' (1934) is printed below
(No. 30).

'The unready would deny tough cords to the wind because
they cannot split a storm endwise and wrap it upon spools.'

This statement exemplifies a part of what gives to the
work of William Carlos Williams, 'a character by itself'.
It is a concise, energetic disgust, a kind of intellectual
hauteur which one usually associates with the French.

The acknowledgement of our debt to the imagination,
constitutes, perhaps, his positive value. Compression,
colour, speed, accuracy and that restraint of instinctive
craftsmanship which precludes anything dowdy or laboured –
it is essentially these qualities that we have in his
work. Burke speaks of the imagination as the most inten-
sive province of pleasure and pain and defines it as a
creative power of the mind, representing at pleasure the
images of things in the order and manner in which they
were received by the senses or in combining them in a new
manner and according to a different order. Dr Williams in
his power over the actual, corroborates this statement.
Observe how, by means of his rehabilitating power of the
mind, he is able to fix the atmosphere of a moment:

> It is still warm enough to slip from the weeds into the
> lake's edge ... and snakes' eggs lie curling in the sun
> on the lonely summit.
>
> Calvary Church with its snail's horns up sniffing the
> dawn – o' the wrong side!
>
> Always one leaf at the peak twig swirling, swirling and
> apples rotting in the ditch.
>
> By the brokenness of his composition (he writes) the
> poet makes himself master of a certain weapon which he
> could possess himself of in no other way.

We do not so much feel the force of this statement as we

feel that there is in life, as there is in Sir Francis
Bacon - in the ability to see resemblances in things which
are dissimilar; in the ability to see such differences, a
special kind of imagination required, which Dr Williams
has. Despite his passion for being himself and his
determination not to be at the mercy of 'schoolmasters',
it is only one who is academically sophisticated who could
write:

> Fatigued as you are, watch how the mirror sieves out
> the extraneous, (and)

> Of what other thing is greatness composed than a power
> to annihilate half truths for a thousandth part of
> accurate understanding.

> Often (he says) a poem will have merit because of some
> one line or even one meritorious word. So it hangs
> heavily on its stem but still secure, the tree unwilling
> to release it.

Such an observation certainly is not the result of pure
intuition or of any informally, semi-consciously exercised
mental energy. It is not, after all, the naive but the
authentic upon which he places value. To the bona fide
artist, affectation is degradation and in his effort to
'annihilate half truths', Dr Williams is hard, discerning,
implacable and deft. If he rates audacity too high as an
aesthetic asset, there can be no doubt that he has courage
of the kind which is a necessity and not merely an admired
accessory. Discerning the world's hardness, his reply is
the reply of Carl Sandburg's boll weevil to threats of
sand, hot ashes and the river: 'That'll be ma **HOME**!
That'll be ma **HOME**!'

> Where does this downhill turn up again? (he says):

> Driven to the wall you'd put claws to your toes and
> make a ladder of smooth bricks.

Though restive under advice, he is resigned under the
impersonal, inevitable attrition of life.

> One need not be hopelessly cast down (he says) because
> he cannot cut onyx into a ring to fit a lady's
> finger.... There is neither onyx nor porphyry on
> these roads - only brown dirt. For all that, one may
> see his face in a flower along it - even in this
> light.... Walk in the curled mudcrusts to one side,
> hands hanging. Ah well.

To discuss one's friends in print may or may not be necessitated by fealty to art but whether there is beauty or not in Dr Williams's discussion of persons as there is in his discussion of life - in citing the idiosyncrasies of friends, note his calmness:

> B. pretends to hate most people, ... but that he really goes to this trouble I cannot imagine.

Additional marks of health are to be found in his use of idiom. He says:

> If a woman laughs a little loudly one always thinks that way of her.

> Throw two shoes on the floor and see how they'll lie if you think it's all one way.

The sharpened faculties which require exactness, instant satisfaction and an underpinning of truth are too abrupt in their activities sometimes to follow; but the niceness and effect of vigour for which they are responsible are never absent from Dr Williams's work and its crisp exterior is one of its great distinctions. He again reminds one of the French. John Burroughs says of French drivers of drays and carts,

> They are not content with a plain matter-of-fact whip as an English or American labourer would be, but it must be a finely modeled stalk, with a long tapering lash, tipped with the best silk snapper.

> It is silly to go into a 'puckersnatch' (Dr Williams says) because some brass-button-minded nincompoop in Kensington flies off the handle and speaks openly about our United States prize poems.

In the following passage, the words 'black and peculiar' would seem to be the snapper:

> A mother will love her children most grotesquely.... She will be most willing toward that daughter who thwarts her most and not toward the little kitchen helper. So where one is mother to any great number of people she will love best perhaps some child whose black and peculiar hair is an exact replica of that of the figure in Velásquez's Infanta Maria Theresa or some Italian matron whose largeness of manner takes in the whole street.

Despite Dr Williams's championing of the school of ignorance, or rather of no school but experience, there is in his work the authoritativeness, the wise silence which knows schools and fashions well enough to know that completeness is further down than professional intellectuality and modishness can go.

Lamps carry far, believe me (he says) in lieu of sunshine.

What can it mean to you that a child wears pretty clothes and speaks three languages or that its mother goes to the best shops?... Men ... buy finery and indulge in extravagant moods in order to piece out their lack with other matter.

Kindly stupid hands, kindly coarse voices,... infinitely detached, infinitely beside the question ... and night is done and the green edge of yesterday has said all it could.

In middle life the mind passes to a variegated October. This is the time youth in its faulty aspirations has set for the achievement of great summits. But having attained the mountain top one is not snatched into a cloud but the descent proffers its blandishments quite as a matter of course. At this the fellow is cast into a great confusion and rather plaintively looks about to see if any has fared better than he.

Dr Williams's wisdom, however, is not absolute and he is sometimes petulant.
'Nowadays poets spit upon rhyme and rhetoric,' he says. His work provides examples of every rhetorical principle insisted on by rhetoricians and one wonders upon what ground he has been able to persuade himself that poets spit upon rhyme? Possibly by rhetoric, he means balderdash; in this case then, we are merely the poorer by one, of proofs for his accuracy.

It is folly (he says), to accept remorse as a criticism of conduct.

One's manners, good or bad, are conventionalized instincts and conduct as a combination of manners and volition, predicates whatever is the result of it, so that remorse is automatically a criticism of conduct; but Dr Williams is essentially a poet. It is true, as he says that 'by direct onslaught or by some back road of the

intention the gifted will win the recognition of the
world.' His book is alive with meaning; in it, 'thoughts
are trees' and 'leaves load the branches.' But one who
sets out to appraise him has temerity, since he speaks
derisively of the wish of certain of his best friends to
improve his work and, after all, the conflict between the
tendency to aesthetic anarchy and the necessity for self-
imposed discipline must take care of itself.

As for leaving nothing unsaid - or to be accurate, something unsaid - there is no topic which a thoughtful person
would refuse to discuss if gain were to result; but so far
as one can see, the peculiar force of Dr Williams's work
does not gain by an allusion to topics of which the average
person never thinks unless inescapably for humanitarian
reasons. Dr Williams is too sincere to wish to be fashionable and that one so rich in imagination should have to be
thrifty in the use of poetic material is preposterous.
One's perspicacity here meets a stone wall.

So disdainful, so complex a poet as Dr Williams,
receives at best half treatment from the average critic or
from the ambitious critic, such untruthful, half specific
approbation as, 'Ah, quite deep; I see to the bottom.'
This is to be expected. There is in Dr Williams an appetite for the essential and in how many people may one find
it? How many poets old or new, have written anything like
January Morning in 'Al Que Quiere!,' like the second
paragraph of Improvisation XVII in the present volume, and
pre-eminently, the Portrait of the Author in a recent
number of 'Contact'? withholding comment upon the title,
this poem is a super-achievement. It preserves the atmosphere of a moment, into which the impertinence of life
cannot intrude. In the sense conveyed, of remoteness from
what is detestable, in the effect of balanced strength, in
the flavour of newness in presentation, it is unique.

8. HELEN BIRCH-BARTLETT, ON WILLIAMS' 'COLOSSALLY NICE
SIMPLICITY', 'POETRY'

Vol. XVII, no. 6, March 1921, 330, 331-2

... Just why these 'Improvisations' are likable is difficult to say. The book holds many sadnesses and bitter-
nesses between its covers; and certain of them, once discovered, find for themselves congenial nooks and resting-
places in the mind.

William Carlos Williams leads us gently, not always gently, by the hand, to nowhere in particular....
... There is a genial and sweet simplicity in the form: 'Go as far as you will with the music, and damn the public!... There's the business of the notes for certain people.... Always some dull wits even among those who pay for their seats.'
I still say there is a colossally nice simplicity about it, and that the change of tonality is utterly agreeable.
There are things to be taken from 'Kora in Hell: Improvisations.' Even after but half a reading it has been possible to go on about this book rather eagerly, and that in itself is almost an introduction to its strong personality, a personality with a sense of something partly eastern about it; but why a flavor of the Orient must cling mysteriously to all writings that conform to a semi-regular change of pitch is unexplained. Perhaps it is that the far extremes of pure lightness and seriousness are so commonly the possession of the Oriental, and so rarely ours.

9. W.C. BLUM, 'SINCE-1914 THE WIND HAS BLOWN ONLY FROM JERSEY', 'DIAL'

Vol. LXX, no. 5, May 1921, 565-6

This is an excerpt from American Letter.
Dr James Sibley Watson ('W. C. Blum') (b. 1894), a financial supporter of the 'Dial' during the 1920s, was also an important editorial influence.

William Carlos Williams has been writing for ten years or more and is by all odds the hardiest specimen in these parts. His poetry actually gets better every year. He was in 'Des Imagistes' in 1914, and has been appearing since in the 'Egoist', the 'Little Review', 'Poetry', the 'Dial', and 'Contact'. Several books of his were published in England by Elkin Mathews, (1) and The Four Seas has published 'Al Que Quiere' and this year 'Kora in Hell'.
At one time passages like this pointed to a wind off London:

for granite is not harder than
my love is open, runs loose among you!

but since 1914 the wind has blown only from Jersey.
   ...His phrases have a simplicity, a solid justice:

Hairy looking trees stand out
in long alleys
over a wild solitude

    the great oaks
lying with roots
ripped from the ground.

This modest quality of realness, which he attributes to 'contact' with the good Jersey dirt, sometimes reminds one of Chekhov. Like Chekhov he knows animals and babies as well as trees. And to people who are looking for the story his poems must often seem as disconnected and centrifugal as Chekhov's later plays; they are very nearly as intense. I offer this comparison as a poor handle to his work, not his personality.

Williams is one of the people who think they know what the U.S. needs in order to ripen a literature. Pound's remedy was for us to parse all the classics, ancient and modern; Brooks, the most gingerly of critics, wanted to improve our morals and let art come as an inconsiderable afterthought. Williams' first suggestion was that someone give Alfred Kreymborg one hundred thousand dollars. Recently, becoming impatient, he started a magazine of his own, in which he advises us to pay no attention to Europe and be thoroughly local. This may be excellent advice, and, in finding the metaphysics to back it up with, Williams appears to be learning a great deal that he never knew before....

Note

1 Mathews published only 'The Tempers'.

'Sour Grapes'

Boston, 9 December 1921

10. KENNETH BURKE, HEAVEN'S FIRST LAW, 'DIAL'

Vol. 72, February 1922, 197-200

Burke (b. 1897) is a critic, literary theorist, philosopher and translator, who made the works of Thomas Mann, Hofmannsthal and others better known in the United States. He was a contributing editor to the 'Dial', and a founder of 'Secession', and is author of 'Counter-Statement' (1931), 'The Philosophy of Literary Form' (1941) and other influential books of literary theory. Burke and Williams exchanged visits and corresponded with each other over a long period of years. J. C. Thirlwall notes that Burke 'has written and received perhaps more letters to and from WCW than anyone living' (SL, 48, headnote).

It had once been my privilege to see a page written by William Carlos Williams on which he undertook to reproduce nine times the lovely sunshine thought, 'Order is Heaven's first law.' Now, by the fifth time, the poet became noticeably impatient, and from the seventh on the copy was completely unreadable. The ninth version was a mere wavy line, broken in four places. At first I took this to be quite damning; but on second thought, what use could Williams make of order? He thinks in an entirely different set of terms. To add organization to his poetry would have no more meaning than to insist that his lines begin in alphabetical rotation.

What Williams sees, he sees in a flash. And if there is any correlation whatsoever, it is a certain determined joyousness in a poet who would find it awkward to weep. For as his arch-enemy has noted, Williams is a bad Freudian case whose poetry is certainly not allowed to come out the way it came in. But beyond this very reasonable prudency, which he shares with no less an artist than Flaubert, consistency falls away.

No, Williams is the master of the glimpse. A line of his, suddenly leaping up out of the text, will throw the reader into an unexpected intimacy with his subject, like pushing open a door and advancing one's nose into some foreign face. Given a subject, he will attack it with verve, striking where he can break through its defence, and expecting applause whenever a solid, unmistakable jolt has been landed. It would be mere idleness to give his *ars poetica* in more presumptuous terms. The process is simply this: There is the eye, and there is the thing upon which that eye alights; while the relationship existing between the two is a poem.

The difficulty here lies in conveying the virtues of such a method, for the method itself is as common as mud. The minute fixating of a mood, an horizon, a contrast; if one finds there any unusual commendation for Williams it is not in the excellence of his poetics, but in the excellence of his results. His first virtue, therefore, lies in the superiority of his minute fixations over those of his ten million competitors. He is a distinguished member of a miserable crew.

Honest people who really think highly enough of words to feel unhappy when they are vague will rejoice that Williams' new volume, 'Sour Grapes,' is more sober in this respect than the 'Improvisations.' For the 'Improvisations' were not finally satisfactory. Clear notes were there in abundance, but they were usually preceded and followed by the usual modern data for mental tests. (How beautiful the association of ideas would have been in art if used in one work, by one man, for one page, and for some end other than that of a beautiful association of ideas.) True, by the mere dissatisfaction of their context, such momentary beatitudes of expression received their full share of enthusiasm, but having twenty sentences of chaos to heighten one sentence of cosmos is too much like thanking God for headaches since they enable us to be happy without them.

'Sour Grapes,' however, skips a generation and takes after the volume, 'Al Que Quiere!' And in these two works, it seems to me, Williams is at his best, since here he is not handicapping his remarkable powers of definition, of lucidity. You may wonder, perhaps, just why the poet is going off in some particular direction; but you are always aware just what this direction is. Here also his inveterate lustiness is up to par; for Williams knows Walt Whitman's smile down to the last wrinkle. If there are logs in the grate, he puts a match to them; if it is a warm Easter morning, he throws off his coat. And if, behind it all, there is evidence of a strong tendency towards transgression, towards, let us say, the mountains of Tibet or a negro harem in Madagascar, such things are there as an irritant rather than as a subject. The face value of the poems will always remain the definition of the poet's own gatepost. His peculiar gifts of expression, if nothing else, dictate this simplification. Williams evidently realizes that his emotions are one thing and his art another, and that those who wish to go beyond his minute fixations can find a great deal more implicated in them; but in the meantime, let the minute fixations suffice.

I should say, therefore, that Williams was engaged in discovering the shortest route between object and subject. And whether it is a flamingo befouling its own tail, or the tired ogling at little girls, or trees stark naked in a wind, one must always recognize the unusual propriety of his poetry, the sureness and directness with which he goes at such things. A fact with him finds its justification in the trimness of the wording.

If a man is walking, it is the first principle of philosophy to say that he is *not* walking, the first principle of science to say that he is placing one foot before the other and bringing the hinder one in turn to the fore, the first principle of art to say that the man is *more than* walking, he is *yearning*: then there are times when scientist, philosopher, and poet all discover of a sudden that by heavens! the man is walking and none other. Now, a good deal of this discovery is in Williams' poetry, and, if I understand the word correctly, is contained in his manifesto praising Contact in art. For I take Contact to mean: man without the syllogism, without the parode, without Spinoza's Ethics, man with nothing but the thing and the feeling of that thing. Sitting down in the warmth to write, for instance, Kant might finally figure it out that man simply must have standards of virtue in spite of the bleakness of the phenomenon-noumenon distinction, and that this virtue could be constructed on the foundations of a categorical imperative. But Williams, sitting down in the warmth to write, would never get over his delight that the wind outside was raging ineffectually; and, in his pronounced sense of comfort, he would write:

[quotes January, CEP, 197]

Seen from this angle, Contact might be said to resolve
into the counterpart of Culture, and Williams becomes
thereby one of our most distinguished Neanderthal men.
His poetry deals with the coercions of nature - and by
nature I mean iron rails as well as iron ore - rather than
with the laborious structure of ideas man has erected
above nature. His hatred of the idea in art is consequently pronounced, and very rightly brings in its train a
complete disinterest in form. (Note: Form in literature
must always have its beginnings in idea. In fact, our
word for idea comes from a Greek word whose first meaning
is 'form.') The Contact writer deals with his desires;
the Culture writer must erect his desires into principles
and deal with those principles rather than with the
desires; the *Urphenomen*, in other words, becomes with the
man of Culture of less importance than the delicate and
subtle instruments with which he studies it.
    Williams, however, must go back to the source. (1) And
the process undeniably has its beauties. What, for
instance, could be more lost, more uncorrelated, a closer
Contact, a greater triumph of anti-Culture, than this
poem:

[quotes The Great Figure, CEP, 230]

Note

1 Mr Burke has drawn my attention to a recent 'footnote'
   to this review. His William Carlos Williams: A Critical
   Appreciation, in 'William Carlos Williams' edited by
   Charles Angoff (Cranbury, N.J., and London, 1974),
   15-19, as he says, 'ends on a redo of "Order is Heaven's
   First Law".' In effect, it reaffirms the earlier piece.

11. HART CRANE, FROM A LETTER TO GORHAM MUNSON

12 October 1922

Crane (1889-1932) is one of the chief American poets of
the twentieth century.
    From 'The Letters of Hart Crane 1916-1932' edited by
Brom Weber (New York, 1952), 102-3.

...Williams wrote Bill [Sommer] a memorable letter accompanying his check (for $25.00) in which he said that Bill got under his underdrawers! - and went on to say that he was potentially greater than Marin. It has heartened Bill wonderfully. Such a letter was worth more than the plaudits of a hundred Rosenfelds. I'd like to meet Williams! (Repeating this statement so many times won't do any good I suppose, but there's that directness about the man that I know I'd find cleansing.)...

'Spring and All'

Dijon, France, Autumn 1923

12. MARION STROBEL, MIDDLE-AGED ADOLESCENCE, 'POETRY'

Vol. XXIII, No. 2, November 1923, 103-5

Strobel (1895-1966) wrote novels, and was associate editor of 'Poetry' 1919-24 and co-editor 1943-9. Wallace notes that Williams' poem A Good Night (CEP, 192-3) in 'Sour Grapes' was 'written for Marion Strobel' ('Bibliography', 15).
    The immediate subject of this review is an issue of a little magazine, 'Manikin Number Two', edited by Monroe Wheeler, devoted to Williams' poems. (Wallace lists it as a separate publication, 'Go Go' ('Bibliography', Item A7), but with one exception all the poems in it had appeared earlier in 'Spring and All'.) In the April 1924 'Poetry', Marjorie Allen Seiffert replied, with a review praising Williams' work.

I remember in one of Williams' early books he used the startling phrase: 'God, if I could fathom the guts of shadows!' Since then I have often wondered why Williams hasn't tried to fathom the obvious commonplaces before bothering about the shadows. And I really believe it is because he hasn't the guts to be simple, that he makes such a muddle of his last poems. It is, moreover, particularly deplorable that a person with delicate sensibilities and genuine emotion should be forever putting up a barrage of words to show that he - by Jove - is no lily-livered ninny singing of love. He even deprecates the rose:

[quotes lines 1-13 of The Rose, CEP, 2492

He is like an adolescent boy, who while loving something
of soft-petalled beauty, scoffs at it, so that he will be
considered a He-Man; yet again and again approaches the
same beauty, and at times - for a breathless moment - dares
to finger it with reverence.
It is perhaps unfair to judge Williams on so slight a
collection - there are only ten poems in all. And of
these, one, The Red Wheelbarrow, is no more than a pretty
and harmless statement:

[quotes The Red Wheelbarrow, CEP, 277]

While another, The Hermaphroditic Telephones, is
equally harmless in spite of the self-conscious naughti-
ness of the title.
On the other hand, ten poems may have so many smart,
tiresome, intricate, swaggering phrases to hide a
frightened spirit and a little beauty!

13. PAUL ROSENFELD ON WILLIAMS' OBJECTIVITY, PERCEPTION
OF TRUTH IN DISSONANCE, 'FLEETING PATTERNS', FROM 'PORT
OF NEW YORK'

1924

Rosenfeld (1890-1946), a literary, art and music critic,
also wrote a novel, 'The Boy in the Sun' (1928). 'Port
of New York', his best-known critical work, was reissued
by University of Illinois Press (1961) with an introduction by Sherman Paul. The essay below, William Carlos
Williams, appears on pp. 103-15 of that edition.

The poems of William Carlos Williams are good biting stuff.
Lyric substance has gotten a novel acidulousness of him.
Scent bitter like the nasturtium's, and like the nasturtium's fresheningly pungent, mounts off his small spikey
forms. The sharp things make gay dangerous guerilla upon
the alkalis coating the brain. Corrosive fluid destroys
the properties characteristic of ubiquitous Huyler's;
leaves crystal of valuable salt. Poems startle with
sudden brandished cutlery. Poems writhe with the movements of bodies vainly twisting to loose themselves from

fixed scorching points. Certain waver indeterminately, blankly, high up in air. Certain murmur faintly, turned in upon themselves. The tone achieves grotesque modulations. It falls unceremoniously from plane to distant unrelated plane; drops out of stars to pin-holes; takes queer, off, sour, turns. Words shock with the unexpectedness of their thrusts, scratch voluptuously an instant, sting with soft sudden fangs. Notes are hammered staccato. Queries and ejaculations enter like bird-shot discharged from the muzzle of a Winchester shot-gun. Color-words come; black, yellow, green, white; but what they impart tastes not of fruit-pulps, but of mineral traces in clear spring-water.

Williams' writings are laconic acclamations of the courage to swallow bitter-flavored medicines, to bear unflinchingly the pain of violent cauterizations. They are the forms wherein a poet has given deep sober thanks to the principle by means of which he has managed to maintain his own spirit intact on a steep inclement bank of life, some Greenland on the verge of the Arctic circle. And the homely magic he wishes to hold before men's eyes is lighthearted self-irony, relentless impersonality of regard, sense of the comic and grotesque in his own career, bald matter-of-factness, willingness to stand evil smells and not run from them. Life has tempted this man with the dope of candies; urged glucose on him, cheap substitute for absent sweetnesses. For the world he inhabits is not liberal with satisfactions. It is a world of lowish climaxes and thin releases; whether from premature agedness or retarded youth, one does not know. Monotonous grey of repetition, of usedness, unrolls its scroll daylong across the firmament. At infrequent intervals, slits are cut in the drabhued curtain. Rose quivers awhile like the ballet of pink slippers with gay pom-poms descending the stairs. A day hops like a yellow bird in April branches. Through the night from afar a spring of towerlights hangs against profoundest blue and utters the salutation of joyful cities. Two hours of golden promenade arrive: Columbus' first walk on new-world ground 'among the trees, which was the most beautiful thing which I have ever seen.' The streets end in the sun, and there is

[quotes CEP, 225, Blueflags, lines 9-22]

But the colors are not permanent nor intense enough to change the aspect of the world. They are merely sufficiently satisfying to keep the organism in motion. That is all

[quotes March, section I, CEP, 43]

No gradual suns nurse the small hardish buds on the black branches, melting their green and tight condition, gathering warm color and sweet flesh until the earth is round and drunk with curving greenery and clustering juiced fruits. And when blaze of July strikes them finally, it arrives upon them with such cruel suddenness that of the unopened things many shrivel and char upon their stalks, and few come to radiant maturity. The grey remains; the earth is month-long scraggly and bare, decked meagerly with a few single separate objects selected by the poet's subconscious from off the Jersey flats: a shad-bush on the edge of a clearing, a solitary track of footprints in the snow, a fire in an ash-can, pools left by the tide, the swirl of wind and the river,

> trees
> always in the distance, always against
> a grey sky.

Truly, a weather-condition which encourages indulgence in dope; and one very prevalent through these United States, to judge by the number of institutions devoted within their bounds to the manufacture of candies of all kinds. Genius has given Williams a hardier, cleaner adjustment. This M.D. has developed the stay of aesthetic perception. He finds release in seeing. A certain quantity of perfectly selfless sympathy is in him. Children exist for him. There are women in labor. There is a bone-wearied, exasperated woman in bed. There is a young man with a bad 'pump.' The doctor is the confessor, to-day. There is

> ...a band of
> young poets that have not learned
> the blessedness of warmth
> (or have forgotten it).

The first impulse may still be:

> You sullen pig of a man,
> you force me into the mud
> with your stinking ash-cart!

Inevitably, the music changes to

> Brother!
> ...if we were rich

we'd stick our chests out
and hold our heads high!

Sublimation of brute desires has made the world less fearful. Flash-like recognition of his proper grotesquerie, dissonance, bondage inside the persons of others; scenes, rhythms, words, oaths dawning tantalizingly upon him, have made the circumstances of the poet's own life less painfully pressing. Capacity for identifying himself with people in their own terms has made him, on one plane, a successful physician, diagnostician, healer. It is his own health for which he is fighting in other bodies, careless of their cries and cringing. On another, it has made him an artist: turned his existence over to him as stuff for contemplation. For he has found himself lifted onto that plane where men become objects to themselves with all the rest of the world. He has viewed himself dispassionately, as though he himself were one of his own cases; placed himself with a not unkindly irony against the remainder of the universe and gotten the exact proportion; applied red-hot irons despite his own fears and outcries to his own gangrened wounds; doused himself with cold water whenever necessary; laughed at his hysterical alarms and abrupt starts; controlled the Madame Bovary inside himself; perceived the effect which he has been having upon those in touch with him as well as the effect they have been having upon himself. He has seen the laws operating in his own life, forcing him to receive the world in certain painful forms. There is no blame laid on time, custom, environment for his leanness, as there is blame in the writings of a poet related to Williams, T. S. Eliot. Williams is aware that if the sum of appeasements in his heart resembles most often the bank-balance of a hand-to-mouth existence: held generally near the two-hundred-dollar mark; occasionally dangerously far below; only rarely up near four hundred dollars, the cause, if there is one, lies in himself. It is

...the madness of the birch leaves opening
cold, one by one

and nothing other.
Because of this singularly mature capacity for insight, Williams's writings have a truthfulness wanting [in] those of certain of his fellows'; wanting, despite the presence of great excellencies, [in] those of T. S. Eliot. His poems give the relationship of things more justly than do those of the émigré's. Williams, for example, does not

repeat Bunthorne's lament that 'nothing poetic in the world
can dwell,' nor represent his spirit as a drowned king.
Kings do not appear upon his horizons, or Christs cruci-
fied. He does not have to cast a grandiose and egoistical
veil over the world; and see in it the Judas to his genius
before he can approach it. He can creep close to the lean
thing which exists and see it dispassionately. He can give
himself, William Carlos Williams, much as he is, without
either simple or inverted pride; give himself in his crassness, in his dissonant mixed blood, in absurd melancholy,
wild swiftness of temper, man-shyness; Americano, Jersey-
ite, Rutherfordian; give himself with a frankness, a
fearlessness, a scientific impersonality, that is bracing
as a shock of needlespray. The fleeting patterns, the fine
breaths, in which destiny manifests itself, contain excitement enough for him. Insight probes

> the guts of shadows;

catches subtle acidulous shades, delicate movements of
life. Carl Sandburg perceives

> ...an ocean of tomorrows
> a sky of tomorrows;

but it takes a maturity as great as Williams's to be able
to put the finger on anything as unobvious and fine as the
vision contained in The Nightingales:

[quotes in full The Nightingales, CEP, 224]

And what exists for him appears in its own tone and color;
finds appropriate verbal imagery and rhythmical accent;
nicely weds vulgarity with lyricism. A poem begins:

> He would enjoy either
> like the others
> to buy a railroad
> or
> in his old clothes to
> chase his wife to
> some such outhouse
> as they still have on the farms...

and we feel lightly the hawk-and-spit of the American
mouth. The crass, unvoluptuous, vitriolic language of
'The Great American Novel' has definitely local color.
It is of the American suburbs as 'Ulysses' is of Dublin.
And verse and prose both realize the existence of the

Sunday-afternoon family motor drive, of the Pullman plate;
glass window in the parlor wall, and the lump of rock-
crystal on the mantelpiece. It is seen not as in the best-
sellers, superficially. It is seen from within. Williams
gives the subjective form.

And, in moments of felt power, in moments of conscious
toughness and sharp will, he breaks 'through to the fifty
words necessary,' and briskly, laconically, like a man
with little time for matters not absolutely essential to
the welfare of the universe, brings into clarity the relation existing between himself and the things seen by him.
Curious harmonies of bitter and sweet, of harsh and gentle,
of sluggish and swift and sharp and soft in word-color and
rhythmical pattern; nude finely viscous little curves of
music in which every line is a decisive stroke, render the
ironic, contained, humorous dance of the spirit amid the
objects of a ramshackle makeshift universe.

Life chants because it can master pain, and move about
through disillusionment like a man going erect and self-
contained through mean sites, and musing and dreaming in

[quotes Pastoral, CEP 121, lines 5-16]

Spring dances like Strauss's 'Till Eulenspiegel' with mor-
dant buffoonery above the hopeless dullness of things.
Intelligence planes sovereign over yards in a fury of
lilac-blossoms. Sore, battered, frozen, life outlasts the
cold, struggles to its feet despite the weights upon it,
lifts itself like the chickory on bitter stems; blossoms
like salvia on ashheaps. It has come finally face to face
with some incapacity of its own; but among the wrecks it
finds a piquant sprightly music:

[quotes in full, Danse Russe, CEP, 148]

It knows its power to live in deserts; knows it can make
much out of next-to-nothing; hang on by the skin of its
teeth:

[quotes in full Youth and Beauty, CEP, 219]

With pride it feels the return of animal health, the good
tickle of the beast-skin:

[quotes in full The Cold Night, CEP, 203]

And with joy we receive the reassurance brought by
these pieces, take the signal of imminent habitable land

they give. The trip from the old to the new world upon
which we are all in spite of ourselves embarked has gotten
most of us not to a city spreading 'its dark life upon the
earth of a new world rooted there, sensitive to its richest
beauty,' or about a temple where 'the tribe's deep feeling
for a reality that stems back into the permanence of remote
origins' has its firm hold: achievement of American civilization. It has brought us it seems no further than a low
smoky shore looking rather like the Bayonne littoral from
the Staten Island ferryboat on a sunless winter's day: a
slatey weed-garden of wharves, gas-tuns, church-spires,
chimneys, gash-like streets, habitations set against
ghostly blueless hills. And we have been standing at the
rail, how often! undetermined to disembark our baggage;
uncertain whether the shore before us is indeed solid
earth upon which one can walk and nourish oneself, or
merely a fume of strangling smoke; worried by the picture
of a silly journey undertaken to a spot which is not firm
land, and can never support the whole weight of man. But
while we have been standing, somebody excited ashore has
sent up some wild signal rockets through the gloom; and
we see the scarlet spikey flowers abloom on the cinder-
piles, and the little human habitation stand snug and
whole in the shadow of vats and chimneys. Life goes on,
behind this forbidding wall. The jumbled piles lose their
dreadfulness. They have been shown rough customers
enough, but beings among whom a sturdy pair of legs can
navigate, and a stout brace of lungs breathe up. And we
know the journey has led us somewhere, at least, and begin
moving up our baggage.

14. ALFRED KREYMBORG, FROM 'TROUBADOUR: AN AUTOBIOGRAPHY'

New York, 1925, 242, 243

A recollection of Williams, this refers to the early days
of Kreymborg's editorship of 'Others' (1916-19), of which
Williams was for a brief space acting editor. (1) Kreymborg (b. 1883), besides editing the 'Glebe', 'Others' and
a variety of other little magazines, was a member of the
Grantwood, N.J., artists' colony, a poet, anthologist and
critic.

...Shy though Bill was in person, blank paper let loose anything he felt about everything, and he frankly and fearlessly undressed himself down to the ground. Not since the days of old Walt had an American gone quite so far, and readers were shocked all over again....

...Among the first contributors to 'Others,' no person gave as much of himself as Bill Williams. Regardless of the many patients who required his attention in and around the gray town of Rutherford, the medico often pointed the blunt nose of his Ford toward Grantwood or wrote incisive letters to Krimmie and aided him critically in the onerous task of choosing and rejecting manuscripts. Krimmie had never encountered a more incongruous American than this artist, scientist and madman. His letters, as outspoken as his poems, attacked and applauded Krimmie in the same paragraph, and for the sake of clarity many a goddam was thrown at the editor - and thrown back in rebuttal. At the close of such an exchange of civilities, Bill would laugh, turn on himself - another favorite pastime - and subject the patient to a surgical operation in which no phase of the raw spirit was spared. Groans would issue from the defenceless ego, and then someone had to treat him like the adolescent he was at such times. Shyness, bravado, imagination, scientific accuracy, childishness, were constantly at war in this son of a Porto Rican woman (Raquel Ellen Rose Hoheb) and an Englishman. One had to develop many shades of responsiveness to cope with the medico's changeable moods and melodies....

Note

1 See SL, 34. Thirlwall's headnote briefly describes the circumstances of the Grantwood 'group', and notes that 'the editorship of "Others" was revolved from poet to poet'. In the headnoted letter, to Marianne Moore, Williams describes the arrangement as Kreymborg's 'letting a few of us who are near at hand take an issue and see what we can do with it'.

'In the American Grain'

New York, 9 November 1925

15. HENRY SEIDEL CANBY, BACK TO THE INDIAN, 'SATURDAY REVIEW OF LITERATURE'

Vol. II, no. 21, 19 December 1925, 425, 430

Canby (1878-1961) in 1924 helped to found 'Saturday Review of Literature' and became its first editor, relinquishing the post to Bernard De Voto in 1936 (see SL, 163). For twenty-eight years from 1926 he was chairman of the editorial board of the Book-of-the-Month Club. A lifelong opponent of censorship, he taught at Yale University for more than twenty years, and published a biography of Whitman and critical work on Thoreau, Twain and Henry James.

American writers usually belong to a minority party - especially the good American writers. From Cooper down through Emerson, Thoreau, Whittier, Mark Twain, Whitman, and Henry Adams, they have been violently critical of the way the country was going. Literary and commercial America in the nineteenth century are not one new world, but two.

Historians have been more complaisant. With the exception of Adams, the major figures have been content to extol like Bancroft, record like Roades, or verify facts like the current school of scientific investigators. Yet any observer who had watched discontent with American civilization spreading through the mid-Western novel, or the vivid rewriting of American social history in the poetry of Masters and Lindsay, might have guessed that a sporadic attack, such as the recent charge of thirty Americans upon their civilization, was only a beginning. We shall have histories and biographies in which the Revolution becomes a brawl, Andrew Jackson, a devil of anarchy, George Washington, an ignorant prig, and the United States is seen to have gone wrong at the beginning and never recovered.

Mr. D. H. Lawrence, some years ago, wrote an extremely suggestive book upon classic American literature which was an attack upon the suppression of instinct in America. According to him, the great Americans were all thwarted by their environment. Pioneer life and a new country bred in them a kind of old Indian devil which was constantly trying to get out, but failing to break through the crust of convention chiefly because there was a Puritan with a shotgun waiting at each crack. Mr. Lawrence is not an academic person, and American literature is still regarded as *infra dig.* by too [many] American scholars, hence his book was not much read by students. If it was sometimes grotesquely wrong in its American estimates, its author was sometimes astonishingly and illuminatingly right.

From this book, Mr. William Carlos Williams, an American poet and modernist, who surveys his home from the perspective of Paris, seems to have drawn a sheaf of ideas for his 'In the American Grain' and added new ones of his own. His disjointed, jolting style comes, at a long remove, from Carlyle, but his point of view is strictly modern in its discontent. In a sweep of free fantasias, from Red Erik down to Poe, he delves toward the roots of American life, and illustrates his comments on American heroes by lengthy quotation from sources often too little known. And always the result is the same. The instinctive, full-blooded people, like Burr and Boone, who did what they wanted - especially with women - were never appreciated. It has been the crafty, prudent folk like Franklin, the cold-blooded conservatives like Hamilton, the godly New Englanders, who together have built a materialistic, hypocritical, puritanical America and got all the praise. The 'swill-hole' of Paterson is a monument to Hamilton's foresightedness, aimless thrift and energy are Franklin's heritage. Prosperity and comfort have merely de-animated us. There was more virtue in the Indian than in the Puritan who slew him.

Mr. Williams is a poet and not a historian, and his book is a poet's protest not a historian's unbiased summary. It would be unfair to subject his brooding criticism to close scrutiny. He is another, if a less original, Rousseau, come to praise the unknown and the might-have-been. It is curious how primitive, instinctive man, with 'the open, free assertion' of originality, keeps bobbing up to threaten stale civilizations. Rousseau made of him the most successful bogey that ever scared a world into revolution. But that he never existed, that the Indians, as Crévecoeur remarked, were only too little like him, did not lessen his influence. He helped to overturn the *ancien régime*.

We need not call Mr. Williams's book another 'Nouvelle Héloïse,' although it has striking passages as well as confused ones. His 'De Soto' is very fine. But we could do well to regard the increasing number of books that deny all the values of what we supposed was our history, which attack the moral impulse as the curse of America, make the uncontrolled frontiersman our only hero, condemn New England intellectualism with every drawn breath, and assert that continence, efficiency, standardization, and progress are equally degrading. These books are not history, not even good sense, especially when the author regards the sober march of civilization across the continent as an unfortunate curtailing of savage liberty, and puts his curse on his native land because he is not allowed to dance naked in the moonlight around a broached rum cask in Gramercy Park; yet there is poetry in them, the poetry of revolt against smugness and too much dull living. It is poetry, but rather muddy poetry. The return to paganism is likely to be rosier in theory than in practice. There is undoubtedly much to cause discontent in the spectacle of America as the fatted calf among the nations, but to choose rampageous Indians and political reprobates as ancestral models by way of a change from puritans, Quakers, and Virginia gentlemen is to strike a Parisian attitude which seems a little absurd in New York.

16. KENNETH BURKE, SUBJECTIVE HISTORY, 'NEW YORK HERALD TRIBUNE BOOKS'

14 March 1926, 7

On the jacket of his latest book, his 'modern account of American heroes', William Carlos Williams announces his program as follows:

> In these studies I have sought to re-name the things seen, now lost in a chaos of borrowed titles, many of

them inappropriate, under which the true character lies hidden. In letters, in journals, reports of happenings I have recognized new contours suggested by old words, so that new names were constituted. [IAG, 5]

And these new names, if I understood Williams correctly, are intended merely to be the old names with their original charge restored. They are new, not for the love of novelty, but through piety, through husbandry of tradition; new only in the sense that one might change the label on a bottle from 'Poison' to 'Deadly Poison', employing a modified statement to produce the same effect.

It is Williams's business, then, to see beyond the label, to see the rolling eye and the quivering muscle behind the word 'Poison'; to replace 'Columbus discovered America in 1492' with excerpts from Columbus's diary which show what it was to be approaching America at the turn of that century and to see a continent not as land, but in terms of seaweed, of river birds heard passing in the night, of clouds which, with a glad outcry, are mistaken for islands; to replace Daniel Boone with the image of a man who tramped through Kentucky alone in constant danger of death and, returning, tried to chronicle in dull language that Kentucky was beautiful when, in reality, he meant that Kentucky was beautiful while there was danger of death; to give us, in place of De Soto, a man who advances in a kind of grim nightmare, taking this virgin country as a woman, his life split into a dialogue with an imaginary, non-existent shape, as it is with those poor devils (tabulated by the savants) who under cover of night converse with themselves in two voices, one deep and the other falsetto. Thus Eric the Red is traded in for a sense of fish-blooded butchery by quotation from original documents, witchcraft is restored not only with its gloom, but with its logic; and Burr, when made human, is automatically made heroic.

I do not mean to imply that Williams's method always works. It tends toward a maximum of 'interpretation' and a minimum of research; his heroes at times are so busy *living* that they neglect to do anything else, and their inventions, or discoveries, or battles, or policies, become an unimportant by-product. The closing chapter on Lincoln is perhaps his process reduced to its farthest absurdity; Lincoln 'done' in five short paragraphs, and the longest of these devoted to a nearly malapropos digression on Mengelberg, the Philharmonic conductor. His complaints against American women are often puerile, although vigorous and picturesque enough.

[quotes IAG, 188, 'They are fit ... wholesale.']

And his respect for brawn and daring has its vicissitudes: on one page it is a brisk and muscular enthusiasm, and on the next we feel that no little girl in a convent ever pondered on these things with a more timid, and a simpler, trust.

The purpose is poetry, not history. Williams seeks bravuras rather than facts. 'Meaning' in his mind is not to observe, but to cry out. Ideology, while it is here, is totally secondary; it is never organized, is low in the evolutionary scale. But splendid wordings turn up continually. I quote from his essay on Raleigh:

[quotes IAG, 75, 'Sing, O muse genius.']

Yet the word 'genius', with which this citation closes, suggests to me that Williams's concern lies elsewhere; at this time, when it is so prevalent a tendency to look over past lives for the evidences of genius, Williams shifts the emphasis, he looks for heroes. The genius is in some way the epitome, the summing-up and concentration point of the forces among which he lives; while in the hero we emphasize rather his struggle against these forces. The two concepts are not opposed, they are different; and being so, they may overlap, separate or totally coincide. In common, however, they possess the quality of energy, of some internal 'drive' or 'demon'.

There is one attitude of mind which sees this demon, this will, as an Olympian trait in man: such will as, translated into the diction of motion-picture titles, becomes the 'lure' or the 'call' of something or other. But this attitude is continually breaking, and as it does so the will becomes no longer a beacon whining in advance, no longer an oasis or a harbor just a little way ahead of us, but is rather something which goads us from behind. People of great will are then *ridden* by demons. Their motion is not the answer to a 'call'; it is flight.

Implicit in Williams's book there is something which fluctuates between these two attitudes, an intermingling of their once divided logics, so that we can no longer distinguish, in these pilgrimages of his heroes, between that which is done in aggression and that which is done in defense, between power and starvation, play and malice.

17. D. H. LAWRENCE, AMERICAN HEROES, 'NATION'

14 April 1926, 413-4

Lawrence (1885-1930) had published his 'Studies in Classic American Literature' in 1923, and many critics (starting with Canby, No. 15 above) have indicated the importance of that work to 'In the American Grain'. Even more crucial is the connection with Lawrence's earlier essay, America, Listen to Your Own, which appeared in the 'New Republic' in 1920. (1) Lawrence urges that Americans make contact with whatever is unresolved and rejected in themselves. The link between Williams and Lawrence is convincingly examined in Thomas R. Whitaker, 'William Carlos Williams' (New York, 1968). Mike Weaver, in his 'William Carlos Williams: The American Background', notes that, 'His review in 1926 of "In the American Grain" was one of the most generous notices Lawrence ever wrote, and two years later the book was one of the very few that he was recommending' (p. 149). Williams remarks in his 'Autobiography' (p. 51) that he once wrote to Lawrence, who never replied. 'The Collected Earlier Poems' includes An Elegy for D. H. Lawrence.

Other artists who were impressed by the book include Hart Crane (whose major poem 'The Bridge' may have been influenced by it;) see No. 18 below, Charles Sheeler (see Constance Rourke, 'Charles Sheeler', New York, 1938, 49), Martha Graham, 'who', Williams tells us, 'wrote me saying she could not have gone on with her choreographic projects without it', and Alfred Stieglitz, who said it had given him the name for his new Madison Avenue Gallery, An American Place ('Autobiography', 236-7).

Mr. Williams quotes Poe's distinction between 'nationality in letters' and the *local* in literature. Nationality in letters is deplorable, whereas the *local* is essential. All creative art must rise out of a specific soil and flicker with a spirit of place.

The local, of course, in Mr. Williams's sense, is the very opposite of the parochial, the parish-pump stuff. The local in America is America itself. Not Salem, or Boston, or Philadelphia, or New York, but that of the American subsoil which spouts up in any of those places into the lives of men.

In these studies of 'American' heroes, from Red Eric of

Greenland, and Columbus and Cortes and Montezuma, on to
Abraham Lincoln, Mr. Williams tries to reveal the experience of great men in the Americas since the advent of the
whites. History in this book would be a sensuous record
of the Americanization of the white men in America, as contrasted with ordinary history, which is a complacent
record of the civilization and Europizing (if you can
allow the word) of the American continent.

In this record of truly American heroes, then, the
author is seeking out not the ideal achievement of great
men of the New World but the men themselves, in all the
dynamic explosiveness of their energy. This peculiar
dynamic energy, this strange yearning and passion and
uncanny explosive quality in men derived from Europe, is
American, the American element. Seek out *this* American
element - Of Americans! - is the poet's charge.

All America is now going hundred per cent American.
But the only hundred per cent American is the Red Indian,
and he can only be canonized when he is finally dead. And
not even the most American American can transmogrify into
an Indian. Whence, then, the hundred per cent?

It is here that Mr. Williams's - and Poe's - distinction between the *national* and the *local* is useful. Most
of the hundred per centism is national, and therefore not
American at all. The new one hundred per cent literature
is all *about* Americans, in the intensest American vernacular. And yet, in vision, in conception, in the very
manner, it still remains ninety-nine per cent European.
But for 'Ulysses' and Marcel Proust and a few other beetling high-brows, where would the modernest hundred per
centers of America have been? Alas, where they are now,
save for cutting a few capers.

What then? William Carlos Williams tries to bring into
his consciousness America itself, the still-unravished
bride of silences. The great continent, its bitterness,
its brackish quality, its vast glamor, its strange cruelty. Find this, Americans, and get it into your bones.
The powerful, unyielding breath of the Americas, which
Columbus sniffed, even in Europe, and which sent the Conquistadores mad. National America is a gruesome sort of
fantasy. But the unravished *local* America still waits
vast and virgin as ever, though in process of being
murdered.

The author sees the genius of the continent as a woman
with exquisite, super-subtle tenderness and recoiling
cruelty. It is a myth-woman who will demand of men a
sensitive awareness, a supreme sensuous delicacy, and at
the same time an infinitely tempered resistance, a power
of endurance and of resistance.

To evoke a vision of the essential America is to evoke Americans, bring them into conscious life. To bring a few American citizens into American consciousness - the consciousness at present being all bastardized European - is to form the nucleus of the new race. To have the nucleus of a new race is to have a future: and a true aristocracy. It is to have the germ of an aristocracy in sensitive tenderness and diamond-like resistance.

A man, in America, can only *begin* to be American. After five hundred years there are no *racial* white Americans. They are only national, woebegone, or strident. After five hundred years more there may be the developing nucleus of a true American race. If only men, some few, trust the American passion that is in them, and pledge themselves to it.

But the passion is not national. No man who doesn't feel the last anguish of tragedy - and beyond that - will ever know America, or begin, even at the beginning's beginning, to be American.

There are two ways of being American; and the chief, says Mr. Williams, is by recoiling into individual smallness and insentience, and gutting the great continent in frenzies of mean fear. It is the Puritan way. The other is by *touch*; touch America as she is; dare to touch her! And this is the heroic way.

And this, this sensitive touch upon the unseen America, is to be the really great adventure in the New World. Mr. Williams's book contains his adventure; and, therefore, for me, has a fascination. There are very new and profound glimpses into life: the strength of insulated smallness in the New Englanders, the fascination of 'being nothing' in the Negroes, the *spell-bound* quality of men like Columbus, de Soto, Boone. It is a glimpse of what the vast America *wants men to be*, instead of another strident assertion of what men have made, do make, will make, can make, out of the murdered territories of the New World.

It would be easy enough to rise, in critical superiority, as a critic always feels he must, superior to his author, and find fault. The modernist style is sometimes irritating. Was Tenochtitlan really so wonderful? (See Adolf Bandelier's 'The Golden Man.') (2) Does not Mr. Williams mistake Poe's agony of *destructive penetration*, through all the horrible bastard-European alluvium of his 1840 America, for the positive America itself?

But if an author rouses my deeper sympathy he can have as many faults as he likes, I don't care. And if I disagree with him a bit, heaven save me from feeling superior just because I have a chance to snarl. I am only too thankful that Mr. Williams wrote his book.

Notes

1 Both it and the present essay are included in
   'Phoenix', a collection of Lawrence's writings edited
   by Edward D. McDonald (London, 1936).
2 Presumably Lawrence's reference is to 'The Gilded Man
   (Eldorado) and Other Pictures of the Spanish Occupancy
   of America' by Adolph Francis Alphonse Bandelier, published in New York in 1893, and possible source reading
   for Lawrence's 'The Plumed Serpent'.

18. HART CRANE, FROM A LETTER TO WALDO FRANK

21 November 1926, in 'The Letters of Hart Crane', 277-8

... Williams' 'American Grain' (1) is an achievement that
I'd be proud of. A most important and *sincere* book. I'm
very enthusiastic - I put off reading it, you know, until
I felt my own way cleared beyond chance of confusions
incident to reading a book so intimate to my theme. I
was so interested to note that he puts Poe and his
'character' in the same position as I had *symbolized* for
him in The Tunnel section. [The Tunnel is a section of
Crane's major poem, 'The Bridge' (1930).]

Note

1 Speaking of 'In the American Grain' to Edith Heal,
   Williams said: 'The chapter on De Soto was used by
   Hart Crane in "The Bridge" - he took what he wanted,
   why shouldn't he - that's what writing is for' (IWWP,
   43). Williams and Crane never met, but they began
   a literary connection in 1916 when Williams accepted
   some of Crane's poems for 'Others'. Their literary
   relationship is fully explored by Joseph Evans Slate
   in William Carlos Williams, Hart Crane, and 'The
   Virtue of History', 'Texas Studies in Language and
   Literature', vol. VI, winter 1965, 496-511, which
   includes a detailed comparison of 'In the American
   Grain' and 'The Bridge', and the suggestion that 'the
   spirit of Hart Crane' is present in 'Paterson (Book
   One)'.
      In his Introduction to the second impression of 'In

the American Grain' Horace Gregory suggests that, like himself,

> several other writers came upon it and kept the memory of its insights and the quality of its prose within the hidden chambers of their own knowledge and imagination. My immediate example is Hart Crane's 'The Bridge', which was published five years later and which carried within it traces of the impression left upon those who first read 'In the American Grain'. These traces are to be found throughout the poem: a fragment of Dr. Williams' quotation from Thomas Morton's 'The New English Canaan' is reproduced on the half-title page of 'Powhatan's Daughter' and like selections of material may be quickly recognized in the concluding pages of Dr. Williams' chapter on Columbus and in the closing stanzas of Ave Maria. Even the quotation from Edgar Poe's The City in the Sea (whose original title was significantly written as The Doomed City), 'Death looks gigantically down', smoulders in a half-line of The Tunnel and also appears in Dr. Williams' book, placed over 'a dead world, peopled by shadows and silence, and despair...' These similarities should not of course be read as plagiarisms, nor should we exaggerate their obvious claims to a relationship....

19. GORHAM MUNSON, WILLIAM CARLOS WILLIAMS, A UNITED STATES POET, 'DESTINATIONS: A CANVASS OF AMERICAN LITERATURE SINCE 1900'

1928, 101-35

Munson (1896-1969), a social and literary critic, taught at the New School for Social Research in New York for many years, and edited successively in the 1920s the periodicals 'Secession' and 'Psychology'. From 1933 to 1939 he edited 'New Democracy', and was an exponent of Social Credit theories. Among his books is a study of Robert Frost (1927).

Munson's view of Williams' work appears to derive from Williams' own remarks in the Prologue to 'Kora' and he cannot have overlooked Wallace Stevens' letter therein, which contains the rather Olympian judgment, 'What strikes me most about the poems themselves is their casual character.... Personally I have a distaste for miscellany.' Stevens' famous remark, 'Well a book of poems is a damned serious affair', also occurs in this letter. See 'Selected Essays', 12-13.

If one stops to survey the touted American writers of the last fifteen years, one is impressed by the failure of most of them to develop. Take the early books of Carl Sandburg, Vachel Lindsay, Sherwood Anderson, Edgar Lee Masters, Theodore Dreiser, H. L. Mencken, Van Wyck Brooks, many others. What have they done, after all, but repeat their first books? Granting to them an initial blaze, the fire can hardly be said to have increased or brightened or become hotter or consumed fuel of a different character. What I mean is that their early work really contains their later work; I mean that no unpredictable element has entered into their 'progress'.

Waldo Frank is one exception. His first novel, 'The Unwelcome Man', does not point specifically to his third novel, 'Rahab', and in fact something very important to him happened in between. He discovered the Jewish prophets in the Bible: he received a powerful charge from an ancient religious culture, higher in level and more intense in character than any stimulus his own culture gave him, and this charge was a shock to his own development. Something came into his work that was not originally present, and this unpredictable element changed his forms, exalted his attitude, and transformed his materials. A criticism of Frank would deal with a development and therefore would find it convenient and best to take the narrative form, moving from book to book in chronological order.

William Carlos Williams exacts the same tribute. The chronology of his books is insistent, for if Williams has not developed in the sense Waldo Frank has, he has at least *changed*, the changes being due to a frantic effort to develop.

The starting point is a small and scarce book of poetry, 'The Tempers', published in London by Elkin Matthews in 1913. After reading Williams's more accessible works, one digs up this little item and discovers that in it Williams employed rhyme schemes and traditional metrical forms! He used 'classical allusions' freely! He sounds very much like Ezra Pound at that date! The Browning influence (with Pound as its probable carrier) had hit him! There are even translations from the Spanish!

Later on Williams was to make the puerile remark that 'nowadays poets spit upon rhyme and rhetoric': he was to

call Pound 'the best enemy United States verse has': he
was to become aggressively contemporary and local, thereby
chucking outside the classical paraphernalia of names,
symbols and associations, and losing all interest in
making translations.
  But when he was composing the nineteen poems in 'The
Tempers', he was, one conjectures, a fellow student of
Pound at the University of Pennsylvania. The little book
then is to be taken as representing Williams in the
Academy, Pound being the teacher. In addition to the
teachings, the pupil shows something of his own - a toughness of personality, a talent for emphatic wordings, a
genuine poetic sap that is just beginning to run. In the
next book this sap will feed surprising foliage, for it
will draw on that surrounding soil that Pound deserted and
produce a poetry quite dissimilar to Pound's work.
  The second poem in 'Al Que Quiere' (1917) is a handy
illustration, though certainly not among the better poems
in that collection.

[quotes Pastoral, CEP, 121]

  This poem indicates first of all that Williams has
found his subject matter, which is none other than the
objects that appear right in front of his eyes, right beneath his nose. Being a practising physician in Rutherford, New Jersey, that means to Williams that his senses
tell him of that locality, of the nearby metropolis, New
York, and of America at large so far as he touches it.
So the choice of subject matter has been definitely
settled in 'Al Que Quiere'. It is the American background
(flora, people, customs, heroes, rigors and scenic atro-
ciousness) from which Williams has never since deviated.
  The second choice was between established verse forms
and vers libre, and Williams committed himself altogether
to the latter. No wonder! Vers libre might have been
made to order for this busy literary doctor, writing poems
in odd minutes between calls, always liable to be interrupted and always on the jump, day and night. For while
vers libre has many difficulties and many possibilities,
this also is true of it: a poet with a fair ear and a
native feeling for form can trust to improvisation in
these respects - rhythm and form - and write good vers
libre, provided his attention bears hard and directly upon
the individual word. That is why Williams prattles so
often and sometimes intelligently about giving freedom to
words, the free word, et cetera. For he is himself only
concerned in a secondary way with combinations of words:
the main thing is a regard for the bite, the weight, the

thrust, the individuality of the successive single words he picks out.

By culling a dozen or so quotations from his critical notes, one could construct a disjointed ars poetica by William Carlos Williams, the first article of which would deal with the necessity for cleansing words and putting weight in them and the remaining articles would explain the psychology of his poetic process. Among psychological processes the correspondent to a technical devotion to the 'free word' would be a devotion to the isolated perception, and that is what we find. To see the thing with great intensity of perception, to see it directly, simply, immediately, and without forethought or afterthought, is the unvarying psychological basis for 'Al Que Quiere' and the later books of poems.

Turning back to Pastoral, we find what I have been saying. The shabby disorder of the poor quarter of an American village. A simple pattern: the autobiographical statement of a changed attitude, a list of objects to illustrate the attitude, and at the end a generality running out a tangent. A very simple rhythm just to set off the clear stark words. The enumeration of bare perceptions of things seen on a walk. And something more: two qualities.

The first is the national flavor, the much sought for American character in writing. To my mind this is achieved as much by the turn of thinking and phrasing in the opening three lines and in the concluding three lines as it is by the veracity of the scenery, for those lines reveal unmistakably a man who has been pressed upon continuously by American sociology, 'marked up' by it. The other quality - that which makes Williams distinctly a poet - is lyrical. He 'admires' these poor streets: if he is 'fortunate', the outhouses will be colored a bluish green, properly weathered. What is it that gets into the poem by means of these words, that gets into the words 'pleases me best'?

I would say, exhilaration, - the exhilaration that all of us have occasionally felt when we have accidentally made an exact perception of some object, seen an object not hazily as in a dream but with clarity, an exterior thing, apart from us, acting upon us. This feeling of exhilaration at the fact that our senses register vividly, occasional with us, appears to be frequent with Williams, and it saves his compositions from flatness and prosaic demeanor, conferring on them the potentiality of flight. Restraint is beautiful only when the potentiality of escape is present.

[quotes January Morning, Section X, CEP, 164]

It is easy to see that there is no principle of selection operative on Williams's subject matter. Given his esthetic of exhilaration induced by sharp and strong perceptions and given his geographical environment as a determinant, he can include everything that affects his sensory equipment ; whether it be harebells or children leaping about a dead dog or the winter wind or rusty chicken wire in a backyard. The one gauge is intensity of perception and since the unpleasant has great power of impact upon nostrils, ears, eyes, and so on, it follows that the unpleasant is generously included in Williams's lines, where however it is redeemed by the same exhilaration that a vivid register of the pleasing objects also creates. This is the reason for Williams's 'unflinching realism' against which sentimental objections have been lodged.

The problem of an advance after 'Al Que Quiere' must have faced Williams quite acutely. He could, of course, go on by refining his instruments of expression and trying for an ever sharper focus, but this would be at best adding to what he had already done or at worst repeating it. Another possibility was to abandon the austerity of bare intense perceptions, without forethought or afterthought, and to make these perceptions work to evoke one emotion or another, one mood or another. This is the ordinary process and Williams himself worked it in a few poems in 'Al Que Quiere' such as In Harbor. Thus, the usual way was already open for him to incorporate in his later poems a great variety of emotions and perhaps eventually to embody an emotional attitude, all this of course without becoming 'intellectual'.

But Williams chose neither of these possibilities for treatment in 'Kora in Hell: Improvisations' (1920): instead he made an unexpected deviation from 'Al Que Quiere'.

'The thing that saves your work is opacity, and don't forget it,' Pound had written to Williams, and in reviewing one of the 'Others Anthologies' he remarked that 'it also displays Mr Williams's praiseworthy opacity'. Apparently Williams valued the counsel and it was bad, for whereas in 'Al Que Quiere' he had written with weight and clarity, in 'Kora in Hell' he set out to cultivate opacity and achieved impenetrability. The opaque is simply the strong man's blur and excusable only if it is the maximum luminosity a recalcitrant and profound subject will yield: profundity is scarcely the term to associate with Williams's writing.

The means employed to gain opacity were of the simplest and may be summed up by the phrase - 'association of ideas'. Williams discovered that a group of remote perceptions had surprising points of contact with each other in his mind, so he consolidated these widely divergent glimpses of things for the sake of the personal connection. Then he found that he could state a similar association in another set of terms and relate the two statements to each other as poem and key. Thus

[quotes 'Kora', 1957 edition, 25. Passage is 42-3 in 'Imaginations', ed. Webster Schott]

I select this improvisation because it seems to me much less opaque than the others, and yet it illustrates my point: namely, that since the 'association of ideas' is accidental in the first place and in the second it is personal, private, excessively subjective, therefore whether or not it produces an intended effect upon an intended reader is purely a hit-or-miss proposition. Or, as Kenneth Burke commenting on 'Kora in Hell' put it: 'How beautiful the association of the ideas would have been in art if used in one work, by one man, for one page, and for some end other than that of a beautiful association of ideas.'

Williams's own remarks about 'Kora in Hell' justify the estimate of it as a detour on which he deviated too far from his path but returned, having learned something from having pushed out so far. On one occasion he was to say: 'Take the improvisations. What the French reader would say is: *Oui, ça; j'ai deja vu ça; ça c'est de Rimbaud*. Finis.' But why should 'light hearted William twirling his November mustachios' mention Rimbaud in this connection. Williams is the child of his mother and he describes her in the Prologue to 'Kora in Hell'.

[quotes SE, 4, para. 3]

Rimbaud was an altogether different type, a prodigy who came to the end of scepticism and saw no way to make an affirmation: he did not take the name of hell in vain when he wrote a title. Whereas Williams, suffering from the ghastly business of war, could yet try to reconstruct a springtime. On another occasion Williams admits of the improvisations that 'their fault is their dislocation of sense, often complete' and with that we may leave them to return to the straight line that joins 'Sour Grapes' (1921) with 'Al Que Quiere', turning over the pages of 'Contact' magazine as we go.

That was a curious magazine! The first issue, ten
multigraphed sheets stapled between dull orange covers,
was dated December, 1920. In January, 1921, there was a
larger number, also multigraphed. In February, one supposes that was the date, a printed and illustrated number
different in format and paper as well. A little later -
who knows just when? - a fourth number came out, printed
on only one side of each page. Then a gap until June,
1923, when the fifth and last (?) (1) number was printed.

'Contact' was edited by Williams in conjunction with a
younger man, Robert McAlmon, 'who has had the peculiar
property of being a magical mirror to Williams. Peering
at the slovenly scripts of McAlmon, Williams sees there -
to everyone's astonishment - the clear hard virtues of his
own writing. So that, in writing about McAlmon's work, he
comes to write excellent statements of himself.

After the fourth number of 'Contact', McAlmon married
an English poet and fortune - a front page story for the
American newspapers at the time - and sailed for Europe to
continue the publication of the magazine. Something, however, caused him to abandon these plans and instead the
Contact Publishing Company was formed in Paris for the
purpose of printing books by Marsden Hartley, Mina Loy,
McAlmon, Williams and others who by contributing to
'Contact' were more or less identified with it.

Besides spawning Robert McAlmon and a publishing company that still publishes, 'Contact' set forth to its two
hundred readers (if there were that many) a program for
American writing. In the first place, beware of the mere
acquisition of information as a culture substitute.
...'Art may be the supreme hypocrisy of an information-
cultured people ... without CONTACT ... justifiable perhaps if it becomes at last actually the way sensitive
people live...' ran the legend on the cover of the first
number. 'Contact' was founded on the conviction that 'art
which attains is indigenous of experience and relations,
and that the artist works to express perceptions rather
than to attain standards of achievement' and it was carried on by a 'faith in the existence of native artists' of
certain specifications 'who receive meager recognition'.
But what was meant by contact? The simplest statement
was - 'the essential contact between words and the locality which breeds them, in this case America'.

All of this was in the first issue. In the second we
read that

> In proportion as a man has bestirred himself to become
> awake to his own locality he will perceive more and
> more of what is disclosed and find himself in a

position to make the necessary translations. The disclosures will then and only them come to him a reality, as joy, as release. For these men communicate with each other and strive to invent new devices. But he who does not know his own world, in whatever confused form it may be, must either stupidly fail to learn from foreign work or stupidly swallow it without knowing how to judge of its essential value. Descending each his own branch man and man reach finally a common trunk of understanding.

And this:

We, Contact, aim to emphasize the local phase of the game of writing. We realize that it is emphasis only which is our business. We want to give all our energy to the setting up of new vigors of artistic perception, invention and expression in the United States. Only by slow growth, consciously fostered to the point of enthusiasm, will American work of the quality of Marianne Moore's best poetry come to the fore of intelligent attention and the ignorance which has made America an artistic desert be somewhat dissipated. We lack interchange of ideas in our country more than we lack foreign percept. Every effort should be made, we feel, to develop among our serious writers a sense of mutual contact first of all. To this also we are devoted.

It remained to broaden the program, as was done in the third issue to mean 'contact with experience'.

contact with experience is essential to good writing or, let us say, literature. We have said this in the conviction that contact always implies a local definition of effort with a consequent taking on of certain colors from the locality by the experience, and these colors or sensual values of whatever sort, are the only realities in writing, or as may be said, the essential quality of literature.

I take the trouble to make these excavations from the file of 'Contact' for several reasons; they make explicit what was already implicit in the working procedure of 'Al Que Quiere' and 'Kora in Hell': they constitute an artistic credo to which Williams has adhered with ardor and fidelity: and, best justification of all, Williams has made the program work with a certain measure of success. That is, his writing has inbred local characteristics and it is good writing.

An outstanding feature of the last decade in American letters has been the working of a nationalistic impulse. We see this most blatantly in Vachel Lindsay, most ravenously in Robert J. Coady and his 'Soil' magazine, most generalized in the allied phenomena of the group that animated the 'Seven Arts', and most mystically in Alfred Stieglitz. Lindsay's 'new localism', however, is a mere proclamation, scarcely a program: it is simply the expression of a wish that the smaller American communities should be inspired to create their own arts and crafts, that the neighbourhood spirit should be directed toward a Campbellite God, a long-skirted Art, and a Wilsonian Democracy. The fruit - that is, Lindsay's verse - has been deplorable. The case of the late Robert J. Coady is much better, but even so it can be summed up as no more than a positive attitude toward a barely differentiated appetite for those phenomena in the environment - works of engineering genius, sports, moving pictures, racy journalism - that seemed flamboyantly national and extraordinarily vigorous in comparison with the official art world with which Coady was disgusted. The 'Seven Arts' group had national aspirations but they were thickened by auras of sociology, psychoanalysis and religion until they lost - in most of the individuals concerned - specific direction and definition. Practically nothing survived the 'Soil': not even its attitude crystallized. Whereas the 'Seven Arts' group diffused its nationalism in all directions and lost whatever purity it originally had. (An exception must be made for Waldo Frank.) In regard to Alfred Stieglitz, his stresses on thorough workmanship, personal integrity and American qualities have been felt with great force in photography and painting, but, owing to Stieglitz's fumbling grasp of the literary medium, they have been almost inoperative on our letters.

Williams differs from all these in that he has observed the limitations of his program and thereby kept it pure, he has confined himself to the strictly esthetic problems of choice of subject matter and the fashion of perceiving and handling it, and he has borne the fruit proper to the aim of his program - in our next instance that fruit being 'Sour Grapes'.

It is hard to hold oneself to the selection of only one poem from this book to show both the continuity with 'Al Que Quiere' and the improvement upon it. No poem in the earlier book seems quite so stripped, so weighted and *physical* in its impact as The Great Figure. No poem in 'Al Que Quiere' seems such a bit of characteristic psychological behavior as January in which the poet opposes to the derisive winds the warm comfort of his study - the only thing in the cosmos that apparently at that moment he *knows*. Again, the Overture to a Dance of Locomotives [CEP, 194] could be quoted, for the sake of showing complication in technic and the approach of a philosophic idea* without loss of firmness. This very good poem, however, begins to thrust away from the main drive of Williams's writing and is a less revelatory example than Blizzard.

[quotes Blizzard, CEP, 198]

I am glad to quote from the best criticism of 'Sour Grapes' I have seen, that by Kenneth Burke in the 'Dial' for February, 1922. 'I should say, therefore, that Williams was engaged in discovering the shortest route between object and subject.' Blizzard, it seems to me, is that shortest route between a lonely man staring back at his isolated tracks across a snowfield and the intense feeling of one's impressions of immensity - in short, a highly energized poem on 'the great open spaces' of America. Its power derives principally from the immediacy of the terms and the uttermost compression of words and technic, or, to state it another way, the smallness of the scale intensifies the feeling of vastitude.

At this point my description of Williams can stand enlargement of the nature that Burke has made. Burke says:

[quotes 'I take Contact to mean ... must go back to the source'; see No. 10 above]

In a word, Williams is a Primitive and practically all that I have written thus far has been a preparation for that word, has been set down to make it safe to use the word. For observe 'The Great American Novel' (1923), his first prose book. He set out, we assume, to write a great American novel. 'If there is progress then there is a novel. Without progress there is nothing. Everything exists from the beginning.' But right there is trouble for him. How can he begin an American novel? What are his own beginnings in the New World? For the rest of the book he keeps trying to start and indicating each time the variety of ignorance or disorder or enormity that blocks progress. In his exasperation he becomes critical or engages in fierce discussion with imaginary opponents: he turns on himself, he sulks, he lunges out desperately. But he never gets the novel under way.

The prose is highly sophisticated. It has similar polarities to those set up in his poetry - one pole being thick and clotted with associations ('Joyce with a difference', Williams calls it) and the other pole (see chapter 17 on the Cumberland mountaineers), a direct emphatic racy simplicity. Between these poles there are many gradations.

But, as we all know, sophistication is not incompatible with primitiveness. Williams couldn't write that novel though he can write a flexible fibrous prose, and the reason is that he is lost in the uncharted American background. He is no master of it: it is not his home: he is trying to become familiar with it. There it is, this huge disorder, this Nuevo Mundo that Columbus's sailors greeted, and he, entranced by its beauty, shaken by its qualities, ferocious or otherwise, but lost in it, utterly lost. To write that novel he feels he must be able to paint the American background: yet he has no pattern for it, only uncoordinated perceptions, impressions, contacts, only a few scattered things that he definitely knows about it. It is the situation of the Primitive. Understanding that, we can understand why Williams sweeps European culture so brusquely aside, even though he is well acquainted with it and responsive to it. Europe is not 'for us', according to Williams, and can give us only sophistication. Williams takes the sophistication, shakes free from it and goes outdoors to discover the new terms that America may present for old or new values.

But no sooner have we tried to encompass Williams with the word - primitive - than this strenuous writer attempts to jump out of the circle. Recall that he began as a poet writing under a freshened academic tradition, then leaped to the straightforward primitivism of 'Al Que Quiere', turned aside for the free association of perceptions in 'Kora in Hell', came back, strengthened, to the primitive contact basis of 'Sour Grapes', and then swerved again into the chaotic prose of 'The Great American Novel'. Late in 1923 he fathered 'Spring and All', a collection of twenty-seven poems held apart by chunks of critical, explanatory and proclamatory prose. 'Spring and All' is his most recent collection of poems and on the evidence it gives one can say that today Williams is veritably thrashing about on the plane he has hitherto written on. One's feeling is that Williams is determined to fly more swiftly and higher than before and that the difficulties are numerous, unyielding and almost intangible.

All his poetic tenets and achievements 'head up' in this book. What is new is a heavier stress upon novelty and the imagination than he stated in 'Kora in Hell', and a critical stress upon composition: and the poetry produced under these stresses.

The emphasis upon newness - it began in 'Kora in Hell' when Williams announced 'nothing is good save the new' and attained capital letters in 'Spring and All' when he shouts, '**THE WORLD IS NEW**' - is easily associated with his creative mood of exhilaration, for to the receptive person novelty is always exciting. It wakes up the senses and they press out the wine which Williams, the poet, drinks. But we should remember that time either evaporates the beauties of newness or cobwebs them into quaint or wayward conceits or imbeds them in the central traditions of literary experience: in other words, the beauties of newness speedily become beauties of another sort altogether or fade out. So that Williams's enthusiastic quest of novelty continually runs the peril of becoming at best a search for poetic conceits.

As for the imagination, one often wonders what Williams can mean by it. As a psychological faculty, the imagination appears to be superior to reason, feeling and action: a higher development. Its processes occur in a flash, and the word for them is simultaneity. The range of its simultaneous perceptions is not less than the whole of the given field. That is to say, the imagination in a flash takes in the whole of a given object - its origin, its history, its constituents and relations, its uses, and its future: it covers at once all the actualities and possibilities included in what was seen. Poe had a true inkling of it when he stressed harmony as its essence and he propounded the acid question for testing the presence of imagination. But Williams appears to have something else in mind when he refers to 'the imagination'. It is a swift combining faculty, a force, a medium, an electricity, that he talks about, but he does not indicate what he regards to be the laws of combination, as Poe did. Judging by the results of his theory - the majority of the poems in 'Spring and All' - the imagination shows its presence by forming unexpected, astonishing, novel combinations, precisely the type of combination that Poe would have named fancy, since it produces the bracing effect of difficulties unexpectedly surmounted.

This is an important point. Williams seeks not to establish a natural harmonious order which covers wholes but an arbitrary composition characterized by independence. He is attempting to leap straight from contact (sharp perceptions) to the imagination (order in the highest sense) without working through culture (the attempt to grasp reality practically, emotionally and intellectually), Thus, to my mind his intense effort to expand his primitivism is leading him back to sophistication, the sophistication of a Parisian cubist painter.

As I have said, he stresses composition in 'Spring and
All' - like a radical modern painter, and it appears to be
the so-called abstract or nonrepresentative painting of
the day that has given him a notion of composition. He
rejects the conception of art as a 'beautiful illusion',
a 'lie', and he rejects the copyist formulae - both
rightly. Nature 'is not opposed to art but apposed to
it', he writes, but his notion of an equal apposition is
to purify art by subtracting elements from it for which
nature has correspondences. This is not the only alternative: subtraction is merely fancy's method for evading the
difficult and tense labor of apposing reality as a whole.

Nevertheless, in spite of the difficulties that a pursuit of novelty, of independent reality, of arbitrary composition has brought down upon Williams there are poems in
this book that rank with the very best of his previous
work. Poem II, a description upon which Charles Demuth
based a painting, is a remarkable union of sensitivity and
force. The light and movement of the major portion of the
poem seems suddenly to fall, but very quietly, to the
center of gravity, the concluding couplet. One might say
that before our eyes these flowers reverse the usual process of growth and take root last.

[quotes The Pot of Flowers, CEP, 242]

If Williams's latest words as a poet show him trying
to transcend primitivism and actually verging toward a
sophisticated fancifulness - to repeat, the arbitrary
purity of 'independent' compositions, when compared to
the organic purity of a complete apprehension of actuality
in all its phases and relations (so seldom achieved!), is
fancy - his latest writing in prose is a vault back to an
intransigent primitivism.

The logic of Williams's position obliged him first to
study American history and then to vivify it, particularly its heroes, as he has done in 'In the American
Grain' (1925). He sets himself against orthodox history
- that is stifling and tyrannous to him: on the contrary,
'history must stay open, it is all humanity'. An artist,
then, he approaches the American past to rename it and
retell it in such a way that its surge and color, its
irony and beauty, its own indecisions and suspenses may
show themselves. But do not think that the book is a
mere exploit in picturesqueness, for Williams is grappling
as hard as he can with the difficulties that frustrated
his attempt to write the 'great American novel'. The past
is made to put its weight directly and heavily upon the
present: a vivid sense of historical determinism is

constantly awake. In the remarkable conversation with
Valéry Larbaud on early Americana which is contained in
one of the chapters, Williams exclaims:

[quotes IAG, 109, 'I said ... upon us.']

This preoccupation with the present gives the book its
drive, inasmuch as Williams, having realized that he has
been formed by history, feels toward history: it is American history with an emotional dimension.
   There were three principal factors. First, the New
World itself, its geography, flora and fauna, its colossal
forces.

[quotes IAG, 7, lines 1-10]

[quotes IAG, 27, opening sentence and lines 7-12]

   They came, the Second Factor, the newcomers from Europe.
The Spaniards with a large gesture, conquerors, outraging
the land. And after the outrages, the destruction of
Tenochitlan and kindred slaughters, the land smiled them on
to an ironic defeat: Ponce de Leon shot in the thigh
searching for the Fountain of Youth. De Soto alone of the
Spaniards married the New World and he was submerged by it
in 'one long sweet caress' of the Mississippi. Then the
French: Champlain curious, exactly noting every detail,
drawing colored maps - a man after Williams's heart. And
Père Sebastian Rasles, still more warmed against the
writer's bosom, Sebastian Rasles the courageous Jesuit who
was supremely interested in the qualities of the new
environment. Also the English came, the Puritans that
Williams detests.

[quotes IAG, 63, lines 1-3 and para. 2, first and fifth
sentences]

   The Third Factor was the Indian, already rooted in what
to him was an old world. Williams does not draw the
Indian directly, but he repeatedly scores this point: the
Indian was 'right', he was the flower of his locality.
The settlers were wrong, for they thieved

[quotes IAG, 136, lines 19-27, 'the problem ... bounty.']

   Almost alone, Daniel Boone, 'by the single logic of his
passion', saw the solution. For Americans are not
Indians, but

[quotes IAG, 137, para. 2]

   Thus, Daniel Boone for the first time becomes a symbol of esthetic and moral worth for American artists. Sam Houston receives the same honor, his career giving the incentive for an urgent plea to American writers of our day to descend to the ground they stand on - 'It is imperative that we sink.' They must go back to the beginning and come up from under, like Sam Houston.
   But the most powerful symbol in the book is Aaron Burr as Williams conceives him. For Burr represents to Williams that for which the American Revolution was fought and that which was squeezed out and dried up as the new nation consolidated itself. There was

[quotes IAG, 193, lines 4-8, 'a half'wild ... possible.']

That deeper matter was in Burr and he was hounded for it. He was an individual. He stood out for liberty. He gave and received to the full of his instinctive nature. There was purity in his functioning.
   What Williams appears to be saying - his psychological reasoning is crude, though sometimes lit by intuitive flashes to the core - is that Burr preserved in his make-up some biological essence, unspoiled by sociological touching, an essence direct and sincere in its action and unwarped and uncomplicated by education. And the axiom is: - he who acts according to his biologic base rather than according to his environmental shell *appears* to be free.
   Hence, the 'teaching' of 'In the American Grain' comes to this: know your sources, know your ground and your locality, know what has shaped you, in order that you may be 'free', in order that like Burr you may live essentially. It is good psychological doctrine *as far as it goes*, just as Williams's poetry and prose are good up to their limits. But I should like to complete my description of Williams's work before entering on the criticism of it just now implied. It would be slighting as fine prose as any American today has written not to give a few sentences to the splendor and force of the prose in 'In the American Grain'.
   As the quotations have disclosed, it is prose with a gusto, prose that puts muscle into its stride. And continually the writer of it spades up superb wordings - sentences with a microscopic accuracy of form and movement, apostrophes and descriptions that attain to romantic eloquence. The eloquence, by the way, is a new facet on Williams's style, and frequently resounds with a dignity

and firmness akin to some well-written wilderness chronicle. On the other hand, there is a full measure of his more usual broken impatient hammering at the subject and the reader. The important thing is that the whole style never loses its propulsion: it keeps doing things: it is an awakening prose in its effect upon the reader.

Surely William's savagery is a unique essence in modern American letters. He has perceived his ground, he has made a beginning, he is riding the forces of his locality. Determinedly, he seeks to be a Daniel Boone in letters, a Sam Houston in method, an Aaron Burr in personal psychology. What threatens him - be it puritanic pressures or the hard exigencies of combining literature with medicine - he barks at: the dog with a bone in its throat is symbolic of his attitude toward all that might interrupt or diminish his poetic pursuit. He will go on, so his career to date guarantees. But where and how?

Very little space is required to define the range of his achievement. Marathon, we are told, looks upon the sea, but - the mountains look upon Marathon. The senses, the emotions, the intellect look upon objects, but the imagination looks upon these: that is, the imagination overlooks experience. This, according to our description of Williams, he has never done and never tried to do. Nor will he ever succeed in so doing by the descent to the ground, the Sam Houston way, unless the laws of psychology reverse themselves. Not by descent into actualized and fragmentary resources but by ascent into our unrealized potentials does greatness in literature come. Descent gives change and renewal, but ascent gives development, and it is precisely development that we miss in this wholly engaging and very active writer.

He is potent enough to originate a needed school of writing in America, a school that will be vigorous and basic, but only basic. The school itself will require fertilization by elements not in Williams and not peculiar to America, elements to which America has not attained, elements that come out of general consciousness and not from the particular ground-contact, if its writings are to span and act upon the whole experience of the reader, if, in short, its writings are to pass from the category of minor to the category of major in aim, scope and power.

Notes

* A feeling for 'eternal recurrence'. This from William Carlos Williams!
1 It was the last number of that first series of 'Contact'.

'A Voyage to Pagany'

New York, 7 September 1928

20. LOUIS ZUKOFSKY ON A PORTRAIT OF AMERICA'S BEGINNING

1928

Included in the commentary on Williams in Zukofsky's 'Prepositions: The Collected Critical Essays' (London, Rapp & Whiting, 1967), this section is dated 1928.
    Zukofsky (1904-78), most influential of the Objectivist poets, was introduced to Williams by Pound in 1928, and influenced Williams towards Objectivism. Later, in his introductory material to 'An "Objectivists" Anthology' (Le Beausset, Var, France, and New York, 1932), Zukofsky included 'Spring and All' in his list of essential reading, and singled out poems in which 'objectification is to be found'. (1) For a long period of years Williams and Zukofsky continued to read and analyse each other's work, perhaps most significantly, from Williams' point of view, in the case of 'The Wedge' (1944), for which Zukofsky (as materials in the Lockwood Memorial Library, Buffalo, show) offered a variety of editorial suggestions.

Writing with a sense of the history and destiny of The United States - as in the Earlier Discoveries of 'In the American Grain' - William Carlos Williams with 'A Voyage to Pagany' impels Americans towards a Beginning. The Curious as to history may find it convenient to draw a parallel between this later effort of sensitized American intellect and the earlier effort of Henry Adams in his 'Mont St Michel and Chartres' (1904).
    As there has been no actual contact of subject matter

the parallel can be no more than metaphor. It points the
fact that two minds, with approximately a quarter of a
century between them, have reacted as Americans, along
different lines, toward what might be termed the European
unchanging - in the words of Williams, 'the ancient
springs of purity and plenty'.

Both writers come to Europe: Adams to the cathedrals of
France to see the Virgin; Williams among other places to
Paris, 'a stitched-up woman hunting a lover'.

'It must be a lover. He must come of machines, he must
break through. Nothing will subdue him.' So they come as
lovers, both from machines. They must break through to
get at what they want, since neither will walk on Nothing.
But there is a difference of twenty-four years.

Son of his New England family Adams voyaged, a mind
replete with education - the heart as though trip-hammered
with its ineffectualness - to preserve intact the spirit
which in the past had preserved his family; in the end a
mind surfeited, prodigal to family, the lover in humility,
submitting (perhaps he did not know) to his own superstructure over French Gothic mind; the spirit mortified,
but somehow complete. In summary he said of it:

> Of all the elaborate symbolism which has been suggested
> for the Gothic cathedral, the most vital and most perfect may be that the slender nervure, the springing
> motion of the broken arch, the leap downwards of the
> flying buttress - the visible effort to throw off a
> visible strain - never let us forget that Faith only
> supports it, and that, if Faith fails, Heaven is lost.

The new voyage to pagany (pagany meaning Europe) is
steered near Adams's original route. Again what was
launched is not the machine, but instinct. 'One thing
about the man, he never argued with his instincts.'
After twenty-four years, it is still the machine which
persists. But no need to be mortified. Wary one must be,
of course - always the check upon the instincts; America
has raised one that way; but one can approach, like the
Indian, circle around, and then attack. Attack at least
with the precision of the machine become instinct.

The Ancient Beauty, yes. At Santa Croce one is 'purified past the walls of any church', but not subdued:
purified for oneself, for one's own Beginning and the
Beginning of one's own ('Spring and All'). Europe,
Venice of Waters, the Pagan underneath the Christian,
Giotto, Cimabue, the world's 'shell of past loveliness',
meet it with distrust! Learn, yes, be penetrated, become
clear on all levels as with the clarity of William's

Viennese doctors, but 'close the eyes sharply to, at the
height of enjoyment, at the peak of understanding. He had
strengthened his understanding of what he had long since
discerned. He carried his affirmation away in his pocket
- with his timetable.' Like an American. Old Europe may
not like it.

What this change means to the writing is clear. The
'Mont St Michel and Chartres' of Henry Adams in submission
attains an imaginative completeness, a clarity originally
foreign and resolves into unity. What might have been a
tiresome itinerary becomes a celestial Baedeker, the plan
of the book chastened as the nervure of the Gothic arch.
What was intended to be impersonal has the element of the
personal diffused through design. The struggle of American mind for the ciborium not its own casts the spell of
tragedy through the calm of structure.

The recalcitrance of William Carlos Williams in 'A
Voyage to Pagany' makes for anything but tragedy. What
is intended to be a novel becomes in structure an animated
itinerary. There is practically no design, since the aim
impelling the book is - to move on to the Beginning.
There can be no lingering for what is final, for what
resolves into unity. Fact - impels from incident to incident, because the Beginning comes only with the finish of
what is Past.

Intellectualism is a by-product of this itinerary and
teases the imagination. The author of that perfect piece
in 'Spring and All'. The Pure Products of America Go
Crazy, might have remained on his own ground and implied
in a novel of the defeat of those 'pure products',
farmers, migrant laborers, substrata of These States, the
defeat of intellectualism itself. The poet's nature compelled him otherwise. For one concerned with the Beginning, a portrait of what is closest to oneself to begin
with is indispensable; it makes for honesty - the welcome
absence of premature sentiment with regard to America's
'peasantry' - rare in recent fiction.

What is good in 'A Voyage to Pagany' breaks through -
despite the hazards of intellect - sees through incident,
surrounds and fathoms objects. The principal character
Dev, a constantly impressionable fellow, irritates himself into thought: 'What does anybody find in anybody?
Something he can't get except through that somebody'; the
words, 'What is it, dear?' making the natural keystone of
a perfect love scene; 'Carcassonne, a rock ruined by
tears'; 'the tan and grime wrestling the hair stuck
together at the ends, growing from the scaly scalps, from
poor soil ...'; the Arno 'river getting broader and going
about its business'; 'music a presence which you feel

occasionally during the playing'; of Bach's 'St Matthew Passion' - 'I heard him agonizing, I saw him *inside*, not cold but he *lived* and I was possessed by his passion.'

Americans might do no better than to emulate the Europeans, and consider the portrait of what is at least their own Beginning - carefully.

Note

1 This may be clarified by a comment of George Oppen's: '"Objectivist" meant, not an objective viewpoint, but to objectify the poem, to make the poem an object. Meant form.' Letter to Mary Ellen Solt, postmarked 18 February 1961, quoted by Weaver in 'William Carlos Williams: The American Background', 55. Williams himself made a similar comment in A Note on Poetry in the 'Oxford Anthology of American Literature', edited by William Rose Benet and Norman Holmes Pearson (New York, 1938), 1313-14.

21. MORLEY CALLAGHAN, AMERICA REDISCOVERED, 'NEW YORK HERALD TRIBUNE BOOKS'

7 October 1928, 4

Callaghan (b. 1903) worked with Hemingway on the 'Toronto Star'. Hemingway encouraged him to write fiction, introduced him to American expatriate writers in Paris (see Callaghan's 'That Summer in Paris', 1963) and helped him to publish in such periodicals as 'This Quarter' and 'transition'. A prolific novelist and short-story writer, Callaghan has been described by Edmund Wilson in 'O Canada' (1965) as 'today perhaps the most unjustly neglected novelist in the English speaking world'.

William Carlos Williams, in 'A Voyage to Pagany,' has marked off another milestone along the road that he is building toward a new discovery of America. In his new novel he is still preoccupied with the word, still unsatisfied to offer merely the external fact and groping toward some kind of an inner reality to explain 'the fact' in a moment of blinding clarity. The prose in the novel has all those qualities which make Dr. Williams a distinguished modern poet.

He wrote a book called 'In the American Grain,' an extraordinary book in which he sought for clarification of American origins in the history of the continent. The book was so free from academic attitude that few critics had on hand a formula that would enable them properly to approach it, and so it fell into the hands of few people. Now the new novel extends the theme. 'A Voyage to Pagany' is the emotional record of an expatriate who went to Europe with a blind and pagan passion for the Old World, its traditions, its art, its landscape, only to discover that it all depressed him like a memory in the calmness of a long twilight, and that he longed for the noonday sun of a new world with all its crassness, chaos, overdose of reality. Such a short summary shows how closely the novel builds upon Dr. Williams's other prose work.

His expatriates have no craze for long and hectic drunken revels, nor have they simply sought the Old World for its tolerance and freedom from American inhibitions. They have gone to Europe with a craze for fresh perception that will arouse new emotions, a deliberate quest for beauty in lands that have an international reputation for beauty and tradition. They find beauty in a calm twilight that is not satisfying enough. Even the love affairs in the book contribute to this theme. For the art of love here becomes the art of concentrating various emotions aroused by a whole train of fresh perceptions, and then releasing them at the very pinnacle of enjoyment.

The chapters on Vienna, aside from their beauty, ought to provoke and forever antagonize the American Medical Association. Rarely have I read such a sharp and effective condemnation of any society, and it is delivered from a stronghold of good medical practice in Vienna. In fact, after reading Dr. Williams's castigation, one has a feeling of sympathy and sorrow for all plodding practitioners in America, something like the feeling one had for a real estate man whose name was actually 'Babbitt.'

The last chapters in the book are the most moving. The principal character, a doctor, in love with his sister, is torn between his desire to live on in Europe with her and his eagerness to return to his own country. Here there is no mere clash of ideas; a young woman of considerable passion struggles desperately to remain with the one man who seems essential to her life. In these chapters Dr. Williams shows how effective his nervous, alert and sensitive style may become when dealing with human drama. The poetry that is in the writing is almost

concealed because it appears to be merely adequate to the
situation, but it remains splendid writing.
   I do not care particularly for the structure of 'A
voyage to Pagany.' In fact, I think that Dr. Williams
has practically disregarded all structure, not deliberately, but as though he wrote the book without giving
consideration to any such problem. In form it is somewhat like a diary, very beautiful, but not an adequate
pattern for a first-rate novel. Such a form does leave
the impression that the events recorded actually occurred,
but that is a poor substitute for artistic organization
from the man who wrote that piece in 'In the American
Grain' about the destruction of Montezuma's capital by the
Spaniards, surely as noble and dignified a piece of prose
writing as has ever been written by an American. 'A
Voyage to Pagany' has not the inevitability of the other
piece of prose, where almost every word, every descriptive
passage, the recounting even of beautiful sights, sounds
and smells simply foretold the destruction of the capital
and the death of Montezuma. That was great writing. The
same author writes 'A Voyage to Pagany' and uses words
deliberately, vividly, so that whole pages are poems that
would astonish, if offered in a book of poetry. But there
is no heroic prose here, by the one man in America who can
and actually has written it without bringing forth a blush
of embarrassment in his readers; not here, probably
because he felt that the characters in the book were far
from heroic and deserved only a more casual treatment.
But now that Dr. Williams, according to his own plan, is
ready to deal with America, everybody in the country
interested in letters should look forward eagerly to his
next novel.

22. UNSIGNED REVIEW, 'TIMES LITERARY SUPPLEMENT'

No. 1,400, 29 November 1928, 932

Mr. William Carlos Williams's novel 'A Voyage to Pagany'
is not a book that is likely to yield all its goodness to
any but an American reader - to a European it is an
interesting curiosity, rather enlightening and rather
pathetic. In its essence it is the debate of an American
with his own soul; in its form it is a record of a voyage
in Europe undertaken by a doctor, Dev Evans, aged forty;

and in its language it is abrupt, staccato, often
exclamatory, the language of a man who feels acutely and
needs to grope after his feelings with an awkward uncouth-
ness.

Dev Evans comes to Europe to shake off his old life for
a year and take stock of himself. He is a writer as well
as a doctor, and his internal drama, as it develops,
appears to be the conflict between that part of the American soul which, in contact with Europe, cannot bear
America any more, and the other part which yearns to get
back to the great fruitful comforting mediocrity of the
United States. Evans is anything but the cultured New
Englander - he is ignorant, so ignorant that he forces
Mr. Williams to spell every other French word he uses
wrong, but not ashamed of his ignorance because aware of
his force. He tries Paris first, and the art-American
world of Montparnasse which has eaten up his sister Bess.
From Paris he blunders on, asking himself bewildered
questions - 'Evans wanted to be let in. Was it literature? To hell with literature. Was it to know the
details of Jack's life? Evans didn't know he had any.
Was it his soul? What the hell is that? It's to get
through something. To get down to it, or up to it.' -
and spends a month on the Riviera with an American girl
called Lou. Lou gets engaged to a rich Englishman while
she is living with Evans as his mistress at Villefranche,
because she feels she is not literary enough for Montparnasse and needs a husband who has a place and money. So
Dev Evans staggers on to Italy with all his devastating
interrogations; and his spiritual convulsions when confronted with Florence, Rome and Naples are faithfully
recorded.

We cannot follow this record of spiritual growing-
pains with anything but a slightly amused sympathy, and
a certain incomprehension, while recognizing a rough
vigorous, sincere mind at work, which is determined to
take nothing at second hand. In Vienna Dev Evans halts,
takes courses at various clinics and finds another lover
who, at the close, sends him away before the splendour of
their moment has dimmed. Mere blundering suddenly stops,
and something besides Dev Evans's soul begins to live -
Vienna in 1924, the poverty, the devotion to science and
healing, the ruthlessness and intensity with which disease
is hunted, and the character of a fine woman, Grace, his
mistress. Her speeches to him when, after the spectacle
in the Spanisch Reitschule, she analyses their respective
temperaments are admirable and eloquent. For about a
hundred pages one has the gratifying sense of being
carried along by something spirited and muscular; and one

only regrets the drop at the end where Dev has to struggle with his own sister to get free. We know already why Dev must go back, and he knows too. 'Fineness, too much of it, narcotizes me. It drives me wild.'

23. UNSIGNED REVIEW, ECCENTRIC NARRATIVE, 'SATURDAY REVIEW OF LITERATURE'

16 March 1929

William Carlos Williams is an extraordinary person; in his literary relations he is probably unique. A practising physician in New Jersey, he should for the sake of his peace of mind be in Paris with his spiritual affinities. Generally speaking, the experimental expatriates are his admirers and at the same time his mentors. 'A Voyage to Pagany' is dedicated 'to the first of us all, my old friend Ezra Pound....' and we are sure that the 'us' means Joyce, Stein, the 'transition' group, et al. It is safe to say that to William Carlos Williams the center of contemporary English literature is Paris. Therefore, as this book shows, he is lonely and bitter. The bitterness, however, is not wholly literary; it is founded in large part on a conviction that he is a wandering soul without the hope of finding a destination.

'A Voyage to Pagany' tells of the pilgrimage to Europe of a New Jersey physician who is something of a *littérateur*; although he is named Evans, he seems to be largely William Carlos Williams. This pilgrimage is a search for the meaning of life. Vague yearnings for the ultimate key to significance drive this unfortunate Evans through Europe and back again to New Jersey, the key unfound and despair blacker than ever in his spirit. Three women fail to suggest any answer to the questions he asks; one of these women is his sister, two are his mistresses. The situation between Evans and his sister is grotesque, implications of incest being inescapable, Evans catches a faint glimpse of satisfaction in Vienna as a medical center, but the fog soon drifts back in again. As we read we are tempted to confuse Evans's literary *préciosité* with his defeat in living, but the two are separate, the latter being by far the more important. The value of this chronicle of a search depends upon the ability of its narrator to make us feel that the search is clear and dignified, that it is not merely frantic and impotent. The writer of this review feels that the narrative is justifiable and worthy of attention.

William Carlos Williams is said by his friends to be a great stylist. He does make us conscious of his manner at all times, but that manner is constantly changing. We cannot say that any one of many styles found in the book is the author's natural style. In this aspect of his writing, as in all other aspects, he exposes himself to the charges of affectation, artificiality, and vacillation. There is no plot, merely a travel-narrative that is intensely spotty in excellence and method. For only a few pages do we see into any other character than Evans. This central figure, however, is as solid and lucid as it could be, considering its peculiarities of temperament. Evans did not know what he wanted, but he knew how he felt during the enervating search. We can follow the twistings and writhings of his spirit, and we sympathize. Therefore we speak well of 'A Voyage to Pagany' as an eccentric narrative of a specially troubled soul; it has no orthodox qualities, but it has better than an even chance of pleasing the literary-minded and the inquisitive.

'The Knife of the Times and Other Stories'

Ithaca, N.Y., March 1932

24. UNSIGNED REVIEW RELATING WILLIAMS' IMAGISM TO HIS TECHNIQUE IN THE SHORT STORY, 'NEW YORK HERALD TRIBUNE BOOKS'

19 June 1932, 7

William Carlos Williams has rounded a turn of his career, from imagism in poetry to the short story. His motion has not implied much change, however, in 'The Knife of the Times' we are given clipped, terse fragments, situations which promise more often than they relate dramatic action, in the manner of his earliest work. The June, 1930, issue of 'transition' included an episode by Mr. Williams that was summary of both his poetry and prose styles. (1) He has retained the point of view of the Rutherford, N.J. doctor, the comprehensive localism that led Alfred Kreymborg to call him 'the most indigenous of modern American poets.' But he has varied the short breathing of his poems, adapting rhythms to the necessities of prose, and finding his medium in a contemporary and matter-of-fact vernacular.

'The Knife of the Times' is a collection of episodes, many of which are impressive in their dramatic suggestiveness. They are all told with clinical calm, in an even-colored tone, which is only slightly shifted as the subjects range from a country marriage contracted with the help of a bureau, a medical examination during which a complete family situation is exposed, to the title-story of the homosexual love of two old friends. There is an emphasis on relationships that have been described before; the tempo of some of the stories has been set by the Hemingway school; but William Carlos Williams has added to these qualities effective dramatic details and an objectivity which distinguish the best stories in this collection. People are presented as being interesting for action expressive of their thought; and the stories are told with a detachment which is in active contrast with the feverishness of our more subjective writers of fiction.

Note

1 The Simplicity of Disorder, 'transition', June 1930, 279-86. Later included in SE.

25. GERTRUDE DIAMANT, MR. WILLIAMS IN HIS CLINIC, 'NEW YORK POST'

25 June 1932, 7

Diamant (1901-69) was a novelist, reviewer and short-story writer, whose chief work is 'Days of Ofelia' (1942).

'The Bandlers had a good many men at Fernycrest since they bought the place ten years back. Most interesting specimens, some of them - if one may speak so of any human being - whose mere list would be a story in itself.' Thus William Carlos Williams begins his story Pink and Blue, giving, in the second sentence, a manifesto of his own attitude and method as a writer. His characters are 'most interesting specimens' to him. Implicit in the *if-*clause is the statement that he is adapting the methods of the scientific laboratory to the human world.

It is, indeed, the doctor's attitude. Mr. Williams treats the psychological complexities of his characters with the objectivity of a physician, neither probing into causes nor attempting to enlist our sympathy. For him the psychological state of each of his characters assumes the morphology and nature of a disease; for, although a disease arises from infinitely complicated causes, the physician must give it form and a name, create it into an artistic whole, before he can proceed to handle it.

Thus Mr. Williams, having accepted each psychological

state that he deals with as a disease, proceeds to hold
it up for our inspection, as a medical lecturer holds up
an exhibit for his class. There is the lecturer's scientific delight in what may be called the ingeniousness,
the cleverness of his specimen, and also the lecturer's
inhumanity and detachment. He is at the opposite pole
from Sherwood Anderson, who has created as his convention
an attitude of bewilderment, and whose purpose is to
understand, and to conciliate others in behalf of what he
finds strange and significant. The purpose of Mr. Williams is to create a slight sense of shock, the congratulatory gasp of the class at the lecturer's exhibit. We
do feel a shock in the sense that he wishes us to, but we
feel it without conviction. We concede it intellectually, as a tribute to his purpose. But we are aware at
the same time of a lack of any emotional entanglement on
our part with the material. We too develop the detachment of an observing and scientific audience.

Within the limitations of this attitude on both sides,
one is free to admire the forthrightness and economy of
Mr. Williams's exposition. The best example of his method
is 'The Knife of the Times,' the story of a woman who has
loved the friend of her girlhood through all their married
life, who writes her passionate letters, and, after twenty
years, at last sees her and declares her love. Here Mr.
Williams's method is most apparent. While the outcome of
this situation is hinted at the end of the story, the
causes of it in the lives of the two women, the analysis
of their feeling for each other, does not concern him.
He applies the technique of the *conte* to psychological
action. The story has the ring of objective narration,
but it is the narration of mental behavior. It is stenographic, essential, like a doctor's report on the progressive symptoms of a disease.

'Contact'

New York, February, April and October 1932

26. AUSTIN WARREN, SOME PERIODICALS OF THE AMERICAN
INTELLIGENTSIA, 'NEW ENGLISH WEEKLY'

6 October 1932, 597

As a successor to 'Contact' (1920-3), which was edited by
Williams and Robert McAlmon, three numbers of a new
series, edited by Williams, associated with McAlmon and
Nathanael West, the novelist (1904-40), were published in
1932.
   Warren (b. 1899) is best known for 'The Theory of
Literature' (1949) which he co-authored with Rene Wellek.

...To Dr. Williams' new series of 'Contact, An American
Quarterly,' I am a subscriber. Its *raison d'être* seems
to be its 'prose fiction,' which belongs to the same
school as that of 'Pagany' and indeed is contributed by
the substantially same list - including Robert McAlmon.
Dr. Williams himself contributes poems, sketches and
rather inarticulate editorials. I regret to say I cannot
share in the eulogy to which this author has been treated
in the columns of the 'New English Weekly.' Williams has
succeeded in getting himself into Untermeyer's anthology
(that 'Who's Who,' 'Blue Book,' 'Brett's' of contemporary
American poets), and has been praised by two critics
whose judgment I must respect - Munson and Kenneth Burke
(whose 'Counterstatement' is the most important book of
criticism produced among us for a long time). But as I
find none of Dr. Williams' defenders able to articulate
the grounds of their admiration, I am disposed to think

their praise the product of loyalty to a veteran leader of
the avant-garde who has never graduated out of the little
magazines, never become a lecturer for the women's club.
Williams is far from possessing the gifts of the now
underrated Amy Lowell; but doubtless, like her, and - I
am tempted to say, like Ezra Pound - his importance is
personal rather than *literary* and by way of instigation
and influence rather than of achievement *in propria persona*.

The attention paid Williams in the columns of the 'New
English Weekly' seems to me distinctly unfortunate. A
notice of 'Contact' in the July 'Criterion' observes,
sharply but accurately, 'For this number at least, violence and energy make "Contact" good reading; nearly every
contributor succeeds in being unlike his idea of a European writer.' And it appears to be for no very different
reason that the 'New English Weekly' has praised Williams:
for writing quite unlike a British writer. It is doubtless quite natural that our trans-Atlantic readers seek
in American literature for something *distinctive*, something violent and energetic and breezy and uncouth; but
however natural, the impulse leads to misunderstanding and
misvaluation. It was, for example, Longfellow and Whittier, not Whitman, who truly represented the American tone
at the middle of the last century.

Today there are innumerable types of Americans. Even
Mr Richard Aldington's caustic 'Soft Answers' credits us
with a Jeremy Cibber as well as a Charlemagne Cox (in
whose characterisation Mr Aldington has painstakingly
reproduced the American language as he conceives it).
Mr Struthers Burt and Miss Ellen Glasgow and Miss Willa
Cather and Mr Tarkington are at least as honest interpreters of the very varied American scene as those European
favourites (favourites in considerable measure because
they depict Americans as barbarians) a Mr Sinclair Lewis
and Mr Dreiser.

Dr Williams' heavily humorous, pretentiously and presumably ironically ignorant 'letter' disposing of contemporary literature in England reminded me of some words of
Arnold's in his essay on Joubert. 'Saugrenu is a rather
vulgar French word, but, like many other vulgar words,
very expressive; used as an epithet for a judgment, it
means something like *impudently absurd*. The literary
judgments of one nation about another are very apt to be
saugrenus.' His flippant patronage was just that -
Saugrenu.

Anglo-American literary alliances, like Anglo-American
friendships, cannot be built upon toleration on the one
hand and Anglophilism and Anglo-apery on the other; but as

little can they be founded upon the desire on the one
hand to write as unlike Europeans as possible and on the
other to invite the youngsters to *show their quaint
tricks*. (1)

Note

1 Williams' letter appeared in the 21 July 1932 issue of
  'New English Weekly'. His reply to the present review
  appeared in 'New English Weekly', 10 November 1932
  ('Bibliography', Items C178, C184).

'Collected Poems 1921 – 1931'

New York, 20 January 1934

According to Williams, The Objectivist Press, publisher of this volume, was financed by the poet George Oppen (see IWWP, 51-2) and its advisory board consisted of Pound, Williams and Louis Zukofsky. The book was largely compiled by Zukofsky.

---

27. WALLACE STEVENS, PREFACE, DEFINES WILLIAMS' POETRY AS BOTH ANTI-POETIC AND ROMANTIC

1934

Stevens (1879-1955) for long was an admirer of Williams' work. Williams was more equivocal, since he felt that Stevens had not fully abandoned traditional measure nor adopted the American idiom. The two poets were aware of each other at least as far back as 1915, but Stevens had refused to write about Williams on at least two earlier occasions. In 1925 Marianne Moore had asked him to review 'In the American Grain' for 'Dial' and Stevens had refused, making his often-quoted remark that 'What Columbus discovered is nothing to what Williams is looking for' (see 'Letters of Wallace Stevens', 246). This remark, and others from the same letters, were contained in the announcement of the 'Dial' award for 1926, which was given to Williams. Stevens had declined to write specifically for the occasion.

Williams was annoyed at Steven's reference, in the Preface, to 'the anti-poetic' and on a number of occasions he repudiated it. In 1948, for example, he wrote to Horace Gregory, 'Frankly I'm sick of the constant aping of the

Stevens' [sic] dictum that I resort to the antipoetic as
a heightening device' (see SL, 265).
    The Preface is reprinted in Wallace Stevens, 'Opus
Posthumous' (New York, 1957), 254-7).

    The slightly tobaccoy odor of autumn is perceptible in
these pages. Williams is past fifty.
    There are so many things to say about him. The first
is that he is a romantic poet. This will horrify him.
Yet the proof is everywhere. Take the first poem, All
the Fancy Things. What gives this its distinction is the
image of the woman, once a girl in Puerto Rico in the Old
Spanish days, now solitary and growing old, not knowing
what to do with herself, remembering. Of course, this is
romantic in the accepted sense, and Williams is rarely
romantic in the accepted sense.
    The man has spent his life in rejecting the accepted
sense of things. In that, most of all, his romantic
temperament appears. But it is not enough merely to
reject: what matters is the reason for rejection. The
reason is that Williams has a romantic of his own. His
strong spirit makes its own demands and delights to try
its strength.
    It will be observed that the lonely figure in All the
Fancy Things and the person addressed in Brilliant Sad
Sun have been slightly sentimentalized. In order to
understand Williams at all, it is necessary to say at
once that he has a sentimental side. Except for that,
this book would not exist and its character would not be
what it is. The Cod Head is a bit of pure sentimentalization; so is The Bull. Sentiment has such an abhorrent
name that one hesitates. But if what vitalizes Williams
has an abhorrent name, its obviously generative function
in his case may help to change its reputation. What
Williams gives, on the whole, is not sentiment, but the
reaction from sentiment, or, rather, a little sentiment,
very little, together with acute reaction.
    His passion for the anti-poetic is a blood-passion and
not a passion of the inkpot. The anti-poetic is his
spirit's cure. He needs it as a naked man needs shelter
or as an animal needs salt. To a man with a sentimental
side the anti-poetic is that truth, that reality to which
all of us are forever fleeing.
    The anti-poetic has many aspects. The aspect to which
a poet is addicted is a test of his validity. Its merely
rhetorical aspect is valueless. As an affectation it is a
commonplace. As a scourge it has a little more meaning.

But as a phase of a man's spirit, as a source of salvation, now, in the midst of a baffled generation, as one looks out of the window at Rutherford or Passaic, or as one walks the streets of New York, the anti-poetic acquires an extraordinary potency, especially if one's nature possess that side so attractive to the Furies.

Something of the unreal is necessary to fecundate the real; something of the sentimental is necessary to fecundate the anti-poetic. Williams, by nature, is more of a realist than is commonly true in the case of a poet. One might, at this point, set oneself up as the Linnaeus of aesthetics, assigning a female role to the unused tent in The Attic Which is Desire, and a male role to the soda sign; and generally speaking one might run through these pages and point out how often the essential poetry is the result of the conjunction of the unreal and the real, the sentimental and the anti-poetic, the constant interaction of two opposites. This seems to define Williams and his poetry.

All poets are, to some extent, romantic poets. Thus, the poet who least supposes himself to be so is often altogether so. For instance, no one except a *surréaliste* himself would hesitate to characterize that whole school as romantic, dyed through and through with the most authentic purple. What, then, is a romantic poet nowadays? He happens to be one who still dwells in an ivory tower, but who insists that life would be intolerable except for the fact that one has, from the top, such an exceptional view of the public dump and the advertising signs of Snider's Catsup, Ivory Soap and Chevrolet Cars; he is the hermit who dwells alone with the sun and moon, but insists on taking a rotten newspaper. While Williams shares a good deal of this with his contemporaries in the manner and for the reason indicated, the attempt to define him and his work is not to be taken as an attempt to define anyone or anything else.

So defined, Williams looks a bit like that grand old plaster cast, Lessing's Laocoön: the realist struggling to escape from the serpents of the unreal.

He is commonly identified by externals. He includes here the specimens of abortive rhythms, words on several levels, ideas without logic, and similar minor matters, which, when all is said, are merely the diversion of the prophet between morning and evening song. It will be found that he has made some veritable additions to the corpus of poetry, which certainly is no more sacred to anyone than to him. His special use of the anti-poetic is an example of this. The ambiguity produced by bareness is another. The implied image, as in Young Sycamore, the serpent that leaps up in one's imagination at his prompting, is an addition to imagism, a phase of realism which Williams has always found congenial. In respect to manner he is a virtuoso. He writes of flowers exquisitely. But these things may merely be mentioned. Williams himself, a kind of Diogenes of contemporary poetry, is a much more vital matter. The truth is that, if one had not chanced to regard him as Laocoön, one could have done very well by him as Diogenes.

28. PHILIP BLAIR RICE ON GROUND-CLEARING IN THE PIONEER AMERICAN TRADITION, 'NATION'

28 March 1934, 365-6

Philip Blair Rice (1904-56) held the Guy Despard Goff chair of philosophy at Kenyon College and was associate editor of the 'Kenyon Review'. He also taught at Columbia and Cornell and, in 1953, conducted a section in humanities at Harvard International Seminar. He was president of the American Philosophical Association in 1952-3. A noted teacher, he was also a frequent contributor to philosophical and literary periodicals. Besides editing the work of George Santayana, he published 'On the Knowledge of Good and Evil' (New York, 1955), and contributed to a number of volumes of critical and philosophical essays.

Of Poe's critical theory Dr. Williams has written: 'It is a movement, first and last, to clear the ground.' This is a concise statement of the direction of his own verse. For the better part of his life as a writer he has been hacking away at all sorts of dead timber. Probably no one but Ezra Pound has done so much to remove the tangle of withered words, stock responses, overripe images, and decayed rhythms that encumbered English and American poetry twenty years ago. Except for one brief excursion from his clearing, Dr. Williams has stuck to the ax with a single-mindedness amounting almost to fanaticism.

While he thus carried on the work of early imagism, in the period represented by the present collection he brought something new: he shaped the fluid impressions of the imagists into the solidity and organization of his favorite contemporary paintings. The result is poetry that is clean and spare and that transmits all the light. If a single poem of his should cling to the mind as typical, it might well be the plain statement about Gay Wallpaper, beginning:

[quotes lines 1-6 of 'On Gay Wallpaper', CEP, 345]

But he does other things besides interiors and still-life; there is the drowsy stir of mean streets and the headlong movement of The Winds:

[quotes The Winds, CEP, 349]

   This poetry springs from more than a technique of looking: there is an ethos behind it. Dr. Williams conceives himself to be giving utterance to an American tradition which has not before found adequate expression in verse, the tradition of the Indians and of the pioneers at their best. He has praised the feeling for life of the early Americans for 'its immediacy, its sensual quality, a pure observation, its lack of irritation, its lack of pretense, its playful exaggeration, its repose, its sense of design, its openness, its gaiety, its unconstraint. It frees, it creates relief.' These are the qualities that the post-impressionists sought in primitive art, and Lawrence in his peasants - qualities, among others, for which some classicists love the Greeks. They are, furthermore, traits conspicuously lacking both in modern life and, until recently, in the modern arts. Dr. Williams believes that we do not need to hunt far afield when we can find them in our own background. For this reason he did not go with his fellow-poets into exile, but kept at his medical practice in a New Jersey town, with an obstinate conviction, doubtless, that some embers of the tradition remained to warm him who could seek them out.
   Like all attempts to revive traditions, like all returns to 'ancient springs of purity and plenty,' this one has its pitfalls. Along with their now almost extinct virtues, the pioneers possessed certain less admirable traits which have been hardier: a suspicion of the intellect, a bluntness of psychological and moral perception, and a submergence of the imagination in present fact. (It may or may not be beside the point here to add that they had no need of economics.) We know that the exigencies of their way of living, together with their heritage, made these defects inevitable, and so we do not cavil at them. But we are more likely to be sensitive to such shortcomings

in a contemporary. Whether it be because he has followed his tradition too slavishly, or because he has confused the functions of poetry and painting, or merely that an aesthetic theory has been pushed to the extreme, Dr. Williams has excluded more from his verse than any other important poet of his generation - and not all that he has excluded is bad.

His search for the immediate presentation, his passion for 'objectivity' (the word has become the slogan of a school), has led him to eschew not only a great many useful poetic tools - even, usually, metaphor - but also the 'subjective' facts about human nature. He gives us the interiors of houses, but rarely more than the outsides of people. The Waitress, one of his best poems, and a very good poem indeed, is a case in point. We have a compelling sense of the woman's presence, and her looks, gestures, and setting are sketched with a poignant delicacy; we also feel the pity that the poet has for her roughened hands, but of true sympathy there is none: we know nothing of what she is feeling, she remains an exterior which arouses in the poet a flare of 'momentary beauty.' Or consider this passage from The Descent of Winter:

[quotes CEP, 300, lines 7-11, 16]

Such facts about the old as force themselves on the young are stated very movingly. But if this poem is compared with Eliot's Gerontion, the limitations of the former are obvious. Eliot, too, makes us see the uselessness and corrosion of old age; but these serve further as a framework to throw into relief the less obvious and more essential facts of senility - for the old have also a history, a tepid inner drama of reminiscence, and an intellectual recognition of their phase; and these more 'subjective' facts, together

> with a thousand small deliberations
> Protract the profit of their chilled delirium,
> Excite the membrane, when the sense has cooled,
> With pungent sauces, multiply variety
> In a wilderness of mirrors....

For all the integrity of his writing, Williams has been ruthless, as the pioneers were ruthless. Cleared ground has a neat beauty of its own, but when every one of the trees has been felled, the landscape tends to have a touch of monotony....

130 William Carlos Williams: The Critical Heritage

29. BABETTE DEUTSCH, WILLIAMS, THE INNOCENT EYE AND THE THING-IN-ITSELF, 'NEW YORK HERALD TRIBUNE BOOKS'

1 April 1934, 16-

Deutsch (b. 1895), a poet, critic and translator, is the author of many books, including 'Coming of Age: New and Selected Poems' (1959) and 'Poetry in Our Time' (1952), which contains a long essay on Williams, with whom she worked and corresponded occasionally.

...These poems make no overtures. They do not seek to flatter, to cajole or to enchant the reader. They may intimidate him by their unexampled nakedness. People, accustomed to the passionate imagery of Yeats, to Eliot's suggestive music, to the panoplied mysticism of Hart Crane or the rich allusiveness of Pound, to name four of the more influential poets of our time, will find themselves at a loss before this stark and unashamed simplicity of statement. For this man the object seen, the clear line, the pure color, is enough. Or the smudged line, the dirty color, if he is looking, as he often must, at the uglier realities of city street and town alley. One must come to his poems with his own quick response to the sensual world in its concrete immediacy. Williams has not, like some of our naive writers, the mind nor the emotions of a child, but he has the child's virgin innocency of the eye. It is as evident in the complex poem about a servant girl, To Elsie, as in the simple scene, Nantucket. He has the abrupt manner that often goes with complete frankness. He offers you the thing, to take it or leave it as you choose. His work is in the French tradition rather than the English. Clarity, incisiveness, the swift contrast, the pleasure in the grotesque, these are its distinguishing marks. Melody is not important to him. The notation about the cat on the jam closet is remarkable for the repeated 'p-s' and 'f's' and 't's' that recall the tentative planting of her careful paws, and there is a certain delicacy of sound in the Portrait of a Lady, but it is the image that is of chief importance.

The reliance on the eye, the singling out of the brief moment, however intense, is a limitation upon his work. There is keenness here, there is energy, there is not the exaltation that comes of a myth-making power, nor do these poems convey the profound excitement that is produced by poetry in the tradition of the metaphysical. The narrowness of attention which makes for concentration also may make for a certain meagerness....

30. MARIANNE MOORE, THINGS OTHERS NEVER NOTICE, 'POETRY'

Vol XLIV no. 2, May 1934, 103-6 (reprinted in 'Predilections', 1955)

Struggle, like the compression which propels the steam-engine, is a main force in William Carlos Williams. He 'looks a bit like that grand old plaster cast, Lessing's Laocoon', Wallace Stevens says in the introduction to this book. And the breathless budding of thought from thought is one of the results and charms of the pressure configured. With an abandon born of inner security, Dr Williams somewhere nicknames the chain of incontrovertibly logical apparent non-sequiturs, rigmarole; and a consciousness of life and intrepidity and is characteristically present in *Stop: Go:*

[quotes CEP, 59, lines 9-14]

Disliking the tawdriness of unnecessary explanation, the detracting compulsory connective, stock speech of any kind, he sets the words down, 'each note secure in its own posture - singularly woven.' 'The senseless unarrangement of wild things' which he imitates makes some kinds of correct writing look rather foolish; and as illustrating the combination of energy and composure which is the expertness of the artist, he has never drawn a cleare self-portrait than Birds and Flowers, part 2:

[quotes Birds and Flowers, Part II, CEP, 356]

William Carlos Williams objects to urbanity - to sleek and nasty effects - and this is a good sign if not always a good thing. Yet usually nothing could better the dashing shrewdness of the pattern as he develops it and cuts it off at the acutely right point.

With the bee's sense of polarity he searches for a flower and that flower is representation. Likenesses here are not reminders of the object, they are likenesses:

> And there's the river with thin ice upon it
> fanning out half over the black
> water, the free middlewater racing under its
> ripples that move crosswise on the stream.

He is drugged with romance – 'O unlit candle with the soft white plume – but like the bee, is neither a waif nor a fool. Argus-eyed, energetic, insatiate, compassionate, undeceived, he says in Immortal (in 'The Tempers'), 'Yes, there is one thing braver than all flowers, ... And thy name, lovely One, is Ignorance.' Wide-eyed resignation of this kind helps some to be cynical but it makes Dr Williams considerate; sorry for the tethered bull, the circus sea-elephant, for the organ-grinder 'sourfaced', for the dead man 'needing a shave – '

> the dog won't have to
> sleep on his potatoes
> any more to keep them
> from freezing

He ponders 'the justice of poverty its shame its dirt' and pities the artist's prohibited energy as it patiently does for the common weal what it ought to do, and the poem read by critics who have no inkling of what it's about. But the pathos is incidental. The 'ability to be drunk with a sudden realization of value in things others never notice' can metamorphose our detestable reasonableness and offset a whole planetary system of deadness. 'The burning liquor of the moonlight' makes provable things mild by comparison. Art, that is to say, has its effect on the artist and also on the patron; and in Dr Williams we have an example of art that disregards crochets and specifications. The poem often is about nothing that we wish to give our attention to, but if it is something he wishes our attention for, what is urgent for him becomes urgent for us. His uncompromising conscientiousness sometimes seems misplaced; he is at times almost insultingly specific but there is in him – and this must be our consolation – that dissatisfied expanding energy, the emotion, the cock-spur of the medieval dialectician, the 'therefore' that is the distinguishing mark of the artist.

Various poems that are not here, again suggest the bee – and a too eclectic disposing of the honey.

Dr Williams does not compromise, and Wallace Stevens is another resister whose way of saying is as important as what is said. Mr Stevens's presentation of the book refreshes a grievance – the scarcity of prose about verse from one of the few persons who should have something to say. But poetry in America has not died, so long as these two 'young sycamores' are able to stand the winters that we have, and the inhabitants.

31. WILLIAM CARLOS WILLIAMS ON HIS OWN SENSE OF RESIGNATION AND PARTICIPATION, LETTER TO MARIANNE MOORE

2 May 1934, SL, 147

...The thing that I like best about your review of my book is that you have looked at what I have done through my own eyes. I assure you that this is so. Had it not been so you would not have noticed the 'inner security' nor the significance of some of the detail - which nobody seems to value as I have valued it.

The inner security though is an overwhelmingly important observation. I'm glad to have had you bring it up. Not that anyone will notice it. It is something which occurred once when I was about twenty, a sudden resignation to existence, a despair - if you wish to call it that but a despair which made everything a unit and at the same time a part of myself. I suppose it might be called a sort of nameless religious experience. I resigned, I gave up. I decided there was nothing else in life for me but to work. It is the explanation for the calumny that is heaped on my head by women and men alike once they know me long enough. I won't follow causes. I can't. The reason is that it seems so much more important to me that I *am*. Where shall one go? What shall one do? Things have no names for me and places have no significance. As a reward for this anonymity I feel as much a part of things as trees and stones. Heaven seems frankly impossible. I am damned as I succeed. I have no particular hope save to repair, to rescue, to complete....

32. BASIL BUNTING, CARLOS WILLIAMS'S RECENT POETRY, 'WESTMINSTER MAGAZINE'

Bunting (b. 1900) is a major British poet whose chief publications are 'Briggflatts' (1966) and 'Collected Poems' (1978).

The virtuoso. Onomatapoeia:

> To
> *a child (a boy) bouncing*
> *a ball (a blue ball)* ...

Rhythmic:

> *Nobody*
> *Nobody else*
>
> *but me –*
> *They cant copy it.*

Lyrical: (This is not the place for a definition)

[quotes lines 1-4 of 'This is Just to Say', CEP, 354]

and

[quotes lines 1-5 of 'Death', CEP, 78]

In diction

> *The pure products of America*
> *go crazy*

or:

> *for I do nothing*
> *unusual*
>
> *I ride in my car* ...

or else:

[quotes lines 20-4 of 'Death', CEP, 78]

Dichtung (condensation):

> she
> opened the door! nearly
> six feet tall, and I ...
> wanted to found a new country....

- this chosen merely because one can measure the exact amount of condensation by the passage in 'Lavengro': Borrow being one of the three or four most condensed English prose writers.
  A writer has to know, he dare not leave it to chance: that is, the language, those aspects grammar as taught cant cope with. A lucky line finder tacks ten misses to his hit or waits ten years for another, it takes knowledge amounting to character to subordinate ready-made inspirations from the unconscious to what is constructed by acquired skill to produce an effect gauged and willed in advance.
  On the other hand a display of skill for its own sake is as odious as billiards. One shouldn't be left exclaiming merely: 'Marvellous!' There are the quasi-musical elements, there's dichtung and diction, and there's having something to say. English poets have at one time or another cultivated all of these except the last, which has always been left to chance.
  Interest in technical experiment tempts writers to over-estimate the importance and instructiveness of French movements. The French relied too much and too long on the dictionary, and are now driven to exaggerate (for purposes of exploration) the properties of words not in immediate connection with a meaning. But what is their antidote is the poison that has kept English back. A disproportionate idea of the power of words in themselves, from the Elizabethan dramatists to Lewis Carroll and from Latimer to the author of Anna Livia Plurabelle has regularly played into the hands of enemies of literature. The Britannic appetite for soufflés and cream puffs has been overindulged continually. Cummings is presumably unable to see that the non-farcical part of Cummings is just Keats and Swinburne over again.
  English needs a treatment quite other than that now being administered (still, after a century) to French: needs stress on the intelligible meaning, the intelligent purpose of words. Don't please, understand 'intelligible to William Ellery Leonard or Carl Van Doren' but 'intelligible to any reasonably quick mind that hasnt been

subverted by a literary education.'

Carlos Williams usually fills the bill. It isn't, fortinately, required that one should agree with him, or be convinced. Indeed, he knows too much to let his mystical Americanism do more than dictate the matter to be treated. That settled, his extraordinary technical virtuosity is used to ensure that the matter shall be matter and not opinion. Writing without motive turns pretty and goes sour in print. But any motive (not 'pretext') married to an adequate technique will beget clear, solid and musical verse.

Nobody else has taken America for a permanent subject. Whitman's was Democracy, an abstraction a much more competent technician would have found as difficult to keep to heel. Philosophy and fact seem to be mutually repugnant. America however is an agglomeration of facts. What Williams thinks about it he has said in prose elsewhere. In his verse he arranges a mosaic of facts, American facts even if most of them are also cosmopolitan.
On inspection the separate stones are very distinct, the cement undissimulated (see Primavera: too long to quote): That is, either there is confessed cement or no cement at all, the cohesion of a perfect fit.

You must get an offing to see the design.

[quotes lines 32-42 of It is a Living Coral, CEP, 326]

(An obvious sample to illustrate the point). Sometimes a long, even syntax provides continuity, carries the eye through without the effort of focussing:

[quotes lines 1-27 of To Elsie, CEP, 270-1]

The sentence is by no means finished yet. One ought to quote the whole of this justly famous poem: indeed, a good review, had any magazine room for it would be an anthology with very few notes (Pound's precept and Zukofsky's practice).

Maybe even such syntax could be made suppler, more continuous, without losing the muscle of common speech that keeps the sentence from going flat or dragging. 'The Tale of a Tub is not read enough.

More immediately necessary to know, as Williams sees,

It is only in isolate flecks that
something
is given off.

The technique that makes such flecks cohere into a To

Elsie is a master's: the collection and arrangement of
flecks concerns apprentices too. 'Minute particulars'
says Blake. Wordsworth adds the caution: 'endeavour to
look steadily at my subject.' Few are the poets who have
understood either of them.

Williams however does not provoke the clash between the
poet and the indulger in literary tidbits to such an
extent as some of his contemporaries. None of his poems
is long enough to get bewildering. It is when mosaic is
practised on the scale of Pound's 'Cantos' or Zukofsky s
'A' (but here mosaic is no longer a satisfactory analogy)
that the academic reader begins to grumble, not finding
the point of focus for himself and consequently unable to
look steadily at any large portion of the poet's subject.
Let him learn for himself, or some wise guy point it out
to him. Williams is readily visible: if not at the first
glance, at the second or third for sure.

This attractive transparency partly from limitations
recognized and acquiesced in. The poems are all short,
the subjects all circumscribed, self-complete, so that no
loose ends need be left. This implies no lack of scope,
seeing that all the poems are American and just as the
separate chunks of fact in each poem project a foreseen
design, the separate poems, or nearly all of them, are
ready to unite at the right focus into the unfinished and
finishable design of their common theme, America.

One of the uses of poetry is to give a design to things
the gods have left lying about in slovenly piles – to take
a directors hand in the business of creating the world.
It is not, I believe, its chief utility but it is an
important one. Whether the Americans like it or no Williams has been tracing patterns their children will have
to fill in. He is like Yeats a national and nation-
making poet. *Nazim* (Arabic) one who sets things in order,
a poet or the governor of a province.

The public will never guess it. Public utterances are
expected to be clumsy, or at least heavy. Williams' work
is light, it has never been retarded by such a burden of
conscious laurels as that Joyce and Eliot now stagger
under. It is eminently graceful, moving easily, even
nimbly, as its arrangement on the page proclaims. It
parades no semi-divine authority. The self-appointed
adjudicators on the New York middleclass-moron weeklies
are not likely to grant it much.

When (rarely) Williams lapses into the dialect affected
by those who are writing about what they don't understand,
in order to get a kick out of words, spell-fashion – a
shabby magic of nebulosities and misapplied epithets pro-
voking a sort of mental narcosis, usually aligned with

Love or Death - when he sets down:

[quotes lines 22-9 of The Botticellian Trees, CEP, 81]

where nearly all the words are too general, too equivocal, too vulgar, and the whole either much below or much above the proper tension, and where the adjective 'hot' in particular links the passage with the whole false literature of 'passion' from Ethel M. Dell to D. H. Lawrence; the shock two or three loose passages give Williams' reader serves to emphasize the perfect absence of such ersatz-poetry from more than nine-tenths of his work.
Enough to contrast The Winds that

[quotes lines 4-14 of The Winds, CEP, 349]

Commonplace exists in its own right and the poet has, as he demonstrates, no need to disguise it. It is mainly a question of diction. Williams knows it too well to trip oftener than once or twice.
In case the implicit intention has been missed let me state plainly that Williams is one of less than a dozen poets now writing who have a reasonable certainly of literary longevity and whose work repays study. He excels in stating a part of America none the less universal for being American. He is the most direct of the first-class poets now writing and his versification, within its chosen limits, that of an acknowledged master.

33. RAYMOND LARSSON, REVIEW, 'COMMONWEAL'

18 January 1935, 350-1

Larsson discusses six books, including an Objectivist Press Press publication, George Oppen's 'Discrete Series' (New York, 1934).

It is the guileless naturalness of William Carlos Williams that is most likely to deceive, and does. His is a simple heart unconcealed, without guile. Saints on the one hand, and bums on the other, would understand his poems, his heart: people with rules and formulae to apply are likely

to understand neither. His heart in wonder and love opens
poem-ly. These poems of his are direct, simple, lacking
in 'fine' writing, full of pure song. In these times, he
remembers: love, that it is direct, full of mysteries when
it speaks commonly the speech of common love. In these
times, his poems are like something of spring's kept for
remembrance against evil days. Nevertheless, he is a
realist, and an 'objectivist'. Nevertheless, love is to
him something communicable in terms of 'the plums that
were in the ice-box and which you were probably saving for
breakfast,' more precisely than in terms of Greece and
eighteen-tube Apollos dead on the sands of Crete. He
knows that 'love is unworldly and nothing comes of it but
love.' He 'at least can understand having sinned will-
ingly.' He is realist in that he knows 'the pure products of America go crazy,' 'objectivist' in knowing 'the
profound detail of the woods,' 'red stars - a several codhead between two green stones - lifting, falling'; and, by
implication, a sort of minor psalmist who knows that
'everywhere Red Lily in your common cup all beauty lies.'
He knows the purity of the actual world of things.
   ...It is the absence of 'interpretation' that distinguishes Mr Oppen's poems from those of William Carlos
Williams, which superficially they resemble. Dr Williams
is, by comparison, a moralist, a critic of ferocity and
acumen....

'White Mule'

Norfolk, Conn., June 1937

34. ALFRED KAZIN, PURE SPEECH, THE POET AS NOVELIST, REVIEW, 'NEW YORK TIMES BOOK REVIEW'

20 June 1937, 7

Kazin (b. 1915), a critic, editor and memoirist, is best known for 'On Native Grounds: An Interpretation of Modern American Prose Literature' (1942). His volumes of memoirs include 'A Walker in the City' (1951) and his most recent book is 'New York Jew' (1978). A former editor of the 'New Republic' and 'Fortune', Kazin has taught at Harvard, Amherst and the New School for Social Research. He is at present Distinguished Professor of English at the State University of New York at Stony Brook.

Poets who turn to the novel face a problem that rarely troubles other members of the guild. There is such a thing as poetic insight. Most of us hover around it like sleepwalkers, respond to it with some common appreciation of its suggestiveness. The poet uses it with a reflex motion. When he turns to dramatic realism he cannot forego the pleasure of seeing men as creatures of light. By seeing the general in every particular, he is oppressed by the pathos or tragedy of the norm. By assuming that all men are eaten by the same worm, he hears the threnody of the world in the pulse of behavior.
    At its worst this means the lyric novel, wherein farmers talk like angels and machinists sing too, too

prettily at work. At its most thoughtful - and 'White Mule' is a superb example - the common material of the novel is given a new texture. The superficially lyric mind distends everything. The genuine poet has a more perceptive feeling for detail, and there, since the novel is built on the odds and ends of temporality, he finds his mission. Open Dr Williams's book and you are in a new world of sound. Accents cling to the air. The harmony is the rough, gravely ironic rhythm of public speech. Like James Joyce, whose blindness has sharpened his extraordinary musical ear, Dr Williams has his characters talk with such a native freshness that the sound is never obtrusive. It is a pure speech because it is so richly characteristic, and its utter realism is therefore deeper, more meaningful than the violent accuracy of naturalism.

The quotation marks have been dropped to bring us closer to every moment in the drama, which is fashioned, after all, by accumulation. In another book the novelist would use quotation marks to tell us that the characters are talking, but here motion is blended with every nuance. We see precisely because we hear. The action evokes so many of the sights and sounds of life that we are stirred at every point by remembrance, but the associations are neither drearily commonplace nor dreamy. The story of Joe Stecher and his wife, Gurlie, may or may not be a parable, but since they are both immigrants, since both are at once restive with nostalgia and determined to follow the promise of a new life, the American dream is part of their story. They may look with scorn at the uncouth aborigine, but they are afraid of him. They, too, want to belong, but the act of adoption costs them something - in pride, in security, in tenderness.

They know that they cannot go back. Their responsibilities have enclosed them. The novel opens, portentously enough, on the birth of their second daughter, a sickly, troublesome child. Joe is frugal, industrious, scrupulously careful to make things go; but his foreman's job at a printing plant does not satisfy Gurlie. The World War is many years away. Expansion is in the blood. Joe was once the co-worker of Samuel Gompers, but when the men in his plant go out on strike, he fights them bitterly. He belongs nowhere. He despises the American workmen, but he hates his own employer. Gurlie's ambition depresses him. The child's delicacy forces them to move from one place to another and prompts a further need of money.

Within this frame of domesticity, Joe and Gurlie try to meet the bleak, hostile scene that is America to them. Joe leaves his employers to start a new business. Gurlie, proud and ironic but not without her moments of deep feeling, is forced to keep special watch over the baby. There are family dinners, a walk in the park, some genial drinking between old friends. Time is measured by the growth of their baby, the increase of their income, the search for old roots. America is a loud stranger, but they would like to know him better. America is not all dollar sign, they see, but some external confusion repels them. Too much noise, heat; too much American laziness. Life for Joe has been an unceasing struggle. He enjoys sweating for his bread. That is the moral law he knows, for from it he gleans purpose and order and the dignity that makes him tick the way he does. But at a Fourth of July double-header he sits thinking about the new business and the crowd heckles McGraw and screams for Mathewson.

Like the millions they live with, Joe and Gurlie would like some sense of citizenship. Their world moves in an orbit around a job, an ill child, a house, a raise. They are too tired, too human, to think of the rest. And so their world, the only one they know, a world of flicker and appearance, encompasses and misleads them. The vague memory of the European past may be solace, but in the end it is an excuse for irony. Joe has to work too hard and too long to make declarations or ask the spiritual question. But he lives before us as most men do in real life: as a gleam in the darkness. He moves in a cycle of sleep, work and dinner: there is a quarrel with Gurlie, many a headshaking over the child, a curse for the enemy of the moment. It is his wry speech that sets the tone, the shiver in his voice that declaims the crisis of his own humanity. But in reality there is no declamation; there is only stasis and the ebb and flow around it, the particular given to us with so much honesty, so much understanding, that what we hear is the echo of a communal whisper.

35. N. L. ROTHMAN, REVIEW, 'SATURDAY REVIEW OF LITERATURE'

26 June 1937

... The effect is as though Joyce were to write 'Studs Lonigan' - suggestive, explosive, briefly illuminating, tantalizingly incomplete.

But the personalities themselves are perfectly realized. Joe, the printing-shop foreman, is an idealist out of an

ancient mould, living according to his fierce, personal
Calvinist ethics. The industrial life of the closing
century is already becoming tense, the battle lines are
forming. Ethics seem suddenly insufficient, isolated, and
Joe stands between the lines, uncertain and bitter. In
the next book we shall perhaps see him move toward some
resolution. Gurlie, his wife, is made of commoner,
earthier stuff. She is certain of life and knows its vulgar secrets; she is proud and exultant, New York's Mrs.
Bloom. The children, Lottie and Flossie, are the book's
crowning excellence. Flossie is born upon the first page,
' - as Venus from the sea, dripping,' and upon the last
she is two. The pages between are filled with a memorable
and probably peerless account of an infant alive, with
that data at once clinical and profoundly intuitive which
only a poet and a doctor could provide. It would be easy
to make much of the story's inconclusiveness, its lack of
recognizable focus, but in the knowledge that other books
are to complete this one, such a criticism must hang fire.
There is enough of vitality and craftsmanship here to bid
us wait....

36. PHILIP RAHV, TORRENTS OF SPRING, 'NATION'

26 June 1937, 733

Rahv (1908-73), co-founder (1933) and co-editor of 'Partisan Review', was an editor and critic, whose chief work
is 'Image and Idea' (1949).

It is a fine thing that Dr Williams's 'White Mule' has at
last been brought out in book form. Dr Williams, though
among the most bracing and original talents in American
letters, has never received the recognition so frequently
according to those who denature and conventionalize the
new attitudes and techniques launched by people like himself. That he is detached from all efforts at popular
appeal goes without saying. Kenneth Burke once said of
Williams that he was engaged in 'discovering' the shortest
route between subject and object', but the reader, unfortunately, having become accustomed to the fatigue induced
by long detours, has come to regard the short cut as an

aberration of literary faddists.

Williams is too hardy a frontiersman of the word to permit himself the idle luxuries of aestheticism. There are too many things to be seen and touched, too many cadences of living speech to be listened to and recorded; and his novel is as busy doing that as his poetry. What happens on the most ordinary level of American living is the theme of his narrative of a man, his wife and their two children. Like the spokes of a wheel all the episodes in the book radiate from the first chapter, called To Be, which describes the birth of the second child and the first few days in the world. As in a microcosm the author's creative credo is embodied in this chapter, so instinct with natural piety and pure in its virile tenderness, so alive with sensory detail recreated in language that is swift, bare, tonic, and elated by its closeness to the object. Such plain and humble subject matter is characteristic of Williams, who has a passion for the anti-poetic, which he sees as the solvent of the unreal in art. Moreover, it is this very quality which causes his elements to move with such simple grace and which releases in him a sensibility of springtime that in itself becomes the source of a new poetics. In this sense, if a good deal of modernist writing represents a vision of the end of the world, Williams's distinct strength lies, conversely, in calling forth a vision of its beginnings. And this would explain why he has been able to work within the modernist medium without sharing its decadence.

The novel as a whole, however, is not content with the perception of facts and the feeling of them. There are certain problems, obviously, that the aesthetics of neo-primitivism cannot encompass. Continuing in a different vein the intense search for America that marked his prose work 'In the American Grain', Williams employs his characters as instruments to register with unwonted sensitiveness the peculiarities of the American scene. Joe Stecher, the foreman of a printshop, is an Alsatian who came to America in early youth, and his wife, Gurlie, is Norwegian. As foreigners, they are acutely aware of the contrast between the old world and the new and singularly perceptive of American qualities. Gurlie is so rife with the natural humors of a wife that she emerges as a veritable goddess of the home, but since it is an American home she is constantly urging her husband to get into the game, beat the other fellow, and make money. Joe's principal motivation, however, is his pride of workmanship; he is the pure artisan, the man who has not yet been alienated from the product of his labor and who thinks of money as the reward of labor and nothing else. Hence he takes a

middle position between employer and worker. He is
assailed by vexatious questions, such as are the unions
merely businesses or do they represent a higher principle
of social justice? Yet essentially he regards both sides
in the struggle as interfering with the efficiency of
production. Ambition stirs him, and despite himself he
gradually becomes more and more involved with the employers. As this is only the first book in what promises to
be a series, it is premature to predict the eventual
resolution of Joe's beliefs.

It is interesting to observe that Williams too, like
most American writers, has not escaped the political bap-
tims of our decade. Patently, there is a correspondence
between Joe Stecher and himself. Joe's philosophy of
workmanship also defines the relation of Williams, a
writer who is primarily a craftsman, to the literary
trends of recent years. It is not difficult to see how to
him the conflict of classes in literature might seem to be
interfering, and perhaps gratuitously so, with the clean
functioning of the written word. He would naturally be
affronted by the automatism with which the phrase springs
to the lips of the political fanatic. Hence, not the
least of the tasks he has set himself in his work is the
discovery of an attitude toward society that will prove
compatible with his creative methods as a writer.

37. FORD MADOX FORD, THE FATE OF THE SEMICLASSIC: THE
SAD STATE OF PUBLISHING, 'FORUM'

Vol. 98, September 1937, 126-8

Ford (1873-1939), besides being a poet and critic, is
chiefly remembered for his novels 'The Good Soldier'
(1915) and the trilogy 'Parade's End' (1924-8) and for his
editing of the 'English Review', which he founded in 1908,
and the 'Transatlantic Review'. An important influence in
early twentieth-century letters, Ford was the first to
recognize the talents of Pound and Wyndham Lewis. For
some years the friend and literary collaborator of Conrad,
he was also friendly with Stephen Crane and Henry James
(who took him as the model for Merton Densher in 'The
Wings of a Dove'). He helped to form Pound's ideas on
Imagism.

According to his bibliographer, Ford made some

observations on 'The Great American Novel" in the 'Chicago Sunday Tribune Magazine of Books' for 24 February 1924, in an article titled Literary Causeries: II. Vill Loomyare, (1) but this piece (which would be Ford's earliest response to Williams' work) has not been traced. In 1928 we find Williams writing to Sylvia Beach about 'A Voyage to Pagany', asking 'Shall I send a copy to Ford?' (He had met Ford in 1924, as he notes in a letter to Marianne Moore, SL, 60.) Later he wrote a poem To Ford Madox Ford in Heaven (CLP, 60) and reviewed 'Parade's End' in 'Sewanee Review' (see SE, 315-23). He also contributed to a symposium on Ford in 'New Directions', no. 7.

In 1939, as Williams relates in 'Autobiography', Ford embarrassed him by founding a group to promote his work, The Friends of William Carlos Williams (see SL, 178-9 to McAlmon). Some time later Williams responded by writing Les Amis de Ford Madox Ford, which eventually appeared in 'Black Mountain Review'. In 1932, in a letter to Pound, Williams described Ford as 'unapproachable' (a strange response to so available a man!) and as 'too much like my father was - too English' (SL, 127), but he wrote to McAlmon in 1939, 'I've gotten to like the man' (SL, 139).

Ford was always willing to promote the work of writers in whose talent he believed and the present review, not so much a review as a commentary on the publishing situation of Williams, Cummings and Edward Dahlberg, is a good example of his generosity, and a gracious tribute to James Laughlin who became the chief publisher for Williams' work from this time on.

... A publisher who is ready to pay for the publication of books that will not pay must be a generous man; and he must be the son of a generous man because he will certainly not have made any money for himself or he would go on making money that way. Such a gentleman publisher, then, has just - four days before the day on which I am writing this - published a novel by one of the three authors of whom I have been thinking for quite a long time now. The publisher is Mr. James Laughlin IV; the writer is my friend Dr. William Carlos Williams; and the book is 'White Mule'.

BOOKS AND BABIES

Dr. Williams is an admirable and abominably overworked physician from the State of New Jersey. I hope that this publicity may, as it would in the country of my birth,

get him struck off the medical register so that he may
produce many thousand fewer babies and many, many thousand
more clear, caustic words. He has been writing for many
years, and the product of his hours between deliveries has
long since drawn to him the consciousness at once of the
intelligentsia and the writers of this country and of the
country across the Atlantic. We have known of Dr. Williams, at first as a fine poet and then as a writer of
lucid, blistering, delightful prose, for twenty years or
so. He is, in short, adored among his patients as a physician and among writers as a writer. That he has never
galled the withers of the large public is in part his own
fault, in part that of the public.

He has taken no steps to let the public know of his
existence. He has let his books be published as a rule by
such semisubterranean private presses as that of the Three
Mountains, (the private undertaking of Mr. William Bird
of Paris, to whom present-day literature owes so great a
debt of gratitude), the private Contact Press of Mr.
Robert McAlmon, the TO Press of somewhere near Toulon, and
the like, so that his books are as difficult to procure as
those of Conrad, Hudson, or James.

But it is still more the fault of the public. If that
public - and it ought to have sense enough by this time,
seeing what happened to Keats and others - if the public,
then, would say to its bookseller, 'No! I will *not* take
that book; I saw a page advertisement of it in the "Literary Supplement" this morning; give me a lousy, home-made-
looking thing, published by no one you ever heard of and
printed on sugar-wrap papers,' then the public would get
hold of something it need not be ashamed of holding - say,
six times out of ten. But that the poor public will precisely like it when at first it reads something like what
I am going to quote immediately I should not care to
swear.

Here is a passage from 'In the American Grain', a book
in which Dr. Williams analyzes the spirit and brilliantly
chronicles the feats of his fellow countrymen from the
day when Red Eric landed at what is now Newport, Rhode
Island, till the present time. It will probably have the
effect - the whole book - of making the obese reader feel
as if he were partaking of a cathartic in an ice-cold
shower bath, with occasional flushes of patriotic pride
running over him as he reads of how his fathers licked
creation, right or wrong. And in the end the effect will
no doubt be that produced in his country, when I was a
boy, by an advertisement that covered the boards from
Sandy Hook to the Golden Gate: *Drink Moxie. You will not
like it at first.* And they did drink!

[quotes IAG, 181-2, 'The ideal woman ... stress'.]

So eventually they may come to read with equanimity this passage from 'White Mule':

[quotes WM, 1, para. 4]

Note

1 D. D. Harvey, 'Ford Madox Ford, 1873-1939' (Princeton University Press, 1952), 232, #D-302.

38. FORD MADOX FORD, FROM A LETTER TO STANLEY UNWIN, WRITTEN FROM NEW YORK CITY

18 January 1939

From 'The Letters of Ford Madox Ford', edited by Richard M. Ludwig (Princeton, N.J., 1965), 307-8.

My dear Unwin:
   Ref. young American writers: I have had sent you in the last week by their authors (1) 'Forward, Children' by Paul Alexander Bartlett and (2) 'White Mule' by William Carlos Williams, the latter published by Laughlin of Norfolk, Connecticut.
   Bartlett seems to be to be a young writer of very considerable merit and one whom I expect to see go far....
   William Carlos Williams is quite another pair of shoes. For at least a quarter of a century he has been regarded by every American and most English writers of any perception as being the best prose writer and one of the acutest minds alive. His work is completely unpopular here and is practically only published by small firms making a speciality of exceptional writers. His first book was published by John Lane at my recommendation in 1913, (1) it attracted very little attention except from poets but it was not a very mature work and I do not think that he has since been published in England at all. The 'White Mule', however, shows Williams at his extraordinary best and so many American writers have received

their first real recognition in England - and not unusually on my recommendation - that I should think that the book might have a good chance of at least a literary success in England. For that reason I do hope you will see your way to publishing it....

Note

1 William Carlos Williams' first book, 'Poems', was privately printed in 1909 in Rutherford, N.J. (see No. 1 above). Elkin Mathews, not John Lane, published 'The Tempers' (London, 1913).

'Life Along the Passaic River'

Norfolk, Conn., February 1938

39. EDA LOU WALTON, X-RAY REALISM, 'NATION'

19 March 1938, 334-5

Walton (1896-1962), American literary critic and poet and friend of Hart Crane. Educated at the University of California, Berkeley, she taught at New York University from 1924 to 1960. Her publications include 'So Many Daughters' (poems, 1952).

Dr. Williams takes no detours around life. Using realism with the precision of a surgeon exposing the vital organs, he achieves art. His materials are those of his own life, the experience of a busy doctor engaged often in clinical and charity work. His vision is stated in his own words: 'I defend the normality of every disease, every amputation. I challenge anyone who thinks to discomfit my intelligence by limiting the import of what I say to the expounding of a shallow morbidity, to prove that health alone is inevitable,' His political position is implied in this bit of dialogue:

'A clear miss,' he said, 'I think if we'd gone in earlier, we'd have saved her.'
'For what?' said I. 'Vote the straight Communist ticket?'
'Would it make us any dumber?' said the ear man.

These sketches - many cannot be called short stories - teem with life, with the urgency, the fury with which life

continues despite all that our general ignorance and our
society do to kill it. Dr. Williams sees the heroism and
the glory in corruptible flesh, among the diseased, the
poor, the ignorant, and the immoral - the people, in
short, who are cuckoo as a funny strip. But at that it is
not so funny.' One of these stories is about a girl with
a pimply face who is cured not only of her pimples but of
ineffectual living by her will to find out causes;
another is an account of a child's violent physical
struggle to keep the doctor from examining her throat
because she knows she has diphtheria. The doctor's anger
at and admiration for the little fighting 'animal' are
both part of the comedy. One could point out that each
of these sketches is, in a way, symbolic, but the reader
discovers this for himself. The impact of these tales is
due to the fact that everything expressed in them is pared
down to the bone, to the essential structure. The shock
of each story is the shock of observing bone suddenly and
cleanly unfleshed. Without any sentimentality, and with
the utmost dexterity, each little piece of the human pattern of living is made significant.

The comedy and tragedy, and always the human dignity,
of birth and death - which a doctor observes daily - are
Williams's subject matter. He stresses the psychology of
the doctor-patient relationship, the exchange of feeling
between healer and diseased. His scene is the Passaic
River town, its tenements, its dirty streets, and its
hospital clinic where the dramatic fight for the preserva-
tion of seemingly worthless lives takes place. Williams's
art lies in his ability not only to paint his picture with
unforgettable exactness but to expose what he himself
makes of his picture. He has been compared to Hemingway
because of his clipped prose. But in truth he is neither
philosophically nor technically like the author of 'The
Sun Also Rises.' He is not a sentimentalist, or a romanticist; he is not disillusioned. He faces life at its
ugliest and reacts to it with a kind of gusto and faith.
In his prose as in his poetry he is an imagist, a painter
of pictures. He so uses commonplace, concrete words that
they live again, expressive of new violence or tenderness,
revealing a new awareness.

Williams's art is realism intensified with a skill as
of X-ray in penetration and analysis - realism, in other
words, vitalized by an imaginative way of viewing life
which is unique, comprehensive, and very American. Despite the evidence in his writings of a clear political
position arrived at through practical experience, Willians is never a propagandist. He lets his material speak
for itself. Because he is a fine artist, he can make the

picture, the action, the facts illuminate his theme; he
need not comment.

40. N. L. ROTHMAN, BRILLIANT STABS AT TRUTH, 'SATURDAY
REVIEW'

19 March 1938, 16

Despite its odd use of the term 'expressionist', this
review supports the common view of Williams' early fiction
in perceiving that its strength lies in the exact rendering of moments of actual experience. Thus, although the
reviewer uses the term 'evocative', he locates accurately
enough the imagist/objectivist concreteness of Williams'
fiction.

These collected sketches are not short stories in the
accepted sense, nor is there in fact any collective term
to convey their special quality. They are stabs, brilliant and inspired, at truth. Their writer is a man whose
aim it is, just as it was fifteen years ago when he pio-
neered in expressionist poetry, to catch in mid-air the
gleaming, immediate spark of life and hold it in the
gleaming, immediate word. His work is supremely evocative, as close to experience itself as writing can be.
That is because it is not literature he is after but
expression; and when he hits the mark his expression is
the best kind of literature. Reading along, you will discover that Williams has scarcely any concern with plot or
background in traditional development. As doctor and poet
at once he has eyes, ears, mind, for only the more basic
experiences, unadorned and unstylized: death, pain, force,
tenderness, lust, exaltation, the vital moments. A sketch
like The Use of Force may be only five pages long, devoted
to a remarkably illuminating description of forcing a
spoon between a child's teeth. Or A Face of Stone, a
little longer, brings to us, almost unwillingly, because
the two characters cannot state it and the writer will
not, an overpowering sense of tenderness between man and
wife. There are more ambitious stories, like that which
gives the volume its title.
   In all of them we can see in simple play those literary

powers which had fuller expression in 'White Mule,' Williams's novel of last year. Here they seem to be exercised in experimental fashion, as though Williams were seeking to test them for new uses, or to discover their limits. Sometimes the result is a failure. The Cold World, for instance, simply doesn't come off. You can just see the objective, and wonder what he left out. Second Marriage, and The Right Thing seem to be fragments. But every one of these is exciting and important. They mark the steady tempering and whetting of a talent that has long been one of the finest our writing affords; perhaps this volume will impel some readers to search out 'White Mule,' a first rate American novel.

41. FRED R. MILLER ON WILLIAMS' LOCALISM, 'NEW REPUBLIC'

20 April 1938, 341

Miller (1903-67) edited the American radical story-magazine 'Blast' (named after an earlier radical review edited by Emma Goldman and Alexander Berkman) in the 1930s and published some stories later included in 'Life Along the Passaic River'. Close friends for many years, in the 1940s Williams and Miller wrote a collaborative novel, which has been published under the title 'Man Orchid' ('Massachusetts Review', vol. XIV, no. 1, winter 1973, 77-117, with an introductory essay by Paul L. Mariani, Williams's Black Novel, 67-75). Miller developed Williams' interest in jazz and put him in touch with New York leftist activity.

These nineteem tales have to do chiefly with the plain (if sometimes violent) people that Williams, as a medico, meets day after day - Polacks whom transplantation has 'mixed up and stunned'; an Italian peasant woman bringing her ninth child into the world; a Negro woman of uncorrupted instinct; Jews; Russians; nurses; babies; an old man, penniless, living in the woods, who has achieved what power and place cannot give, great human dignity and worth (Under the Greenwood Tree).

Character is the thing Williams looks for - and finds more often than not - in these mongrel isolated Americans

along the Passaic. *They* represent the America of his
dogged belief, which has no truck with defeatism, morbidity, cynical anemia, bigoted partisanship or any of
the other easy sentimental 'outs.' His social awareness
has grown considerably since 1932, when he published his
first collection of short stories, 'The Knife of the
Times.' Nor has its growth hampered his artistry - The
Greenwood Tree is among the most esthetically gratifying
pieces he has done; so are A Night in June and The Dawn
of Another Day. Every suggestion of the preciousness
that, here and there, tinged 'A Voyage to Pagany' (1928) is
absent. And by now even blind men and professional critics can see that Williams has triumphantly solved, in the
downright classical clarity of his prose, the problem of
harmonizing style and realism. He has shown again that
the more truly localized the art, the more it is universal.

42. ROBERT MCALMON RECOLLECTING WILLIAMS IN PARIS IN 1924, 'BEING GENIUSES TOGETHER'

1938, 180-1 (1)

McAlmon (1896-1956) was co-editor with Williams of the
first series of 'Contact' (1920-3). McAlmon collaborated
with William Bird in the Three Mountains Press and Contact
Editions (Paris) which published Williams' 'The Great
American Novel' (1923, see above) and 'Spring and All'
(see 'Being Geniuses Together', London, 1st edition,
270-1). McAlmon himself published a number of novels,
short stories and articles, but nothing after 1938. The
last ten years of his life were spent in the United
States, at first working for his brothers in a surgical
supply house in El Paso, Texas. One of the few of
McAlmon's literary associates to remain in touch with him
in these later years was Williams, who wrote the introduction to Robert E. Knoll's 'Robert McAlmon: Expatriate
Writer and Publisher' (revised edition, Lincoln, Nebr.,
1959).

... Williams would tell amazing experiences which occurred to him through his years of doctoring. On the outskirts of his town was a colony of settlers intact

throughout a two-hundred year period, ingrowing and interrelated, with the customs of long ago. Because Williams is kindly and understanding he had quantities of patients amongst Italian settlers and negroes, and some of his stories were weirdly amusing or tragic, but deeply based in life. Now and then he wrote poems about these characters, or short stories, but these stories he seemed not to rate so highly himself as some precious poem inoculated with nostalgia for something Greek or poetic in a way that pedants conceive poetic: that is, poetic in a way that they have been taught was metrical and had 'beauty', in a convention.

Williams, as an organism was and is one of the most interesting 'sensibilities' which America has produced. He was over-impressionable, in that the quiverings of his sensibility were so constant that he never had time to clarify his observation, but instead was lost in a species of life-wonder, bewilderment and torment. He has written many fine poems and short stories, but he is apt to think his best not worth publishing because it has come straight from a direct and stark impulse, it does not perplex and torment and irritate him and make him restless. In New York I kept him from destroying one such poem, one of the most beautiful in any language. It was the Portrait of the Author, which appeared first with 'Contact', and later in his book, 'Sour Grapes'. Marianne Moore later commented on it, saying, 'It preserves the atmosphere of a moment, into which the impertinence of life cannot intrude'.

But Williams thought it too intricate, or not art, or whatever. Miss Moore, I believe, forced him to save various others of his better poems which he was inclined to reject....

Note

1 This passage from the text of the first edition of 'Being Geniuses Together' differs extensively in detail of writing from that in the New York edition (Doubleday, 1968) revised and with supplementary chapters by Kay Boyle. In that edition, the corresponding passage, which differs in no way in substance, is on pp. 185-6.

'The Complete Collected Poems of William Carlos Williams 1906 – 1938'

Norfolk, Conn., November 1938

This book is a watershed in Williams' career as a poet. James Laughlin of New Directions had already published Williams' fiction, but this is the first Williams poetry collection to be published by other than a 'small press', and it is a handsome book. Williams commented later in 'I Wanted to Write a Poem', 'The "Collected Poems" gave me the whole picture, all I had gone through technically to learn about the making of a poem' (p. 65).

---

43. PHILIP HORTON ON WILLIAMS' INNER CONFLICT BETWEEN ANTI-POETICISM AND SENTIMENTALISM, 'NEW REPUBLIC'

21 December 1938, 208

Horton is the author of the pioneering biography 'Hart Crane: The Life of an American Poet' (1937).

It is no easy matter to estimate the achievement of William Carlos Williams. One cannot feel that he is an important poet, and one knows that he is not an insignificant one. The name-callers have dubbed him an 'objectivist,' which has been wildly defined as one who adapts to his poetry the principles of pragmatism. By rebuttal this became: one who applies to his poetry the doctrines of pure empiricism. Then along comes Dr. Williams with a definition of his own: 'A poem is a whole, an object in itself, a "word" with a particular meaning old or new. The whole poem image and form, that is, constitutes a single meaning. This is the full meaning of the term "objective" as I employ it. This very neatly cancels out the other definitions by what is apparently a total, tautological eclipse.

Now Dr. Williams' poems are very rarely 'objects in themselves' in any meaningful sense of the phrase. More usually they are observations and reactions, simple or complex, diatribes, fantasies, divertissements, occasional pieces - collected, they are the remarkable anthology of the experience of a highly individual mind. Like E. E. Cummings, Williams is an aggressive individualist, and his poetry, like Cummings', is most successful when most personal. True, like all individualists, he has consistently refused to be consistent and has written in as many manners as he chose.

Unfortunately, the manner habitually associated with his name is the stripped style, the end product of his early imagism and later naturalism. In its extreme form this style is little more than experimental, the application of a theory; its poetic achievement is almost nil. The Locust Tree in Flower is one example of it; Young Woman at a Window is another:

[quotes 'Young Woman at a Window', CEP, 369]

The paradox involved here is that this style aims at pushing to its logical extremes one legitimate element of his poetry at the cost of those other elements that occasionally combine to raise his work to its most distinguished level. It eliminates the vision that makes Flowers by the Sea, particularly in its last two lines, one of his best pieces:

the sea is circled and sways
peacefully upon its plantlike stem

and it eliminates the humor and pathos that bring his portraits of the poor so intimately to life; the irony of To a Dead Journalist, the sarcasm, the passion, even the wealth of visual detail that has been one of his chief fortes. The key to this paradox is to be found in Wallace Stevens' Introduction to Williams' 'Collected Poems 1921-1931,' where he defined Williams' poetry in terms of the conflict between the 'anti-poetic' and the 'sentimental': between what I prefer to call here the fidelity to the concrete impersonal fact and the seductions of the complex personal perception. Mr. Stevens acutely noted that the 'anti-poetic is his spirit's cure' which he needs 'as a naked man needs shelter or as an animal needs salt.' As a passing commentary on the dilemma of modern poets, it is worth remarking that the opposition governing Williams' creative activity is very much the same as the dichotomy with which Yeats has struggled, and the function of Williams' 'anti-poetic' very much like that of Yeats's Mask or Anti-Self.

Dr. Williams' extreme 'objectivism' then, is the deliberate stylization of the anti-poetic state of mind. In such a poem as Young Woman at a Window the poet is wearing his most impersonal mask; his manner, even his intention, may be overtly 'objective,' but his motivation, one suspects, is sentimental. He attempts to solve the conflict by arbitrarily eliminating the personal in favor of the impersonal, with the result that the poem, though it may sometimes hit off an effective ambiguity or implication, is more often nothing but an exercise in spiritual hygiene, essential to the well-being of the poet, but in itself hardly poetry. It is not when the conflict is eliminated, but when it is sustained in equilibrium and made to function as a physical law of the poet's universe that the most fertile condition for poetry is attained. Dr. Williams has attained this condition often enough to have added a small body of distinguished poetry to our literature. For the rest, his work is valuable as a public record of a private conflict that happens also to be common to most modern poets. His anti-poetic naturalism, his localism and his tough-minded humanity may well serve as astringents and tonics for many of the ailments of contemporary verse.

44. YVOR WINTERS, POETRY OF FEELING, 'KENYON REVIEW'

Vol I, no. 1, Winter 1939, 104-7

Winters (1900-68) taught at Stanford University 1928-66, and established solid, though controversial, reputations both as a critic and poet. For him the function of criticism is moral evaluation of the work, and he felt that poetry also should be a rational and moral statement about human experience. Besides studies of E. A. Robinson, W. B. Yeats and J. V. Cunningham, the main body of Winters' criticism is included in 'In Defense of Reason' (1947). His 'Collected Poems' were published in 1952 and he was awarded the Bollingen Prize for poetry in 1960.

In 1965 Winters added a postscript to Poetry of

Feeling, for inclusion in 'William Carlos Williams: A Collection of Critical Essays', edited by J. Hillis Miller (1966). He notes that 'my general remarks stand', but speaks of 'Williams' foolish and sentimental ideas' and restricts his own choice of the poems he regards as successful. Winters was himself quite widely regarded as increasingly reactionary and even idiosyncratic in his judgments of modern poetry. For this reason his final comment is included here rather than later, since it has not marked a general tendency in the evaluation of Williams' work. Winters concludes: 'To say that Williams was anti-intellectual would be almost an exaggeration: he did not know what the intellect was. He was a foolish and ignorant man, but at moments a fine stylist' (p. 69). Writing to Kay Boyle in 1932, Williams had said: 'Yvor Winters seems to me bogged in ideas. His line has a self-inflicted tendency to become short and to stay so. It excludes too much. It has no largesse for the mind or the emotion' (SL, 132).

W. C. Williams, in his view of life and of poetry, is an uncompromising romantic. He believes in the surrender to feeling and to instinct as the only way to wisdom and to art: The Trees is one of his many explicit statements of this notion. He believes that art is the product of a character which is 'automatically first rate' ('Blues' for May, 1929). (1) Such a character would have, of course, no need for ideas and no awareness of them; indeed, one may ask whether he would display any consciousness whatever. In any event, Dr. Williams distrusts all ideas and seeks value as far as may be in the concrete: in the poem called Paterson he reiterates the phrase 'no ideas but in things.' And he distrusts the entire range of feelings which is immediately motivated by ideas, for he is in no position to distinguish good ideas from bad, and hence, in this realm, sound feelings from false. In A Poem for Norman McLeod, [sic] he writes: 'The revolution/is accomplished/noble has been/changed to no bull.' Any feeling arising from the contemplation of an idea, whether moral, metaphysical, or religious, appears to him merely sentimental: this is a defect, but he at least displays the virtue of his defect and almost wholly eschews the realm of experience which he does not understand, so that his poetry, though in certain ways limited, is at its best not confused or sentimental. He distrusts traditional form, as a kind of restraint or inhibition: since he fails to grasp its significance, it

appears to him another mechanical sentimentalism; and he
desires that the theme create its own form. But in this
desire he has in part fallen short of his ambition, for
his own excellent ear has made of free verse a complex
accentual meter, very difficult to control, and creating
very binding conventions of feeling.

His poetry therefore concentrates on the concrete; the
only ideas which it occasionally expresses are those which
I have outlined, and since the ideas are bad, the poetry
is best when Dr. Williams follows his favorite formula and
eschews ideas altogether. At its simplest, it resembles
nearly all of his prose: that is, it offers merely sharp
impressions of objects observed, either in isolation, or
in accidental sequence, or forced by a purely rhetorical
violence, as in Romance Moderne, into a formal and emotional unit. In such a case as this last - and there are many
such - the form, or emotion, which enacts the violence is
unmotivated, and the whole effect, in spite of much brilliant detail, is one of excited overstatement. Some of
the simplest, and purely isolated, descriptive notes are
among the best; as for example, many of those in the
sequence called January Morning; and occasionally, as in
Complaint, by virtue, perhaps, of some metrical or otherwise rhetorical miracle, one will take on inexplicable
power. Dr. Williams' belief in this kind of thing no
doubt accounts for his own high opinion of the poem about
the red wheelbarrow in the rain, as compared to his other
and often more valuable poems. Often his confidence in
the intrinsic value of the physical object results in a
poem composed of perfectly unrelated items, a passage of
crystalline chaos, amusing but empty, as in the sixth poem
of Descent of Winter. He has not been without doubts in
this connection, however; in This Florida: 1924, he
writes: 'And we thought to escape rime/by imitation of the
senseless/unarrangement of wild things/the stupidest rime
of all.'

His theory, however, seems to permit his dealing with
certain richer material; that is, with some of the simpler
events of human relationship, chiefly love, seen primarily
as something deeply desired but which passes. The best of
these poems is probably The Widow's Lament in Springtime,
a poem both rich and somber, and one of the most moving
compositions of our time. There are many others nearly as
fine, among them The Bull, A Coronal, Arrival, Portrait of
a Lady, The Hunter, The Lonely Street, To Mark Anthony in
Heaven, To Waken an Old Lady, and Waiting. In spite of
the simplicity of theme, when the poems are viewed in bare
outline, the sensuous and emotional awareness is extremely
rich and is perfectly controlled; in style, the poems are
masterly.

Here and there something else occurs that is even more
impressive. His romantic view of nature and of art
results in his experimenting with symbols of elemental
forces and instincts. When, as in The Trees, he passes an
explicit judgment on these symbols in relationship to the
intellectual values which he misapprehends and derides,
the result is sentimental and essentially unsatisfactory.
When, however, he represents the force in isolation,
defining merely the power and the terror, he is perfectly
sound and defensible; on at least three occasions, he has
succeeded brilliantly with such symbols: in 'Spring and
All,' No. I (On the Road to the Contagious Hospital) and
No. XXVI (The Crowd at the Ballgame), and in The Sea-
Elephant. In these poems the violence of the theme supports even his most rapid and muscular rhetoric, and he
raises the metrics of free verse and poetry in free verse
to the highest level at which they may be found. No other
poet using free verse is even comparable to him on these
occasions.

The romantic principles which have governed Dr. Williams' work have limited his scope in the ways which I
have mentioned. The combination of purity and of richly
human feeling to be found in his language at times reminds
one of Hardy or of Bridges, and in beauty of execution he
is their equal, though in so different a mode; but his
understanding is narrower than theirs, and his best poems
are less great. On the other hand, when poems are so
nearly unexceptionable in their execution, one regards the
question of scope regretfully: Herrick is no less great
than Shakespeare, but he is probably as fine, and, God
Willing, should last as long. If I may venture, like
Arnold, to make a prediction, it is this: that Williams
will prove as nearly indestructible as Herrick; that the
end of the present century will see him securely established, along with Stevens, as one of the two best poets
of his generation. He is handicapped at present by the
fact that the critical appreciation of free verse has not
got beyond the long and somewhat obvious rhythms of Pound
and of the less expert Eliot, so that Williams' artistry
goes all but unperceived with most readers.

The present collection contains 313 pages and nearly
all of Williams' poems. There are no regrettable omissions that I can discover; there are few omissions of any
kind. There are no poems butchered by hasty revision at
the last minute, and a few that were so butchered in previous volumes have been repaired. The book is essentially
complete and definitive, and it brings the author's work
down to date. It is thus indispensable to anyone seriously concerned with American poetry. In regard to

physical appearance, the book is beautifully and durably
made, without being in any way pretentious; it is a
luxury to handle it after having dealt for twenty years
or so with the other volumes in which many of these poems
have appeared.

Note

1 This remark occurs in Williams' uncollected essay, A
  Note on the Art of Poetry, 'Blues', vol. I, no. 4,
  May 1929, 77-9. Williams was a contributing editor to
  the magazine.

45. PAUL ROSENFELD ON 'THE LEAST NAIVE OF MEN ... AN
INTELLECTUAL POET', 'SATURDAY REVIEW'

1 February 1939, 16

... The language not only is the vernacular. The very
style of the verse corresponds to that of manifestations
of American life. And both the manner and the phraseo-
logy reflect and communicate the inner forces and the ways
of being of Americans.
   Technically, as a poet Williams appears to stem from
imagism. He has the nudity of vision, the strict, intense observation, the direct impressions of the poetic
aspect of the object characteristic of the band headed by
Pound; and its manner of seizing the image, the fusion of
reality in the expression, with the most concise means of
the language and, as it were, with but a single swoop.
He shares these poets' almost deliberate non-melodious-
ness, indifference to the beauty of sound and periodic
arrangement, preference for mute and verbal harmonies.
His cadences tend to be prose cadences; his line-lengths
to be arbitrary. The cantilena and the singing voice in-
frequently sustain themselves in his poetry. The emotion
too, while forceful, is often latent and dissimulated:
from the first, Williams must have been among the least
naive of men. Yet his sensibility differs from that of
Pound, H.D., and other representative American imagists.
It not only is more realistic and both more sardonic and
warmer than theirs, and more acridly sensuous; it is
deeply rooted in the soil. Both as a man and a poet

Williams is more profoundly related to American life and
limited and conditioned by it than are the wanderers.
 The inner truth he most regularly comprehends and
strives now lovingly, now humorously, now ironically to
form, is that of the fierce, nervous, and emotional tension of American life: its fitfulness, spasmodic motion,
'bursts of fragrance from black branches' - itself the
consequence of the abruptness with which American earth
passes from the bitterness of winter to the sweetness of
spring and onwards again to the fierceness of summer:
this, and its coldness, cruelty, and power of endurance.
He recognizes their forces in the features of his own
landscape, industrial northern New Jersey. The landscape
mixing in his imagination with persons and his own inwardness gives his poetry its peculiarly regional quality.
And he hears American life in the inflections of the
American language. Since he is an intellectual poet,
these essences embody themselves in the style, the way of
motion of his verses. It is high-tensioned, extremely
energetic, with plenty of dynamic punch, ascending
cadences, and irregular rhythms of short and stabbing
lines. It is swift, leaping from thought to thought, and
of a javelin-like sharpness. And it has sardonic humor.
 Perhaps not all this poetry is wholly unsatisfactory.
Williams is not always touched in the depths and suffused
with the feeling which gives scope and density to form.
But the volume contains a number of lyrics, among them
Portrait of the Author, Man in a Room, A Goodnight, Eve,
Cyclamen, and others, which rank with the poetry of our
time highest in quality. The whole of the poetry has
worth. All has texture, truthfulness, subtle consciousness of life. Mr. Williams has a sovereign gift for animating his emotions.

46. R. P. BLACKMUR ON WILLIAMS' 'UNEXPANDED NOTATION',
'PARTISAN REVIEW'

Vol. VI, no. 2, Winter 1939, 114

Blackmur (1904-65) was an influential critic, and poet.
His chief collection of critical essays is 'Language as
Gesture' (1952), which contains the present review.
Blackmur was a theorist of the New Criticsm, who did much
to determine the proper relation between literary

criticism and scholarship. His other works include 'The Lion and the Honeycomb' (1955), 'New Criticism in the United States' (1959) and 'American Short Novels' (1960), which includes Williams' 'The Great American Novel'.

... almost everything in Dr Williams's poetry, including the rendering, is unexpanded notation. He isolates and calls attention to what we are already presently in possession of. Observation of which any good novelist must be constantly capable, here makes a solo appearance: the advantage is the strength of isolation as an attention-caller to the terrible persistence of the obvious, the unrelenting significance of the banal. Dr Williams perhaps tries to write as the average man - that man who even less than the normal man hardly exists but is immanent. The conviction which attaches to such fine poems as The Widow's Lament in Springtime, Youth and Beauty, or the first section of 'Spring and All', perhaps has its source, its rationale, in our instinctive willingness to find ourselves immanently average; just as, perhaps, the conviction attaching to tragic poetry is connected with our fascinated dread of seeing ourselves as normal. Dr Williams has no perception of the normal; no perspective, no finality - for these involve, for imaginative expression, both the intellect which he distrusts and the imposed form which he cannot understand. What he does provide is a constant freshness and purity of language which infects with its own qualities an otherwise gratuitous exhibition of the sense and sentiment of humanity run-down - averaged - without a trace of significance or a vestige of fate in the fresh familiar face....

'In the Money'

Norfolk, Conn., October 1940

47. F. W. DUPEE, W. C. WILLIAMS AS NOVELIST, 'NEW REPUBLIC'

18 November 1940, 700

Dupee (1904-79), an editor of 'Partisan Review' during its early years, was author of 'Henry James' (1951), 'The King of the Cats and Other Remarks on Writers and Writing' (1965) and co-editor of 'The Selected Letters of E. E. Cummings' (1969).

'In the Money' is Part II of the projected long novel, 'White Mule.' The whole work is an experiment in applying to sociological fiction the strict objectivity and plastic effect that are Williams' *forte* as a poet. When the first instalment appeared in 1937, it proved to be a somewhat overelaborated version of a conventional plebeian story, and one complained that Williams was merely rewriting Dos Passos according to Imagist principles. With 'In the Money,' however, his experiment seems to be justifying itself. Either the material of this volume is more favorable in itself or else Williams is now better able to realize the possibilities of his story, for 'In the Money' is a tense, finely written little novel of domestic and business life in the years of the first Roosevelt.

Part I dealt with the Stechers in their semi-proletarian phase. Part II relates the efforts of the German-born printer-hero to buck established capital and set up his own shop. Joe Stecher, who used to be a spokesman for labor, now represents small private

enterprise in its contest with monopoly. He is the same
shrewd, reticent, attractive plebeian, but his innocence
seems to be taking leave of him as a result of his bitter
experiences. In Joe's household, too, there is tension,
as if the conflicts of the business life were reproducing
themselves in that smaller world. Joe has a Norwegian
wife, Gurlie, a kind of Molly Bloon, romantic, sensuous,
aggressive, whose ego expands in proportion as her husband
rises in the world. She begins to have dreams of travel
and high life, and she is getting very sensitive and
quarrelsome. There is a remarkable scene in which she
sends her tragic old-country mother packing, and indeed
she appears about to fly out of the family orbit
altogether. Joe Stecher is a good character, too, and the
Stecher children are almost clinically exact studies of
small animals in the process of acquiring human masks; but
Gurlie Stecher thus far is the life of 'White Mule.'

On the whole, Williams seems to be engaged not in turning up any new experience but in rehabilitating, on principle, the commonplace. And reliving the commonplace with Williams is a simple experience of the senses and sentiments, involving no challenge to our intellectual patterns. One may not agree that his literary program is quite the Great Mission that his most fanatic admirers represent it to be. But he does bring to his writing many fine gifts: an immaculate craftsmanship, an ear for common speech as exacting as Ring Lardner's, a physician's knowledge of people's behavior, a faculty for combining lyrical feeling with the most careful observation of reality. And Williams' precise realism is certainly a relief after the big murals of John Steinbeck and other belated workers in the American folk-epic tradition.

48. PAUL ROSENFELD ON 'A SORT OF SPIRITUAL PROLONGATION OF THE VOYAGES OF COLUMBUS', 'NATION'

23 November 1940, 507-8

Few reviews of 'In the Money' add new judgments or insights to the assessment of Williams. Rosenfeld, one of the few frequent reviewers of the early and middle work, became increasingly aware of Williams' quest for 'the essential America'.

The Friends of William Carlos Williams can now be certain
of his approaching reception of a widespread recognition.
This probably would have come to him long since but for
the fact that the opportunism of the publishing world,
while it may not extinguish a man of letters whose public,
like Dr. Williams's, at best grows slowly through the
years, does help to keep him in obscurity. True, because
of its prevailing sexlessness the poetry of this half
Anglo-Saxon, half French and Spanish-Jewish pediatrician
might never have been popular. Still his prose is strong.
Despite the singularity of the style, little of it is
esoteric in character. That much of it achieves forces of
perception and expression new to American literature could
have been plain to many readers.

Plain and peculiarly satisfactory; since these intensities are the fruit of a sort of spiritual prolongation of
the voyages of Columbus and the conquistadors. Williams's
object steadily has been that still imperfectly charted
new world, the essential America. On native character,
affections, manners, especially on the minutiae of lower
and middle-class existence, he has leveled an acute, warm,
unvaryingly truthful feeling. Basic forces have been discovered by him near the core of things American; abundant
cruelty but also miraculous toughness and power of growth.
With a certain force of imagination he has visualized his
discoveries in symbols derived from history but more frequently from the life and landscape of his special region,
industrialized northern New Jersey, and seized them in a
swift, lean style immediately connecting reality and the
word and more than occasionally heroic.

What assures one that a wide sense of his importance is
at hand is first of all the circumstance that Williams
lately has found a publisher with the will to keep him
before the world and the ability to do so. Secondly, it
is the discerning praise bestowed on 'White Mule' and the
reimpression of 'In the American Grain.' Most assuring of
all is the fact that by sheer dint of effort the author is
continuing to enlarge his scope as proseman. His latest
novel, 'In the Money,' indubitably is his best and one of
his most comprehensive performances. A sequel to 'White
Mule' and like that fine book a scenic and dramatic, half-
humorous narrative, it continues its massive characters
and situations. The soft idealistic German, Joe Stecher,
who loses his socialistic feelings in his relations with
labor, figures prominently. So does Gurlie, his Norse
wife, the lusty lady of more Hunnish than Norweigan stateliness. (Her harshness grates on the reader's sensibility
as her name does on his ear and eye.) Again we meet the
well-nigh Shakespearean personage, the baby girl Flossie,

mysterious parallel of the spring and the landscape.
Placed in 1900, the actions revealing these characters,
through which they change and learn and visibly increase
(even poor Gurlie's stunted being finally expands), are
the events in Joe's battle to pass into the capitalist
class at the instigation of his own growing individualism
but also of Gurlie's unleashed selfishness and ambitions:
these and the natural events in which their infant attains
self-consciousness and the unnatural, hateful scene between Gurlie and her old mother that deals the baby its
first mental blow. What again is intended as a measurement of the forces transforming the characters of immigrants and recapitulating the life of the race. The still
incomplete series continued by 'In the Money' promises to
prove Williams's 'The Making of Americans.'

   The story's faults may be the familiar ones. The tension occasionally weakens: from chapter five to chapter
thirteen the continuity approaches the loose one of a
chronicle. The frequency with which the dramatic method
of the bare dialogue is exploited also fatigues at times.
There still is a superfluity of medical moralizing. However, these faults are less obtrusive here than heretofore. By and large, the well-varied scenes are cumulatively built up, fully conveying the author's meanings.
Pictorial touches oftentimes lend atmosphere to the
stretching dialogues. The wonderfully truthful expressions of character and manners and speech again include
contrasts of city streets and countryside, but this time
represent fragments of the political as well as of the
business and domestic spheres; and the intuition in the
realm of the semi-conscious life of small children verges
on the prodigious.

   Meanwhile, the driving style functions as an all-pervading image of the author's general feeling. Perfectly it conveys the tones of the drab, periodically
brightening and smiling range of life under observation:
and from time to time movingly develops a lyricism above
its constant symbolic stature.

'The Wedge'

Cummington, Mass., September 1944

Apart from the booklet 'The Broken Span' (1941), 'The Wedge' is Williams' first collection of poems for six years. The well-known definition contained in his Introduction, 'A poem is a small (or large) machine made of words', owes something to the influence of Louis Zukofsky. (1) Typescripts in the Lockwood Memorial Library, at Buffalo, N.Y., suggest that Williams sent Zukofsky the manuscript of the poems for comment, suggestion, and even editing.

---

49. RANDALL JARRELL ON THE AMERICA OF POETS, 'PARTISAN REVIEW'

Vol. XII, no. 1, 1945, 122-3

This is part of a composite review titled Poetry in War and Peace. Jarrell (1914-65) was an American poet, novelist, translator and writer for children. His 'Poetry and the Age' (1955) is an influential collection of critical essays on American poetry. His other work includes a novel, 'Pictures from an Institution' (1954), translations of Rilke, Mörike and Corbière, and 'The Complete Poems' (1969).

William Carlos Williams is almost too much of a fact to be criticized. In the best of his poems the Nature of the edge of the American city - the weeds, clouds and children of vacant lots - and its reflection in the minds of its inhabitants, exist for good. His ironic (but certainly correct) *Am I not/the happy genius of my household?* suggests

the charm, honesty and rather astonishing limitations of
his work. These limitations are neither technical nor
moral but intellectual. (Even his good critical remarks
sound as if they had been made by Henry Ford; his critical
sense seems kinaesthetic, only intermittently conscious,
so that he is unable, generally, to exploit his regular
style for dramatic monologue, as he most effectively
might.) His poems are, in a way, the diaries of another
Sally Beauchamp; but the tough responsible doctor-half
that says and does, the violent and delicate free-Freudian
half that feels and senses, have their precarious connection in one of the great mythological attitudes of our
country: Brooklyn, the truck-driver looking shyly at the
flower. *In the suburbs, there one feels free*: his optimism comes not from closing his eyes to the serpents but
from strangling them. He is young forever; so this optimist of ability and courage - touchingly wrong in the old
Hercules, dying in his shirt of fire - is still precariously right for the young one. He is the America of poets.

Note

1 It also bears an interesting resemblance to Paul
   Valery's dictum: 'A poem is really a kind of machine
   for producing the poetic state of mind by means of
   words', in Poetry and Abstract Thought (in 'The Art of
   Poetry', translated by Denise Folliot, London, 1958,
   p. 79), first published, in England, in 1939 after
   being given as a lecture. The closing pages of
   Valéry's essay contrast illuminatingly with Williams'
   Introduction.

50. R. P. BLACKMUR ON WILLIAMS AND THE PERCEPTION OF
ORGANIC FORM

1945

This is part of a composite essay, Notes on Seven Poets,
which is included in Blackmur's 'Language as Gesture'
(1952), 353-5. Acknowledgments are made in that volume
to periodicals wherein some essays have previously
appeared, but specific attributions are not made. Notes
on Seven Poets is also included in Blackmur's 'Form and

Value in Modern Poetry' (1957), wherein four of the essays are noted as having appeared in periodicals and specific acknowledgments are made. This essay is not one of the four.

... William Carlos Williams has been publishing almost as long as H.D., and has been writing perhaps longer; his work represents another course, just as limited but differently, of the Imagism that started H.D. off. Where H.D. is, to repeat, cold, 'Greek,' fast, and enclosed, Williams is warm, 'primitive,' of varying speed, and open to every wind. He is so excited with actuality at the minimum remove possible to the machine of language that it does not occur to him that reality is other than immediately contingent and equal to the actuality. Sometimes, by grace of insight, it is; more often, by the fouler accident of mere observation, it is not. In the sense that H.D. depends on a mode of poetry - that the description of her formal verbal means assigns the area of significance to her work - Williams does not employ modes; out of the private abundance of his perceptions his poems take each their forms for, almost, the mere sake of print. This is only to say that Williams takes a great, but unredeemed, care for the underlying modes that inhabit the language itself: the modes that give magnanimous reality to the *report* of a conversation; but it is a spoiling care, it lets the modes do as far as possible all the work; and what it spoils is the chance of that high level of performance which is possible, apparently, only to purposive and convicted minds, with just so much of a felt need of order as makes anarchy actual. Williams ignores the sense of order that goes with the long history of the craft of verse by transposing it to the belief that each poem has an intimate order of its own, which it is the business of the poet to make out of the ardor of his direct perceptions. There is no reason why he should not be right for himself, in his own relation to his verse; he can, as he does, find the sonnet as dead as dead; but he is wrong for his readers in their relations to his poems, because his readers, finding the relations (not the substance) of the verses uncontrolled, cannot tell whether or not they are in intelligent contact with the intimate form of the verse. To the reader it seems no more likely that a piece of verse has an intimate form *de novo* than a woman has, and if either did it would not excite him. The most intimate form underlies common flesh. Some of Williams' poems know this for themselves even if their maker did not.(1) Here is one:

[quotes The World Narrowed to a Point, CLP, 20]

Here, as you might say, intimate form and common form are identical, and are so because of the uniting force, the warming relish, of an old convention about love and drunkenness. There is something a little more in the third quatrain of The A, B and C of It. The first quatrain says 'Love's very fleas are mine,' and the second says the fleas recoiled from the odors of the lover.

[quotes The A, B & C of It, CLP 45, lines 9-12]

The little more is in certain musical and rhetorical conventions like those in the dead sonnet; that is to say, conventions or habits of perception itself. Form is a way of thinking. It may be observed, too, for what it is worth, that to the accustomed ear Williams' four lines tend to rearrange themselves as three iambic pentameters, with the second and third rhyming. What it suggests is that the poetic mind gets ahead somewhat by counting....

Note

1 In a letter to Norman Macleod in July 1945 Williams complains that the critics want him to produce poetry in 'some neo-classic *recognizable* context' and accuse him of 'formlessness'. 'That's why I despise the crew! I won't offend again by naming any', he says; but two paragraphs later he does name Blackmur (SL, 238-9).

'Patterson (Book One)'

Norfolk, Conn., June 1946

51. ISAAC ROSENFELD, THE POETRY AND WISDOM OF PATERSON, 'NATION'

24 August 1946, 216-17

Rosenfeld (1918-56) was a short-story writer and literary critic. His 'An Age of Enormity: Life and Writing in the Forties and Fifties' was published posthumously in 1962.

... There is an obvious scrap-book advantage in this method; it permits running back and forth in time, leaps from man to this-man to the self, and provides a sociological or historical distillate of the city which the poetry, essentially lyrical, could never undertake to do. But the success of this attempt, a generalizing lyricism with an *ars poetica* as its motive, cannot as yet be determined. It will depend on how freely the poetry detaches itself, in the subsequent parts, from the prose conveyor belt and works out its own designs. There is already some spontaneous generation of material in the lyrical sections; thus, a reconstruction of a National Geographic snapshot of native women, which develops into a delicate passage on marriage and the communication between lovers.

Of course, devices are essential, for the lyric has short wings. But more important than the sustaining of the lines is the sustaining of the mood, which is here one of summary and wisdom: whether it can grow, circle out, and return on itself with real gain....

52. RANDALL JARRELL, REVIEW OF 'THE BEST THING WILLIAM CARLOS WILLIAMS HAS EVER WRITTEN', 'PARTISAN REVIEW'

Vol. XIII, September-October 1946, 493-8.

Six other volumes of poetry are considered in the composite review, The Poet and His Public, from which this is taken. Jarrell's review of 'Paterson (Book Four)' is included below (No. 78). Perhaps the balance between these two very different judgments of 'Paterson' is held by the essay with which Jarrell chose to conclude 'Poetry and the Age', where he considers, 'this poet is as odd as he is good ... one of the clearest and firmest and queerest, the most human and real, of the poets of our time'.

... 'Paterson (Book I)' seems to me the best thing William Carlos Williams has ever written; I read it seven or eight times, and ended up lost in delight. It seems a shame to write a little review of it, instead of going over it page by page, explaining and admiring. And one hates to quote much, since the beauty, delicacy, and intelligence of the best parts depend so much upon their organization in the whole; quoting from it is like humming a theme and expecting the hearer to guess from that its effect upon its third repetition in a movement. I have used this simile deliberately, because - over and above the organization of argument or exposition - the organisation of 'Paterson' is musical to an almost unprecedented degree: Mr. Williams introduces a theme that stands for an idea, repeats it over and over in varied forms, develops it side by side with two or three more themes that are being developed, recurs to it time and time again throughout the poem, and echoes it for ironic or grotesque effects in thoroughly incongruous contexts. Sometimes this is done with the greatest complication and delicacy; he wants to introduce a red-bird whose call will stand for the clear speech of nature, in the midst of all the confusion and ugliness in which men could not exist except for 'imagined beauty where there is none': so he says in disgust, 'Stale as a Whale's breath: breath!/Breath!' and ten lines later (during which three themes have been repeated and two of them joined at last in a 'silent, uncommunicative,' and satisfying resolution) he says that he has

> *Only of late, late! begun to know, to*
> *know clearly (as through clear ice) whence*
> *I draw my breath or how to employ it*
> *clearly--if not well:*
>
> > *Clearly!*
> *speaks the red-breast his behest. Clearly!*
> *clearly!*

These double exclamations have so prepared for the bird's call that it strikes you, when you are reading the poem, like the blow which dissolves an enchantment. And really the preparation has been even more complicated: two pages before there was the line 'divorce! divorce!' and half a page before the birds and weeds by the river were introduced by

> *... white, in*
> *the shadows among the blue-flowered*
> *Pickerel-weed, in summer, summer! if it should*
> *ever come ...*

If you want to write a long poem which doesn't stick to one subject, but which unifies a dozen, you can learn a great deal from 'Paterson.' But I do not know how important these details of structure will seem to an age which regards as a triumph of organization that throwing-out-of-blocks-upon-the-nursery-floor which concludes 'The Waste Land,' and which explains its admiration by the humorless literalness of believing that a poet represents fragments by eliminating metre, connectives, and logic from the verses which describe the fragments.

The subject of 'Paterson' is: How can you tell the truth about things? - that is, how can you find a language so close to the world that the world can be represented and understood in it?

[quotes P I, i, 14, lines 1-6]

How can he - this city that is man - find the language for what he dreams and sees and is, the language without which true knowledge is impossible? He starts with the particulars ('Say it, no ideas but in things') which stream to him like the river, 'rolling up out of chaos,/a nine months' wonder'; with the interpenetration of everything with everything, 'the drunk the sober; the illustrious/the gross; one':

[quotes P I, Preface, 12, lines 21-5]

The water falls and then rises in 'floating mists, to be
rained down and/ regathered into a river that flows/and
encircles'; the water, in its time, is 'combed into
straight lines/from that rafter of a rock's/lip,' and
attains clarity; but the people are like flowers that the
bee misses, they fail and die and 'Life is sweet, they
say' - but their speech has failed them, 'they do not know
the words/or have not/the courage to use them,' and they
hear only 'a false language pouring - a/language (misunderstood) pouring (misinterpreted) without/dignity,
without minister, crashing upon a stone ear.' And the
language available to them, the language of scholarship and
science and the universities, is

[quotes P I, ii, 28, lines 6-12]

Girls walk by the river at Easter and one, bearing a wil-
low twig in her hand as Artemis bore the moon's crescent
bow,

[quotes P I, ii, 29, lines 18-21]

(How could words show better than these last three the
touching half-success, half-failure of their language?)
And Sam Patch, the drunken frontier hero who jumped over
the Falls with his pet bear, could *say* only; 'Some things
can be done as well as others'; and Mrs. Cumming, the
minister's wife, shrieked unheard and fell unseen from the
brink; and the two were only

[quotes P I, ii, 31, lines 9-12]

The speech of sexual understanding, of natural love, is
represented by three beautifully developed themes: a
photograph of the nine wives of a Negro chief; a tree
standing on the brink of the waterfall; and two lovers
talking by the river:

[quotes P I, ii, 36, lines 3-11]

But now the air by the river 'brings in the rumors of
separate worlds,' and the poem is dragged from its highest
point in the natural world, from the early, fresh, and
green years of the city, into the slums of Paterson, into
the collapse of this natural language, into 'a delirium
of solutions,' into the back streets of that 'great belly/
that no longer laughs but mourns/with its expressionless
black navel love's/deceit.' Here is the whole failure of
Paterson's ideas and speech, and he is forced to begin all

over; Part II of the poem ends with the ominous 'No ideas but/in the facts.'
   Part III opens with this beautiful and unexpected passage:

[quotes P I, iii, 41, lines 1-8]

The underlying green of the facts always cancels out the red in which we had found our partial, temporary, aesthetic victory; and the poem now introduces the livid green of the obstinate and compensating lives, the lifeless perversions of the industrial city: here are the slums and the adjoining estate with its acre hothouse and weedlike orchids and French maid whose sole duty is to 'groom/the pet Pomeranians - who sleep'; here is the university with its clerks

[quotes P I, iii, 44, lines 10-13]

Then (in one of the fine prose quotations - much altered by the poet, surely - with which the verse is interspersed) people drain the lake there, all day and all night long kill the eels and fish with sticks, carry them away in baskets; there is nothing left but the mud. The sleeping Paterson, 'moveless,' envies the men who could run off 'toward the peripheries - to other centers, direct' for some 'loveliness and/authority in the world,' who could leap like Sam Patch and be found 'the following spring, frozen in/an ice cake.' But he goes on thinking to the very bitter end, reproduces all the ignorance and brutality of the city; and he understands its pathos and horror:

[quotes P I, iii, 49, lines 16-25]

Yet he contrasts his own real mystery, the mystery of people's actual lives, with the mystery that 'the convent of the Little Sisters of/St. Ann pretends'; and he understands the people 'wiping the nose on sleeves, come here/ to dream'; he understands that

[quotes P I, iii, 51, lines 12-15]

Then Paterson 'shifts his change,' and an earthquake and a 'remarkable rumbling noise' frighten but do not damage the city - this is told in the prose of an old newspaper account; and, at the end of the poem, he stands in the flickering green of the cavern under the waterfall (the dark, skulled world of consciousness), hedged in by the pouring torrent whose thunder drowns out any language; 'the myth/that holds up the rock,/that holds up the water thrives there/in that cavern, that profound cleft'; and the readers of the poem are shown, in the last words of the poem,

> standing, shrouded there, in that din,
> Earth, the chatterer, father of all
> speech....

It takes several readings to work out the poem's argument (it is a poem that *must* be read over and over), and it seemed to me that I could do most for its readers by roughly summarizing that argument. There are hundreds of things in the poem that deserve specific mention. The poem is weakest in the middle of Part III - I'd give page numbers if good old New Directions had remembered to put in any - but this is understandable and almost inevitable. Everything in the poem is interwoven with everything else, just as the strands of the Falls interlace: how wonderful and unlikely that this extraordinary mixture of the most delicate lyricism of perception and feeling with the hardest and homeliest actuality should ever have come into being! There has never been a poem more American (though the only influence one sees in it is that of the river scene from 'Finnegans Wake'); if the next three books are as good as this one, which introduces 'the elemental character of the place,' the whole poem will be far and away the best long poem any American has written. I should like to write a whole article about it; I leave it unwillingly....

53. PARKER TYLER, FROM THE POET OF PATERSON BOOK ONE, 'BRIARCLIFF QUARTERLY'

No. III, October 1946, 169-70

Tyler (b. 1907), American poet, biographer and critic. A writer of several books on film, Tyler was for some years film critic for the 'Kenyon Review'. Williams reviewed Tyler's 'The Granite Butterfly: a Poem in Nine Cantos' (1945) in 'Accent'. Tyler's 'The Will of Eros: Selected Poems 1930-1970' was published in 1972.

... In practice, Williams reversed the orientation of Mr. Eliot's objective-correlative by trying to piece together, in an inspired 'jig-saw' fashion, the picture of the material out of which American poets should write their poetry. If addressed by the criticism of the Eliotian objective-correlative, Dr. Williams could only defend this view by saying: 'My theory of poetry was that it arises from immediate environment, and in the case of *my* environment, America, the poetic formulas for familiar (or "objective-correlative") emotions did not exist. Why not? Because the emotions themselves, and the very imagery of their implicit situations, were elusive and unformed.' This theory is the inevitability of Dr. Williams' *style*. This style was a radical effort to establish the concrete elements from which feelings arise, in the sense that a cry arises from a person in one specific situation and in no other. If the situation is not self-evident, the 'cry' is hollow: musical in the limited, abstract sense. The Swinburnian 'voice' in poetry is the effeteness of the objective-correlative; nothing but the 'cry,' the typical epithet and the closed vocabulary, emerges. Twentieth-century poetry, not only here but also in France and England, was a reaction against the Swinburnian voice, authentic in itself but inapplicable to human development.

The last and most bravura effeteness of poetic tradition was in the high art of Mallarmé's memory-mechanism, which compressed and ellipsized the situation from which the emotion was derived into what might be termed a capsule synthesis of image and emotional reaction. A correlation which, I believe, has gone unnoticed is that Williams is a naive or imagistic 'Mallarmé.' Assuredly, the lyrics of both reveal the same smallness of physical area, the same concentration on a very simple, typical, and vivid gesture, stated by both elliptically. The great difference is the assurance of Mallarmé's emotional reaction, the demonstration - absent from Williams - that art is 'emotion recollected in tranquillity.' Williams' 'poetic evidence' is not essentially transformed by the symbolic formulas of language, remaining often brutally *untransformed*. Reading a Williams lyric, we are in the presence of the action or of the object in a sense in which we definitely are not while reading a Mallarmé lyric. In Williams' case there is effort to recreate the physical décor, the concrete scene, whereas Mallarmé writes precisely to disguise the physical event and replace it with a formula of sensation.

For this reason, I feel that William Carlos Williams has always been progressing towards a poetry whose form finally stands revealed in his latest volume, 'Paterson'

(Book One), a poetry that is mythical while being epic only in the Joycean sense of 'Finnegans Wake'. The obvious parallel between Joyce's Finnegan dreaming of the Liffey and Williams' Patersonized man, lying 'on his right side, head near the thunder of the waters filling his dreams!' is not to be ignored. Yet while Joyce approached his transcendence of narrative action through all the incidental conventions of drama and novel, Williams has remained exclusively within the data-collecting definition of the lyric....

54. EDWIN HONIG, THE CITY OF MAN, 'POETRY'

Vol. LXIX, no. 5, February 1947, 277-84

Honig (b. 1919), who teaches at Brown University, Rhode Island, is a poet, academic writer and translator of Calderon and Lorca.

Through 'Paterson (Book One)' one may walk or fly or stagger a dozen times - one proceeds in a different way at each reading of the poem - and emerge each time with a different set of meanings, a different sense of the fusion of the parts, and a different feeling of exaltation and exasperation.

As the first unit of a long philosophic poem, it calls for a special kind of attention and evaluation. Though published in book form, it obviously cannot be treated as any other book of verse which does not similarly point to a still unpublished and larger design. One must also dodge the momentarily fruitless question of its unity or fragmentariness as a part in order to determine first what the poet promises and what the poem itself suggests of purpose and direction. Then, because the promises, like those of the magician, are but the invitations to suspend belief, which is swept up in the miracle of performance, it might better serve to show how the incredible richness of the poet's effects exalts by mystification and exasperates by seeming deception.

Williams proposes to prove 'that a man in himself is a city, beginning, seeking, achieving and concluding his life in ways which the various aspects of a city may

embody - if imaginatively conceived - any city, all the
details of which may be made to voice his most intimate
convictions.' Thus a man may become a treasury, a legend
taking unto himself all the proportions of a city, historical and contemporary, animate and inanimate, moribund
and waking. The city becomes the focal myth wound out of
the poet's consciousness, or, like the dreams of the hero
of 'Finnegans Wake', the myth becomes the consciousness
itself.

But what of the philosophy, the poetic logic, the use
of guiding symbol, referents, central images, and artifice to bind the whole together? These do not appear
according to any conventional pattern. The events of
history themselves - with which the poet interlards his
verse: letters from friends, snatches from old newspapers,
archival records, the documents of past and present - provide the links, the scattered facts which the broad imaginative conception seeks to co-ordinate. Tentatively,
however, some such rough scheme may be delineated: for the
philosophy: 'no ideas but in things'; for the poetic
logic: 'to make a start,/out of particulars/and make them
general'; for the guiding symbol: man as a city; for the
referents: (what Williams has said in another place) 'my
sources .../the secret of that form/interknit with the
unfathomable ground/where we walk daily'; for the central
images: the river, the falls, the rocks, the green things
separately growing; and for the artifice: a language, to
use Williams' quote from J.A. Symonds, of 'deformed verse
... suited to deformed morality.'

Like any long-festering preoccupation with life which
erupts into art, the poem is both a personal confession
and a challenge to the forces which besiege the poet's
creative faith. In a life which proves only that 'we
know nothing, pure/and simple, beyond/our own complexities,'

[quotes P I, ii, 28, lines 1-12]

As with another 'divorced' contemporary, T. S. Eliot
(whose resolution may be clearer because his faith is
orthodox, though his knowledge is no fuller), the personal
problem with Williams is to discover and constantly re-
discover a language which will embody the forms of fluxive
reality. Eliot seeks the language fitting the imagination
to God; Williams, the language fitting the imagination
to things. For Williams it is not the language of the university, of the scholarly 'non-purveyors,' 'the knowledge-
able idiots' who restrict knowledge, but of one who feels
like the branch of a sycamore, trembling

[quotes P I, ii, 31-2, four lines beginning 'among the rest ...']

who would rescue something of the waste of moment-to-moment reality:

[quotes P I, ii, 34, lines 9-17]

He would believe in 'The vague inaccuracy of events dancing two/and two with language which they/forever surpass,' and would seem to demand that his own crotchety choice of quotations be judged, however faulty their language, as records of that reality embedded in events which the poet at best only occasionally grasps in his own verse.
   They are his proof of an ever-present and ever-past activity of spirit which has penetrated the inanimate world: the sentimentality with which the knowledge of the prior penetration there by others invests the scene, *e.g.*, the heroic and pathetic deaths of those in the past which make the waterfalls over the river legendary, and the perverse assumption of some accredited accomplishment in the obscure persons and events which re-enact the poet's sense of wonder in the place, forever absorbed and rejected as he is by his environment. Obsessed with the sources of things, and with the mystic's proprietary rights, he seeks to maintain the balance between sheer surface illusion and sharp plunging insight into their being. Although at times admitting with others his failure to find what 'laughs at the names/ by which they think to trap it. Escapes!/Never by running but by lying still,' he is often rewarded by the scrupulous intensity of his vision with lines like

[quotes P I, ii, 36, lines 12-15, 23-5, and 37, lines 1-15]

Pointing to the harmony that must be created out of the eternal sense of the duplicity in things, the poet, doctor-like, with skill and passion, and without cheating himself, affirms his power to control the flux by defining and ministering to it.
   Williams' verses insist on themselves, insist on their own self-distractedness, their own 'deformity'; they insist on their own explosions from sense and their own sure bringing together of the strands of sense, like music more than verse, like fluid water color, trembling with motion while at rest, themselves part of all motion when motion momently, quixotically freezes into rest.
   'Book I,' which 'introduces the elemental character of the place,' thereby also introduces the poet's magical

paraphernalia, his reiterative symbols, his episodic
devices, the links in his Man-City chain. Several readings will ostensibly justify the growing magnitude of
poetic conception. But though one is willing to applaud
the achievement, it becomes increasingly difficult to
validate as integral parts of the poetry the successive
chunks of prose interlardings, which one instinctively
wants to skip on rereading the poem. And one is made
conscious of the faltering gestures of objective relationship between the poet and his human surroundings. His
love of the human is fixed, alien, and cold, a pity self-
magnified; yet he persists in that identification as an
almost classic necessity. The reason is perhaps not far
to find. It is not love of the human, but a recognition
in their actions of the forces in men by which they try
to extend themselves, their fumbling illiterate use of the
language of sex ('an incredible/clumsiness of address,/
senseless rapes'), of imagination (Sam Patch, the inspired
professional jumper, who at last failed because he had
lost words), curiosity and knowledge, forces which wealth
and poverty cut short and divorce from living. Facing
people, the poet confronts the complicated equations of
their lives, 'controlled' but unmanageable. Wishing to
embrace in order to sustain them, like the City, he finds
that the problem resolves itself into a personal 'mathem-
atic.'

[quotes P I, ii, 30-1, four lines from 'The thought
returns...']

Make the pathetic leap? End up in the river frozen in an
ice cake, 'incommunicado'? But he has only lately discovered his voice,

[quotes from P I, ii, 31, lines 13-16]

And through the lover who sits by the bank of the river at
the side of his beloved, proposing

[quotes from P I, ii, 35, lines 15-21]

- the poet comes to know the language which failed the
others, which fails the people who 'have not the courage'
to use it. This sense of discovery is extremely personal,
welding together as it does the poetic esthetic with a
criticism of man which subsumes the poet's very acceptance
of the living condition. It accounts for the marvel of
the poet'c recreation of things through a consciousness
inbred with the underlying shifts of nature. But it does

not reconcile that sense with any sense of solution of the 'problem of language' in man.

If the City is ultimately made to embody the Man, it will be because the time and events which identify the place have been surpassed by the universality toward which the Man-as-City strives. Though possibly violating Williams' conception and effectively bypassing the inconclusiveness of the objective human relationship, this statement may perhaps explain the insistent power of the poetry. For when all the apparatus which has been created to implement it has faded from the design, the mystery of the poet's creation remains, as in the last lines, an attainment of personal faith: the reawakened knowledge that only through a penetration to the sources of being, the active acknowledgment of primitive earth forces, does life, the language of thought and action, become real or intelligible:

[quotes P I, iii, 51, lines 24-7, and 52, lines 1-13]

55. ROBERT LOWELL, 'A SORT OF ANTI-CANTOS ROOTED IN AMERICA', 'SEWANEE REVIEW'

Vol. LV, Summer 1947, 500-3

Lowell (1919-77), American poet, translator and playwright, and a cousin of the Imagist poet Amy Lowell. Lowell won the Pulitzer Prize in 1946 for 'Lord Weary's Castle'. His most influential single work is probably 'Life Studies' (1959), a book of autobiographical poems.

In a review that I imagine will become famous as an example of 'the shock of recognition,' Randall Jarrell has said about all that can be said in a short space of the construction of 'Paterson'. I feel no embarrassment, however, for repeating, poorly but in different words, what has already been written. 'Paterson' has made no stir either in the little magazines or in the commercial press; and yet I can think of no book published in 1946 that is as important, or of any living English or American poet who has written anything better or more ambitious.

When it is completed, 'Paterson' will run to over a
hundred pages, and be in four parts. As only Part I has
been published, the critic is faced with many uncertain-
ties, and forced to make many conjectures.* Williams'
own rather breathless and incoherent introductory note
will, perhaps, be of little help. 'A man in himself is a
city, beginning, seeking, achieving and concluding his
life in the ways which the various aspects of the city may
embody - if imaginatively conceived - any city, all the
details of which may be made to voice his most intimate
convictions.' The poet beings with a slightly different
statement of this purpose: 'Rigor of beauty is the quest.
But how will you find beauty when it is locked in the mind
past all remonstrance?' The answer is 'to make a start
out of particulars ... no ideas but in things.' This may
appear crude and vague, but Williams has nothing in common
with the coarse, oratorical sentimentalists, most favor-
ably represented by Carl Sandburg, who have written about
cities and the people. More than any of his contemporaries, he resembles Wordsworth in his aims and values; and
in its maturity, experience, and sympathy, 'Paterson'
appears to me to be comparable to the 'Prelude' and the
opening of the 'Excursion.'

I am not sure that I can say very clearly why, or even
how it is that Williams' methods are successful. By per-
sonifying Paterson, and by 'Patersonizing' himself, he is
in possession of all the materials that he can use. First
the City is his: all its aspects, its past, its present,
its natural features, its population, and its activities
are available for him to interrelate and make dramatic.
But also he can use his whole life in the City - every
detail is an experience, a memory, or a symbol. Taken
together, Paterson is Williams' life, and Williams is
what makes Paterson alive.

For Williams, a man is what he experiences, and in his
shorter lyrics he has perfected a technique of observation and of empathy. He can move from man outward;
'The year plunges into night/and the heart plunges/lower
than night/to an empty, windswept place/without sun,
stars or moon/but a peculiar light as of though/than
spins a dark fire....'/ Or the observed is personified:
'Lifeless in appearance, sluggish/dazed spring approaches
- They enter the new world naked,/cold,uncertain of all/
save that they enter.' Which end he starts from matters
little. Williams triumphs in his sense of motion, his
ability to observe, and to fit his observations to the
right rhythms.

But if the short poems show Williams as an excellent
stylist, there is nothing in them to indicate that their

thematic structure could be extended to a long poem. How this has been done and how 'Paterson's' various themes are stated, developed, repeated, opposed, broken, and mingled, has been demonstrated at some length by Jarrell in 'Partisan Review.' Here I shall confine myself to quoting passages in which the principal themes are expressed and to pointing out a few of their more important connections and meanings. The theme on which all the others depend is threefold: a city - Paterson, New Jersey -, a mountain, and a river that flows from the mountain into Paterson - a man, a woman, and the man's thought. First the city:

[quotes P I, 14, lines 1-10]

The mountain is introduced in a parallel passage:

[quotes P I, 17, lines 5-14]

The passage introducing the river is too long to quote in full.

[quotes P I, 16, lines 4-11]

The Man-City and the Woman-Mountain are easier to understand than the river which symbolizes thought. It is the elemental thought that lacks a language, the source of life and motion. It is described again and again, always with such powerful precision that one is in no doubt of its grimness and strength. It is intercourse between Paterson and the mountain, and above all, it is Paterson's thoughts, his population - the primal vitality behind their lives and speech. The two lovers later meet under its falls, and in the prose records that are interspersed with the poetry, one reads of the men and women who were drowned in it, and the pearls and fish that were taken out of it. This three-fold main-theme is repeated in smaller themes, such as the African chief with his seven wives on a log, and 'the lightnings that stab at the mystery of a man from both ends.' It is broken up in the two divorces: the university, 'a bud forever green,/tight-curled, upon the pavement, perfect/in juice and substance but divorced, divorced/from its fellows, fallen low -'; and the 'girls from/families that have decayed and/taken to the hills.... Life is sweet/they say: the language!/ - the language/is divorced from their minds.' 'In ignorance a certain knowledge and knowledge, undispersed, its own undoing.'

    This is the tragedy of 'Paterson', what the poem, is really about. It is the divorce of modern life, of intellect and sensibility, spirit and matter, and of the other

stock categories that come to mind. His 'quest for
beauty' is a search for the whole man, whose faculties are
harmonious, and whose language corresponds with the particulars and mystery of reality. Williams is liberal,
anti-orthodox, and a descendant of Emerson and Whitman.
But if a man is intense and honest enough, the half-truth
of any extreme position will in time absorb much of its
opposite. Williams has much in common with Catholic,
aristocratic and Agrarian writers. For all his sympathy
with his people, he makes one feel that the sword of
Damocles hangs over Paterson, the modern city and world.
As with Yeats, 'things fall apart.' The educated lack
connection, and the ignorant are filled with speechless
passion.

Williams has had much to say about Ezra Pound, one whom
he may have envied for being able to 'run off toward the
peripheries to find loveliness and authority in the world
– a sort of springtime toward which his mind aspired.'
Some of his pronouncements seemed unfair and hysterical,
but in 'Paterson' his position has paid off, when compared with Pound's. It is a sort of anti-Cantos rooted
in America, in one city, and in what Williams has known
long and seen often. Not only are its details enriched
and verified by experience, but the whole has a unity
that is analogous to the dramatic unities of time, place,
and action.

'Paterson' resembles 'The Bridge'; but Hart Crane's
poem, for all its splendor in its best moments, will not
stand up to the comparison. It seems relatively inexperienced, chaotic and verbal. Even as a rhetorician
Williams is much superior. It would be fruitless to compare 'Paterson' with the best writing of Eliot, Stevens,
Tate, or Auden, for the ways of writing very well are
various; but for experience and observation, it has,
along with a few poems of Frost, a richness that makes
almost all other contemporary poetry look a little second-
hand. If Parts II, III, and IV are as good as Part I,
'Paterson' will be the most successful really long poem
since 'The Prelude.'

Note

*As the poem stands, it has many insufficiently related
odds and ends. It is a defect perhaps that human beings
exist almost entirely in the prose passages.

'Patterson (Book Two)'

Norfolk, Conn., April 1948

56. ROBERT LOWELL ON WILLIAMS' 'PLATONISM', REVIEW, 'NATION'

19 June 1948, 692-4

'Paterson, (Book Two),' is an interior monologue. A man spends Sunday in the park at Paterson, New Jersey. He thinks and looks about him; his mind contemplates, describes, comments, associates, stops, stutters, and shifts like a firefly, bound only by its milieu. The man is Williams, anyone living in Paterson, the American, the masculine principle - a sort of Everyman. His monologue is interrupted by chunks of prose: paragraphs from old newspapers, textbooks, and the letters of a lacerated and lacerating poetess. This material is merely selected by the author. That the poetry is able to digest it in the raw is a measure of power and daring - the daring of simplicity; for only a taut style with worlds of experience behind it could so resign, and give way to the anthologist. The didactic chapters in 'Moby Dick' have a similar function, and are the rock that supports the struggles of Captain Ahab.

The park is Everywoman, any woman, the feminine principle, America. The water roaring down the falls from the park to Paterson is the principle of life. The rock is death, negation, the *nul*; carved and given form, it stands for the imagination, 'like a red basalt grasshopper, bootlong with window-eyes.' The symbols are not allegorical, but loose, intuitive, and Protean.

'Paterson,' like Hart Crane's Marriage of Faustus and Helen, is about marriage. 'Rigor of beauty is the quest.' Everything in the poem is masculine or feminine, every-

thing strains toward marriage, but the marriages never come
off, except in the imagination, and there, attenuated,
fragmentary, and uncertain. 'Divorce is the sign of knowledge in our time.' The people 'reflect no beauty but
gross ... unless it is beauty to be, anywhere, so flagrant
in desire.' 'The ugly legs of the young girls, pistons
without delicacy'; 'not undignified'; 'among the working
classes *some* sort of breakdown has occurred.' The preacher
in the second section, attended by the 'iron smiles' of his
three middle-aged disciples, by 'benches on which a few
children have been propped by the others against their running off,' 'bends at the knees and straightens himself up
violently with the force of his emphasis - like Beethoven
getting a crescendo out of an orchestra' - ineffective,
pathetic, and a little phony. He has given up, or says he
has given up, a fortune for the infinite riches of our Lord
Jesus Christ. Interspersed through his sermon, as an
ironic counter-theme, is Alexander Hamilton, whose fertile
imagination devised the national debt and envisioned Paterson as a great manufacturing center. Nobody wins, 'The
church spires still spend their wits against the sky.'
'The rock-table is scratched by the picnickers' boot-nails,
more than by the glacier.' The great industrialists are
'those guilty bastards ... trying to undermine us.' The
legislators are 'under the garbage, uninstructed, incapable
of self-instruction.' 'An orchestral dulness overlays
their world.' 'The language, tongue-tied ... words without style!'

This is the harsh view. Against it is the humorous, the
dogs, the children; lovely fragments of natural description; the author's sense of the human and sympathetic in
his people.

Williams is noted as an imagist, a photographic eye; in
Book One he has written 'no ideas but in the facts.' This
is misleading. His symbolic man and woman are Hegel's
thesis and *antithesis*. They struggle toward *synthesis* -
marriage. But fulness, if it exists at all, only exists
in simple things, trees and animals; so Williams, like
other Platonists, is thrown back on the 'idea.' 'And no
whiteness (lost) is so white as the memory of whiteness.'
'The stone lives, the flesh dies.' The idea, Beauty, must
be realized by the poet where he lives, in Paterson. 'Be
reconciled, Poet, with your world, it is the only truth,'
though 'love' for it 'is no comforter, rather a nail in
the skull.'

'Paterson' is an attempt to write the American Poem. It
depends on the American myth, a myth that is seldom absent
from our literature - part of our power, and part of our
hubris and deformity. At its grossest the myth is

propaganda, puffing and grimacing: Size, Strength, Vitality, the Common Man, the New World, Vital Speech, the Machine; the hideous neo-Roman personae: Democracy, Freedom, Liberty, the Corn, the Land. How hollow, windy, and inert this would have seemed to an imaginative man of another culture! But the myth is a serious matter. It is assumed by Emerson, Whitman, and Hart Crane; by Henry Adams and Henry James. For good or for evil, America *is* something immense, crass, and Roman. We must unavoidably place ourselves in our geography, history, civilization, institutions, and future.

The subjects of great poetry have usually been characters and the passions, a moral struggle that calls a man's whole person into play. One thinks of the wrath of Achilles, Macbeth and his conscience, Aeneas debating whether he will leave Dido, whether he will kill Turnus. But in the best long American poems - 'Leaves of Grass,' 'The Cantos,' 'The Waste Land,' 'Four Quartets,' 'The Bridge,' and 'Paterson' - no characters take on sufficient form to arrive at a crisis. The people melt into voices. In a recent essay Eliot has given his reasons why a writer should, perhaps, read Milton; Williams has answered with an essay that gives reasons why a writer should *not* read Milton - Eliot and Williams might learn something from 'Paradise Lost' and 'Samson Agonistes,' how Milton populated his desert.

Until Books III and IV are published, it is safer to compare 'Paterson' with poems that resemble it; not with 'The Bridge,' that wonderful monster, so unequal, so inexperienced - dazzling in its rhetoric at times in the way that Keats is dazzling; but with a book in which its admirers profess to find everything, 'Leaves of Grass' Whitman is a considerable poet, and a considerable myth. I can never quite disentangle the one from the other. I would say that Whitman's language has less variety, sureness, and nerve than Williams's; that his imagination is is relatively soft, formless, monotonous, and vague. Both poets are strong on compassion and enthusiasm, but these qualities in Whitman are *simpliste* and blurred.

'Paterson' is Whitman's America, grown pathetic and tragic, brutalized by inequality, disorganized by industrial chaos, and faced with annihilation. No poet has written of it with such a combination of brilliance, sympathy, and experience, with such alertness and energy. Because he [Williams] has tried to understand rather than excoriate, and because in his maturity he has been occupied with the 'raw' and the universal, his 'Paterson' is not the tragedy of the outcast but the tragedy of our civilization. It is a book in which the best readers, as well as the simple reader, are likely to find *everything*.

57. LESLIE FIEDLER, SOME USES AND FAILURES OF FEELING, 'PARTISAN REVIEW'

Vol XV, no. 8, August 1948, 924, 927-31

This is part of a composite review, in which three other books are considered at lesser length.

Fiedler (b. 1917) is an American literary critic whose chief works are 'An End to Innocence' (1955) and 'Love and Death in the American Novel' (1959). His most recent book is 'Freaks' (1978).

The sense of how much any poem is at the mercy of large sightless shifts in feeling outside the poet's will or the exigencies of his poem mocks us who were brought up to regard poems as structures, that is in their aspect of autonomy taken as a total definition. The concept of structure has been a handsome and useful fiction, sustaining two, perhaps three generations of poets in the style to which we have become accustomed, but it begins, I think, to assume already a slight air of the old-fashioned; defending it we seem inevitably - a little truculent. For we submit now, willing or not, to a revolution in sensibility, called sometimes with moderate accuracy neo-Romanticism, which involves in the aspect these poets chiefly illuminate a restoration to legitimacy of the more dangerous uses of emotion and the consequent difficulty in the discrimination of sentimentality. There is a point at which that revolution is self-conscious, interested in giving itself names and canonizing forerunners, but almost everywhere its pressures are manifest, at least as distortion or dismay, and it forces us uneasily to recognize the sense in which the poem is spectacularly not autonomous, but must yield to changing fashions in emotion, themselves prompted by inscrutable adjustments in the gross social mind that does not feel responsible for, or indeed even interested in, the production of poetry.... In this context of shifting feeling William Carlos Williams assumes a new meaning; and it is fitting that he consummate at this precise moment his life's work with the appearance (this is the second volume; there are two more to go) of his long poem 'Paterson,' parts of which have been appearing over the last twenty years.

For Williams has long been testifying to the uses of sentimentality. He is, in a sense, the Dashiell Hammett

of American poetry; there exists in his work the precise
mixture of realism and sentimentality, the masculine soup-
iness under the hardboiled surfaces (The Raper from
Passenack defines in a short lyric all that James M. Cain
was ever after) of the boys in the back room. 'Noble,' he
says someplace in praise of another poet, 'has become No
Bull!' And that's Bill all over.

It is good for us, I think, to see Williams in such a
setting (though it is by no means the whole truth about
him), for his reputation has flourished among those who
have despised manifestations of the same complex of feeling in prose fiction - and Williams has in the meantime
attained the status of a Grand Old Man, a survivor, who
saw the young Ezra plain, who dates back to the almost unimaginable heyday of Imagism, and who has persisted (unlike the Hammetts, to be sure), uncommercialized, doggedly
outliving the little reviews that have continued to print
him. That modernist poetry has already survived long
enough to have produced Old Men, is a fact that in itself
constantly astounds us, and we fail perhaps to evaluate
them precisely, carried away by our adulation of them as
original Witnesses.

But it is with Williams' unswerving sentimentality, his
role of the hard-shelled doctor with the secret sympathetic heart, that we must begin: his sentimentalization of
the working-class, bulls, the New Jersey landscape - and
the balancing crustiness: the crabbed forms, the use of
anti-poetic detail, the guttural grunts, the constant
self-mockery, in short, the attributes of realism.

That we have had only this one respectable realistic
poet in twentieth-century America confuses us; we are
always lumping Williams with the wrong people, for it
seems utterly improbable that one highly admired by, say,
Wallace Stevens, could have radically less in common with
him than with the obsolescent Carl Sandburg - and, of
course, there is the bent and coloration given once and
for all to the realism of Williams by the Imagist movement and the Japanese short poem as they imperfectly
understood it. 'Imagism' - the word comes up out of that
darkness in which we store a handy vocabulary for discussing (if improbably pushed to it) what no longer interests
us - and clinging to it the dead and the mad and the honest: Amy Lowell, Ezra Pound and W. C. Williams. Well, we
like to think of Pound; madness has been at least optional
among poets for a long time - but Amy Lowell!

Yet we cannot reject what Williams' astonishing persistence evokes - the questionable ghost of *vers libre*, the
tyranny of the eye. The realist is ultimately the *voyeur*
- for seeing is the most literal of the senses, the

remotest from abstract or symbolic thought ('No ideas but
in things,' Williams intones at the beginning of 'Paterson,' his lifelong credo), and it is happiest of coincidences that the Hammett hero is the Private Eye, precisely
as in the center of Williams' long poem the watcher whose
vision makes the body of his world: the Shamus, the Private Eye, unnoticed epiphanies embedded in our speech.

What the exploitation of that single sense, plus an
unmitigated honesty, can do, Williams has done all right,
and the simple devotion to seeing gives to some of his
poems a magnificent, a manic vividness. But how far can
you go on *one* sense! This is not quite fair, perhaps;
though the visual obsesses Williams, sounds occasionally
touch him: the noise of water, the mythic pissing of his
Falls, grunts, the thick voices of his wise wops talking,
but there is no song in him. His entirely visual concept
of poetic form inhibits what incipent melody comes (a few
honorable exceptions, noticeably some stanzas from the
center of the Beautiful Thing sequence in 'Paterson II,'
come to mind); he pursues absolutely the seen poem: speech
that rejects the illusion of being heard; lines broken on
the page regardless of cadence to make the eye's pattern
or emulate plastic form; at last, the absurd periods set
off by chaste white space . , as if they were the poem
ultimately reduced and framed by a respectful silence.

It was, I suppose, Pound who started it all, or rather
through him Ernest Fennollosa with his Sinologist's myth
of the Ideograph: the presumed unity in Oriental verse of
the drawn shape of the characters and the poem as sound,
as sense. But proposed in our world where not the brush,
intimate with the hand, but a remote machine composes the
poem on the page, there is an inevitable air of nostalgia,
or even parody about the attempt to unify the seen and
heard forms of the poem - and in the end what is involved
is a kind of betrayal, a surrender to typography of music
and resonance:

[quotes This is Just to Say, CEP, 354]

Whis is a parody of Williams, to be sure, but oddly
enough, written by Williams himself in his pursuit of the
ultimate, the utopian Skinny Poem; beyond this there is
only

```
* * *
* S *
* O *
* S *
* A *
* * *
```

whose obvious aspiration toward the phallic (think of it
up or down, tumescence or detumescence) perhaps defines
an ulterior meaning of Williams' form.

What on the face of it seems more incredible than that
the supreme practitioner of the reduced poem among us
should be tempted toward the Long Poem; what seems less
probable than his success, especially when he proposes,
who has fled all but the sentimental-ironic picture, a
dissertation on the mythic city and the definition of man
- tempted toward philosophy as well as discursiveness.
And yet here in hand is the second volume of 'Paterson,'
already substantially realized, in the most literal sense
- a wonder! To be sure, there was a form ready to solve
the dilemma of the short breath and the long intent without teaching an old dog new tricks of substantial structure; the pattern had long been set for what I suppose we
might as well call the Ezra-istic poem: the collage of
fragments whose architecture is a continuing irony of disjunction, set once and for all when Pound revised for
Eliot 'The Waste Land,' confirmed in Pound's own 'Cantos'
and in 'The Bridge' of Hart Crane. It has been a long
time since any serious poet among us has attempted any
other strategy for the long poem - and we recognize the
convention in Williams, adhered to with a basic conservatism that gives his poem a classic, an expected air.
Here are the rapid shifts in point of view, the urban
subject, the intruded quotations, the counterpoint of a
formal diction and the overheard brutalities of common
speech; here are the harsh distorted forms and the Greek
allusion to justify the fallacy of imitative form (sufficient unto the day is the incoherence thereof) that
promts them.

It is so far a work with real virtues, above all a kind
of unflagging candor, a freshness of vision from which
Williams astonishingly does not wither, and all the charm
of a personality that at his age he can afford to inflict
upon us with a lucid self-confidence unavailable to the
young. He is, as we say, a self-made man. There is a
certain appeal too in his conjunction of a radical
vagueness of ideas and a sensual precision, real charm in
his respect for language, his ironic and tender regionalism. But the poem's faults are even now apparent, disturbing: the lack of a felt necessity in its transitions and conjunctions, and a pervading wilfulness, a
self-indulgence most usually discreet, but occasionally
blatant as in its injection into the work's progress of
some old letter given at needless length, or even an impassioned irrelevance about Lilienthal and the 'guilty
bastards' in our Senate completely out of the poem's time

assailing its fictive integrity. It is doubtful if in the
end the total credibility of the poem can survive such
lapses; if we think even for a moment 'Padding!' - all is
imperilled. Besides, the old faults persist: the failures
of flatness and sentimentality, the philosophical weakness, the impulse to subsume everything into sight.

Of one thing I am sure: that there is no point in being
as extravagantly kind to Williams as the reviewers apparently were to the first volume of 'Paterson.' A muddled
sort of sentiment seems to me to blur any possibility of
definition in the page-full of excerpts from critics New
Directions sends along with this volume to bully us by
creating an atmosphere in which any dissent from absolute
enthusiasm appears am impiety. To be sure, we owe something to the conscientious practitioner who has survived
our own vagaries of taste through half a dozen minor aesthetic revolutions, but what we owe him is, I suspect, a
devotion equal to his own, but in our case turned to the
difficult and sometimes impious business of discrimination.

58. LOUIS L. MARTZ, ANTICIPATING WILLIAMS' CONCLUSION THAT 'THE VIRTUE IS ALL IN THE EFFORT', 'YALE REVIEW'

Vol XXXVIII, no. 1, Autumn 1948, 147-50

Martz's composite review, Recent Poetry, deals also with
books by Randall Jarrell and Robert Horan and with Pound's
'Cantos' and 'Pisan Cantos'.

Martz (b. 1913), Sterling Professor of English and
American Literature at Yale University, is the author of
notable studies in seventeenth-century meditative poetry,
and of 'The Act of the Mind' (1966) which includes two
chapters on Williams. Writing to thank Martz for The Road
to 'Paterson' (first published in 'Poetry New York',
no. 4, 1951), Williams said (SL, 299):

> You give me confidence. The first effect is in the
> writing itself. I begin to see what I have been after,
> by evidence of the sense of smell mostly, but which now
> is coming more and more into view. Verse form, the
> actual shape of the line itself, must be ... the first
> visible thing. I'm finally getting to understand what
> I want to do. Such writing as yours supports me.

It is perhaps true that our interest in a great part of
the new cantos lies at the edge of the poetical; we feel
the interest aroused by the journal or the letters of an
important writer who has intimately known the greatest
artists of his time. It is perhaps true that the 'Pisan
Cantos' are really a brilliant note-book held together by
the author's personality, with poems scattered throughout:

>   and there was a smell of mint under the tent flaps
>   especially after the rain
>   and a white ox on the road toward Pisa
>   as if facing the tower,
>   dark sheep in the drill field and on wet days were
>   clouds

But the poetry can also be sustained for many lines, as in
the great lynx hymn that concludes Canto LXXIX, or the ode
on vanity that concludes Canto LXXXI with these significant lines:

>   To have gathered from the air a live tradition
>   or from a fine old eye the unconquered flame
>   This is not vanity.
>   Here error is all in the not done,
>   all in the diffidence that faltered ...

This and a notable sentence from Pound's essay on Williams
seems to summarize all that need be said of Pound's failures and achievements: 'Art very possibly *ought* to be the
supreme achievement, the "accomplished"; but there is the
other satisfactory effect, that of a man hurling himself
at an indomitable chaos, and yanking and hauling as much
of it as possible into some sort of order (or beauty),
aware of it both as chaos and as potential.'
   That sentence describes the core of Williams's poetry
as well; together with a wise passage at the end of
Canto LXXVIII, it defines the essentials of the long
association between these two poets, now both in their
sixties:

>   and as for the solidity of the white oxen in all this
>   perhaps only Dr Williams (Bill Carlos)
>   will understand its importance,
>   its benediction. He wd/have put in the cart.

Exactly: Williams understands and agrees with Pound's
insistence that logical abstraction is the enemy of
poetry, that poetic understanding must arise from grasping
the particular image, that poetry cannot exist without the

impact and focus that such particularity gives. 'No
ideas but in things,' Williams says in the opening of his
important new poem, 'Paterson,' a poem cast in the form of
Pound's best cantos, with, as Williams says,

>   a mass of detail
> to interrelate on a new ground, difficultly;
> an assonance, a homologue
>   triple piled
> pulling the disparate together to clarify
> and compress.

But Williams, unlike Pound, has made a firm and strict
delimitation of materials. He has no interest in seeing
life through books, after Pound's fashion; he explicitly
regrets in Book II of 'Paterson' that 'the poet, in disgrace, should borrow from erudition,' Williams will
admit very little to his poem that is not, like himself,
bred in the grain of the region near Paterson, New Jersey.
Truth for Williams resides primarily in what he has seen
directly, immediately, in this region where he was born,
and where he still practices skilfully his twin arts of
medicine and poetry. Both are in Williams the result of a
lifetime spent in acquiring a self-discipline that Pound
could never achieve.

'Paterson,' Williams tells us, is to be a long poem in
four parts, written on the symbolical principle 'that a
man in himself is a city, beginning seeking, achieving
and concluding his life in ways which the various aspects
of a city may embody.' Book I, which appeared in 1946,
presented 'the elemental character of the place' with a
power and brilliance that surprised even his strongest
admirers. One always knew that he could do well with
short pieces, and perhaps the shorter the better; but here
he displayed a power that seemed capable of integrating
lyrics with poetical meditations and prose anecdotes. The
basic image of Book I was the Passaic River, metamorphosed
into a symbol of the flow of all human mind, including the
mind's half-conscious sense of power of the poet to interrupt, refract, and coalesce this flow into a quivering and
terrifying scene of beauty. Some elements of Book I were
left dangling, and some remained obscure; but one trusted
that Williams would use them and clarify them as the poem
proceeded.

Book II suggests that Williams deserves our trust.
The hideous dwarf of Book I has become a symbol of the
poet defeated and crushed by his environment; the minister's wife who fell from the rocks and drowned now suggests some vital principle which 'leaped (or fell) without

a language, tongue-tied/the language worn out.' And the
roar of the river sounds throughout the scene, which is
here transferred to Sunday in the Park 'upon the rock,/
female to the city.' Williams is working out a complex
of analogies. Paterson the city is to the park as man is
to woman; this relates the larger scene to the prose letters that run throughout, describing the painful need of
a woman for intimate friendship with a man (Dr. P.), who
has seen her not as a human being but as material for
literature. The theme of this book is love, in all its
forms. Everywhere the speaker looks in the park he sees
attempts to communicate, to make contact with something
other than the self: Paterson (the city) attempts for a
day to communicate with nature; Paterson (the man-poet)
seeks for imaginative understanding of all he sees, to
find the true poem in the whole scene. And there, in the
centre of the book, is the poor old evangelist, preaching
to his sparse and bored audience, 'calling to the birds
and trees,' while

> The picnickers laugh on the rocks celebrating
> the varied Sunday of their loves with
> its declining light –

That shabby, pitiful preacher is the hero of the book, the
symbol that binds together all the rest, prose and poetry:
a last, faded apostle of charity. Thus in its unity of
scene and symbol, Book II of 'Paterson' seems to surpass
the impact of Book I. We may be watching here the growth
of one of the most important works yet written by an
American poet.

'A Dream of Love'

Norfolk, Conn., September 1948

59. MAURICE H. IRVINE, REVIEW, 'NEW YORK TIMES BOOK REVIEW'

27 February 1949, 14

This review also contains comments on 'The Clouds'.
  Irvine (1906-60) was a Professor of Literature and colleague of Horace Gregory at Sarah Lawrence College.

... This three-act play in prose, often highly charged with emotion and symbolism, is about the love and death of a middle-aged doctor, a poet who was trying to write a play. In essence, the play seems to be a dramatic showing forth of the extended connotations of a simple love poem that the doctor reads to his wife. The frank dialogue is realistic to the point of tediousness and verbosity. Though there are fine bits in it, the effects are produced too slowly. The protagonist, tied up in the ambiguities of love, marriage, and his profession, seems at the last most concerned with verse - 'multiplex, efflorescent, varied as the day in its forms.'

60. R. W. FLINT, 'A FATAL INCOHERENCE AT THE CENTRE', 'KENYON REVIEW'

Vol. XII, no. 3, Summer 1950, 541-2

Part of a composite review, this places the play alongside 'The Clouds' and 'Paterson (Book Three)'. Vivienne Koch's pioneering study, 'William Carlos Williams' (1950) is also mentioned in the review.

... 'A Dream of Love,' the latest of three published plays, is rated next to 'Paterson' by its author. Certainly it is full of Williams' obstinate wisdom and paradoxical selflessness.

> *Doc:* Don't be profane. Every man is like me. Don't try to hand me than bunk. I know too much. I'm just the run of the farm, dull average. I'm not neurotic. That's just what I'm not. I'm just like everybody else. That's my pride. I'm proud. Hellishly proud that I'm just the core of the onion - nothing at all. That's just what makes me so right. And I know I'm right.

Yet a few scenes before, the same Doc makes the following speech:

> *Doc:* Our relationship? Something horrible in all probability - if it isn't magnificent. Perverse. Insane - of which we shall never know anything. Murderous perhaps but inevitable ... I love you! - the second word being an eternal lie.

Lastly, the Doctor regales the Other Woman, just before they consummate their fatal affair:

> *Doc:* (growing more and more excited): the Greeks. Here's one of the most famous lines from their most famous poem: **KAI SAY GAYRON TOW PREEN MEN HAKOIOMEN HOLNION EENAI.** Sounds like a horse coughing, doesn't it? Achilles said that to Priam. Or does it, after all, remind you of Hiawatha?

So we have almost exclusively in this play the agony and

bloody sweat, without the grateful compensation of 'Paterson.' Here and there a turn of humor or poetry, especially in a none too relevant scene between the negro cook and a lady evangelist, but the main action is grueling. That it illuminates Williams as a poet of the anti-poetic and a hero of the anti-heroic is incontestable. He has absorbed several devices of naturalistic-expressionistic theatre, the trouble being that the play doesn't *reveal* enough for its type of theatre. A fatal incoherence at the center of the plotting forces it back on its thinness, as to a kind of penance. 'Doc: "Because I will not lie. Cost what it may, I will not lie"!' To put it bluntly, the play exploits Williams' minor vices at the expense of his major virtues; everything suffers, the language most of all....

'Selected Poems'

Norfolk, Conn., March 1949

61. ROBERT FITZGERALD COMPARES AND CONTRASTS THE POEMS OF WILLIAMS AND WILLAM EMPSON, 'NEW REPUBLIC'

25 April 1949, 22-3

Fitzgerald (b. 1910) is an American poet, translator and teacher. This article is titled Bejeweled, the Great Sun.
   Writing on Rhythm and Imagery in English Poetry in 'Journal of the British Society of Aesthetics' in 1962 (vol. II, no. 1), Empson said of Williams, 'He has renounced all the pleasures of the English language, so that he is completely American; and he only says the dullest things, so he has won the terrible fight to become completely democratic as well.'

If we were to work out a coherent view of modern poetry, if it were only to recognize and put a proper value on our various appetites and pleasures, we would have to keep the works of William Empson and William Carlos Williams simultaneously in mind. Each is a true and brilliant poet, to be looked to for delight and revelation, but not much has been said about either in terms applicable to the other; they represent the extremes of formal difference in contemporary verse. It is also true that each is peculiarly native to his own English-speaking region and has a style inimitable by the other; obviously, no Englishman has ever got the hang of Williams' kind of writing and, less obviously, no American writes as Empson does. We do more than differentiate - we classify - when we think of the two men.

One is a Yorkshireman educated in the twenties at Winchester and Magdalene College, Cambridge, a more than donnish wit, at home in mathematical and scientific abstractions, passionate in his study of the treasurable stuff of English poetry, a teacher and wanderer to the East, where he lives in China's Holy City. The other is a Yankee with an infusion of Latinity, for thirty years a practising physician in a small American city, very much on his own and on the loose from poetic tradition, no student, no teacher, but as close to concrete life - and as immaculately unstuck by it - as quicksilver in your palm. No photography could do his kind of job with the American street scene:

[quotes January Morning, VI and VII, CEP, 163]

The good thing about the intelligent anti-intellectual is that he scents with appropriate alarm the dangers of committing himself to abstract attitudes that a later or rougher or rounder experience would show up; he distrusts not only 'those large words that make people unhappy' but all the apparatus of ideas that can get in between us and the things that we do or witness, all stereotypes and, in the extreme case, all stereotypes-to-be. For the poet Williams this apparently meant consigning to the ashcan even such neutral instruments as the iambic line, which may be potentially either dead or alive for others but for him must have carried an uncontrollable threat of blight and blather. For more than three decades, then, Williams has been using his acute and cleanly art to render the visible, the sensuous particulars of the world in motion and the equally predictable, odd responses that usually go unspoken in the heart or in the throat. He has done so in poems like strings of beads or notations for plain chant, the notes well separated, slight in themselves, but with startling emotive effects as they tumble out, leap up, or coil and pool together. The 'Selected Poems' that Randall Jarrell has edited is an excellent introduction to and anthology of Williams.

It would seem at first that Empson's 'Collected Poems' ... is a body of work as dissimilar from Williams' as any could possibly be, but it is important to notice that the two poets can be united under one large heading; if they are at extremes, what makes them so is the refusal in each case to adopt the formulae that come most easily to the mind, with the most specious comfort or the most fashionable portentousness. Empson's poems are famously difficult. A few of them resemble quartzlike fusions that will

resist analysis almost as long as they will decomposition.
All there is to say on this point, is that every one of
them means more the more it is studied, and that the study
is always worth making. The unprepared reader might not
believe it, but patience - and Empson's Notes - will bring
profound sense out of the magnificent energy and enigma of
such a passage as this:

> Fall to them, Lucifer, Sun's Son. Splash high
> Jezebel. Throw her down. They feast, I flee
> Her poised tired head and eye
> Whose skull pike-high mirrors and waits for me.

In sequence, these poems, the fruit of more than twenty
years' work, offer a sustained and dazzling display of
intelligence avoiding false commitments and premature
plumpsings, in the knowledge that

>   the spry arts
> Can keep a steady hold on the controls
> By seeming to evade.

In Empson's case the evasion is indeed only a seeming, and
nobody has a steadier hold on the controls. The notion
that such a poetry cannot be a 'poetry of affirmation' is
misguided, since what the poetry would affirm is the exact
and elusive truth of the matters with which it is concerned, and these are often serious:

[quotes Your Teeth Are Ivory Towers, 'Collected Poems',
46-7, lines 19-25]

Empson has lived, and knows he has, in a physical world
that has yielded to methodical thought, at last, only the
principles of relativity and indeterminacy, and in a moral
world equally at sea. His intelligence, being sane and
large, has drawn away from that overwhelming dither toward
a recognition of absolutes, but with honest hesitation,
holding carefully to small dignities:

[quotes Your Teeth Are Ivory Towers, 'Collected Poems',
47, lines 37-43]

The wrung-out, colloquial dryness of this diction has its
own firm music, capable of being heightened, in more
elaborate poems, to a grand polyphony. (He has, for
example, taken over and extended E. E. Cummings' structural stunt of writing one poem in parenthesis inside
another.) What is always humming underneath is the verse

tradition itself, nowhere so obtrusive that you can sense, in particular, Hardy or Donne or Rochester or Dryden, but everywhere deepening the effect - a poetic language of many minds renewed in a single one.

This tradition of metrical form is precisely what Williams has done without, but it does not follow that his work has no tradition behind it; it has the rich tradition of prose. He is not a verse writer and knows little about versification, but he has an ear for prose rhythms more delicate and various than most of his contemporaries, and the free verse he has made is prose transformed by arrangement. For a long time nobody who admired Williams' work cared to say this for fear of being misunderstood; it should be understood that Williams is a poet. Shaking the prose notes out and down the page, placing words and phrases in space, the writer calls attention to them one by one and is assisted by this in evoking, likewise one by one, the details of his notation. He can speed up or slow down the movement according to how much white space he offers to the eye or breath to the reading voice. When he prints his piece in lines and stanzas, with roughly the same number of beats to a line, he counterpoints his prose with the rhythm suggested by verse form.

Empson 'conceptualizes,' as the psychologists say, works in metaphor, concentrates allusion to make diamonds of verse 'until the star replies.' He is a metaphysical poet. Williams is a physical poet; he 'tries talk,' but mainly leaves the talking to the things he presents. When he does talk, he often does so under his breath, interruptedly, like a man pausing to gaze, whistling or exclaiming, before he compresses his lips again and makes the incision or moves on. If you trouble to listen carefully you will from time to time hear great emotion in the doctor's little, broken-off reflections, as here in a country churchyard:

[quotes from A Unison, CLP, 239, lines 2-12, 'a white ... rise ...']

The life of such writing is in the realities brought together (the weakness of a dying child, the freshness of morning) by sudden transitions, quickening the mind that will remain relatively asleep through commonplace prose. If you take a simple passage in Empson you may see much the same thing happening, only here in a metaphor that makes two disparate scenes interpenetrate and by so doing enlarges the world. The poem is called The Beautiful Train (a Japanese one, in Manchuria, in 1937); Argentina is the Spanish dancer and 'call' means a curtain call, the applause set in motion by her impact:

> Argentina in one swing of the bell skirt,
> Without visible steps, shivering in her power,
> Could shunt a call passing from wing to wing ...
>
> So firm, so burdened, on such light gay feet.

62. ROLFE HUMPHRIES ON ORGANIC FORM AND THE 'MACHINE MADE OF WORDS', 'NATION'

9 July 1949, 44

This review points to an interesting and unresolved question in modern poetics: the possibility that a traditional form may, in a given instance, be organic to the particular poem. Williams, as is well known, rejected the traditional forms, and many of the traditional means, of poetry. Humphries' point about The Yachts is similar to that made earlier by R. P. Blackmur in regard to Williams' The A. B & C of It (see No. 50 above), although, in that instance, one doubts Blackmur's ear.

Humphries (1894-1969) was an American poet, translator and teacher, whose work includes translations of Ovid and Virgil and 'Poems Collected and New' (1954).

... The 'Selected Poems' of William Carlos Williams ... are introduced with an essay, both enthusiastic and convincing, by Randall Jarrell. A job well done; one can believe every word, and yet - . And yet, having read the introduction with delight, and the poems with new interest and attention, I find myself of the same opinion still with regard to Dr. Williams's work: this is the kind of poetry I think I should admire rather than the kind I know I do enjoy. If this is not sheer obstinacy of temperament, the clue to an almost embarrassing sense of dissatisfaction perhaps lies in a remark of Dr. Williams, quoted by Mr. Jarrell, about the nature of poetry: 'A poem is a small (or large) machine made of words.' And then too, in spite of Dr. Williams's admirable, and lauded, boldness, I seem to detect a certain amount of

diffidence. A reluctance, however great, to commit the
sentimental cliché does not quite justify turning a deaf
ear to some of the demands, in music, in metric, in rhyme
even, that one's content seems to be making; The Yachts,
for instance, a poem that Mr. Jarrell praises as 'a para-
digm of all the unjust beauty, the necessary and unnecessary injustice of the world,' is a poem that seems, at its
beginning, to be practically demanding to be heard in
terza rima, a demand so insistent that even Dr. Williams
recognizes it, and permits it, for a few introductory
lines, and once in a while thereafter seems to be listening to, however uneasily, even while giving it summary
dismissal. I wish Dr. Williams's generosity and exactness would carry him a little farther, and feed into his
work as much excellence of ear as there is, already,
importance of eye.

63. RICHARD WILBUR ON WILLIAMS' 'ESSENTIALLY MYSTIC OR
MAGIC FEELING', 'SEWANEE REVIEW'

Vol. LVIII, no. 1, Winter 1950, 137-40

This is part of a composite review, Seven Poets. The
Lawrence work under review is New Directions' edition of
'The Selected Poems'.
    Wilbur (b. 1921) is an American poet and translator.

Respecting the 'otherness' of creatures and things was a
perpetual crusade with Lawrence; to W. C. Williams it
seems to come naturally. In no contemporary poet do we
find more credible objects. 'No ideas but in things,'
says Williams. He devotes a poem to the perception of the
behavior of sparrows on the pavement, and of an old man's
'majestic' gait as he goes gathering dog-lime along the
gutter; and he closes by saying

             These things
    astonish me beyond words.

Of course they don't astonish him quite beyond words,
because he has just given them words. But then the
expression affords an insight into Williams' aesthetic.

He insists always on the priority of the object. The
objective situation has something to say, and the poet's
business is to make words measure up to the situation.
Williams sees words in everything: in the voluble Paterson
waterfall; in the sea ('waves like words'); in trees,
which are sometimes like letters and spell things, and
sometimes have raucous voices which 'guffaw and curse' at
us.

   A perfect poem for Williams is a perfect translation,
the rendering into written words of an inherent utterance
in things.

[quotes Between Walls, CEP, 343]

This is Williams in the extreme. Here we find no comparison: none of that comparison which Wallace Stevens has
said is the essence of poetry. At any rate, hardly any
comparison. The ideas of growing and greenness make us
half-consciously contrast the cinder-lot with a garden,
and the poem seems to imply that cinders and bottle-
shards, spontaneously regarded, are as important and
beautiful as a garden. But on the whole this poem is a
direct translation from an observed reality. Not a nexus
of thoughts and images but an act of strict outward focus
and realization. The full enjoyment of the poem depends
on one's sharing with the poet an essentially mystic or
magic feeling - a feeling that words, rightly arranged,
become one with the things they signify. (In respect of
this attitude toward words, Williams goes quite beyond
the Imagists.) Clearly such a poem as this above is a
risky thing to write: for the reader will either feel in
the words that rightness and perfect correspondence which
the poet did, or he will find the poem appallingly flat.
Since the success of many Williams poems depends on their
'clicking' with the reader in this magic way, the usual
experience in reading one of his books is alternate elation and blankness.

   It doesn't seem to me that Williams' successes, at
least in the extreme genre of Between Walls, are suscep-
tible of analysis. His rhythms are frequently mystic or
magic like his words, and are approximate to motions,
actual or potential, which Williams finds in the experience thereof. In his poem (called Poem) about a cat
climbing over a jamcloset, Williams' rhythm parallels,
and seeks identity with, the movement of the cat. In
Young Sycamore, Williams finds the proper movement for his
poem by imaginatively hunching down inside the bole of the
tree and then growing and branching upward. Where this
kind of thing works, and it does wonderfully often, one

can only say (as one must say of Lawrence's best free
verse) that the form is quite inexplicably - and quite
undemonstrably - perfect.

Life is more than art for Dr. Williams, as the object
is prior to the word. He is no goldsmith making timeless
birds. Part of the exhilaration in reading his poetry
comes of its formal and logical incompleteness (this is
at the same time its greatest drawback). Many of his
poems seem notes to a text - to the dense and fluid text
of reality; they seem gestures and exclamations in appreciation of something beyond the poem, insistences that we
use our sense, that we be alive to things. The poem Rain
is partly a rebellion against the selectivity and egotism
of art, against art's tendency to make its own precious
and stuffy world. Williams would like to see justice done
to the beauty of the commonest things, and he knows the
rewards of such virtue in an urban society: for one of the
most oppressive things about city life is the affective
neutrality of one's surroundings. A selection of Williams' poems might be made which would be our best Baedeker to the possibilities of sense-experience in the city
world....

'Patterson (Book Three)'

Norfolk, Conn., December 1949

64. VIVIAN MERCIER, REVIEW, 'COMMONWEAL'

3 March 1950, 565

This review deals also with Vivienne Koch's book on Williams.
    Professor of English at the University of California, Santa Barbara, Mercier (b. 1919) is author of 'The Irish Comic Tradition' (1962) and 'Beckett/Beckett' (1977).

... To me, the prose extracts which interrupt and illustrate Williams' verse are more truly poetry than the verse itself. They present concrete particulars, whereas the verse too often deals in abstractions - in striking contrast to so much of Williams' earlier verse. Book Three is the least satisfactory - giving the impression that Williams is writing a poem about how difficult it is to write a poem. In fact, says Williams, 'the brunt of the four books ... is a search for the redeeming language by which a man's premature death ... and the woman's (the man's) failure to hold him (her) might have been prevented.' This redeeming language appears to be symbolised by the sound of the Falls. 'The poet alone holds the key to their final rescue.' All of which seems to me to say that human consciousness can change human consciousness by direct action....

65. RICHARD ELLMANN, 'THE MOST PRO-POETIC OF POEMS',
'YALE REVIEW'

Vol. XXIX, no. 3, Spring 1950, 543-5.

Ellmann (b. 1918) is Goldsmith's Professor of English
Literature at Oxford University. A distinguished
authority on modern literature, his chief work is his
biography 'James Joyce' (1959).

... Dr. Williams has achieved his distinction in a different tradition. He is a good deal more concerned than Miss Sitwell (1) and most other poets with the actual look of things around him, and he delineates them with a clean, sinewy, brash line. But 'Paterson,' of which the newly published Book Three is the next to last section, contains like Miss Sitwell's verse an apocalyptic note, though set in a different key. Where Miss Sitwell uses religious imagery to portray her feelings about the present and future, Dr. Williams, less sibylline, views everything from the point of view of the language. We must, by act of love, change the language, for a change of language is a change of world; the language must be refitted to suit life rather than, as at present, death.
Some of Dr. Williams' poem must remain obscure until the fourth and final part is published. It is evident, however, that the book's pattern is loose but insistent; images recur and interweave. Only a man so rooted in everyday experience as Dr. Williams would conceive the hero of the poem: it is the city of Paterson, New Jersey, variously envisaged by the poet as the city itself, as a giant on the order of Blake's Albion, and as a man. Paterson's emanation, female to his male, is the city park. The municipal relationship of these two is one of the many in the poem which has to be remedied. Only the Passaic Falls which overlook the town, and the river of which they form part, are in tune. Elsewhere are dislocation and blockage: divorce rather than marriage, unsuccessful attempts of a woman poet to find herself and to write poetry; and, historically, the irreverence for life of the white man and the reverent, ritualistic attitude towards it of the Indian. This panorama is sketched with power in irregular verse, often based on a short line of three or four accents, with occasional prose passages interspersed.

In Book Three of 'Paterson' occurs a culmination of the city's disasters, and of the psychological problems of modern man. Non-residents of Paterson will discover from their encyclopedias that in 1902 most of the town was destroyed by fire, and a month later swept by flood. Dr. Williams converts these calamities into symbols, and finds along with their dreadfulness a purgative value in them, for they at any rate destroy the stale and dead. Among other things the fire destroys the public library, beneficently, for Dr. Williams sees libraries, like universities, as burial grounds. The fire is not, however, the true fire, but like it; the flood not the true flood, but like it. By fire and flood we can, the poet says, begin to begin again. We must turn words inside out in search of the phrase 'that will lie married beside another for delight.' The poet must find his meaning, must comb out the language or succumb. 'Let me out!' he cries at the end.

Dr. Williams asserts, then, that the poet holds the key to redemption. Wallace Stevens long ago referred to him as anti-poetic, but 'Paterson' is the most pro-poetic of poems. It must be said, however, that by poetry Dr. Williams seems to mean a form of creation which is more dependent upon observed data than most poets would allow. It is the reliance he puts upon accuracy of description that makes Paterson, so difficult to visualize in detail, a less adequate symbol than the Falls. But Dr. Williams secures an immediacy which is available to only a few writers of our time. The structure of the poem remains to be justified by the last book, but the poetry is palpable from the beginning. If the giant Paterson is still lacking a few lineaments, Dr. Williams, a physician as well as a poet, can be depended upon to supply them.

Note

1 The Sitwell book under review is 'The Canticle of the Rose: Poems 1917-1949'.

66. MONROE K. SPEARS, IMITATIVE FORM AND 'THE FAILURE OF LANGUAGE', 'POETRY'

Vol. LXXVI, no. 1, April 1950, 39-44

Spears (b. 1916), Moody Professor of English at Rice University, Texas, was editor of 'Sewanee Review' 1952-61 and is author of 'The Poetry of W. H. Auden: the Disenchanted Island' (1963) and 'Space Against Time in Modern American Poetry' (1972).

The reader may need to be reminded of the plan of whole poem as stated by Dr. Williams:

> Part One introduces the elemental character of the place. The Second Part will comprise the modern replicas. Three will seek a language to make them vocal, and Four, the river below the falls, will be reminiscent of episodes - all that any one man may achieve in a lifetime.

The title of Book I is The Delineaments of the Giants; of II, Sunday in the Park. For the present book, The Library, Dr. Williams has supplied an explanatory note:

> *Paterson* is a man (since I am a man) who drives from cliffs and the edges of waterfalls, to his death - finally. But for all that he is a woman (since I am not a woman) who *is* the cliff and the waterfall. She spreads protecting fingers about him as he plummets to his conclusions to keep the winds from blowing him out of his path. But he escapes, in the end, as I have said.
> As he dies the rocks fission gradually into wild flowers the better to voice their sorrow, a language that would have liberated them both from their distresses had they but known it in time to prevent catastrophe.
> The brunt of the four books of 'Paterson' ... is a search for the redeeming language by which a man's premature death, like the death of Mrs. Cummins in Book I, and the woman's (the man's) failure to hold him (her) might have been prevented.
> Book IV will show the perverse confusions that come of a failure to untangle the language and make it our own as both man and woman are carried helplessly

toward the sea (of blood) which, by their failure of
speech, awaits them. The poet alone in this world
holds the key to their final rescue.

The subject of Book III is the search for expression, for
a language; the difficulties of writing poetry in an
industrial civilization, and ultimately the difficulties
of Dr. Williams. Vivienne Koch suggests in her new book*
that the keyword of Book I is 'divorce' and that of Book
II is 'blocked'; perhaps the keyword of III is 'cost' -
the cost of beauty to the artist and of failure of language to a civilization. The book describes the library
and the surrounding city as ravaged by cyclone, fire and
flood. The structure is essentially symbolic, each of the
three parts of the book being dominated by one symbol;
the symbolism, however, is loose, the major symbols under-
going constant accretion and shift of meaning and, in an
approximation of musical structure, being interwoven with
each other and with minor symbols throughout. Part I
establishes the basic themes and introduces the three
symbols; its dominant symbol is Wind, the desire for and
urgent drive toward expression and beauty. The Library
is a source of beauty, but chiefly its tomb; its **SILENCE**
sign represents the cost of dreams, the failure of language. Beauty in the modern world is impractical, non-
conformist, useless, like the 'Castle' of the individual-
istic businessman; it is precarious and dangerous like
tight-rope walking. This theme is summed up in the first
Beautiful Thing episode; beauty is feared and therefore
bought, debased, raped. The city's lack of love (lack of
water in the dry, hot summer) can be remedied only by
expressive language.

>What language could allay our thirsts,
what winds lift us, what floods bear us
>   past defeats
>but song but deathless song? (fol. 10v.)†

The situation of the artist is embodied in a specifically
autobiographical passage; and the section ends with the
fulfillment of the wind symbol as a tornado strikes the
city.
  The third part is dominated by Water: relief, fulfillment, successful language. After some elaborately paradoxical prose passages, there is an effective description
of a flood (of water and of words). A dead dog represents, presumably, the cost of beauty. The poem then
degenerates into broken fragments askew on the page (Dr.
Williams, still following the principle of Imitative Form,

represents chaos by chaos, breakdown of language by breakdown of language) and a technical report on an unsuccessful attempt to bore a well (i.e. to find expression). The mud, detritus of the flood, is powerfully described; it suggests the bitter after-taste of failure to write adequately. There is a clever burlesque of a conventional romantic song (fol. 27 r. & v.) an example of hopelessly inadequate expression. The final passage is autobiographical, expressing the poet's worship of and compulsion to find language. 'Not until I have made of it [language] a replica/will my sins be forgiven and my/disease cured... And yet, unless I find a place/apart from it, I I am its slave...'

Dr. Williams appears to me to be a genuine poet, and one peculiarly deserving of respect for his honest, integrity, and devotion, throughout a long life, to his art.‡ But he seems to me a very limited and therefore very minor poet, and one who has been praised far beyond his deserts. It may be said that we should appreciate Dr. Williams for what he is instead of criticizing him for not being something different, particularly since he is too old to change his ways. I assume, however, that the interested reader will have seen plenty of appreciation (certainly he can find it in Miss Koch's book), and I intend my remarks on the other side of the picture as a contribution toward a balanced view.§ Although no judgment of 'Paterson' can be final until the poem is completed, I think it can be said now that the work is a long poem only according to the Poe definition. Book III consists of some magnificent passages, some silly passages, and a great mass of undigested material. It is true that repeated readings bring out subtle effects of repetition and variation, and reduce much of the apparent formlessness to order; but the final impression remains one of lack of discipline and organization. As I have indicated in my skeleton exegesis, the symbolic structure is intended to unify the book; but the symbols are related more by free association, with the prose passages as food for reverie, than by any real analogy to musical structure. Sometimes the repetition of symbols appears mechanical; sometimes variation proceeds so far that the symbols shift their meaning and melt into one another; frequently they are buried beneath gobs of raw material. Eccentricity and willfulness are constant threats to their integrity.

At the beginning of part II the symbols are recapitulated and applied to the creative act: ' - the cyclonic fury, the fire./the leaden flood and finally/the cost -' (fol. 13 v.); books are 'men in hell,' as Paterson under cyclone, fire and flood has earlier been called/'Hell, New Jersey' (fol 5r.). The dominant symbol is Fire, Beauty in its destructive, anarchic aspect (as I have indicated, it is also the fire in the blood that forces one to write). There is a fine description of the fire consuming the city and library. The work of art is symbolized in a bottle, formed by the fire and surviving it ('Poet Beats Fire at Its Own Game! The bottle!'). Only art survives. But language is never completely successful; books incorporate little of the beauty originally in the poet's mind ('We read: not the flames/but the ruin left/by the conflagration/Not the enormous burning/but the dead (the books/remaining).' (fol. 19 r. & v.). The Beautiful Thing refrain is now incarnated in a sick Negro girl attended by Dr. Williams in a basement; then there is a passage about a Beautiful Thing (presumably the same one, since she is described as 'a dark flame') in a white lace dress getting involved in tough company and having her nose broken 'till I must believe that all/desired women have had each/in the end/a busted nose.' (Perhaps I should admit that this episode [most of which was published separately long ago] is not entirely clear to me. The theme of pathos, degradation of beauty, seems obvious enough; and apparently the Negro girl is intended to contrast with the earlier Beautiful Thing (presumably white) who would not take off her clothes (ff. 8v.-9v.), the dark flame being preferable because an outcast and more natural.)

The symbolic structure fails to sustain the poem adequately, I think, because it is based on no coherent pattern of ideas. The concepts of the poem seem, in fact, curiously anachronistic; Dr. Williams is still shocking the bourgeois, revolting against Suburbia, preaching the gospel of Beauty as 'a defiance of authority' and poetry as the only salvation. He continues the Whitman tradition of celebrating the natural man, complete self-expression, freedom from all restraint; there is the same mystical sense that everything is equally important and everything is somehow everything else, the same generous egotism. In attitude as in technique, he has an almost mystical regard for 'facts' and 'experience' and a corresponding scorn of ideas; since one cannot escape ideas, this means in practice that the ideas implied are often naive. 'No ideas but in things' is rather dated as philosophy.

A comparison with T. S. Eliot is inevitable, though absurdly disproportionate. Eliot has been moving during the last two decades toward a complex musical elaboration of language; Dr. Williams is still throwing off shackles in the style of the twenties, moving toward the common

speech, rejecting the distinction between poetry and
prose. His verse technique has not progressed far beyond
Imagism. And Eliot's point of view, whether one agrees
with it or not, has a range and depth, a coherence and
maturity, not to be found in the though of Dr. Williams.
To use Collingwood's terms, Dr. Williams's poetry is too
limited to bring emotions to consciousness for many
people; it cannot express the attitudes of an age as does
Eliot's. It is not only *about* the failure of language; it
is a failure of language.

In view of the high praise that Dr. Williams and
'Paterson' have received from critics whose work I admire,
I must remind the reader candidly that my own prejudices
and limitations of taste may be responsible for this un-
favourable judgment. The variable factor of individual
tastes and reactions (which are never perfect) makes completely objective evaluation an impossible ideal. Let me
say at once that I am not a critical relativist; I believe
that absolute standards exist, and that taste should be
checked by analysis as objective as possible. Analysis,
however, seems to me often neutral; that is, it may be
made to prove whatever the critic wants it to prove, and
support a judgment arrived at on other grounds. Some of
the recent analyses of Dr. Williams make it evident, I
think, that an ingenious and subtle critic can, if he
wants to, discover complexity and unity in almost anything; they are demonstrations of how the machinery *might*
work, regardless of the question of whether it does nor
not. For instance, the reading quoted by Miss Koch (I
leave the author anonymous) of **THIS IS JUST TO SAY**

[quotes This is Just to Say, CEP, 354]

The irony of this poem was that precisely that which preserved them (the plums) and increased the deliciousness
of their perfection (the refrigeration) contained in its
essence the sensuous quality most closely associated with
death; coldness. So the plums' death (or formal dis-
appearance and disintegration) was symbolically anticipated in the charm of their living flesh. This is, I
believe, the exact pathos of this brief poem... (pp.
64-5)

What could this critic do with a more significant note -
or with a poem?

Notes

*Vivienne Koch, 'William Carlos Williams', New Directions.
†Since the pages are not numbered, I have (not without
 malice toward New Directions) employed the usual system
 of manuscript folioing.
‡I derive some consolation, in thinking of the parlous
 times in which we live, from the fact that many contemporary poets have been able to continue their development
 into their middle and later years. For Dr. Williams, as
 for Yeats, Eliot, and others, an increase rather than a
 diminution of powers has been evident with advancing age.
 The phenomenon is sufficiently unusual, historically considered, to encourage us in thinking of our own as one of
 the great ages of poetry.
§I do not mean that nobody has pointed out Dr. Williams's
 faults and limitations. Excellent analyses have been
 written by, for example, Frederick Morgan ('Sewanee
 Review', 1947) and Leslie Fiedler ('Partisan Review',
 1948 - reviewing (Paterson II').

67. HAYDEN CARRUTH ON THE VERSE LINE 'HUNG OVER, LIKE A
DALI WATCH', 'NATION'

8 April 1950, 331-2

Carruth (b. 1921), American poet, critic, editor and fiction writer. His books include 'Journey to a Known Place'
(1961) and the anthology 'The Voice that is Great Within
Us' (1970).

This third book in Dr. Williams's projected long poem (the
fourth and final book is promised 'by 1951') is at first
reading the most difficult of the three we now have, and
at the eighth reading some details of structure and
aspects of symbol remain unclear. Nevertheless, we can
begin to perceive what will be the shape, scope, and texture of the finished work; this book helps greatly to expand and clarify a number of themes, heretofore obscure,
in the first two books. When the three are read together
in sequence, they reveal, through an interlacing of symbols and a thematic reference back and forth, a close and
compact development. More than ever, it becomes apparent

that Dr. Williams has in mind a whole, inseverable poem, not a discrete tetralogy, as many of those who reviewed the first two books were led to assume.

The meaning of the poem so far can best be elucidated by a compressed, doubtless defacing examination of its symbols. Paterson, then, is a city and also a man, a giant who lies asleep, whose dreams are the people of the city, whose history is roughly coterminous with, and equal to, the history of America. He is diseased with slums and factories and the spiritlessness of industrial society; his character - usually as observer - walks about, sometimes as a plain citizen, sometimes as a hero, often as 'Dr. Paterson' - the poet himself. Beside Paterson lies a mountain, which is a woman, upon whose body grow trees and flowers, with the city park at her head. The city-man and mountain-woman are the two basic facts of the poem; they are activated by the four elements. A river, broken by a falls, flows between them, and has, beyond its obvious secual meaning, the further significances of flowing time and of language, the fundamental or pre-mental language of nature. Earth is the speaker that knows this language, the 'chatterer.' Fire is the creative act, in love or art. Wind is, if my reading is correct, inspiration, the integrator, the carrier of sounds and smells. Though generally benign, these forces may be malevolent too, for fire, flood, cyclone, and earthquake all occur in this poem.

Another dichotomy of ideas, which is enforced upon these basic symbols, is that of marriage-divorce. As divorce is a principal symptom of social disorder, so it is also of historical disorder: man has been divorced from his beginnings, his sources. Dr. Williams also uses the word *blockage*: man has been blocked from an understanding of his real self in nature by the modern institutions of church, university, commerce, et cetera. Dr. Williams seems to be saying that the only way to escape these blocks is to ignore them, to sidestep them and experience marriage directly. Thus, in the river, it is the falls which is important, the present act and present moment which unite immediately the man and the woman, the city and the mountain, the 'plunge' which 'roars' now with a language that lies hidden in the past above and the future below.

This third book has been described by Dr. Williams as a search for a language. Yet much of it is spent in inveighing against what we ordinarily call language. The technical abstractions of scholarship are the poet's primary anathema, but he extends his disgust to include almost all human speech. 'No ideas but in things,' he

says repeatedly - the Objectivist doctrine carried to its
extreme. Abstract 'meaning' is the enemy, 'an offense to
love, the mind's worm eating out the core.' The dead
authors in the library are 'men in hell, their reign over
the living ended,' their thoughts trapped in a hull of
inflexible, dead rhetoric. Even the poet's own work is
suspect; at one point, he admonishes himself: 'Give up the
poem. Give up the shilly-shally of art.'

This would seem to put the poet in a rather difficult
spot, since there honestly isn't much reason to be writing
a poem (much less to publish it) if one must write in a
bad language. Dr. Williams's conclusions on this head are
not so clear as one would wish, but he appears to be saying that the poet can resolve his difficulty through a
doctrine of invention. The good language is the language
of the river, articulated by the falls. The poet cannot
hope to imitate the falls, but he can learn from it. By
forgetting the past, by writing instantaneously, even
carelessly, by grounding all speech firmly in natural
objects, the poet can create a language in nature which
is essentially an act, not a meaning - an act of love and
union. By working constantly at a peak of inventiveness,
he can elevate this language to a level of independence
which is its own justification.

'Paterson,' when it is finished, will make a great
hunting ground for the explicators. There are virtually
hundreds of symbols and allusions to be tracked down,
related, explained - all of which will, if he sticks to
his text, annoy Dr. Williams profoundly. Essays will be
written, for instance, on the many uncomplimentary allusions, often devilishly hidden, to T. S. Eliot and his
works. There will likewise be essays on the other writers
mentioned (I detect Pound, Stevens, and perhaps others),
on the various flowers, on the dog. Yet I should like to
suggest one question to the explicators before they begin.

Perhaps I can put it best this way. Twenty-five years
ago Eliot felt that he should explain some of the symbols
and meanings of 'The Waste Land' in accompanying notes;
for Dr. Williams this is not necessary. We are better
readers now. Furthermore, Dr. Williams's symbols are
made from objects we all know, and the meanings assigned
to them are drawn from a common fund of romantic ideas.
But I think we should call on Dr. Williams for another kind
of note - a definite note on prosody. He himself sees the
trouble, and at one point he says to the reader, rather
sharply: 'Use a metronome if your ear is deficient, one
made in Hungary if you prefer.' I think he misses the
mark, for any reader with an ear for poetry will easily
discern Dr. Williams's astonishingly pure feeling for the

rhythms of the American language. It is not meter that
bothers me, but the line. These lines are not run over,
in the Elizabethan sense; nor are they rove over, in the
Hopkinsian sense; they are hung over, like a Dali watch.
They break in the most extraordinary places, with no textual, metrical, or syntactical tension to help us over.
If this is done for typographical effect, as it sometimes
appears, it is inexcusable, for it interferes with our
reading. If it is done to indicate a certain way of reading the poem, then we should be told what it is.

Dr. Williams has explained in the past that he uses
this device of the short, oddly broken line to obtain the
effect of speed in a lyric poem. But 'Paterson,' by a
rough estimate, will be 5,000 lines long when it is
finished. In such a large dose, the effect is, instead,
limpidity, constantly bolstered by interjections and typographical waggeries; real power is seldom obtained.

Perhaps I am a dull reader; if so, these matters can be
explained. And in fairness to me, they must be explained
- if not by Dr. Williams, then by some modern prosodist
sympathetic to Dr. Williams's method. The question of
'Paterson's' value as poetry should at last put the critics face to face with the problems they have been dodging
for twenty years: What kinds of lines and sentences does
one put next to each other to create a long poem? Is it
an arguable prosodic concept that the metrical beat, to
the exclusion of the line, is the basic unit of poetry?
What, precisely, has experimental technique added to our
knowledge of ways to say our thoughts?

'The Collected Later Poems'

Norfolk, Conn., November 1950

68. JOHN FREDERICK NIMS, REVIEW, 'CHICAGO SUNDAY TRIBUNE'

17 December 1950, 4

Nims (b. 1913) is an American poet, teacher and translator. Since 1978 he has been the editor of 'Poetry'.

... These later poems continue the excellences of his many earlier volumes: an intensity of interest in all kinds of people and all kinds of things; a more than photographic precision in the descriptions of places and objects; a directness and terseness of language that owes nothing to the conventionally poetic; an independence that makes the poet contemptuous of forms of poetry that are established and therefore not personal, not spontaneous, not determined by the peculiar needs of the individual poem.

The later poems also suffer from Dr. Williams' limitations: an occasional tone-deafness for which the visual brilliance is no full compensation; a sense of rhythm that is of the logical intellect rather than of the impulsive heart; a prosiness of content and statement which I suppose Dr. Williams would admit and defend and which no doubt does come from the all-inclusiveness of his sympathies. These very limitations make the poems more lively and readable than the conventional poetry whose insincerity he detests....

69. UNSIGNED REVIEW, AN AMERICAN POET, 'TIMES LITERARY SUPPLEMENT'

23 March 1951, 178.

Dr. William Carlos Williams has introduced the collection of poetry which he has written in the last 10 years with a few clear, and several turgid, sentences; and it is important to understand these in order to follow his verse with that complete sympathy which implies for the moment a sharing with the author of the principles on which his poems have been made. Between us and our appreciation of American poetry there is often the difficulty that we are unresponsive to the subtlest effects of the American language. With diffuse poetry the barriers are lower: with terse, lyric poetry the obstruction which prevents our appreciation is sometimes insuperable. Dr. Williams is never diffuse. As he tells us in his preface, his poems are like machines; there is nothing in them that is sentimental, nothing that is redundant. Probably for this reason more alertness to the American language and feeling than an outsider can develop is necessary to appreciate his poems properly. Many English readers will find it hard to reach the centre of the poems; yet they are not difficult poems in their own context of the American language and society.

The emphasis falls on form rather than on content. Dr. Williams raises this question in the preface, where he writes: 'To me all sonnets say the same thing of no importance. What does it matter what the line "says"?' But his forms are so irregular in outline that there is no way of measuring them. Any metrical ideas which the reader retains while reading him will be an interruption. Nor is the machine a good example of these forms, apart from the absence of redundancy in each: they resemble more nearly the unpromising figures of pruned rose trees. He does not use the ordinary combinations of sounds such as we are accustomed to in English poetry; and his words give at first a false impression from their almost unstyled manner, their lines of two or three words: -

    It's all in
    the sound. A song.

The detachment of the poet from the thing he is writing about is sometimes so definite that it might almost amount to a lack of interest. Instead of engaging his sensibility to his subject the author seems to have disengaged it. This is one aspect of the emphasis on form rather than on content, which is also found in the poetry of his contemporary Mr. Ezra Pound.

It would be hard to say exactly what his style is. He draws few clear pictures, and the kind of image he presents reached its climax in an early poem, from which he has here quoted the lines: -

> Your thighs are apple-trees
> whose blossoms touch the sky!

Only in one poem is the sound of his songs really memorable: ;

> In Breughel's great picture, The Kermess, the dancers go round, they go round and around....

In the rest it is elusive. But what, after all, does the effort of lyric poetry aim at but the perfection of one or two poems? And this aim Dr. Williams has achieved.

70. DAVID DAICHES ON WILLIAMS' AMERICAN POETIC 'INSCAPE', 'YALE REVIEW'

Vol. XLI, no. 1, Autumn 1951, 153-5

This review goes on to consider 'Nones' by W. H. Auden and Robert Lowell's 'Lord Weary's Castle'.

Daiches (b. 1912) was Professor of English and American Literature at the University of Sussex 1961-1977. His many books include 'A Critical History of English Literature' (1960) and studies of Milton, Burns, Scott and Stevenson.

'When a man makes a poem,' Dr. Williams wrote in 1944, 'makes it, mind you, he takes words as he finds them interrelated about him and composes them - without distortion which would mar their exact significance - into an intense expression of his perceptions and ardors that they may constitute a revelation in the speech that he uses. It isn't what he says that counts as a work of art, it's what he makes, with such intensity of perception that it lives with an intrinsic movement of its own to verify its authenticity.'

This explains both the virtues and the difficulties of Williams' poetry. For Williams a poem has always been an intensely individual structuring of language to correspond to a perception or state of mind of the author. It is not the expression of a state of mind so much as the construction of a pattern of words which at the same time resolves it and bears witness to it; and the emphasis is always on the integrity and the unqiueness of the finished poem. 'A poem is a small (or large) machine made of words,' and there is nothing sentimental about a machine - or about a poem. 'When I say there's nothing sentimental about a poem I mean that there can be no part, as in any other machine, that is redundant.'

He puts the matter perhaps more persuasively in his Writer's Prologue to a Play in Verse:

[quotes from CLP, 13, lines 29-35, and 14, lines 1-10]

With this view of poetry, so scornful of traditional helps, so insistent on the poet's individual responsibility for using language altogether in his own way, so contemptuous of any formal structure that is not uniquely contrived for the individual occasion, Williams is both the most truly original and the most profoundly American of our poets. His idiom is not the idiom of the English poetic tradition (as, for example, Eliot's is, for all its originality), but the idiom of Wiliam Carlos Williams at this moment of time in the United States of America.

There are certain dangers in this excessive poetic independence: sometimes the poetic structures he so carefully builds are so idiosyncratic in expression that they testify to nothing except that there is something here that presumably had significance for the author. Sometimes the transitions between parts of a poem are utterly obscure, the structure being so individual as to be meaningless to any outsider. This kind of obscurity which we occasionally find in Williams' poetry is not willful or pedantic or eccentric or precious, and it has nothing to do with the search for a language of symbols which has bothered poets from Yeats to Auden: it arises entirely from his insistence on using language in the way that seems proper and inevitable to him.

Williams' successes - and they are many - are, by the same token, quite remarkable: there is nothing really like them in modern American poetry - certainly nothing at all like them in British poetry. To someone brought up on British poetry (even modern British poetry), he is an acquired taste, for the ear must be retrained, and the mind accustomed to a kind of poetic 'inscape' different from anything found in those modern poets who have debts to Donne or the French Symbolists. But the taste is worth acquiring, and the special kind of purity one finds in Burning the Christmas Greens, A Woman in Front of a Bank, For a Low Voice (a wonderful little poem, with a kind of humor all its own), or The Clouds, yields a genuine delight.

For all his preoccupation with the uniquely appropriate poetic structure, Williams is no mere verbal artificer. He is a humanitarian observer of the human scene, interested, quizzical, shrewdly vulgar, iconoclastically honest, and what he puts into his poems constitutes the record of a life of rich curiosity about himself and others. The flavor of his best poems lingers on the palate, providing both relish and illumination.

'Make Light of It: Collected Stories'

New York, November 1950

71. BABETTE DEUTSCH ON THE TECHNIQUE OF CARELESSNESS, 'NEW YORK HERALD TRIBUNE BOOKS'

3 December 1950, 5

In the opening passage of 'Paterson (Book Three)' (1949), Williams had written: 'Only one answer: write carelessly so that nothing that is not green will survive' (155).

It is natural to link Dr. Williams with Dr. Chekhov. Both storytellers, looking at the daily commonplace with the alert, amoral eyes of the doctor, both setting down their observations with rare fidelity to the facts, indifferent to the well-turned phrase, the polished paragraph, the tale tapering to a considered end; offering, instead, something casual, even tumbled, in appearance, odorous of a living thing, dirty or clean. For all these likenesses, there is a gulf between the two writers, as this volume of William Carlos Williams's collected stories makes plain. Here are none of Chekhov's twilight moods, nor the piercing pathos of his sketches of the deprived and outraged. Nor is the most ample of these stories as detailed as some of his studies of the folk he knew. Not a few of the inclusions are mere anecdotes, and all of them from the least to the longest and saddest, have an exuberant vitality. It is this, among other things, that distinguishes Williams's work not only from that of Chekhov but also from Joyce's 'Dubliners,' with which these stories have more than once been compared....

... The majority of the stories in the second section

are those you might hear one doctor telling another. A
few are mere thumbnail sketches. These are the stories
most like 'Dubliners,' not because of their subject matter
or their style, but because Williams, like Joyce, catches
the very accent of the people talking. They are not lower
middle class characters but all kinds, many of them with
nothing to lose, and the story-teller handles his material
with a carelessness not to be expected from one who writes
such notable poetry. He will introduce irrelevant details,
tack on superfluous comment, dwell on trivia that have
caught his fancy. Nevertheless, his ear for the vocabulary, the speech rhythms, the tone of voice of ordinary
men and women, boys and girls, in the midst of situations
important to them, makes these pages startlingly come alive
alive....

... It is characteristic that Williams doesn't ask
questions. He makes statements. Here is the crux of his
stories. What are you going to do with guys and girls,
scenes and situations like these? Why want to do anything
with them? Except not miss them.

The book is not lacking in compassionate understanding.
But its chief quality is the gusto that is Williams's
signature. If this collection does not show him at his
best, it helps us to realize the distinguishing features
of his contribution to American writing.

72. ROBERT HALSBAND, I LIVED AMONG THESE PEOPLE,
'SATURDAY REVIEW'

9 December 1950, 14-15

The review also considers briefly Williams' booklet 'A
Beginning on the Short Story' (New York, 1950).

Halsband (b. 1914) teaches at Columbia University, is
the author of 'The Life of Lady Mary Wortley Montague'
(1956) and editor of 'The Complete Letters of Lady Mary
Wortley Montagu' (3 vols, 1965-7).

In 'Make Light of It' Dr. Williams has gathered stories
from two previous books,'The Knife of the Times' and the
better known 'Life Along the Passaic River,' and added to
them twenty-one previously uncollected. Altogether the

stories are an exciting experience, for we are constantly surprised, even startled, by their flashes of insight, of humanity, and of poetry. And what makes this excitement substantial and satisfying is that there is nothing meretricious in his tough and honest vision of life.

If by a story is meant a plotted and structured narrative, then it would be difficult to find one in this collection. They are sketches, ranging from the merest impression or anecdote to full episodes of character and incident. In Dr. Williams's notes on the short story, jottings prepared for a lecture, we can see his theory and compare it with his practice. He defines a short story as 'a medium for nailing down a single conviction'; again, as a 'single flight of the imagination, complete: up and down down.' His stories contain so much conviction and imagintion that in spite of their fragmentation they hold together as a single book with a unified impact.

His stories have the utmost flexibility of subject matter and style, with the utmost rigidity in the truthfulness of both. He describes the lives of Polish immigrants (probably his favorite subject), or the thoughts of a lascivious woman, or the trip of a nursemaid to the zoo, or the emotional hunger of a weak man, or, frequently, his own work as a physician. And his tone always has true pitch; it is so beautifully tempered to the story he is telling that we are unaware of the changes in modulation but aware of their rich variety. A sentence may have an ungainly simplicity: 'Year. I know, I said. But I can't go three places first.' Or it may have a solid density: 'Death is difficult for the senses to alight on.' But it is always right for its time and place. His poetry has been described by Wallace Stevens as showing a 'passion for the anti-poetic'; and in his stories he is as passionately against the prose equivalents of the poetic - the stereotyped character of formulated stories in a slicked-up style.

If his stories lack these hallmarks of socially successful writing today, they have instead the genuine gleam of what Joyce described as an epiphany: 'a sudden spiritual manifestation, whether in the vulgarity of speech or of gesture or in a memorable phase of the mind itself.' Several of Dr. Williams's sketches come close to being clinical case histories, several are inconsequential trivia, but most of them light up with flashes of this sort. It is not an easy thing to achieve; certainly it can never be reduced to a formula or pattern. That is why, probably, he advises his audience in one of his notes: 'And be careful not to imitate yourself.' In his own case he always imitates nature, never himself.

The adjective 'compassionate' - so glibly attributed or denied to writers recently - is only a cliché of sentimentalism. Dr. Williams has no compassion for his people; he has what is far better, a feeling of respect and involvement. It is the fundamental conviction of his writing, and here is how he explains it in his Notes:

> I lived among these people. I knew them and saw the essential qualities (not stereotype) the courage, the humor (an accident) the deformity, the basic tragedy of their lives - and the *importance* of it. You can't write about something unimportant to yourself. I was involved.

His sympathy, and not his sentimentality, is usually with the underdog. His Jersey outcasts, though authentic, are familiar American pariah-heroes - like the outcasts of Bret Harte's Poker Flat or Steinbeck's 'Tortilla Flat.'

There is still another traditional element in his writing which brings him into the mainstream of our literature. He is a writer of the Twenties who has maintained his integrity; staying close to the ground and true to his craft (as well as his profession) through the Thirties and Forties. How many others have? He stems from the same rich soil as Sherwood Anderson, the early Hemingway, Gertrude Stein before she departed from intelligibility; and he has retained what was so valuable in their gifts: vigor, humor, and humanity. Whatever his ultimate reputation will be, he is one of the hardiest and healthiest shrubs on the landscape of American writing today.

73. ROBERT GORHAM DAVIS, STORIES, TO MR. WILLIAMS, ARE SWIFT EXPERIENCES, 'NEW YORK TIMES BOOK REVIEW'

17 December 1950, 1, 12

Davis (b. 1908) is an American teacher, editor and critic.

... Williams makes no effort in his stories to create any sort of aesthetic distance, to separate the author as author from the author as doctor, ...
 ... Williams doesn't play with vernacular speech for

its own sake, like Ring Lardner and Sinclair Lewis, nor does he give it the poetic rhythms and recurrences of Hemingway and Gertrude Stein. He doesn't even use the skilled raconteur's arts of suspense and climax. He satisfies the formal canons of neither slick fiction nor the New Criticism. There is much emotion but no 'objective correlatives'; much insight but no developed symbolism. Stories end as abruptly and casually as they begin. The form is almost nothing, the human facts everything. When the facts are not enough, the stories can seem flat or insignificant.

The whole book, nevertheless, has a keen, rich, tough humanity. Minimal and transparent though the medium is, it lets Williams define precisely his attitude toward his material.

'Patterson (Book Four)'

Norfolk, Conn., June 1951

74. RICHARD EBERHART, A VISION WELDED TO THE WORLD, 'NEW YORK TIMES BOOK REVIEW'

17 June 1951, 5, 18

Eberhart (b. 1904) is a noted American poet, whose books include 'Collected Poems 1930-76' (1976) and 'Selected Prose' (1978).

'Paterson' is one of the few original long poems of the mid-century. Its difficulties are not abysmal and may be surmounted; these enforce its fascination. The reader has to learn the technique of an experiment. The boldness and scope of the poem are already legendary. In this last book the work is pinned to the earth.

Dr. Williams does not leap to Cathay and he places no improbable strain on our imagination, no such strain as that which broke Crane's 'Bridge' and made it finally unusable. The fourth installment of the poem, subtitled The Run to the Sea, upholds a logical burden of meaning projected for it in the plan of the work as announced in Book I. The lyrical passage at the end sums up a lifetime of poetic perception. The larger symbol of the sea is entertained; time runs to history as life runs to death. Yet Dr. Williams, ever the stubborn lover of the world, reiterates 'The sea is not our home.' Our home is Paterson, the city, the man, the history, in short, fullness of life. By stepping back, he has leaped farther than Crane. He has thus humanized the imagination and has given us a philosophy of probability and use.

Book IV is a masterful section of the work, thoroughly consistent with the others, rich in esthetic materials, less given to moralizing than was Book III, and fairly dancing with shifts and turns of suggestion, taking up earlier motifs to bind them in, then delivering new themes. The first three parts of this section provide delightful exchanges between Corydon and Phyllis, Phyllis and Paterson, in the usual elliptical glance-style, feints that give on lattice-works of perception.

An old dowager, who likes to be massaged, takes a young nurse on a yachting trip to Anticosti. The themes weave back and forth. There are prose letters reminiscent of those in Books I and II. A satirical use of the word invention occurs at the end of the second section, reminiscent of the passage on invention in Book II.

The second section sports the author's findings and dynamic pronouncements on money and credit. He enters a prose 'Advertisement' beginning 'The Constitution says: *To borrow money on the credit of the United States.* It does not say: To borrow money from Private bankers.' He then sets forth a scheme to prove that 'We can build 100 airplanes for the price of one.' This ends on a whacking Williams fiat: 'I would like to have some smart economist or banker stick out his neck and contradict one single claim I present herewith to the nation.' In capitals we are adjured to 'Enforce the Constitution on money.'

The third section is about the river flowing to the sea, with a long passage on the history of Paterson, ending on the lyrical and philosophical passage mentioned above.

Book IV is richly satisfying and draws one back to a study of the three previous books and to an appraisal of the whole. The books have appeared in the years 1946, 1948, 1949 and 1951. They represent the sustained culmination of the ingenuity and invention which Dr. Williams has lavished on method and insight. He has taken the stony path of trying to define a new context. He has mastered a very large area of experience. And he has brought us closer to grips with imaginative vision, refined in things, welded to the world.

75. DUDLEY FITTS ON 'A MORE OR LESS TRIUMPHANT CONCLUSION', 'SATURDAY REVIEW'

21 July 1951, 23

Fitts (1903-68) was an American classicist, translator and critic, chiefly noted for his translations of the plays of Sophocles (with Robert Fitzgerald) and Aristophanes.

The Fourth Book of 'Paterson' brings Dr. Williams's ambitiously planned epic to a more or less triumphant conclusion. More or less: for, in spite of the brilliance of individual passages and the passionate human warmth which irradiates the work as a whole, the materials are so mixed and so undigested and the tensions and motives are so variously at war with one another that the total impression is one of colorful noise-shapes in a dream. Nevertheless, there are many positive qualities. Of the major poets of our time only Marianne Moore rivals Williams in clarity of perception and accuracy of tone; though his material is confused, each of the widely disparate ingredients has its own startling vitality bursting from the page. And there is a young eagerness here, an engagingly audacious sexuality, which gives the lie to the poet's personal calendar. Finally, for all the basic incoherence, there does emerge a philosophic and artistic credo which is sane and forceful. In a sense 'Paterson' is an 'Ars Poetica' for contemporary America. It is a pity that those who might benefit most from it will inevitably be put off by its obscurities and difficulties.

76. HAYDEN CARRUTH ON 'PATERSON' AS LYRICAL MEDITATION, 'NATION'

25 August 1951, 155-6

... The great questions raised by 'Paterson' are technical ones, and this in itself should have a momentous effect on contemporary criticism, our science of nebulosities - if, that is, the critics will meet the challenge. The question of prosody, for instance: Can a poet, as Dr. Williams contends, invent a new poetic language, free from traditional meters, free even from traditional syntax, based solely on contemporary American speech? Is the American ear truly as anti-European or as anti-classical as all that? We need many essays, good ones, on this subject. Furthermore, the question of structure, especially Dr. Williams's use of prose passages. These occur frequently. They are documentary - letters, newspaper clippings, medical records, and the like - and they are well chosen and interesting. But one does not want to read them twice. Do they derive literary value from their juxtaposition with verse? Is this not perhaps carrying the catalogue-of-ships device too far? Can a poem survive in the public mind which contains so much unquotable - that is, unrememberable - material?

A word should be said about Book Four itself. Unfortunately, it seems to me less satisfactory than the preceding books. It is less well integrated and gives the impression of having been more hurriedly written. It begins with a mock pastoral, satiric and sardonic in intent. The middle section concerns the paradox of science that both heals and destroys, and it contains also a digression on the similar faculties of money and credit. The final part is a long lyric of recollection; Paterson, the man-city, remembers the many murders that have occurred and thinks of the sea of blood toward which his people are flowing. All these phases refer to aspects of the previous books. The poem ends with a last picture of the poet who bathes harmlessly and carelessly in the sea.

Among the lines of an episode about his son, the poet give us, in Book Four, this parenthetical prose sentence: '(What I miss, said your mother, is the poetry, the pure poem of the first parts.)' This happens to be a true statement, for the final parts of 'Paterson' do not have the lyric intensity of the two first books. But my reason for quoting it here is not to illustrate something about the quality of the poem but rather to give an instance of something that Dr. Williams does over and over again and to point out another, rather unusual problem for the critics. Dr. Williams utterly destroys the convenient fiction that the poet and the man are separable. What are we to say honestly about this sentence except that the poet is giving us a criticism of his own poem, made by his wife? Such intimacies occur often, some of them much more pointed than this, all of them expressed in the most direct manner. Nothing could be more precisely contrary to the common practice of poets who think they are more important than themselves and therefore give themselves, even when they are dealing with obviously personal experience, a larger character and a more public decorum than the individual can claim in reality. Dr. Williams is more unassuming and more difficult. For this practice has several effects: it obstructs our understanding, since most of us are not lucky enough to know the poet; it embarrasses the critics, who do not want to discuss such matters even if they can; and it restricts the applicability of the poem's meaning, which is much broader than the personal.

'Paterson' has been called a 'personal epic.' I think this is a contradiction in terms, and I should prefer to call it a long, often superlatively good, lyrical

meditation. Parts of it will seem to every reader both
puzzling and foolish, yet in the end it becomes an expression of mature and convincing emotion, a poem in a versatile language that is often beautiful.

77. M. L. ROSENTHAL, IN THE ROAR OF THE PRESENT, 'NEW
REPUBLIC'

27 August 1951, 18

Rosenthal (b. 1917) is an editor, critic and poet, and
Director of the Poetics Institute at New York University.
His publications include 'The Modern Poets: A Critical
Introduction' (1960), and 'The New Poets' (1967). He is
the editor of 'The William Carlos Williams Reader' (1966).

'I'm just the core of the onion - nothing at all,' says
the hero of one of William Carlos Williams' plays. Good
poetry usually finds a center and starting point in some
immediacy: a direct statement, a narrative or dramatic
moment, a concrete image or emotion. Dr. Williams'
immediacies (and he is our master of the spontaneous
effect) are so often colored by his unpretentious humanity
that he seems almost to be improvising, as if he were not
one of the very few really accomplished poets in English
today:

[quotes P I, preface, 11, lines 319]

Well, that is one way to begin an epic poem! And yet,
in a sense it is the only way if the poet is to keep himself as free as possible of sentimental and purely literary assumptions while exploring the meanings of his own
time and place - 'the roar,/the roar of the present, a
speech - /is of necessity, my sole concern.' 'Paterson'
is not 'strictly' an epic, but a long poem in four parts.
(That is its first unpretentiousness.) Structurally, it
is loose though not uncontrolled. The poet takes a specific locality in New Jersey and personifies its geography,
sociology and history, identifying himself both as just
one of the many inhabitants and as the sensibility and
consciousness of the area. Readers of his novels and

short stories will agree that Williams knows its life.
As a local doctor and baby specialist, he has come closer
to the people than any other of our poets - far closer
than Sandburg, for instance - and the knowledge he must
grapple with is simply too intractable to allow of easy
triumphs or solutions.

Williams, as has been said often enough, is a pragmatic thinker. ('No ideas,' he writes, 'but in things.')
At the same time and like other pragmatists, he is a
mystic - at any rate, a would-be mystic. In 'Paterson' we
see writ large the kind of human-ecological mysticism that
a few scientists have been toying with recently. The
entire poem is an attempt to see what meaning, if any, can
be read into a given cultural unit, in its way symbolic of
life in American and in the modern world as a whole. Can
the life force realize itself fully in our society, the
poet asks, or do the violent gestures of graceless lust
and hatred and self-destruction define irrefutably a
'world of corrupt cities' lacking continuity with past
tradition or future perspectives? And can the poet himself find a 'language' in it comparable to certain
achievements in the past and to the vital relationships of
primitive societies, a language commensurate with the
terrible need of individuals to communicate the nature of
their love?

'No ideas but in things.' And so private memories,
extracts from letters and documents, close-ups of sex and
family relations in America, marvelous lyric outbursts and
afterbeats, vigorous social comment and satirical vignettes punctuate the poem explosively. In its surface
multiplicity it bears a family resemblance to Pound's
'Cantos.' It does also in some of its rhymes and attitides, but the personality speaking is entirely different.
Williams' America is indeed tragic, but at least in part
that is seen as the basic human condition; and he holds
fast to what is alive and solid in his country, with a
firm grasp on the American idiom.

The poem is finally a unit - humane, passionate, self-humbling, assertive of a minimum value - the intellectual
and esthetic possibilities arising in counter-dream age
against the dulling rituals of our society. Not as compressed or 'designed' as 'The Waste Land,' it nevertheless has a similar dramatic force and is perhaps the product of as rigorous a discipline....

78. RANDALL JARRELL, '... "PATERSON" HAS BEEN GETTING RATHER STEADILY WORSE', 'PARTISAN REVIEW'

Vol. XVIII, no. 6, November-December 1951, 698-700

This is the concluding part of a considerably longer review-essay, A View of Three Poets, in which volumes by Richard Wilbur and Robert Lowell are also discussed.

... 'Paterson (Book One)' seemed to be a wonderful poem; I should not have supposed beforehand that William Carlos Williams could do the organizing and criticizing and selecting that a work of this length requires. Of course, Book I is not organized quite so well as a long poem *ought* to be, but this is almost a defining characteristic of long poems - and I do not see how anyone could do better using only those rather mosaic organizational techniques that Dr. Williams employs, and neglecting as much as he does narrative, drama, logic, and sustained movement, the primary organizers of long poems. I waited for the next three books of 'Paterson' more or less as you wait for someone who has gone to break the bank at Monte Carlo for the second, third, and fourth times; I was afraid that I knew what was going to happen, but I kept wishing as hard as I could that it wouldn't.

Now that Book IV has been printed, one can come to some conclusions about 'Paterson' as a whole. My first conclusion is this: it doesn't seem to *be* a whole; my second: 'Paterson' has been getting rather steadily worse. Most of Book IV is much worse than II and III, and neither of them even begins to compare with Book I. Book IV is so disappointing that I do not want to write about it at any length: it would not satisfactorily conclude even a quite mediocre poem. Both form and content often seem a parody of those of the 'real' 'Paterson'; many sections have a scrappy inconsequence, an arbitrary irrelevance, that is extraordinary; poetry of the quality of that in Book I is almost completely lacking - though the forty lines about a new Odysseus coming in from the sea are particularly good, and there are other fits and starts of excellence. There are in Part III long sections of a measure that sounds exactly like the stuff you produce when you are demonstrating to a class that any prose whatsoever can be converted into four-stress accentual verse simply by inserting line-endings every four stresses. These sections *look* like blank verse, but are flatter than the flattest blank verse I have ever read - for instance: 'Branching trees and ample gardens gave/the village streets a delightful charm and/the narrow old-fashioned brick walls added/a dignity to the shading trees. It was a fair/resort for summer sojourners on their way/to the Falls, the main object of interest.' This passage suggests that the guidebook of today is the epic of tomorrow; and a more awing possibility, the telephone book put into accentual verse, weighs upon one's spirit.

Books II and III are much better than this, of course: Book II is decidedly what people call 'a solid piece of work,' but most of the magic is gone. And one begins to be very doubtful about the organization: should there be so much of the evangelist and his sermon? Should so much of this book consist of what are - the reader is forced to conclude - real letters from a real woman? One reads these letters with involved, embarrassed pity, quite as if she had walked into the room and handed them to one. What has been done to them to make it possible for us to respond to them as art and not as raw reality? to make them part of the poem 'Paterson'? I can think of no answer except: *They have been copied out on the typewriter.* Anyone can object, *But the context makes them part of the poem*; and anyone can reply to this objection, *It takes a lot of context to make somebody else's eight-page letter the conclusion to a book of a poem.*

Book II introduces - how one's heart sinks! - Credit and Usury, those enemies of man, God, and contemporary long poems. Dr. Williams has always put up a sturdy resistance to Pound when Pound recommended to him St. Sophia or the Parthenon, rhyme or metre, European things like that; yet he takes Credit and Usury over from Pound and gives them a good home and maintains them in practically the style to which they have been accustomed - his motto seems to be, *I'll adopt your child if only he's ugly enough.* It is interesting to see how much some later parts of 'Paterson' resemble in their structure some middle and later parts of the 'Cantos': the Organization of Irrelevance (or, perhaps, the Irrelevance of Organization) suggests itself as a name for this category of structure. Such organization is *ex post facto* organization: if something is somewhere, one can always find Some Good Reason for its being there, but if it had not been there would one reader have missed it? if it had been put somewhere else, would one reader have guessed where it should have 'really' gone? Sometimes these anecdotes, political remarks, random comments seem to be where they are for one reason: because Dr. Williams chose - happened to choose - for them to be there. One is reminded of that other world in which Milton found Chance 'sole arbiter.'

Book III is helped very much by the inclusion of Beautiful Thing, that long, extremely effective lyric that was always intended for 'Paterson'; and Book III, though neither so homogeneous nor so close to Book I, is in some respects superior to Book II. But all three later books are worse organized, more eccentric and idiosyncratic, more self-indulgent, than the first. And yet that is not the point, the real point: the *poetry*, the lyric rightness, the queer wit, the improbable and dazzling perfection of so much of Book I have disappeared - or at least, reappear only fitfully. Early in Book IV, while talking to his son, Dr. Williams quotes this to him: 'What I miss, said your mother, is the poetry, the pure poem of the first parts.' She is right.

I have written (sometimes in 'Partisan Review') a good deal about Dr. Williams' unusual virtues, so I will take it for granted that I don't need to try to demonstrate, all over again, that he is one of the best poets alive. He was the last of the good poets of his generation to become properly appreciated; and some of his appreciators, in the blush of conversion, rather overvalue him now. When one reads that no 'living American poet has written anything better and more ambitious' than 'Paterson', and that Dr. Williams is a poet who gives us 'just about everything,' one feels that the writer has in some sense missed the whole point of William Carlos Williams. He is a *very* good but *very* limited poet, particularly in vertical range. He is a notably unreasoning, intuitive writer - is not, of course, an intellectual at all, in either the best or the worst sense of the word; and he has further limited himself by volunteering for and organizing a long dreary imaginary war in which America and the Present are fighting against Europe and the Past. But go a few hundred years back inside the most American American and it is Europe: Dr. Williams is just as much Darkest Europe as any of us, way down there in the middle of his past.

In his long one-sided war with Eliot Dr. Williams seems to me to come off surprisingly badly - particularly so when we compare the whole of 'Paterson' with the 'Four Quartets.' When we read the 'Four Quartets' we are reading the long poem of a poet so temperamentally isolated that he does not even put another character, another human being treated at length, into the whole poem; and yet the poem (probably the best since the 'Duino Elegies') impresses us not with its limitations but with its range and elevation, with how much it knows not simply

about men but about Man - not simply about one city or
one country but about the West, that West of which America
is no more than the last part.

79. UNSIGNED REVIEW, POET OF AN INDUSTRIAL SOCIETY,
'TIMES LITERARY SUPPLEMENT'

No. 2,609, 1 February 1952, 95

As is noted in its opening paragraph, the occasion of this
review was the publication within a short period of time
of four separate titles by Williams. Because the reviewer
focuses chiefly on 'Paterson' this summing-up, for British
readers, of Williams' position is included here.

The recent publication in America of four books by William
Carlos Williams should for several reasons by interesting
to British as well as American readers. 'Paterson (Book
Four)' completes the major work of Dr. Williams's life,
'The Collected Earlier Poems' and 'The Collected Later
Poems' make available to the general reader the whole
range of the poet's work from 1906 to 1946, and the
'Autobiography' supplements the details given by Richard
Aldington, Harriet Monroe and Ezra Pound. We are now in a
position to evaluate the contribution to American letters
of this prolific New Jersey physician who, during the past
45 years, in 30 or so books of verse, novels, short stories, and studies of the American past, has expounded his
artistic philosophy of 'no ideas but in things,' and whose
prolonged and sometimes violent contact with the currents
of American urban life early prompted a search for some
'reply to Greek and Latin with the bare hands' which might
convey the aspirations and despairs of man in an industrial society.
 During a period of eclecticism, a poet's choice of subject and technique will be watched with great attention.
His critics will tend to ask whether he has, in the Keatsian manner, sought to embrace as much of this world as
lies within his reach, or whether he has, for his art or
his conscience's sake, narrowed his range - problems which
earlier poets sometimes found settled for them. It can,
of course, be argued that all poets must make a selection

– must, as T. E. Hulme pointed out, be subject to some conception of limit. The narrow stream, it is said, often runs deep. This is undoubtedly true. But when, says the drift of Dr. Williams's work, whole classes of objects are treated as irrelevant vulgarities, when the facts – unpalatable as they may be – of twentieth-century life are misinterpreted and when, most significant of all, there is nostalgia for things past, then the reader is at liberty to question not only the present wholeheartedness but also the ultimate significance of a poet who turns such a wishful eye upon the present scene. Dr. Williams himself does no such thing. From the start he embraced that noisy fraternity ' who ride ten in a compartment to a football match at Swansea,' as he did their more fastidious brethren. Living among machines, he neither ignored nor enshrined them. Like Blake championing the cause of the Minutely Particular, he said, 'I believe all art begins in the local and must begin there, since only then will the senses find their material.'

It is this belief which has guided Dr. Williams since his youthful association with the Imagist group, from which he retained a preference for the sharp image and the ring of poetically heightened 'ordinary speech.' It is this which has earned him the label of 'anti-intellectual,' for he distrusts abstractions, 'the craft subverted by thought,' and seeks instead a direct contact with the thing itself. This direct contact he wishes to communicate, moved perhaps by the same conviction which led Miss Gertrude Stein to cry, 'A rose is a rose is a rose.' And yet the honest violence of this reaction against the stale image, the refusal to follow the paths of men 'content with the connotations of their masters' has, like Wordsworth's, sometimes overstepped itself. When Dr. Williams writes of the wheelbarrow one is reminded of the poetic youth in one of Mr. Saroyan's plays who wrote poems with single words – 'tree,' for example, and 'sky.' Poetry, one need hardly say, is not so simple and the reader might be tempted to ask himself whether Dr. Williams's notorious 'non-poetic' style was less a deliberate device than a confession of inadequacy, were it not for the lyrical splendour of such poems as The Yachts.

In the writings of 'Paterson,' which was projected for several decades and began to appear in 1946, Dr. Williams has used a rich and varied series of techniques and it is felt in some quarters in the United States that he has produced the first long poem in this century with enough weight and purpose behind it and enough poetic cunning in it to challenge the thought and style of 'The Waste Land' and the 'Four Quartets.' The theme of 'Paterson,' 'that man is himself a city,' could hardly have been more suitable to these urban times. Paterson is an industrial town in New Jersey. When it is added that through it there runs a river, the Passaic, and that outside it there are Falls, it will be at once apparent how many levels of meaning may be illuminated by the conjunction of the river and city symbols. Paterson undergoes metamorphoses. He is Dr. Paterson, Mr. Paterson; 'butterflies settle on his stone ear.'

From Book One, The Delineaments of the Giants, the poet passes to The Modern Replicas, Book Three discusses the language which may make vocal both the awareness of Paterson's colonial and nineteenth-century past and the facts of its present. Book Four encompasses:

>   .... the blast
> the eternal close
> the spiral
> the final somersault
> the end.

The poetic narrative, itself quick-darting and breathless, is broken by flashing impressions, which are awakened by key-ideas. 'Divorce' is one - of language from meaning, of man from his essential nature, 'blocking' is another - of the essential life-force, and of communication. Excerpts from chronicles of Paterson are interspersed with long self-searching letters from a woman who represents the self-consuming introversion of those intellectuals who work against, rather than with, the facts of their time. Symbols and theme-words are reiterated; their mutations and connotations make an increasingly intricate pattern. At first reading, the extent of this weaving of meaning-patterns can only be vaguely apprehended, but with closer study selected words and ideas take on a depth of meaning which grows more precise as it grows more complex. The bud in Part II of the first book:

>   ... Forever green,
> tight-curled, upon the pavement perfect
> in juice and substance but divorced, divorced
> from its fellows, fallen low ...

appeared first as:

> (The multiple seed,
> packed tight with detail, soured ...

which

> ... is lost in the flux and the mind
> distracted floats off in the same
> scum)

In his impatient pilgrimage 'from mathematics to particulars' Dr. Williams is apt to put a personal interpretation upon words which in common currency bear rather different connotations. But since the words so selected are threads which appear again and again to illuminate the vivid impressionistic scenes of the poem they explain themselves and live their own life in the poem.

It is harder to read 'Paterson' than many long poems, not only because of the difficulty but because the element of 'incantation' is absent. Even the lyric passages are taut and bare:

> On this most voluptuous night of the year
> the term of the moon is yellow with no light
> the air's soft, the night bird has
> only one note ...

The English reader, therefore, with the clanging rhetoric of Marlowe, the organ-note of Milton or, in more recent times, the verbal savouriness of Mr. Dylan Thomas in his ear will at first be disappointed. He must therefore accept the fact that this poem, written in English, is as little in the English tradition as are the poems of Federico Garcia Lorca. The Americanism of William Carlos Williams is, however, not militant but fundamental. It illuminates rather than affords an excuse for his art. The reader senses in the jutty images and rapid impressionistic flashes that vastness and many-sidedness, the feeling of embroilment that so many American artists convey. The verse breathes contact with life, understanding and humanity. It is as if the page is not big enough, nor life long enough, for the poet to note it all down.

Dr. Williams who, in his earlier years, limited himself as severely as Ernest Hemingway to the sharpness of things, to smallness and accuracy of detail, now, in the fruition of his talent, takes upon himself the subject of Man in America. But, consistently, it is through 'local pride,' the New Jersey microcosm, that he works. And it is with a ruthless attention to the themes that arise from the 'things' of Paterson that he writes, for the sensuous attractions of words for their own sake were rigidly excluded from his artistic consciousness a long time ago. Dr. Williams has all the attributes of a major poet. All his life he has been persistently and seriously concerned with the philosophical problem of man's position in the world he

has made for himself. He gives a sense of having a consis-
sistent view of what that position is and, finally, his
'style' is something which includes but surpasses his
technical manner. The very flavour of his writing is
recognizable and is as intrinsic to his work as are his
themes. It matters little that he has had small public
acclaim during his lifetime; Gerard Manley Hopkins was in
the same case.

And yet, for some reason, the serious critic withholds
the final cachet. Is it from a belief that poetry at its
greatest must be noble utterance as well as brilliant
sense? Is it from annoyance at the starkness of Dr.
Williams's technique, the 'fallacy of imitative form'? Or
is it from a sense of disappointment at the kaleidoscopic
quality, the lack of verbal density - even the absence of
memorable and quotable passages? Perhaps it is mainly for
this last reason, for tradition dies hard and the effect
of Dr. Williams's verse is largely cumulative. Moreover,
the English reader will have an additional difficulty,
since the poet in his country is not subject to quite the
same spiritual and physical pressures as the poet in
America. It is possible for the English poet to feel in
his blood a tradition which includes medieval order, the
Line of Wit and Augustan elegance. The American poet may
re-live such a tradition intellectually, but feels with
more immediacy the Puritan conscience and the legacy of
Twain and Whitman. The English poet has no racial turmoil to contend with. The past lives for him in the monu-
ments as well as the literature of his ancient country.
He lives on the legacy of times when literature was both
privileged and respected, and however insecure his position in fact, he holds it proudly. The American, having
no such legacy, feels much more acutely the danger of
being swamped by cultural barbarism. He therefore goes
out to meet its challenge more rawly, more fiercely and
perhaps more knowledgeably.

William Carlos Williams is such a poet, a man who tries
to deal intelligently with the world of men as he finds it
in his own country. He advances like a worldly prophet,
crying out against the severing of man from his ancient
roots, and his vocabulary and his manner subserve his
honest attempt to 'be reconciled, poet, with your world.'
It is perhaps for this example of reconciliation and of
immersion in the life of the people that Dr. Williams's
work is most valuable. In a democracy the poet enjoys
no aristocratic immunity, and if he is to exist as a vital
force in his community he must do more than make brilliant
copy out of the flounderings of his fellow men.

'Autobiography'

New York, September 1951

80. HARVEY BREIT ON 'AN UNEMBELLISHED, HONEST MAN OF LETTERS', 'ATLANTIC MONTHLY'

October 1951, 82-3

From a Reader's Choice book column, this is preceded by a review of a reissue of Ford Madox Ford's 'The Good Soldier'.
    Breit (1913-68) was an American poet, playwright, novelist and critic.

It is not irrelevant that Ford saw something of William Carlos Williams in Paris in the twenties, and later, in the States, started a Friends of William Carlos Williams club. Williams must have been a fine, fresh, indigenously American breath of air for the expatriates and collective upper Bohemia that wrote, painted, drank, and mostly talked in those Paris days. In 'The Autobiography of William Carlos Williams ..., published on the 17th of last month, which was the author's sixty-eighth birthday, you see the autobiographer plainly. The book is immensely honest, reminding me, peculiarly, of Stendhal's 'Memoirs of Egotism,' in which that autobiographer promises the reader he will only put down honest lines.
    The autobiography takes in Williams's childhood, boyhood, and youth, his efforts to become a doctor, his various internships, his in-the-meanwhile attempts to write, his eventual triumph as a first-rate doctor and a first-rate writer. It also includes, with complete naturalness, some of Williams's main esthetic ideas. The result is,

first of all, refreshing; second of all, absorbing; and
last of all, informative. Ezra Pound, a schoolboy chum
of Williams, appears in the memoir frequently and always
commands interest. Williams, by the way, has continued
to see Pound at St. Elizabeth's Hospital in Washington.
The partial record of these meetings is fascinating. For
example, Williams reports that Pound refuses to entertain
the idea of reopening his case, because 'he knew he would
be shot by an agent of the "international crew" the moment
he stood outside the hospital gates.' And Williams adds:
'Maybe he's right, for one thing is certain: he'd never
stop talking.'

The autobiography contains fascinating vignettes of
Joyce (a memorable one, when Robert McAlmon says, 'Here's
to sin,' in a half-drunken toast, and Joyce suddenly says,
'I'll not drink to that'); of H.D. (sitting in the grass
in the rain, 'and I behind her feeling not inclined to
join in her mood. And let me tell you it rained, plenty.
It didn't improve her beauty or my opinion of her ...');
of a hilarious Yeats-Gosse incident. (1) Best of all, the
memoir shows you the memoirist, an unembellished, honest
man of letters, whose opinions you don't always agree
with, but whose opinions you nevertheless value in themselves and because they are the product of a tough-minded,
warmhearted, intransigent, and wonderful human being.

Note

1 The 'Yeats-Gosse incident' refers to an occasion when
   Sir Edmund Gosse chaired a lecture by Yeats on the work
   of some younger Irish poets. Objecting to Yeats'
   approval of the 'drunkenness, lechery or immorality' of
   Lionel Johnson and others, Gosse rang a bell on the
   table beside him. Yeats hesitated, then continued; but
   after Gosse had rung the bell a third time Yeats was
   forced to discontinue the lecture. Williams, 'Autobiography', 115.

81. LAWRENCE FERLINGHETTI, REVIEW, 'SAN FRANCISCO CHRONICLE'

7 October 1951, 20

Ferlinghetti (b. 1919) published this review before he resumed the original Italian form of his surname, which had been anglicized by his family to 'Ferling'. Well-known as a poet, reader and lecturer, an originator of the Beat movement and the founder-owner of City Lights Bookshop, in San Francisco, Ferlinghetti has had many volumes of his own poetry published, including 'A Coney Island of the Mind' (1958) and 'Landscapes of Living and Dying' (1979).

An edition of Williams' 'Kora in Hell: Improvisations' was published in the Pocket Poets Series by City Lights Books in 1957.

William Carlos Williams is at once more and less than the Poet Laureate of New Jersey, as one university president dubbed him. Besides practicing medicine with distinction for 40 years in his home town, he has written 36 books of prose and poetry, and has had a large influence upon American writers of our time, sometimes beyond his own talent as a poet.

His slightly elliptic though delightful 'Autobiography' reveals why this is so. It is the personal history of Dr. Williams, poet and physician, from his boyhood in Rutherford, N.J., to his present 68 years. Yet it is more than this. The 'Autobiography' is significant, as Dr. Williams is himself, in representing the 'other side of the coin' in American literature.

On one side, Europe and the expatriate writers, Henry James, Ezra Pound, T. S. Eliot, ...; on the other side, America and Whitman and all those with their roots in American soil. Dr. Williams is in the Whitman camp. He calls the appearance of T. S. Eliot's 'Waste Land' in 1922 'the great catastrophe in our letters.'

'Only now, as I predicted, have we begun to catch hold again and restarted to make the line over. This is not to say that Eliot has not, indirectly, contributed much to the emergence of the next step in metrical construction, but if he had not turned away from the direct attack here, in the western dialect, we might have gone ahead much faster.'

This is not to say Dr. Williams never left home. He spent more than one year in Europe and knew many of the Americans there, especially in the 1920's, and was well up on all their movements. Yet he was for the most part an unhappy expatriate. By his own description, he is happiest when hard at his medical practice, letting the poetry germinate while he works, finding the resolution of medicine and poetry in the final, limitless search for poetic essence in the life he is able, because of his profession, intimately to touch.

What he has to say of the other artists of his generation, especially of his good friend Pound, illuminates the division among them. Both he and Pound would have no one tell them how or what to write; they took appositive ways to their objective. How Dr. Williams succeeded is his 'Autobiography.'

'I would continue medicine, for I was determined to be a poet; only medicine, a job I enjoyed, would make it possible for me to live and write as I wanted to. I would live, that first, and write, by God, as I wanted if it took all eternity to accomplish my design. My furious wish was to be normal, undrunk, balanced in everything ... I would not court disease, live in slums for the sake of art, give lice a holiday. I would not "die for art," but live for it, grimly and work, work, work (like Pop), beat the game and be free (like Mom, poor soul) to write, write as I alone should write, for the sheer drunkenness of it, I might have added. And complete defiance of the world or what might come after it, if anything.'

In this choice which most artists must make, Pound followed no separate profession to earn a living; he went abroad. Williams approached poetry through poetry. Pound's poetry is greater, but does this prove Pound's path more direct, or harder, than that of Williams? Their ends are disparate: Williams in the sane, snug harbor of Rutherford; Pound alienated from his country in St. Elizabeth's Hospital, Washington, D.C., and symbolically resembling in appearance (by Williams' description) the beast in Jean Cocteau's version of Beauty and the Beast.

As in the story of the young novelist who lived with two grandmothers and wrote as an old woman talks, a poet, in some measure, writes the way he lives. The 'Autobiography' has that infectious warmth of local humanity, coupled with curiosity and great intellectual honesty, which makes the Rutherford poet a continuing influence.

82. MATTHEW JOSEPHSON, WILLIAMS AS AN EMBODIMENT OF THE 'AMATEUR SPIRIT', 'SATURDAY REVIEW'

20 October 1951, 10-11

Josephson (1899-1978), American editor and biographer, was associated with a number of influential periodicals in the 1920s and 1930s, such as 'Secession', 'Broom', and 'transition'. His books include 'Portrait of the Artist as American' (1930) and 'Life Among the Surrealists' (1962). Josephson reviewed 'The Great American Novel' in 'Broom' in October 1923.

The memoirs of the inimitable family doctor and poet of Rutherford, New Jersey, range widely in time from impressions of the arty set at the University of Pennsylvania in 1903 to those of personages figuring in the latest *avant-garde* reviews, just arrived from Paris, Rome, or Bleecker Street. You being with Ezra Pound as an uncomfortable and sulking sophomore and William Butler Yeats in spruce middle age; you end up half a century later among the slender saplings of 'New Directions.' Along the way there is the the excitement of the historic Armory Show of 1913 with its Post-Impressionists and Cubist painters; there are the Imagists of the 'poetry Renaissance'; the 'Others' group, including Wallace Stevens; the 'Little Review' and its unrestrained experimenters; 'Contact,' featuring mainly Williams himself; and of course, Paris, with its 'expatriates,' who weren't really that; and the whole 'springtime of the little magazines.' In addition there are galleries of wonderful minor characters, bohemians, anarchists, panhandlers, who were eternally on the verge of writing another 'Ulysses' (after James Joyce), now unjustly forgotten. Thus it is a literary banquet of no mean proportions Dr. Williams offers; and here, as always in his later writings, literature is interlarded with thick slices-of-life - served very rare - American life as observed by a keen-eyed obstetrician in the dreary industrial slums of New Jersey. To Williams the environs of New Jersey. To Williams the environs of Paterson were the chosen native ground of which he was to sing; he himself was the son of transplanted English and West Indian parents.

Williams is an excellent physician by reason of the same qualities that have made him a good poet: imagination, independence of mind, quickness of eye and hand. Though he turned out poetry in gushers from boyhood on,

he vowed that he would never seek to earn money with his
pen, but would live by some other calling rather than by
the low shifts of professional and 'commercial' writers.
Some of his best lines were written in the hours of waiting for an accouchement. Thus Dr. Williams has embodied
in literature what we used to call the 'amateur spirit,'
which is now so rare. Today our budding writers train
themselves from high-school on to be professionals in
corporate prose for institutions of mass entertainment.
But to Williams writing has been a cult and not a trade.
Since he generally went unpaid and had few readers, he
wrote for his own amusement or relief - which encourages
originality rather than imitation. The recent 'revival'
of Williams before a somewhat expanded public is surely
one of the pleasanter things that have happened in our
literary scene.

One recalls meeting Williams for the first time, during
a walk along his favorite Jersey swamps, when he was still
in his thirties - though a small-town doctor and pater-
familias - and finding him exceedingly 'boyish' in his
ebullience, his enthusiasms, his sudden laughter. He is
as young of voice and as eager-beaver at sixty-eight.
This candor of spirit and quickness to love or hate en-
livens his autobiography, as also his growing 'saga' of
'Paterson.' It would be unduly optimistic, however, to
estimate this book as great autobiography.

To the good autobiographers we turn usually for their
intimate analysis and appraisal of their contemporaries.
Williams' approach is too 'spontaneous' and impatient to
permit balanced judgments of complex personalities such
as Pound and Gertrude Stein, before whom he appears at a
loss. In detail he is often negligent. The play of
ideas, the intellectual content of artistic movements is
not familiar ground to him. One might say that he is
more at home in giving us the 'inside story' of a hospital
clinic than of a literary group. But he is a masterly
story-teller, as in a digressive anecdote of the delivery
of twelve-pound twins by a tough, three-hundred-pound
gangster of a woman.

The unpredictable element in Williams's writing, though
affording many a pleasant surprise, has made him a
problem-child for those New Critics who are disposed to
rules of order and good taste as established by T. S.
Eliot. (A 'catastrophic' influence Williams has called
Eliot, perhaps rightly.) How, they ask, can he write
first-rate poetry or prose by methods so unorthodox? And
yet he plainly does; for he has the painter's eye and an
ear for swift, terse American speech. A 'primitive' he
may be, as the critic-technicians hold, but many of his

poems and tales will live.

His fairly simple *ars poetica* demands that he 'contact' nature and life as quickly, as directly as possible; and he manages this well at times. His method, in essence, was evolved toward 1918.

> I decided that I would write something every day, without missing one day for a year. I'd write nothing planned, but take up a pencil, put the paper before me, and write anything that came into my head. Be it nine in the evening or three in the morning, returning from some delivery ... I'd write it down.
> Not a word was to be changed ... but I did tear up some of the stuff.

This is close enough to the 'automatic' writing and drawing practised by Dadaists and Surrealists at about the same period. One of their gifted painters once explained the system to this reviewer as follows: 'You simply go fishing in the subconscious stream: sometimes you catch a fine carp; sometimes all you bring up is an old shoe.' Williams's swiftly-paced recollections have some of the defects as well as the virtues of this method.

In this solid, respectable doctor, anchored to his duties, there is always a pathetic, hidden rebel, who seems to gaze longingly across the Jersey meadows at the pink lights of lower Manhattan, where his heart also lies. At regular intervals he would commute from Rutherford to Greenwich Village to join those relaxed gatherings of choice spirits there who paid honor to free art, free poetry, and cheap wine. And often Williams was the only one who had the price of the wine. One feels this dual personality in many a passage of painfully honest confession, such as the priceless account of his abortive 'romance' with the Baroness Elsa von Freytag-Loringhoven. When Williams first met her, an admiring reader of his early verses, she was momentarily residing in the Tombs for having stolen an umbrella. On her release, to save her and her dogs from starving, he kindly gave her a little money - then had to fight his way back to Rutherford, happy at escaping unscathed. But our Baroness pursued him there.

You see him sitting at dinner on a Sunday evening with his rosy-cheeked family, when an emergency call comes by telephone. He hurries off with his bag, to meet the Baroness just outside the door, emerging from behind the bushes. She seizes his arm. (According to a different account from that in this work, which he used to give verbally toward 1920, she cried: 'Villiam Carlos Villiams,

I vant you!') In the present account she asks him to accompany her; when he refuses: 'She hauled off and hit me alongside the neck with all her strength. I just stood there thinking. But at the moment a cop happened to walk by.' She flees, but returns to her ambuscading some days later. Dr. Williams, meanwhile, having practised with a punching bag, is ready: 'I flattened her with a stiff punch to the mouth. I had her arrested, she shouting: '"What are you in this town? Napoleon?"'

When she was released soon afterward it was on her promise to return no more to the Rutherford scene. Exit the Baroness. This is but one specimen of Williams, as storyteller, at his best, as in many an unguarded passage of reminiscence, unaffected, sometimes naive, always truthful.

83. MAXWELL GEISMAR, A TALENT OF MATURITY, 'NEW REPUBLIC'

24 December 1951, 19-20

Geismar (b. 1909), an American critic, has written a series of studies of the American novel from 1890 through the twentieth century.

The success story of William Carlos Williams after a lifetime of devotion to both the practice of medicine and of poetry almost justifies the old-fashioned virtues that he has clung to in the changing values of contemporary art. Another transitional figure in the Middle Generation, and practically alone among the modern poets, he reminds us of the American scene of Dreiser and Sherwood Anderson at its turning point. 'These were the years just before the great catastrophe to our letters - the appearance of T. S. Eliot's "The Waste Land,"' Williams says here. 'Our work staggered to a halt for a moment under the blast of Eliot's genius which gave the poem back to the academies. We did not know how to answer him.'

He figured Eliot had set him back twenty years in the development of a new art form rooted in the locality which should give it fruit, and he was just about right. Ezra Pound's influence, too, from his college days with Williams, runs through this chronicle just as Williams

himself - a blunt, sturdy and perhaps naive figure that
would not be persuaded or subdued - is a persistent source
of torment in Pound's letters. The two men represented
antithetical poles of the poetry group in this country,
and their relationship, often comic or absurd, finally
tragic and grim (Williams lately visited Pound at St.
Elizabeth's and was still drawn to the paranoiac prophet),
has a nice undertone of historical drama. In this sense
of course, the four books of 'Paterson,' the publication
of Williams' collected poems and short stories, and the
present volume, are a final vindication of his divergent
and unpopular point of view in a central esthetic controversy.

Why, then, do we hestitate to cheer? - since the
'Autobiography' is in many respects also an admirable
book. Williams was serious about his medical career.
There are excellent sections on his early training in New
York hospitals and first experiences with 'my wonderful
friends, the Wops of Guinea Hill' in Rutherford, among
whom he was to practise for the rest of his life and from
whom he drew so much material for both his stories and
poems. Poverty, human misery and ignorance brought home
to him at first hand the meaning of a social-economic
framework, that sense of 'culture' and of history from
which so many modern poets had claimed to exempt themselves. From this area, as well as from his Spanish-
French ancestors, Williams drew one of his distinctive
traits: a completely flexible and frank view of the
flesh, suffering and lusting in its most grotesque and
secret passages.

The literary movement of the 1920s is at the center of
the book; in the discussion of such figures as H.D.,
Marianne Moore, Alfred Stieglitz, Marsden Hartley, Charles
Demuth, Margaret Anderson, Bob McAlmon and many other
major and minor personages, the 'Autobiography' is more
direct and illuminating than most informal histories of
the period. Williams, in his vacations at least, followed the expatriates to Europe, and he provides interesting side-lights on the artistic and bohemian circles of
Paris. Yet to a certain degree he felt as 'out of place,
self-conscious and alone' among such people as he did at
the large dances, drinking parties and charity shows he
mentions. 'I was a rustic in my own eyes, completely
uninitiated,' and again, speaking of such restless,
devouring women of this society as Nancy Cunard or Iris
Tree, he mentions the men who served as their counter-
foils 'from the piddling French surrealists of the day to
myself standing in the mere outskirts of the picture.'

Williams' talent developed slowly - it was a talent of

maturity, perhaps, as against all the bright talents of youth that marked the postwar generation - and to a certain degree we have this sense of the outsider, the spectator, rather too limited, cautious and reserved, all through his chronicle. What we miss, at any rate, is a kind of bolder judgment and self-assurance on Williams' part, a wider range of values than he shows, and perhaps even a more reckless thrust of creative energy that would have put both the 'Collected Stories' and the 'Autobiography' into the class of major works. They are not; and what they lack is simply the style and the imprint of a free and original personality to complement what is, after all, an admirable but somewhat limited and even conventional mind.

Maybe it is unjust to suggest this about Williams' work on the basis of his prose narratives. (He warns us that 'what I believe to be the hidden core of my life will not easily be deciphered' in the narrative of its outer circumstances). Perhaps, too, he has deliberately omitted, as Pound's correspondence did also, the story of his single greatest experience, poetry itself, and a final judgment will obviously have to be made there. But it is a shame that the 'Autobiography,' good as it is, should leave us with a sense of disappointment, while our praise falls a little flat.

84. RICHARD ELLMANN, THE DOCTOR IN SEARCH OF HIMSELF, 'KENYON REVIEW'

Vol. XIV, no. 1, Winter 1952, 511-12

... In his preface Dr. Williams suggests that the hidden center of his life 'will not easily be deciphered, even when I tell, as here, the outer circumstances.' Yet some deciphering may be ventured. His progress is from the child who discovers that the emperor has no clothes on to the adult who knows that no one can cover his nakedness. Nakedness is in fact a principal theme for him. The novel, he whimsically informs us, is a strip tease, each chapter removing a layer of clothes but with a last garment still left on at the end. And it is just here, he says, that poetry begins, flicking off what is left, disclosing 'the underlying nudity of patriotic or economic stress, or reality of other sort.' Poetry has to 'see

through the welter of evasive or interested patter.' He
recalls a cartoon by Tenniel with three parts, the first
showing Louis, 'a skinny-legged, bald and toothless old
man,' the second Rex, 'a huge curled wig supporting a hat
with plumes, an embroidered coat, below pads for the
legs,' and last 'Louis Rex, in full regalia, the king
himself - Louis XV.' The poet deals only with the first,
essential Louis.

Consequently Dr. Williams cannot understand why so good
a poet as Pound should have 'side' or pose instead of con-
tenting himself with unembellished personality. For Dr.
Williams the pursuit of nakedness has been a dominant
quest. Hence he presents a naked red wheelbarrow, or a
funeral coach stripped of decoration, or, as in the last
book of 'Paterson,' several scenes in which people are
undressing or undressed. Rebelling against the wardrobe
of poetic tradition, he has abolished rhyme and all
rhythms that do not sound like plain American speech.
Even the sentence has too much 'side' to be retained. As
he writes in 'Paterson,' 'Kill the explicit sentence,
don't you think? and expand our meaning - by verbal
sequences. Sentences, but not grammatical sentences:
dead-falls set by schoolmen.' While the 'Autobiography'
is not so radical in its grammar, it abounds in slang
phrases whose exclusion Dr. Williams would perhaps consider unAmerican or Jamesian: 'medicine, a rat race, if
ever there was one,' 'an excellent Chambertin that nearly
ruined me,' 'the scholarship is appalling. I'd go crazy.'
These lapses contribute to the informality of the tone,
they show that Dr. Williams is a good guy, but they don't
demonstrate that bare precision which he achieves in his
best verse.

The danger of keeping one's clothes off is suffering
from exposure. Dr. Williams' detestation of philosophy,
of abstraction, of generalization is so strong that it
affects his work adversely. His method, like Pound's
in the 'Cantos,' is to amass particulars until generalizations form themselves, but they don't necessarily do so.
The experiences in this book are good examples. He sup-
plies several interesting sketches of Pound, yet Pound
remains a collection of particulars, his motivation unexplored. There are vivid pictures of hospital life in
New York City, of American writers in Paris or this
country, yet they remain half-interpreted at most. His
stories about homosexuals and transvestites are interesting but unfocussed. His book is chatty, leisurely, sometimes exciting, not often dull; it takes on the irregular
rhythm of a doctor's day, separate episodes occurring like
house calls, some routine, some out of the ordinary, all

strung together rather fortuitously. Because he has clung
tenaciously to the imagist doctrine of 'no ideas but in
things,' Dr. Williams tends to give us the things alone.
These, left unadorned, are often impressive or startling.

But nakedness, too, as Dr. Williams knows, is frequently
a deception. Layers of skin as well as of clothing have
to be removed, and there is the possibility that after
removing all the layers we will discover, like Peer Gynt
peeling the onion to find its core, nothing at all.
Cleansing the gates of perception is a useful remedy for
certain literary disorders, but Dr. Williams, who is dis-
trustful of wonder cures, might distrust this one too. He
assures us that there will always be, when all superfici-
alities are removed, 'the radiant gist,' but may that not
depend upon the presence not only of an honest eye and
ear, but also of all the finery of the intellect?

'The Collected Earlier Poems'

Norfolk, Conn., December 1951

85. I. L. SALOMON, CANDOR & SCIENCE, 'SATURDAY REVIEW'
15 March 1952, 14

Salomon (b. 1899) is an American poet and translator.

To increase the prestige of William Carlos Williams, the winner of the National Book Award for Poetry (1950), his publishers have issued this collection of his earlier poems. It is a good thing they have done so, for in this book the work of thirty-three years stands exposed, revealing the importance of Dr. Williams as a poet even had he never written a line after 1939.

The essentiality of Dr. Williams lies in his approach to the poem, his union of idea and form, and his unceremonious insistence that the things seen spring alive imaginatively by the proper distillation of emotion into words. He has gathered sustenance from the arts, from music and painting, as well as from his environment, yet not solely from Rutherford, New Jersey, where he is a practising pediatrician. He brings to his poetry the candor of his science, and his themes are concerned with people and their customs in America in the large, and with the flora in the microcosm of the locality he lives in. He is constantly breaking the principles of his esthetic canons. A good old-fashioned romanticist in his earliest work, he becomes an anti-poetic primitive. An imagist with H.D. and Ezra Pound, he becomes an objectivist, the spare line and primary color being essential to his delineation of objects. In fine, the various sections contain enough first-rate work to prove he is a poet who has never stopped growing. That is his virtue, his prime distinction.

If the influence [sic] is drawn that Dr. Williams has preserved too much of his early work, the charge cannot be wholly denied. Yet in this book of approximately three hundred poems, there are at least fifty that will appeal to the modern reader. His best poems are the crystallization of his principles of writing, change as these did. His lyrics in one of the earliest sections, The Tempers, are among the finest that have appeared in our generation. They are cast in the traditional mold, yet note how the form, suggesting a variant idea of Matthew Arnold, does not impede the movement of the verse in this song from The Birth of Venus:

[quotes CEP, 20, lines 1-4]

and how seventeenth century is this example from The Fool's Song:

[quotes CEP, 19, lines 1-5]

In 'Al Que Quiere (To Him Who Wants It)' Dr. Williams forsakes rhyme and again shows his mastery in a lyric, Spring Song, that has the metaphysical quality of Donne:

[quotes CEP, 119, lines 9-16]

To Dr. Williams form is all, whether it is measured in traditional rhythm and rhyme or bears its own cadences in free verse. There is a sardonic bitterness that shows his large humanity in Impromptu: The Suckers, a poet's savage reaction to the Sacco-Vanzetti miscarriage of justice. There is a satirical and acidulous quality in Tract, a poem that tears the sham of indecency that surrounds modern-day funerals, a poem that restores man to dignity in burial.

86. G. S. FRASER, NEW FORMS, NEW FORMS!, 'NEW STATESMAN'

12 April 1952, 440

Consideration of Williams in this composite review is

led into by a brief evaluation of 'Collected Poems' by
Oliver St John Gogarty. Interestingly, too, Williams'
figure for the Muse was Venus emerging from the sea.
   Fraser (b. 1915) is a British teacher, poet and critic.
His books include 'The Modern Writer and His World' (1958)
and 'Vision and Rhetoric' (1959), and, most recently,
'Essays on Twentieth-Century Poets' (1977) and 'Alexander
Pope' (1978).

... His Venus, he says,

>   fell and broke to many pieces:
> Discovered later by a Professor,
> He cried, 'New forms, new forms!' And wrote
> a thesis.

The Professor might have written his thesis on William
Carlos Williams, whose 'new forms,' at their most char-
mingly impudent, suggest democratically that you might as
well write this poem yourself. The audience is not the
proud and tall, but the sensitive and average:

[quotes This is Just to Say, CEP, 354]

Yet Williams has his own rhetoric. Consider the obvious
and effective irony of this passage about the Sacco and
Vanzetti case. One of the points against these two was
that they were scared of policemen:

>   For you knów that évery
> Américan is innocent and at péace in his
> ówn heart. He hásn't a damned thing to be
> afráid of. He knows the góvernment is fór
> him. Whý, when a cóp steps and grábs
> yóu late at night, you just laúgh and think it's
> a héll of a góod jóke -

My stresses indicate these three rhetorical thuds to a
line which Professor Dobrée also finds overlying the five
conventional metrical stresses of Elizabethan blank verse:

   I come to bury Caesar, not to praise him.

Perhaps it is a formal criticism that there is nothing so
definite for them here to overlie, but Elizabethan blank
verse also stretches and contracts a lot, and the important point is that Williams, like a dramatist, seeks to
convey the impression of thinking while he speaks; not of
speaking what he has thought out in advance. The memory

test does not pass him: what stick are images, not words. But between the extremes which I have illustrated of notation and vehemence, he does throw a fresh and innocent light on most aspects of the American scene. Almost unknown here, he is the poet whom I would recommend a visitor to America to study.

87. JOSEPH BENNETT, THE LYRE AND THE SLEDGEHAMMER, 'HUDSON REVIEW'

Vol. V, no. 2, Summer 1952, 295-307

An essay-review on 'The Collected Earlier Poems', 'The Collected Later Poems', the first four books of 'Paterson', 'Make Light of It', 'Autobiography', and Vivienne Koch's 'William Carlos Williams', this in effect sums up the critical 'case' against Williams just at the moment when his late high reputation had begun to develop. Bennett's opening paragraph is omitted.

The gift was, to begin with, purely lyric. It was small and clear, pure and true. It was there; and it flashes through occasionally in the later poetry. It was a single string, delicate and sure, matched with a fine ear and watched with a discriminating eye. The villain was the vice of grandeur, the attempt to forge out of a single metal string a sledgehammer which could beat against the major anvils. Let me begin by trying to show what Williams started out with

[quotes the last four stanzas of Wild Orchard, CEP, 88-9]

There are a number of imagist poems in Williams' texts which are as good as this one - lithe and deft, with a sense of the variations of rhythm. Impressionism - the sensitive registering of nuances of color, sound, taste, smell and touch - is the technique by which the images are built up, and they are left, completed, untouched, stuck on the page with Chinese clarity and precision. Poems such as The Bull, Metric Figure, Winter Trees, and The Dark Day show that Williams perfected the imagist technique beyond any of the group who were working with it before 1914. These poems are excellent and should be preserved.

But in the later work, the images lose their edge, grow pointless - 'the back wings/of the hospital where/ nothing/will grow lie/cinders//in which shine/the broken/ pieces of a green/bottle' - fail to 'come off'. Williams attempts to move beyond the picture - 'Twenty sparrows/ on//a scattered/turd://Share and share/alike.' - and the imagist technique will not carry the 'moral'. The desire to 'be profound' overwhelms, somewhat rancidly, the very sure, restricted range of his talent - 'Round white eyes dotted with/jet live still, alert - in/all gentleness! unabated/beyond the cackle/of death's stinking certainty.' At last we reach the point where his technique, designed for cold and clear-cut sequences of sense-impressionism, breaks down constantly as he stresses it with psychological or emotional burdens?

[quotes CLP, 40, lines 8-17]

By this time, the imagist zeal, the pure fervour for tight clean expression, has been replaced by an attempt to grapple with the major themes, an attempt at 'profundity', at the handling of world-shaking events and crises:

[quotes from Russia, CLP, 93-6]

Williams, prophet and teacher of the nations, salutes Russia as he is about to die, proclaiming 'the power of my dream'. The lines are worthy of Edith Sitwell; they show how much bad poetry is alike the world over. Miss Sitwell has staked out the atom bomb as her literary property and there are hints and references to The Bomb in this poem which suggest that Williams may shortly be in danger of hearing from her solicitors. The touch of self-pity near the end, the grandeur of the old dying genius, adds a final note of vulgarity to a garish piece of self-exhibitionism.

Williams' journalism presents the most conventional and fashionable social attitudes, cliches of social observation served up as profound wisdom, often in a vituperative tone. As a journalist - take his poem Impromptu: The Suckers as an example - he writes in the heat of the moment, for quick consumption, raging and ranting, bombastically, with crude, primitive irony, without reflection, without care, expressing his moral self-righteousness at the expense of some 'current event'. Inevitably the note of self-pity creeps in, and he is off commiserating the hard plight of poets and poetry in general, at random, in any cross-section of his work, without relation to his immediate text.

As a poet, Williams is intensely self-preoccupied, entranced with the image of his own ego. This preoccupation has its roots in his Romanticism, as does the concept of the self as hero - 'I pick the hair from her eyes/and watch her misery/with compassion' - he is always *pitying* someone. It reaches its characteristic development in the sentiment of self-righteousness. The *persona* of the neurotic poetess who appears so persistently throughout 'Paterson' exhorts him.

> to take all your own literature and everyone else's and toss it into one of those big garbage trucks of the Sanitation Department, so long as the people with the top-cream minds and the 'finer' sensibilities use those minds and sensibilities not to make themselves more humane human beings than the average person, but merely as means of ducking responsibility toward a better understanding of their fellow men.....
> [P II, iii, 101]

That is to say, the criterion of value of a literary work is a biographical one, determined by the study of the author's personal life to decide whether he is a more 'humane human being' than the average. Some sort of a norm of average 'humane human' behaviour would have to be established, and then the moral life of the author in question weighed to determine whether it falls short of, or exceeds this norm. The exhortation - an unusually cantankerous display of priggishness, of moral superiority - is made against himself through a *persona*, indicating a split attitude on this question.

Implicit throughout much of Williams' work, and part of his priggishness, is the self-congratulatory feeling that he is more sensitive to moral values than the general run of writers. Self-pity is naturally associated with this attitude, and the theme of the poet as a sacrificial victim of society grows until it becomes one of the major obsessions of his work. This incestuous preoccupation with the pathos of the existence of poets - a preoccupation Romantic in origin - adds to the inwardness of his work. The duties, the destinies, the miseries of poets - the poetry breeds upon itself for subject matter.

The Romanticism which is the mainspring of Williams' compulsions manifests itself in the most obvious ways - zest for the Gothically gruesome; fascination with the natural functions of defecation, and, to an incredible degree, of urination; the loud anti-intelligence

harangues. Such phrases as 'But who are You?' are likely
to occur at random, in any of the poems, and then disappear in a mass of blurred, foggy images, confused ideas,
turgid rhetoric, pathetic fallacy, and sentimentality of
a moaning, sobbing type. He poses in Shelleyan attitudes,
echoes Swinburne, and, Delphically inspired, prophesies
like Elizabeth Barrett Browning.

The Strawberry Hill Gothic is presented with such zest,
in all the gruesome details and incidents of the shorter
poems and 'Paterson', and in such quantity, that it lends
a determining strain of its own to Williams' Romanticism:

[quotes These Purists, CLP, 41, lines 5-9]

What aesthetic effect is secured, what dramatic point is
made, what emotion is expressed or underlined escapes me.
I cannot see in such writings as 'Twenty feet of/guts on
the black sands of Iwo' any care or any patience, anything
but a childish pleasure in the gruesome for gruseomeness'
sake.

The obverse face of the gruesomeness is the sentimentality; an age which takes pleasure in gruesomness is
generally a sentimental age. In Williams' work, there is
a maudlin quality which is not exceeded by any other writer of our time:

[quotes P III, ii, 154, lines 10-17]

The sentimental is often directly mixed with the gruesome,
and in one interesting case, both are combined with the
mail carrier's motto. Occasionally, the indulgence in
raw emotion reaches the point of hysteria:

>   Your face! Give me your face, Yang Kue Fei!
>   your hands, your lips to drink!
>   Give me your wrists to drink -
>   I drag you, I am drowned in you, you
>   overwhelm me! Drink!
>   Save me!

More often it is at the level of the maudlin, incessant
repetitions of the Beautiful Thing motto in 'Paterson', or
in the constant emphasis throughout his work on the passive suffering of helpless victims, the pathos of tortured
creatures who cannot fight back and who do not provide a
subject for dramatic development.

Williams continually uses the word 'love' as a slogan
or a label, but it remains a *word* only - it is never
achieved in the context of the poem. It does not arise

as the supreme unifying crux of a train of symbolism, of
a series of carefully conceived images, or of a dramatic
action. The word is merely tossed in at random - whenever
there is a slow spot - whenever, as in 'Paterson', the
ramble of language, the adventitious succession of images,
the babble of opinions and moralizing hits a slow spot and
will no longer flow. Coagulated, choked with detritus,
the thing grinds to a halt of its own inanity, and the
word 'love' is tossed up into it. The use of the term is
so paltry and disfiguring that the ear is dulled to it;
it becomes a dead word, a killed word, four letters merely
of black print on the page, as harsh and stuffless as any
of the verbal counters knocked about in commercial advertising that once were part of the living language.

Williams' anti-intellectual attitude is puerile in its
implications. 'Let the metaphysical take care of itself,
the arts have nothing to do with it,' he warns in his 1944
Introduction, and proceeds to his old whipping boy, the
university. The dreary, repeated attack on the university throughout his work amounts to a phobia in 'Paterson',
with the hammering repetition of its motto 'No ideas but
in things.' It reveals a pompous, bigoted mind, not
merely anti-intellectual in attitude, but dedicated to the
principle of non-intelligence. Note again that these
attacks occur without relation to their context in the
work itself.

In the long discordant babble of 'Paterson', a Whitmanesque celebration of the Self occurs - 'What shall I
become,//Snot nose, that I have/not been? I enclose it
and/persist, go on.//Let it rot, at my centre./Whose
centre? I stand and surpass/youth's leanness.//My surface
is myself.' [P I, iii, p. 43] This celebration is interrupted, without relevance, by a typical harangue against
the university - that which opposes the Self in its divine
non-intellectual compulsions. The university is made up
of 'clerks/got out of hand forgetting for the most part/to
whom they are beholden.' [P I, iii, 44] This harangue,
the Self versus lowly clerks, is in turn interrupted by a
prose sequence in which a doctor examines a specimen of a
patient's urine. There had been no hint of a medical
theme in the 44 pages of 'Paterson' preceding. This is
immediately followed by a scene in which a young naked
coloured woman proposes copulation. The copulation
sequence is cut short by a Technicoloured picturization
of luxury life, with political overtones. This hackneyed
bit of poster art is then superseded by a prose inventory,
by items, of a small estate left in 1803, to contrast with
the luxury. And so on, for the 228 pages of 'Paterson'.

Williams' use of repetition is perhaps his most

pronounced anti-intellectual device. Such passages as

> Level it down
> for him to build a house
>
> on to build a
> house on to build a house on
> to build a house
> to build a house on to... (Sic. End of poem)

babbling away senselessly, are in their inanity an affront
to the intellect. The overwhelming repetition of sententious phrases - *I believe*; *So be it*; *Beautiful Thing* -
especially marked in 'Paterson', has an effect of sledge-
hammering the mind into eclipses so that it functions as
a sensory organ only.
    The use of onomatopoeia - *Cha cha,*, *chacha, cha*! - seems
an extension of this technique, as do various devices
employed to give an air of pseudo-profundity to simple-
minded statements:

[quotes P IV, ii, 235, lines 1-11]

The passage* is from 'Paterson' and illustrates Williams'
habit of trying for an air of 'profundity' by making a
pompous statement and then reversing it - 'the sea is *not*
our home'; 'the sea *is* our home'. Elsewhere in the same
poem, the Furies are dropped in here and there, as with an
eye-dropper, and splattered irrelevantly over the page:

[quotes P I, i, 19, lines 19-27]

    Williams is quick to pick up and transmit echoes of the
important writers of his time. He depends heavily on
surrealist techniques; there is much in 'Paterson' that
resembles a bad reading of Cocteau or Apollinaire. Joyce,
Eliot and especially Pound reverberate off and on throughout his work, and Marianne Moore will find some of her
fish turning up among Williams' 'undulant seaweed'.
Joyce provides him with the portmanteau word and Anna
Livia's river, but without the intellectual force and con-
cision which made them vivid. Eliot is alternately
attacked, parodied and imitated - almost every style of
Eliot's long career is copied in parts of Williams' verse.
    Pound's influence is extensive. There are a number of
direct references, and there is a full page letter from
Pound which constitutes all of page 165 of 'Paterson'.
Occasionally Williams utilizes typical rhythms of the
'Cantos' - page 65 of 'Paterson' derives rhythmically

direct from the 'Usura' canto. The technique of Williams' page set-up is now and then like that of the 'Cantos' and there are a number of passages in 'Paterson' which are, stylistically, close imitations. The extended section on money and credit theories in 'Paterson' is heavily influenced by the 'Cantos' in page set-up, rhythm and style. Another letter from Pound is quoted briefly, and the credit theories, which are hysterically presented, are essentially the same ones which Pound has attempted to popularize in the 'Cantos' and elsewhere. Unfortunately, their presentation lacks the vivacity and clarity of presentation that Pound was able, earlier, to give the same material.

No doubt Williams had the 'Cantos' in mind in making up his own long poem, 'Paterson', with the ambition of producing a work as inclusive and powerful. But in the 'Cantos', even in the Inferno sections, it is seldom that there is a lapse of intelligence. The material is always organized with an aesthetic, or narrative, or ideological intent, and the less glamorous, even the repellent, sections of the 'Cantos' remain passable and negotiable, to become eventually rewarding. The splendour and accuracy of the 'Cantos' do not justify their occasional failures and their eccentricities of composition. But the splendour and accuracy do tend to mitigate these faults. The point is, that in Williams there is little splendour and little accuracy; and there is not the eccentricity of an intelligent, cunning artisan, but merely incoherence.

Space prevents a detailed formal analysis of 'Paterson'. The poem clearly established Williams' descent from Whitman and Sandburg. It purports to take a city - Paterson - as a type of the world-city, and incorporate this city in various *personae* - a man, Paterson; his daughter, Phyllis; a river at the Falls; a neurotic poetess; a neurotic young male poet; and a myriad set of lesser *personae*. The poetess and the poet correspond at great length - apparently with Mr Williams - discussing their special neuroses. The poetess is the most exasperating of these correspondents - one of her letters, covering pp. 105-113 of 'Paterson' continuously, is nearly nine pages long. At times Wagnerian, at times folksy, the poem flows on, shifting confusingly from one of these *personae* to another, and introducing at haphazard, wholesale prose sections of local history, about forty percent. of which have a gruesome slant. Inexplicably, the poem returns constantly to the voice of Mr Williams himself, apparently *not* as one of the *personae* incorporating the world-city of Paterson, and we get both self-pity and Whitmanesque paeans to the Self; as well as cantankerous opinions and harangues on banking and credit, labour relations, the atom bomb and theories of literary composition.

There is nothing wrong with the idea of taking one city as the world's city, and developing its character in the direction of universals through *personae*. It could, if intelligently developed, be a fruitful and original theme. But to put this stamp on the formless morass of 'Paterson' and claim that it describes some rational plan behind the non-sequential babble is impossible.

Much of it is purely capricious - there is the 'slant' page, where each line of type is slanted at a different angle on the page, and another full page of the poem is devoted to the drilling log of an artesian well. As an example of all that is worst in Williams, take the Madame Curie-Atom Bomb sequence in Part II of Book IV of 'Paterson'. This ridiculous mélange is openly derived from the Hollywood extravaganza, starring Greer Garson, on Madame Curie

[quotes P IV, ii, 202, lines 20-8]

It goes on for twelve pages, a curious mixture of popular science and sentimentality, sprouted in a movie-house, and interspersed throughout the section with harangues on labour relations and banking, and a full-page circular on credit theory presumably provided to Williams for insertion in 'Paterson' by one 'August Walters, Newark, N.J.' Also to be found between the Greer Garson-Madame Curie episodes is a long letter from the young neurotic male poet, continuing for three pages; passages from St Luke and Chaucer; references to Sappho, Sophocles, Woodrow Wilson, Carrie Nation, Artemis, Liberia, the Abbess Hildegard, Tate, the Spanish Civil War, Phideas, Reuther and Ben Shahn; part of a Pound letter; a diarrheal case history in prose concerning 'a stool submitted by the nurse for the usual monthly examination'; and a prose account of an early explorer's landing on the shores of what is presumably New Jersey.

The question arises as to whether Williams' intent is poetic - that is, is he attempting, fundamentally, to write poetry:

When a man had gone up in Russia from a small town to the University he returned a hero - people bowed down to him - his ego, nourished by this, mounted to notable works. Here in the streets the kids say Hello Pete! to me - What can one be or imagine? Nothing is reverenced, nothing looked up to. What can come of that sort of disrespect for the understanding?

This is a short poem of the late Forties, The Unfrocked Priest, written out without any line breaks. Read as prose, the lines are a limply-phrased statement of comparison of the social attitudes towards university graduates in Russia and the United States, with definite overtones of self-pity. Try it as a 'poem':

[quotes The Unfrocked Priest, CLP, 148]

... Or is the arrangement of words into broken lines a hoax; that is, is the arrangement purely adventitious, casting prose - and pretty bad prose, at that - into the 'form' of poetry, but not altering its structure?...
   I think that Williams avoids poetry, for the most part, sidestepping it, and substituting for it sentimentality, pathos, self-revelation, self-pity, surrealism, raw emotion, gruesome anecdotes, and hammering repetition of grand-sounding phrases. In 'Paterson' this is especially marked. His 'poems' are headless and footless. Cut them anywhere, excise their middles, slit them in half, and like amoebas, the jelly flows back together and the animal is the same. Cut off their heads, take off their tails, put their elbows down where their knees should be - no harm is done because the animal is formless, plastic; it all flows together, and any part of 'Paterson' can be taken out and put elsewhere in the poem. The poem can be started at any point in its text, run around its entire circle and brought to a conclusion at the starting-point; and no harm is done.
   Williams' stories are somewhat better than his poetry; a number of them are honestly conceived and unpretentious, particularly the earlier fiction, which displays a conscientious regard for realistic observation, and provides an accurate tone for the subject in hand. There is a certain amount of control; at times humour, and good close-mouthed tough dialogue. But nothing remarkable; at their best, the earlier stories do not rise above the mediocre, with the possible exception of An Old Time Raid, a picaresque piece, vividly executed. The later stories tend to become rambling reminiscences, generally in the first person, disconnected and autobiographical.
   The one long story in the collection, Old Doc Rivers, is an interesting account of the life of a versatile country physician, addicted to dope. Done in a factual, honest style, the piece gives an amusing inside story on medical eccentricities and practice, medical codes and shibboleths, etc. Of the fifty-one stories in the collection, eighteen are directly concerned with medical cases, presented with full clinical detail. The novelty soon

wears off, and the tireless repetition of medical deaths
and disasters seems morbid and dull, unimaginatively
treated. Mere pointless horror - the physical misery and
agony of the moribund and the helpless sick - is often the
only impression that is created by the vignette. The
grotesqueness of medical freaks and freak accidents is
exploited, seemingly for no other purpose than to shock
and stun a reader whose appetite has been numbed by the
long succession of atrocities. A bedbug crawls around on
a coloured boy's eardrum; a prematurely born foetus is
visible through the mass of membranes. And so on.
    Sections of it are straight medical journal material:

> acute purulent mastoiditis of the left side, going on
> to involvement of the left lateral sinus and finally
> the meninges. We might, however, have taken a culture
> of the pus when the ear was first opened and I shall
> always, after this, in suspicious cases. I have been
> told since that if you get a virulent bug like the
> streptococcus mucosus capsulatus ...

The material is not used as Flaubert would have used it,
structurally, to develop a theme, an effect or a character,
but merely for display in itself: an inert mass of medical
information. Williams takes us through a post mortem,
obligingly cutting open a brain, and lets us assist at an
enema - 'Mix up a little soapy water. We'll need some
vaseline.' There are dialogues on socialized medicine -
pro and con - and discussions of Science Vs. Humanity
written in a stilted schoolboy 'essay' manner.
    Williams, in these frankly autobiographical anecdotes,
frequently visualizes himself as a hero. He contrasts
other physicians' money-grasping attitude with his own
deep sacrificial sympathy, his own unselfish outpouring of
loving time and care on the poor and the oppressed. He
defends an injured workman against a wicked, ruthless
corporation. And so on, generally with a sobbing undertone.
    The overall impression of this collection of stories is
one of pointlessness; of haphazard jottings set down at
spare moments without any attempt at dramatic development
or conscious integration. The autobiographical slant is
considered to be enough; it pardons, even justifies, the
most serious lapses. I cannot believe that Williams is
any longer seriously attempting to write fiction.
    His bent is autobiographical; throughout his poems and
prose an intense preoccupation with his own personality is
the compelling impulse in his work. The 'Autobiography',
as printed in a separate volume, is a haphazardly written

account of his prejudices and opinions, unreasoned and un-argued, with more material on the messianically inspired, mystically compelled figure of the poet. In it there is the recurrent tendency to develop situations in which he appears as a hero, a tendency psychopathic in its implications. The *minutiae* of his existence are liberally ladled out. Unrestrained emotion, philosophising in sophomoric platitudes, crass ignorance and stupidity are here given free play; and the passages describing his mystical poetic inspiration and rapid techniques of composition point up many of the faults in his other work.

Vivienne Koch's painstaking study of Williams is a sensible and orderly book, collecting a great mass of facts and references about Williams, and treating the poetry through extended paraphrase and close textual analysis. There is a minimum attempt at evaluation, other than her statement that Williams' poetry is his most enduring achievement, and her rather tentative subscription to the theory that in 'Paterson' Williams has performed a function messianic in nature, consistent with his mystical calling. At this point, and to reinforce such a view, she quotes from the Sermon on the Mount, concluding her study of his poetry with this quotation. The general tone of her book is mildly favourable, and cautious. She is not afraid to censure Williams on occasion, but in the main it is a sympathetic and inconclusive study.

Williams is not without his virtues; the equipment he started out with is still with him. No doubt if he dug far enough into the detritus he could refurbish that pure talent for images, sounds, colours and textures which he enjoyed in earlier years. But the 'serious' work is a failure, and a complete failure, utter and ignominious. To hammer against the major anvils requires intelligence, rational discrimination, dramatic skill, psychological acuity, and emotional subtlety - especially intelligence. And patience and care. These qualities simply do not form a part of Williams' poetic equipment. The verdict of criticism must inevitably be to link Williams with Sandburg; and the difference between them - Williams' relative superiority - will be seen to be one of degree, not of kind. That is to say, Williams has a better ear and uses a more subtle and evolved technique.

Note

*Note the imitation of Joyce - *whither*, (*wither*), and the 'borrowing' of theme. Also the open lift from the 'Cantos' -*Put wax rather in your ears* and the *Thalassa!* echoes.

'The Build-Up'

New York, October 1952

88. WINFIELD TOWNLEY SCOTT, 'A JOY IN PEOPLE AND A PASSION
FOR LIFE', 'NEW YORK HERALD TRIBUNE BOOKS'

2 November 1952, 6

Scott (1910-68) was an American poet, author of 'Collected
Poems' (1962).

Any reader of 'The Autobiography of William Carlos
Williams,' published last year, is in a position to know
that Dr. Williams' trilogy of novels - begun fifteen years
ago with 'White Mule,' continued with 'In the Money' and
now concluded with the 'Build-Up' - is biographical. The
'Autobiography' contains an abundance of clews that the
German-born printer, Joe Stecher, and his ambitious,
Norwegian-born wife, Gurlie, of the novels are Dr.
Williams' in laws, the Paul Hermans; that their relatives
and children and friends are all drawn from life, as are
even the events of these novels, and that their daughter
Flossie is, of course, the Flossie of Dr. Williams' poems.
'White Mule' opens with the birth of Flossie, and her mar-
riage to the poetry-writing 'Doc' (herein known as Charlie
Bishop) occurs near the end of 'The Build-Up.'

This information is not irrelevant literary gossip; it
bears directly, and with revelation, on what Dr. Williams
has attempted in these novels. All but plotless, they
narrate an American 'success story,' 1893-1917, of an
immigrant whose solid abilities, goaded by a money-loving
wife, carry him to prosperity; a story typical enough, and
sufficiently of its era, to rate as a genre piece. 'The

Build-Up' is a model of how infrequent the historical or
sociological touches need be to achieve the flavor of past
times. But more profoundly, these novels are exercises in
the recreation of memories long viable within a family.
They are a record of actual lives. And where the 'imagination' superimposes its creativity on this material what
in fact we have are still further extensions of Dr. Williams' ability as recorder - the clean objectivity of
description, really tactile, which distinguishes his best
poems; his remarkable ear for speech; above all, an unsur-
passed skill at setting down exactly how babies and small
children behave.

The method of the novels, then, is a clinical purity of
observation: the thing, the moment, the person seen
directly, each for its own sake. Reality is to be
achieved as nearly as possible as though it were not fil-
tered through an observer.

The disadvantages are evident. 'The Build-Up,' excus-
ably plotless except as biographical narrative, sometimes
seems planless. Incidents are spun out without apparent
relation to the integrity or meaning of the novel; presumably they are here because they 'really happened.' At
such points the novel meanders in non-functional anecdote.
Sometimes events are touched upon - such as stolen money
orders at Joe Stecher's printing plant - without further
mention after what would seem to be ominous preparation;
or a minor character - such as the flirtatious Elvira -
is brought on thoroughly enough to arouse curiosity but
is banished as though forgotten. The sharp ear for small
talk sometimes records more than is needed. Finally, how
to conclude this sort of novel? Dr. Williams' solution is
a rather hurried transcript, a petering-out: stop.

One disadvantage of the clinical method - the chill air
of detachment - is triumphantly avoided: these novels
shine with a joy in people and a passion for life. The
emotion is simply not sentimental. The innocence with
which the common trivia of middle-class life are seen
gives them the importance and beauty of authentic thing....

89. ERNEST JONES, 'THE EXCITEMENT OF THE FACTS IS ALL THERE IS', 'NATION'

8 November 1952, 434

... Unhappily, just as Dr. Williams's short stories are only so many sights, sounds, and actions wonderfully observed and set down, so 'The Build Up,' like the novels which preceded it, is, with the exception of the last badly written chapters, a sequence of similar sights, sounds, and actions which never becomes a novel. The reader, while admiring the superb talent which contrives to make the daily facts of daily life so exciting, is regularly disappointed because the excitement of the facts is all there is to hold his attention. This writing assumes that any experience is, somehow, meaningful, and that any recaptured fragments of experience, put together, will somehow constitute a novel. But the details, the sketches, and the episodes do not result in character and action. Gurlie is for a while an exception. She starts out as a magnificent and irresistible natural force; and then, because the last chapters lapse into a series of notes, she disintegrates into a stock figure, someone's mother-in-law, brainless, destructive, and driving....

'The Desert Music'

New York, March 1954

90. KENNETH REXROTH, A POET SUMS UP, 'NEW YORK TIMES BOOK REVIEW'

28 March 1954

Rexroth (b. 1905) is an American poet, playwright, translator and essayist. His publications include 'The Collected Shorter Poems' (1966) and 'The Collected Longer Poems' (1968). Some years after the present review, in his The Influence of French Poetry on American (1958, written as an introduction to an anthology of American poets in French translation) (1) Rexroth wrote: 'Today it is William Carlos Williams who emerges as the greatest of this group - the classic American modernists - and as America's greatest living poet' ('Assays', Norfolk, Conn., 1961, 160). Rexroth won the Copernicus Award of the Academy of American Poets in 1975. 'The Morning Star' (1979) is his most recent book.

It is a long time, in fact over a generation, since it has been possible to take seriously any American poet as both an accomplished and a genuinely popular artist. The last writers to lay claim to such a role were Robert Frost, Amy Lowell and Carl Sandburg. As all the world knows, American poetry is over-specialized, academic, ambiguous in the worst sense. It reaches only an audience of specially favored academicians who like to call themselves poets - if it reaches them. T. S. Eliot reaches a temporary audience of spiritually puzzled middle-class adolescents who soon outgrow him as their fathers outgrew Ernest Dowson before him. Ezra Pound is read by a similar audience, largely for the uncritical reason that he is known to be 'agin it.'

It is possible that in William Carlos Williams modern poetry in the United States has the only writer who stands any chance of being assimilated into our culture permanently at his face value. Certainly once the reader has adjusted to the novelty of Williams' metric, he is the living poet who looks most like a classic. The novelty is only superficial. In actual fact his poetic line is organically welded to American speech like muscle to bone, like the choruses of Euripides were welded to the speech of the Athenians in the market place.

Since Baudelaire, poetry in the Western World has concerned itself with the spiritual ills of a demoralized society. Williams has always concerned himself with the same things that gave Herrick and Theocritus and Horace their subject-matter. Dr. Williams has diagnosed what so many poets have interpreted as a metaphysical crisis of the Spirit and the Absolute as a simple disorder in our human relationships, acute but temporary.

Throughout his earlier career Williams was content to construct poems as independent esthetic objects. He worked in what Whitehead called the realm of presentational immediacy. There was little discursive expository writing as such. General ideas, philosophical notions, exhortation were all implicit. In recent years, beginning with his long poem, 'Paterson,' he has veered slowly around toward a more discursive style. 'Paterson' is a philosophy of life and a criticism of society, but these aspects emerge most distinctly from the juxtaposition of objective images.

In 'The Desert Music' it would seem that Williams has decided to write about the meaning of his own work - to embark on a sort of summing up and stock-taking of his career thus far. So the title poem is an explicit statement of the irreducible humaneness of the human being - a sort of manifesto of humanism in the guise of a description of a visit to Juarez. To a Dog Injured in the Street is an explicit statement of what the other great doctor of our time called reverence for life. The Host is an explicit statement of the sacramental nature of reality.

Deep Religious Faith and the following poem, The Garden, are an explicit statement of Williams' own brand of Franciscanism - the transcendence of nature in nature. Work in Progress is apparently a continuation of 'Paterson' - a summing up of a whole personal world outlook. And, not least, to confound the critics who didn't know he was a classic, Williams has included a translation of the first idyll of Theocritus - probably the best in English to date, certainly the best in America - the point of course being that Williams sounds just like Theocritus and Theocritus sounds just like Williams.

In many ways this is the best book except 'Paterson' and his 'Collected Poems' that Williams has ever published. It is very wise, very mature, very quiet, very relaxed and extremely unpretentious and unworried. These have always been his outstanding qualities, but hitherto they have not been brought so much to the fore. This masterful easiness shows in everything. The metric flows as smoothly as water and is completely obedient to his will. There is no torment in it whatever. The images have a clarity and an inevitability that make them seem completely uncontrived, like the events in a sequence of sublime happenstance, rather than details in a work of art.

The ideas are simple, indisputable, presented with calm maturity. All the cracker-barrel flavor of small town eccentricity which Williams sometimes shared with Ezra Pound has vanished. Again the schism between Williams the artist and Williams the suburban doctor, which sometimes disturbed his balance, has been healed. He speaks about himself, his practice, his children, his friends all in the same tone. All of his life is assimilated to one set of values.

This description sounds like a set piece, 'a definition of great poetry, or how to write like a classic.' That is precisely what it is intended to be. I prophesy that from now on, as Williams grows older, he will rise as far above his contemporaries as Yeats did above his in his latter years. The fruit has ripened on the tree.

Note

1 See 'Bibliography', Item T22.

91. JOHN CIARDI, THING IS THE FORM, 'NATION'

24 April 1954, 368

Ciardi (b. 1916) is an American poet, teacher, editor and translator.

[quotes closing 12 lines of To Daphne and Virginia PB, 78-9]

'There is no form. *Thing* is the form.' I have heard him argue it a dozen times, waving his arms at the audience. 'Sonnets, iambic pentameter, couplets - you have to do away with all that old stuff!'

And Williams does away with it. And wins. But at a cost, too. Rejecting every traditional measure, he not only has to play out his game but has to invent it at the same time. That he succeeds so often is a tribute to his own immense inventiveness. And, even more, to the fact that he is richly stored with the very traditions he sweeps away with a wave of the arm. Down with meter, yes. But the Williams poems that really lift and go are the ones whose free cadences are haunted by the memory of meter:

>   A pair of robins
>   is building a nest for the second time this
>   season.
>   Men against their reason, speak of love
>   sometimes,
>   when they are old. It is all they can
>   do.
>   - Or watch a heavy goose who waddles,
>   slopping
>   noisily, in the mud of his pool.

To typeset it closer to metric form is no help. I like the poem better in Williams's own triple-split line. But resetting will at least serve to indicate that it is not so far from metric as the wave of the arm would indicate.

Not long ago Williams appeared on a television show to discuss Robert Penn Warren's 'Brother to Dragons' and insisted over and over again: 'There has to be some principle of regularity.' Warren argued back that the poem was written in a loose five-beat line, but Williams would have none of it. It remains my impression that most of the poems in this book could be reset into a near-regular line no looser than Warren's, which, God knows, is loose enough to be nearly aimless.

Certainly to question what one admires is no irreverence. Williams is one of our great ones. But I cannot help thinking that his achievement is possible only because he ignores most of his aesthetic pronouncements and relies on his own ear and pulse beat, and because he has stored himself so richly with the great measures of iambic pentameter that their march-and-go asserts itself just under his own best cadences.

The danger is that the rush and immediacy of the fact for its own sake may overwhelm that management-of-the-fact which we call poetic measure - whether metric or cadenced. Watching the magazine appearances of Williams's poems in the triple-split line he has been working of late has been an exciting experience. The three parts of the line, if not measurably the same length, *feel* equal. A nice principle of containment seems to be at work, neither too demanding nor inadequate. Yet Williams allows himself to break away at many points from even as simple a measure as this.

That wave of the arm again: 'You have to do away with all that old stuff.'

And on the other hand Williams on Warren: 'There has to be some principle of regularity.'

And so there must. And though a man of great intuition may persuade himself that he is following no rule while his very breath-groups observe a real regularity, the problem remains from the root. Williams first found himself as an Imagist. And Imagism may almost be defined as a poetic movement that died a-borning because it could never decide what made a poetic line. Everything else was there - at least in the good ones and certainly in Williams. The passion, the perception, the wish-in-motion. But not the line. The Imagists, and Williams with them, set themselves a heartbreaking task: they not only had to win the wrestling match with form, they had to invent their opponent every time....

92. WILLIAM CARLOS WILLIAMS EXPLAINS HIS THEORY OF MEASURE IN A LETTER TO RICHARD EBERHART

23 May 1954, included in SL, 325-7

... I have never been one to write by rule, even by my own rules. Let's begin with the rule of counted syllables, in which all poems have been written hitherto. That has become tiresome to my ear.

Finally, the stated syllables, as in the best of present-day free verse, have become entirely divorced from the beat, that is the measure. The musical pace proceeds without them.

Therefore the measure, that is to say, the count,

having got rid of the words, which held it down, is returned to the *music*.

The words, having been freed, having been allowed to run all over the man, 'free', as we have mistakenly thought. This has amounted to no more (in Whitman and others) than no discipline at all.

But if we keep in mind the *tune* which the lines (not necessarily the words) make in our ears, we are ready to proceed.

By measure I mean musical pace. Now, with music in our ears the words need only be taught to keep as distinguished an order, as chosen a character, as regular, according to the music, as in the best prose.

By its *music* shall the best of modern verse be known and the *resources* of the music. The refinement of the poem, its subtlety, is not to be known by the elevation of the words but - the words don't so much matter -- by the resources of the *music*.

To give you an example from my own work - not that I know anything about what I have myself written:

> count: not that I ever count when writing but, at best, the lines must be capable of being counted, that is to say, *measured* - (believe it or not) - At that I may, half consciously, even count the measure under my breath as I write. -

(approximate example)
(1) The smell of the heat is boxwood
      (2) when rousing us
            (3) a movement of the air
(4) stirs our thoughts
      (5) that had no life in them
            (6) to a life, a life in which
(or)
(1) Mother of God! Our Lady!
      (2) the heart
            (3) is an unruly master:
(4) Forgive us our sins
      (5) as we
            (6) forgive
(7) those who have sinned against

Count a single beat to each numeral. You may not agree with my ear, but that is the way I count the line. Over the whole poem it gives a pattern to the meter that can be felt as a new measure. It gives resources to the ear which result in a language which we hear spoken about us every day....

93. LOUIS L. MARTZ, IN THE PASTORAL MODE, 'YALE REVIEW'

Vol. XLIV, no. 2, Winter 1955, 303-5

Dylan Thomas' 'Under Milk Wood' is one of the five other works Martz reviews in this essay.

There is a startling, almost uncanny kinship between 'Under Milk Wood' and the poems that make up Williams' 'Desert Music.' The clue, perhaps, is best found in Williams' translation here from the first Idyll of Theocritus, the opening dialogue where shepherd and goatherd invite each other to pipe and sing. Williams' superb translation ends with the goatherd's invitation, promising as a reward a bowl whose decorations symbolize 'the pastoral mode': leaves, flowers, a girl courted by two youths, an aged fisherman, a vineyard, a boy plaiting rushes.

But Williams speaks of more than these things: he builds a stark background of sickness, age, and imminent death, while the poems carry out the theme announced on the first page:

> No defeat is made up entirely of defeat - since
> the world it opens is always a place
>   formerly
>   unsuspected.

The poems move to create such a place, where, as in the poem of affection for his daughters-in-law (To Daphne and Virginia) the 'healing,' 'penetrant' odor of boxwood 'on an old farm' grows to indicate the bond of love. Elsewhere an orchestra of bird-songs tunes up for the sunrise; Catholic veneration of Mary is sympathetically described as veneration for a profound natural 'principle of the world'; an 'ungainly' yellow flower, seen through glass in winter, becomes a sign of cure; a long, intimate reminiscence with his wife is given chiefly in terms of flower-images; while perhaps the best poem in this florilegium is set in

[quotes lines 24-36 of The Mental Hospital Garden, PB, 97-8]

The poem (The Garden) tells of human recovery under the

bounty of nature and the 'kindly spirit' of St. Francis -
patron saint of this hospital. Young couples, conval-
escing, embrace on the spring-lawns; then, as summer
matures and they grow stronger, 'The lovers raise their
heads,/at that which has come over them,' and 'Blinded by
the light/they walk bewildered,' 'incredulous,' as they
sense their cure. 'Filled with terror' at the sight of
the new world before them, they shrink away, but at last

>   emboldened,
>   parting the leaves before her,
>   stands in the full sunlight ...

The spacing of these poems is a subtle form of punctuation, giving just the right pace and emphasis when the
poem is read aloud. And Williams' poetry (like Thomas's)
must be read aloud: the music will never come right otherwise. Every poem here, after several such readings, will
come right - except for the title-poem, where Williams
tries to weave a harmony-amid-tatters out of sounds and
glimpses from a visit to El Paso and Juarez. I cannot
make this poem work: the fragments will not form the
'dance' that the poet announces.

'Selected Essays'

New York, November 1954

94. NICHOLAS JOOST, THE DEVELOPMENT OF AN AMERICAN POET, 'COMMONWEAL'

Vol. LXI, no. 10, 10 December 1954, 291-3

Joost (b. 1916), who was on the editorial staff or 'Poetry', 1951-4, is the author of several books on the history of 'Dial' magazine, notably 'Scofield Thayer and the Dial' (1964).

The essays in Dr. Williams' present book span the years from 1920 to 1954. The first and earliest (1920) is Prologue to Kora in Hell; on through the dates we read the titles: George Antheil and the Cantilene Critics of 1927; Marianne Moore of 1931; Pound's Eleven New 'Cantos' of 1934; Carl Sandburg's Complete Poems of 1948; and among the latest, in 1954, a memorial essay on Dylan Thomas. Both Miss Moore and Mr. Pound are allotted two essays apiece- single essays are devoted to esthetic contemporaries - Sandburg, Cummings - and to poets too young to be contemporaries - Shapiro, Lowell, Thomas, Charles Henri Ford. There are essays about painters - Charles Sheeler and Pavel Tchelitchew - and about theories of art - The Basis of Faith in Art, The Poem as a Field of Action, On Measure - Statement for Cid Corman. But even this extended inventory of the contents of the 'Selected Essays' can only begin to categorize the subjects and ideas that, quite literally, run riot through the book. It is rich and varied fare, a salmagundi of esthetic fashions in America since 1920.

Actually Dr. Williams' work begins much earlier than his first essay indicates. His first volume, 'Poems,' was issued in 1909, and he contributed to 'Poetry' in the year of its inception, 1912-13, as an acquaintance of the group surrounding Ezra Pound, whom he met at the University of Pennsylvania, but the poet and his coterie were, we learn, 'important' to the young medical student. In short, Dr. Williams was intimately concerned with the beginnings of the great revolution in American poetry, a movement as influential for American literature as the 1913 Armory Show proved to be for American art. This revolution-spearheaded by Pound's Imagist group of poets and critics - was of course much more complex and comprehensive than the Imagist program and its adherents; there were other influences and poets as well. But the Imagists were the dominant, the best organized, the best or at least most vociferously led, and the most intelligibly programmatic.

Dr. Williams, however, has always stood outside coteries. We find him in these essays passionately involved but involved as an individual rather than as a member of a group writing according to its poetic canons. He was, he tells us in the Preface to this book, raised in a 'religious training [that] was, as they say, liberal.' The reluctance to categorize himself even as a 'liberal' by religious training is typical of his cast of mind, and the ambivalence it reveals is basic to an understanding of this poet-critic's work.

Dr. Williams, with his scientific background, is completely at home in dealing with the concrete, the singular, the sensible. Despite his wonderful enthusiasm for ideas, despite his redoubtable learning and his wide experience of life, despite even his wide charity gained from that learning and experience, his sympathies obviously lie with eternal flux rather than with eternal order. His cast of mind is Heraclitean - not Aristotelian, not Platonic. He tells us that 'modern poetry ... and especially the free verse of Walt Whitman, opened my eyes.' It is true, that remark: Whitman's ambivalent romantic heritage is the heritage not alone of Dr. Willians but of Americans in general.

Whitman believed that our life is a Long Journey into the unknown - eternal, without beginning and end, except that we moved upward from some vague primeval slime toward some vague union with the Great Camerado. Unlike Emerson, Whitman remained enough of a Christian still to be interested in beginnings and endings, even though his romantic idealism obviated the possibility of an eschatology. Inheriting the optimism of the eighteenth-century Deists,

Whitman was obssessed with the Journey itself, eternal
progress toward the ideal; yet the fact of idealism pre-
sumes stasis, and the Long Journey becomes not progress
toward a goal but a squirrel's nimble padding inside its
little treadmill. Beyond Whitman lies the ultimate self-
indulgence; for the artist, of solipsism - the poem about
its own significance, or about the poet's psychological
processes in creating it.

'Whitman was right in breaking our bounds but, having
no valid restraints to hold him, went wild. He didn't
know any better. At the last he resorted to a loose sort
of language with no discipline about it of any sort and
we have copied its worst feature, just that.' We must,
then, forget Whitman, who nevertheless instinctively was
on the right track, which was to find a 'new discipline.'
We must get on our own course, must invent new modes to
take the place of those now outworn. Whitman, we see,
was the cause of many poetic failures, for: 'No verse can
be free, it must be governed by some measures, but not by
the old measure.... We have to return to some measure but
a measure consonant with our time and not a mode so rotten
that it stinks.'

One can only agree firmly with Dr. Williams, with the
qualification that he is being unfair to Whitman, who did
not write free verse. 'I among the rest have much to
answer for,' writes Dr. Williams in this context. And
assuredly his poetic generation must come to a reckoning
for not having seen, as Gerard Manley Hopkins, that
Whitman at his representative best wrote not free
verse but a finely controlled polyryhthmic verse with its
own laws developed in consonance with the inner nature of
English speech and poetics. The fault lies not with Whitman, but with the poets who failed to understand his prosody and his esthetics.

But where is 'measure'? 'Relativity gives us the cue
... We have today to do with poetic, as always, but a
relatively stable foot, not a rigid one.' Is Dr. Williams
explaining that the discoveries of Whitman and Hopkins
were after all, the ones we ought to make for ourselves?
Are Whitman's polyrythmic verse and Hopkins' sprung rhythm
the poetic standard for our century? But surely they have
nothing to do with 'relativity,' mathematical or otherwise, in the cant sense of the word; and any systematic
esthetics takes into account the fact that words and
sounds and meanings exist in a complex of relatedness.
A reading of good poems - or, if one wants to fall back on
theory, of the 'Poetics' - leads to such a conclusion more
readily than any vague appeal to mathematics to come to
the rescue of the arts - which, it would seem, are fully

capable of rescuing themselves and living by their own laws. And as for this standard of 'measure,' it is well-known. Its law has always been both musical and mathematical, as Plato and Coventry Patmore were aware, and wrote.

'Without measure we are lost.' Yes. But no 'new measure' is a true measure unless it partakes of the eternal as well as the revolutionary. Dr. Williams' fashionable talk about relativity makes one rather uneasy, for it displays the gaps and patches and tatters in the robe of that magician, Secular Liberalism, whose want is Science. Dr. Williams' quick, warm charity one can only hope to emulate. His scientifically trained eye is, paradoxically, at the service of poetic art; he creates some of the finest poems in the American grain; and it is this magic music which enchants us.

95. JOHN R. WILLINGHAM, PARTISAN OF THE ARTS, 'NATION'

22 January 1955, 78

Willingham (b. 1919) is an American teacher, editor and critic.

... The major concerns of the essays are the nature of poetry in general and the development of a specifically American tradition. Dr. Williams asserts the essential contemporaneity of all great poetry. The major poets of the past provide for the poet of today an achievement not for imitation but for attempted outstripping. Since it is in the structure of the art form that modernity or lack of modernity is manifest, the art of the past offers a proving-ground: 'As writers we shall find in writing our most telling answers, and as writers it is we who whould uncover them. That is our business. If, as writers, we are stuck somewhere, along with others, we must go back to the place, if we can, where a blockage may have occurred.'

On the subject of American art and poetry Williams offers some sound advice for the reinterpretation of American literature and reveals not a little about his own poetic aims. Whitman, he says, freed American verse from an obsolete, restrictive, and hence meaningless poetic; as a pointer, 'a key man to whom I keep returning,' Whitman

brought the glow of health and vitality to American
poetry. When, in reckless enthusiasm for the iconoclasm
he had begotten, he allowed his own poetry to degenerate
into meaningless catalogues and structural confusion, he
failed; when the later *vers librists* built upon the failures of Whitman, they emphasized and extended the failure.

But in Williams's view Eliot and his followers were
guilty of a worse crime: in their horror at the softness
and looseness of free verse they set out to assassinate
the achievement of Walt Whitman. They fomented a poetry
for the 'instructed few'; 'and instructed poetry is all
secondary in the exact sense that Dante's "Commedia" is
secondary where it is archaic and fettered against a broad
application of the great tradition.' It is to be expected
that Williams, if he had to take sides somewhere in this
basic conflict, should always line up with Whitman in
spite of his failures.

Grenades are tossed, with considerable premeditation,
right and left. But it is clear, I think, that as both
artist and critic Williams is carrying on an attack against
an intrenched, baneful, derivative art - an attack first
formulated clearly in 1916 and 1917 by the men associated
on the 'Seven Arts' magazine. Significantly, Waldo Frank
in both 'Salvos' (1924) and 'The Rediscovery of America'
(1929) recognized a close connection between Williams's
inclinations and the aim of the 'Seven Arts'group; the
writings of Williams, Frank said, 'partake of a promising
apocalyptic method,' whose practitioners 'must literally
make the plastic form of their vision from the plasmic
substance of their experience - without obedience to con-
ceptual heritage or aesthetic tradition.' As Williams
pointed out in his 'Autobiography' (1951), he has found
meaning as both individual and poet in 'the fates of ideas
living against the grain in a nondescript world'; he has
never been quite comfortable in an alliance with any
school or party line. Like Whitman he has preferred to
follow his own bent with 'creeds and schools in abeyance.'
Though he admires and has profited by some aspects of the
Imagists, of the work of Eliot, Pound, Stevens, Marianne
Moore, and others, Williams has never found it necessary
to be an expatriate or to ransack the literature of the
past for images and forms. Emerson's demand for a writer
to saturate himself with reality is probably met more
nearly by Williams than by any other living American poet.
If 'Paterson,' 'In the American Grain,' and the collected
poems have not made clear the basis for his constant
approach to the universal through the local, these essays
will certainly show that Williams, the artist and the
thinker, is American in the best sense - a sense shared by

Thoreau, Emerson, Whitman, Alfred Stieglitz, Randolph
Bourne, and Hart Crane.

96. THOMAS H. CARTER ON WILLIAMS' 'CAMPAIGN BULLETINS',
'SHENANDOAH'

Vol. VI, no. 2, Spring 1955, 72-7

The review concludes with a brief consideration of 'The
Desert Music'.
Carter (1931-63) edited 'Shenandoah' for two years.
His posthumous 'Essays and Reviews' (1968) includes, as
Professor Ashley Brown says in the introduction, a 'long
essay on William Carlos Williams, which owes something
to Yvor Winters' "Primitivism and Decadence", and is one
of the most judicious examinations of Williams that have
yet been made'.

This rich selection of Williams' prose papers is in the
nature of an event. It will do him honour. But we must
not mistake these essays and notes for literary criticism,
at least in the ordinary sense: they are rather strata-
gems, or campaign bulletins, issued over a period of years
by a poet closely associated with the 'modern' movement in
literature; 'modern', in fact, is one of his key terms.
Williams himself, in a 1920 manifesto, gives us the clue:

> Nothing is good save the new. If a thing have novelty
> it stands intrinsically beside every other work of
> artistic excellence. If it have not that, no loveli-
> ness or heroic proportion or grand manner will save it.
> It will not be saved above all by an attenuated
> intellectuality.

I doubt that Williams means us to take this dogma
altogether seriously; but these essays demonstrate that it
has remained an integral part of his procedures. It is
the remark of a poet, not a critic. Yet most of the
pieces in this collection do deal with literature; and
once we grasp their essentially polemical nature, we may
safely enjoy their art. Williams has one great advantage
over the mere critic; he has known well so many of the

major figures in contemporary letters, and he blends his
memories of them -

> Marianne had two cords, cables, rather, of red hair
> coiled around her rather small cranium when I first
> saw her and was straight up and down like the two-by-
> fours of a building under construction.

- into his commentary on their work: he deals in startling, sometimes significant juxtapositions of detail and
theory, like Ford Madox Ford on Conrad. The result is a
sort of pre-criticism with a fine novelistic texture.
Many of Williams' judgments are shrewd. Here he is on
Miss Moore:

> The 'useful result' is an accuracy to which this
> simplicity of design greatly adds. The effect is
> for the effect to remain 'true'; nothing loses its
> identity because of the composition, but the parts
> in their assembly remain quite as 'natural' as before
> they were gathered. There is no 'sentiment'; the
> softening effect of word upon word is nil; every-
> thing is in the style.

It will be noted that Williams salutes Miss Moore for
those qualities which distinguish the best of his early
verse. And now Pound's first 'Cantos':

> It stands out from almost all other verse by a faceted
> quality that is not muzzy, painty, wet. It is a dry
> clean use of words. They are themselves not dead.
> They have not been violated by 'thinking'. They have
> been used willingly by thought.

Williams' criticism, like his other work, is crippled
finally by a lack of formal design; it is a thing that he,
with his hard eye for the small fact, cannot see clearly.
The form of most of Williams' short, early lyrics was
imported into the poem together with its subject; the
subject, not so much organized as perceived by the imagination, did not become part of a design, it dictated its
own characteristic structure; so, here, Williams' best
criticism sticks close to its matter. He doesn't soar
very well.

From these essays, written at random over thirty-four
years, there emerge two major concerns; they dominate
Williams' thought so completely, in fact, that what is
called a collection has the implicit unity of a tract.
The relationship with his verse, we may incidentally

observe, is intimate.

First there is his conception of an America which is the combined sum of the gains and regressions of an alien people trying to erect a new life, and a new language, in a strange, hostile land. Their limited successes are authentic, primary, good; their failures, false, secondary, bad. The question can nearly be stated in Laurentian terms of 'becoming' and 'Being'. For the artist, says Williams, 'the local is the universal'; and he writes lovingly and well of what, escaping Europe's dead hand, he finds to be truly *local*. Hence Pound and Eliot, raiding all time and many cultures for the foundations of excellence, erred at the start; Kenneth Burke, relating Laforgue to an American environment, was right: ' ... criticism must first be in contact with the world for which it is intended.'

With Rebecca West, Williams is very severe: her English background, threatened by advances it couldn't cope with, blinded her to Joyce's achievement. This may be so; but we are justified in wondering if this is purely an *English* sin. The burden of Williams' remarks here, as I follow them, is that the American *by definition* operates from a vantage point beyond the grasp of the European writer. It would appear that Williams, as an artist, felt impelled to resist the pressures of the tradition represented by Miss West; such a struggle, against a pervasive cultural climate, has elements of the heroic. And the artist - though not the critic - can afford to be provincial. If Williams is ultimately unconvincing, it is because he, in response to personal need, has indulged in a mystique of America. Like Lawrence, he strikes off fine sparks, but finally it is all too simple.

Williams' dominant concern, I imagine superior even to his preoccupation with the American background he has rendered with such immediacy, has been properly with the nature of language, of style, even to the subversion of subject matter: a strange emphasis, perhaps, for the man who, defending the integrity of *things*, first introduced us to the importance of red wheelbarrows and the precise movements of a cat; he must mean that the subject resides, sometimes casually, in the election of the poet, but the poem is created by its style. There is also structure, a formal ordering, which he mentions in passing. Williams' marvellous responsiveness to words leads him to an extremist position, similar to Pound's when the latter declared that the painter's brushwork will reveal the degree of usury manifest in a particular epoch. Here Williams speaks of Sylvia, Tietjens' foil in 'Parade's End':

Sylvia is the lie, bold-faced, the big crude lie, the
denial ... that is now having its moment. The opponent
not of *le mot juste* against which the French have today
been rebelling, but something of much broader implications; so it must be added that if our position in the
world, the democratic position, is difficult, and we
must acknowledge that it is difficult, the Russian
position, the negative position, that is, the Communist
position is still more difficult. All that is implied
in Ford's writing.

That is true enough, in a sense, if by writing we mean
also what the book is about, and the environment that is
implicit in it; but it states the case far too strongly.
It posits a burden that the language, whose purpose lies
elsewhere, may carry only incidentally, and that the
critic locates perilously, beginning from a position, I
would judge, arrived at by a cultural determinism and
supported by evidences inferred from below the executive
level of style. I sympathize with Williams, and I believe
him; but I don't think the critic's job, as he implies it,
can be honestly done, at least not without endangering
the poem or fiction. It is at this level I would like to
see critics make their attack; but he will be an agile man
who emerges with the poem unviolated.

Throughout the 'Selected Essays', Williams turns again
and again to the problem of an American language, distinct
from an outmoded English and competent to grapple with the
bare, hard fact; a new language for a new world. As evi-
dential support, he adduces Whitman, who made the first
break but, crippled by a lack of formal intention, ran
rapidly to wind. Auden migrated to this country seeking
an authentic language, one not snarled in dead apparatus,
but had the sound of English too much in his ears and so
lost.

If Williams, speaking out of his need as an artist,
means the poet must work with the idiom as he hears and
fashions it, we can only agree. If he means that the poet
wastes himself who lets a convention alien to him vitiate
his work, we shan't argue; this is sound enough. But I am
not sure that this is what Williams has in mind at all; I
think it is, partly, bound up with his mystical approach to
to America. There *is* an American language, if it is compared with that of England (or France or Italy) - loose,
connotative, tending to become shapeless, but with unique
effects inherent in it. One can begin with minimum essentials and make it say almost anything; Hemingway taught us
that. Actually, however, as Williams must know, there are
several American languages, of which Hemingway represents

only the midwestern variety: it is surely commonplace to note that Hemingway and Faulkner, both drawing on local idioms, achieve singularly dissimilar effects.

I have been harsh about these 'Selected Essays', deliberately so, for their actual human attractiveness (especially since Williams is being institutionalized by many young writers) tends to disguise his weakest points, areas where the inexperienced may be, and are being, side-tracked. In prose and verse, Williams' acute sensitivity to language, to words but not always their meanings, often betrays him into what Joseph Bennett has called, with some fairness, 'compulsive babbling'. (1) Several essays in the present volume, most of them previously unpublished, amount to little more than an affected prose stutter. I can see no excuse for this kind of thing; like certain of Williams' bad poems, it represents self-indulgence at its most debilitating.

It may be interesting to inquire into the cause of the these lapses. First, at the heart of Williams' writing (and perhaps of his thinking), there is a core of genuine incoherence, a real inability to deal in logical relations; this has made his poems, generally speaking, most effective when he allows his meaning to emerge from the juxtaposition of several objects, or ideas treated as objects. At the same time, it seems hardly necessary to point out that there is a good deal more to poems than logic, or that they sometimes get along very well without it. But not without structure of some kind, as 'Paterson' - which began well enough but collapsed as it grew longer - showed us.

I make these points for a reason. There is little doubt in my mind that Williams is one of our finest minor poets, or that his 'Selected Poems' is a book to treasure. Yet I wonder if he is not a true eccentric, a sport - whose methods work *for him* again and again, miraculously; but which for other poets only skirt that chaos into which they had better be careful not to drop. If there are any lessons to be learned from Williams, they should derive from his strictures on the poetic line, suggesting not, as he would contend, the only way to write verse but one of many usable strategies. As I understand him, Williams would abolish the traditional metered line, but still avoid the rhythmic laxity of free verse; like Eliot, he believes that no *vers* is *libre* if the writer wants to do a good job. For the poetic foot ('a mode so rotten that it stinks'), he would substitute a new - or very old - *measure*: that he fails to specify. The remark is notable because Williams is not bluffing; and his new volume of poems, handsomely got up by Random House and called

'The Desert Music', nearly persuades me that he is right.

Note

1 The phrase occurs in Bennett's essay (No. 87) above, in the omitted opening paragraph. Bennett attributes the term to Northrop Frye.

'Journey to Love'

New York, October 1955

97. WALLACE FOWLIE, THE WORLD IN HIS HANDS, 'NEW YORK TIMES BOOK REVIEW'

18 December 1955

Fowlie (b. 1908) is an American teacher, critic and translator, whose writings include studies of Mallarmé and Rimbaud. His most recent book is 'Journal of Reversals: A Memoir' (1977).

Dr. Williams' first volume of poems was published in 1909, and yet this last volume, 'Journey to Love,' seems one of the youngest. When the wisdom of poetry reaches, as it does in this book, a unity of vision and purpose, a consonancy, an inner identity, it is by definition an expression of youthfulness. It is not 'literature' in any of its derogatory aspects. It is that kind of writing with which one does not trick or deceive or dazzle. The homogeneous work has grown into a style which we recognize as the man, William Carlos Williams.

The book is made up of fifteen shorter poems, in which the poet is still the familiar champion of the vernacular, the energetic and compassionate singer; and one long poem on love, Asphodel, That Greeny Flower. This is, beyond much doubt, a major poem. The riches the poet has known in the experience of love he narrates to the beloved in terms of the flowers they have known together during a long time. He reverts even to the flowers he pressed as a boy, among which the asphodel 'forebodingly' has its place. The poets speaks at great length, as if he is speaking against time, as if, were he to stop, time also would

stop. Because 'only the imagination is real,' asphodel
opens for the poet and for his wife after a lifetime.

98. RICHARD EBERHART ON MEASURE, THE SPEAKING VOICE AND
DIRECT WISDOM, 'SATURDAY REVIEW'

18 February 1956, 49

... Williams has tried to break down the iambic line. His
substitute is what he calls measure. Poetry, he says, is
based on measure. He seems to mean something like the
natural and subtly varying rhythms of the spoken voice,
based on the natural rhythms of breathing....
... It is mature man speaking direct truth. Yet I do
not mean that there is not a great deal of strategy in the
way he makes his verses.
 His wisdom is made to inhere in his racy lines, palatable to our sense because of the directness and concentration of his images. And because of the swiftness of
the timing. And because of the general lack of ambiguity.
And because of the rational propositions behind the airy
gauze and flow of the poetical language.
 You think his lines are light and easy, being read with
such direct intake and pleasure, and they are light and
easy; but read them over and over again and they will be
seen to have a very tough and tensile strength which cannot be broken down. They have a magical virtue and are
full of life. Williams has learned to say what he means
with a maximum of poetical reality.
 In 'Asphodel' he has ripe things to say about love,
about the garden, harking back perhaps inadvertently to
Marvell's. 'There is no power/so great as love/which is a
sea,/which is a garden.' 'The whole world/became my
garden!' 'and the will becomes again/a garden.' A mark of
his mature wisdom is in the line 'What power has love but
forgiveness?'
 His imagination everywhere 'celebrates the light.' And
what could be more typical than these three lines from
'Coda':

   Only the imagination is real!
    I have declared it
      time without end.

99. PAUL GOODMAN, BETWEEN THE FLASH AND THE THUNDER-STROKE, 'POETRY'

Vol. LXXXVII, no. 6, March 1956, 366-70.

A novelist and poet, Goodman (1911-72) is best known for his writings on education and the problems of communal living. Among his many books are 'Growing Up Absurd' (1960) and 'The Lordly Hudson: Collected Poems' (1962).

All these poems have a uniform versification, so we can take it this is an achieved norm for Williams, and let me devote most of this review to discussing it. It is repetitions of the triplet

```
    ----------------------
        ----------------------
            ----------------------
```

where each dash is a beat of meaning that may contain from one to about ten ametric syllables, one to six or seven words. By 'a beat of meaning' I mean any word or group of words that can momentarily, and relatively to its sentence, be attended to in itself. Pauses fall most frequently at the end of the first or second dash, but only sometimes at the end of the triplet: the versification is such as to keep you running on.

Now to understand this meter, we must at once observe that it is laid across a serious nervous common speech given just as it might actually be spoken, without inversion, compression, or other alteration by which poets tailor speech. For instance, omitting the versification: 'I should have known, though I did not, that the lily-of-the-valley is a flower makes many ill who whiff it.' 'This would be a fine day to go on a journey. Say to Florida where at this season all go nowadays.' 'She fed the King's poor and when she died left them some slight moneys under certain conditions.' 'In the name of love I came proudly as to an equal to be forgiven. Let me, for I know you take it hard, with good reason, give the steps if it may be by which you shall mount again to think well of me.'

By 'actual common speech' I do not mean prose. It is more profitable to regard common speech as the matrix from which both prose and verse are formed (and back towards

which certain species of prose and verse aspire.) You can
hear this when you listen to Eliot or Gertrude Stein or
William Carlos Williams and then notice that people sound
like that when they talk. Stein more catches overheard
voices, Eliot both social conversation and musing to oneself; but Williams gives you mostly the speech of a man
explaining to you, perhaps over a cup of coffee, how it is
with him, and trying to be accurate, clear, quick, and
modest.
    Here are some verses:

[quotes lines 40-7 of The Sparrow, PB, 130]

I think this versification has a twofold genealogy and is
a fairly viable compromise of the conflicting demands of
both lines.
    (1) These are the three beats of meaning to a line of
normal English blank verse. (As in blank verse, Williams
occasionally has two beats and occasionally four.) Quite
often Williams's triplets are perfect pentameters: 'cannot
surpass/the insistence/of his cheep'; 'more than a natural
one./His voice,/his movements'; 'keen eyes,/serviceable
beak/and general truculence'; 'does it portend?/A war/will
not erase it.' There is, I choose quite at random, a pervasive blank verse with the usual variations. And within
the poetic program of achieving the actual common speech
unaltered, the most direct way of writing blank verses is
to keep the triplets of meaning but to give up the pentameter ..., rather filling each beat with whatever is
required ametrically. This is just what Williams does.
Thus Milton, in the sonnets also employing a nervous earnest style close to speech, writes

    to serve therewith/my Maker/and present
    my true account/lest He returning/chide;

but Williams allows also

    I cannot say/that I have gone to Hell/for you
    but often/found myself there/in your pursuit.

    (2) If, however, we consider the blank verse

    throws back his head
        and simply -
            yells! The din

we see at once the other genealogy of this versification:
each beat of meaning is to be if possible taken also in

isolation, as an image. Such brief bursts are the direct heir of the imagist poetry of the beginning of the century, and especially of the Chinese influence. Compare, e.g., Florence Ayscough's translation of Tu Fu, where the attempt is made to keep the ideograms intact (so that the couplets of ideograms can be read both vertically and horizontally.) At the start of his career, to be sure, Williams was concerned with the common objects, generally pictorial and generally static, and he used to construct them handsomely with these isolating phrases. Or we can take these little bursts as a kind of pointillism, every spot a color, every color a spot; from this beginning Cummings and Pound went off in their own directions - to bursts of surprise, shapes of words, glancing references and fragmentary allusions, etc. But Williams has taken up a program of actual common speech that does not fragment into little entities in exactly this way; he has accordingly tried to get back to a regular underlying flow, in which the sudden accents and turns and digressions can sound out more like the actuality of talking.

This versification does manage to give Williams an imagist blank verse serviceable for his purposes. I question its widespread utility. In the first place there is a difficulty of breathing. The bread-and-butter virtue of pentameter blank verses - or Alexandrines or Greek iambic trimeters - is that each verse is one breath; this is the modulus for dramatic recitation, and to maintain it poets have been willing to make large alterations of what is actually spoken. By contrast, many of Williams' lines have to be rehearsed, or contrariwise, there is the temptation to disregard the versification altogether and recite straight on, a very sweet melody but swifter than he intends. But secondly, and more important, it is very difficult to make these cut-up ametric little units flow and grow into true paragraphs, the way blank verses grow with power and intensity into large wholes.

This makes little difference here, for mostly Williams is interested in a more glancing and unimpassioned effect, darting from aspect to aspect, shifting his point of view. But this versification too can achieve paragraphs of power and intensity. For example: 'It is ridiculous//what airs we put on/to seem profound/while our hearts//gasp dying/for want of love./Having your love//I was rich./Thinking to have lost it/I am tortured//and cannot rest./I do not come to you/abjectly//with confessions of my faults,/I have confessed,/all of them.//In the name of love/I come proudly/as to an equal//to be forgiven' and so forth. Here the gasping, the interruptions and the turns, that are in the verse are in the situation itself, and you cannot arrange the words better.

So much for Williams' versification; but finally let me add a few remarks about 'Journey to Love' as a whole. I find it a disturbing book. As he tells us frequently in these poems, Williams is now seventy years old; and the case is - whether he likes it or not (my guess is that he would both like it and not) - he is a sage. For that's what a sage is, a person who keeps growing and producing and nevertheless manages to live a long time; as Rilke said, the point is not to be happy but to persist. A sage has got the trick of it; we open our ears and say, tell *us*.

He has curious things to say about eyes and looking; here are some passages: 'To look in my son's eyes - /I hope he did not see/that I was looking - '; and 'we dare not stare too hard/or we are lost./ The instant//trivial as it is/is all we have'; and 'He kept looking at me//and I at him ... His eyes/which were intelligent/were wide open//but evasive, mild ... my father's face!' Is this, then, the trick of it? Look and see, but do not let on that you're looking, and you daren't let on to yourself that you see. Elsewhere he projects this feeling onto the Others: 'It would be/too much//if the public/pried among the minutiae/of our private affairs.//Not/that we have anything to hide//but could *they* stand it?' The motive here, to spare the Others, sounds like a rationalization; certainly at least poets first blurt it out to the Others and then find out what it is we mean to say. Williams knows this, of course, and his advice seems to be, 'Don't give yourself away too far (to yourself); take it easy and you'll live long.'

You can see it in a structural device that recurs half a dozen times. He starts out with a forthright picturesque excited affirmation; then suddenly he stops and asks a question, much weaker, and doubtful: 'What is she/but an ambassador/from another world?' or 'And who but we are concerned/with the beauty of apple-blossoms?' or 'Are we not most of us like that?' or 'What was he intent upon/but to drown out/that look?' Frankly, I cannot help feeling that these questions are spurious, they are smoke-screens. He doesn't ask because he wants to know, he asks because he knows something *else* too well and he is changing the subject; or closer, he has trapped himself into saying something that makes him suddenly feel very lonely and unsafe, and so he covers up with a modest question to get back to the animal warmth of agreement.

The most exciting and affirmative poem in this volume is The Sparrow, dedicated 'To My Father', and a very fine poem it is. And what a busy, sexy, decisive, truculent,

and independent bird that sparrow is! even though he does
end up the dried-out victim of a female. As a figure for
himself, however, our poet chooses a flower. The Pink
Locust: 'I'm persistent as the pink locust,/once admitted/
to the garden//you will not easily get rid of it.' And
this is a fine poem too; but the ending of it has a certain
doctrinal abstractness, and I, at least, can't help asking,
'Who's he kidding? and why is he kidding himself?' Also I
give myself the answer, 'Say! who is supposed to know the
trick of persisting, you or he?'

    The longest and most ambitious poem in this volume is
Asphodel, That Greeny Flower. This is a curious poem,
much too elaborate to explore here in a few words. But it
seems to be founded on a simple enough premise: the old
poet is seeking for forgiveness from his wife and rein-
statement in her affections, since this love is after all
the main thing in life. (What the devil sin did he commit
anyway?) Now if this *is* the premise, I'm damned if it's a
sage one. If at the age of discretion we are still making
this particular Journey to Love, it's too bad, it simply
isn't worth it. But I don't believe it (and I don't think
he believes it).

'The Selected Letters'

New York, August 1957

100. WINFIELD TOWNLEY SCOTT, 'FOR THE LOCAL, THE REGIONAL, AND FOR AMERICAN SPEECH', 'SATURDAY REVIEW'

7 September 1957, 14

'Hell,' William Carlos Williams wrote one spring day in 1926, 'some days I can write what I want to and some days I write "In the Am. Grain" - and when I'm very low I can write a letter.' There are pages in the 'Selected Letters of William Carlos Williams,' ... which show the belly-crawling weariness of a hard-working physician, pages (even into the 1930s) which show the discouragement of a poet who, though reasonably well-famed, combed New York in vain for a publisher. Yet, on the whole, the mood isn't low at all. These are the spirited, hasty, offhand, high-tempered letters of a busy man. Sometimes the high temper is rude or angry; much more often it is the ebullience of a richly endowed sensibility, keenly pitched to the experience of poetry and all the time deeply involved in the workaday life of suburban New Jersey.

Let us regard that for a moment in terms of a comparison. Though setting one poet up against another too often turns into a useless stick-beating, sometimes a juxtaposition can be instructive - as, I think, in the case of Dr. Williams and Wallace Stevens. The two were near-of-an-age, both caught the ears of the small body of poetry readers at about the same time and had many years to wait before, later on, general recognition was heaped all over them; and each man, through his adult life, was occupied by a full-time profession. I have become convinced that no complete understanding of either man's poetry is plausible without taking into account the duality of the life, and that the end results in the two poetries are fascinatingly different.

Stevens's insistence was upon a complete divorce between his poetry and his life as an insurance company lawyer and executive. Therefore he was driven to the position of erecting the imagination as 'the reality'; and therefore his poetry became increasingly an exercise in esthetics. A poetry about art, a poetry about poetry: the great bulk of his work became that. As usual, time will judge it; but already it seems, granting him a handful of uniquely beautiful poems, that most of his work will fade like so much elegant embroidery in the real sun of authentic poetic necessities.

His friend William Carlos Williams, on the other hand, has never been weaned from the daily life of Rutherford. From the smallest red wheelbarrow out in the rain to the massive structure of 'Paterson,' Williams has sucked into all his art the Sunday-through-Saturday doings of people and place. His writing has been completely involved with his profession as a physician. This, no doubt, just came naturally. But he, as most writers do, justified it in theory. He saw it as decision for the local, the regional, and for American speech. He himself once set up one of these illuminating contrasts - and he could have used Stevens - when he said Ezra Pound wanted poetry as caviar whereas he himself wanted it as bread.

With Williams, the work is the man; if possible, the whole man. It is so, of course, with a special intimacy in these 'Letters,' more informally so even than in his 'Autobiography,' to which this book makes a companion portrait, focussed on the life through a fortuitous gathering up of the present tense. Here, you feel, is a simple man, albeit a many-sided simple man made up of not unusual proportions of vanity and arrogance, of failures and successes. He has somehow managed to look and act - indeed, to be - like any of the nicest family doctors you have ever known, little black bag in hand, in and out of his car on his daily rounds; yet all the time one of God's spies....

101. KATHERINE HOSKINS, SWEATING OUT A BIRTHRIGHT, 'NATION'

5 October 1957, 226-7

Hoskins (b. 1909) is an American poet and reviewer.

... They are not letters to be picked up at random and savoured for a bit of gossip here, an aphorism there. They should be begun at the beginning and read through to the end. In that way the reader may have the extraordinary experience of watching a life build, stone after difficult stone, to nobility.

The drama is made the more accessible to us by a remarkable job of editing on the part of John C. Thirlwall. The stages of the doctor's life as man are presented in blocks of related letters - from college to his mother and brother, then to his young wife, then to his sons, first at school, later in the armed forces. And through these, from start to finish, thread letters to his friends and acquaintances, most of them fellow writers and editors. Sometimes a name will appear but once, others weave in and out of the whole life, as to Marianne Moore, to Kenneth Burke, and the involutions of a friendship are adumbrated. In a letter to his mother in 1904, he mentions his new friend Ezra Pound and adds a brief characterization of him that stands up wonderfully through the years. Throughout there are letters to Pound, mention is made of him and the last letter in the book is to him.

The recurrence of Pound acts like a fictional device to point up the intense Americanism of the Williams story. Whatever may be the truth of our presidents, the American artist has, until very lately, been born and reared in a cultural log cabin. He has been self-made and has missed few of the advantages and disadvantages the phrase connotes. He has been, he has had to be, lonely, cantankerous, obstinate. He has had to waste motion and to direct and tutor his originality with very little aid from the outside. And he has had to earn his living in the market place. It is a tough proposition. But those who have evaded or escaped it have seemed doomed to expatriation and that has often proved in the end to be even tougher.

Clearly, Dr. Williams never regretted this American fate of his, though he often regretted its barrenness,

wished like any artist that he could enjoy, just for a
little, green lawns and noble friends and a life ordered
to his highest capabilities. He 'embraced his lion' and
if his insistence on Americanism was folly, he at least
pursued it to where he joins the classical line of men of
action plus letters, of Chaucer, Montaigne, Shakespeare,
Stendhal, Flaubert. Though it takes the extremes of the
new country and the new era to demand that a man deliver
two thousand babies in addition to being a poet. Surely,
none of the old masters was quite so driven. Still, as
one considers this line, the career of pure man of letters
looks new and decadent when it doesn't look hieratic and
hermetic. And it is hard for an American to remember that
the priest and decadent are also invaluable to our poetic
economy. In 1932, Williams wrote, 'Let us once and for all
understand that Eliot is finally and definitely dead - and
his troop along with him.' Twenty years later, he writes,
'I'm glad you recognized my affection for Pound and saw
what I intended to make known of him. He too was an
orchid in my forest, he had no interest, really, for my
trees, no more than did Eliot. They both belonged to an
alien world, a world perhaps more elevated than mine, more
removed from my rigors. I have always felt as if I were
sweating it out somewhere low, among the reptiles, hidden
in the underbrush, hearing the monkeys overhead. Their
defeats were my defeats, I belonged to them more than to
a more mobile world....

'Eliot could have saved me many years ... had he been
willing to remain here and put his weight behind the working of the thing out. [i.e. a new poetic line] Pound
helped at the beginning and has, it must be said, not
weakened. Both Pound and Eliot ... are top men in the
craft. But I must go beyond that.'

Lost though he may have seemed in the underbrush, Dr.
Williams emerges triumphant, having done what he set out
to do. He gave the local an airy habitation and a name;
and, for his own needs at least, arrived at a new and
satisfactory metric. These are immense achievements. And
one must add to them such humane virtues as the courage
with which he sustained his many, many years of unsuccess,
years when often even his colleagues scorned him; his unfailing kindness to young poets; his sensitivity to work
for which he had little temperamental sympathy. Perhaps
his great strength shows best in his ability to meet and
incorporate change. For years he berated the 'academies';
lately he writes, 'we are ignorant, we British ex-
colonials' and suggests that a generation of formal schooling in poetry may not hurt us after all. Change is for
him an enriching, an including, rather than a shift from

one attitude to another. And so he can write wisely, as
in 1951 to Marianne Moore: 'It is inevitable that, in the
end, individuals, brothers though they be and closely
allied as they have lived, will finally arrive at the
place where their separate individualities are revealed
and they will find themselves strangers. That will be the
moment when their love and their faith is most tested.
Let it be so with us.' ...

102. REED WHITTEMORE ON WILLIAMS AS AN EXPERIMENTAL POET
AND A CONVENTIONAL LETTER WRITER, 'YALE REVIEW'

Vol. XLVII, no. 2, December 1957, 286-7

The composite review, Five Old Masters and Their Sensibilities, from which this is an excerpt, also includes consideration of Wallace Stevens' 'Opus Posthumous' (1957).
 Whittemore (b. 1919) is an American poet, editor and critic. He has edited 'Furioso' (1939-53) and the 'Carleton Miscellany'. His books of poetry include 'The Boy from Iowa' (1962). His biography 'William Carlos Williams, Poet from Jersey' was published in 1975.

... In verse Williams is a bundle of carefully chosen
eccentricities. He likes to pick subjects for poetry
that somebody else might not think poetic; he likes to
experiment with new cadences, new line dimensions, new
kinds of poetic logic or continuity; and he is the most
exuberant living despiser of the sonnet. All of this
should put him on Stevens' side, and indeed he is, at
least theoretically. Throughout his selected letters one
finds him exhorting young poets and young editors to be
'new' and to be themselves. Criticizing the first issue
of 'Furioso' he says (and rightly): 'the issue seems to me
a little tight, too ordered - coming from two kids. I want
to see what might be presumed to be more of you, as you, in
it.' Writing to James Laughlin he says,

> It is hard ... to grasp that we know, that we are able,
> that others are barriers to our progress right from the
> beginning. I for one have hung back just from a lack
> of conviction of the dullness of others. I have said,

> Why should I presume? when I should have said, For.
> God's sake, get the hell out of my way and at once!
> So much time is lost.

Such statements make him a clear advocate of poetry which is the expression of a personal sensibility. Together with his poems they defend oddity (which is, after all, achieved by not conforming) even more strenuously than do the works of his correspondent, Pound. And yet the statements of the letters belie the manner of the letters, which is not really odd at all.

This is not to their discredit. They are good letters; they are full of all that energy that has permitted the good doctor to live two lives at once; and they are full also of a kind of good will toward the right enterprises (and sometimes the wrong poets) that few persons not about to be canonized can manage. But they are nonetheless conventional letters - the letters of a conventional father advising his son, of a conventional elder advising his juniors, and of a conventional rebel recommending war. They are thus very different in spirit from his poems; one cannot imagine a poem of his in which he addresses his readers as follows:

> Your difficulties arise from a lack of balance in your daily life, a lack of balance which has to be understood and withstood - for it cannot be avoided for the present. I refer to the fact that your intellectual life, for the moment, has eclipsed your physical life....

103. HUGH KENNER, COLUMBUS'S LOG-BOOK, 'POETRY'

Vol. XCII, no. 3, June 1958, 174-8

Kenner (b. 1923), Distinguished Professor of Modern Literature at Johns Hopkins University, is an authority on the life and work of Ezra Pound. In addition to 'The Pound Era' (1971), Kenner's work includes books on Eliot, Joyce, Beckett and Wyndham Lewis, and a number of essays on Williams. Three of these are contained in 'Gnomon: Essays on Contemporary Literature' (1958).

Dr. Williams's letters don't, except slantingly, reveal a
personality, in the sense in which the potato which grew
in the shape of a dumb-bell exhibited a personality,
differentiating it from other potatoes sufficiently to
gain it photographic commemoration in the Sunday supplements. The letters register something much more interesting, a continuous, directed, unfaltering intention. ('For
I know,' Williams wrote Norman Macleod, 'that whatever my
life has been it has been single in purpose, simple in
design and constantly directed to the one end of discovery,
if possible, of some purpose in being alive, in being a
thinking person and in being an active force.') The
potato, like a minor poet, merely happened in the tuberous
stage of its career to pass through a buried curtainring;
its diverting subsequent development may be categorized as
'response to environment.'

To categorize Williams in this way is a temptation the
editor of the 'Letters' has not escaped: 'His mother and
father had inculcated an ideal of absolute purity ... the
nonattainment of which left William Carlos Williams uncomfortable for life. To compensate, he adopted a tough,
external pose, a Whitmanesque hail-fellow-well-met attitude....' Which is about as important as Shakespeare's
deerstealing, though intimates whose impressions have not
survived may have speculated on the Bard's habit (in his
cups) of vamping ex-con argot and ribbing Jonson about the
branded thumb. The important Williams shines through and
around the man preoccupied with talking 'animal to animal.

The intention, the drive toward discovering 'some purpose ... in being an active force,' never shifts or weakens, but for Williams's first fifty years it thrusts forward invisibly, disrupting the social surfaces a little
without properly revealing itself. For two-thirds of a
lifetime we see Williams doing the right thing (in his
writing) by instinct, or doing the wrong thing and by
instinct discarding it. About everything of permanent
interest he is inarticulate until quite late: until he
begins to gain the upper hand in a long fury of struggle
to identify and master consciously what he could intermittently do. His instincts dictated a complex mode of
poetic apprehension: there has been too much stress on
his experiments with sensationally curt postage-stamp
impressionism, the red wheelbarrow or the green bottle.
It is more important to notice that the intricate pattern-
ing of sound in Spring Strains -

In a tissue-thin monotone of blue-grey buds ...

was achieved nearly forty years ago. Yet bull-necked

activism ('Life is ... always new, irregular. Verse to be
alive must have infused into it something of the same
order....') is the only thing we find him articulating
consciously at that epoch: or, 'My liking is for an unimpeded thrust right through a poem from the beginning to
the end, without regard to formal arrangements.' He is
forty-eight before he writes to Pound that he has been
playing with a prosodic theory –

> ... that the inexplicitness of modern verse as compared
> with, let us say, the Iliad, and our increasingly difficult music in the verse as compared with the more or
> less downrightness of their line forms – have been the
> result of a clearly understandable revolution in poetic
> attitude. Whereas formerly the music which accompanied
> the words amplified, certified and released them, today
> the words we write, failing a patent music, have become
> the music itself, and the understanding of the individual (presumed) is now that which used to be the
> words.... (SL, 126).

He is sixty before he is noting for another correspondent
that there is no such thing as freedom in verse, that to
rebel is to claim freedom to do something in particular,
and that what he has been all his life trying to do is not
express W.C.W. but perfect a necessity forced on the
responsible writer of his generation by the facts of the
present:

> We've got to know that we have to invent for ourselves
> ... a new prosody based on a present-day world and real
> in a present-day world which the English prosody can
> never be for us or the world. That is our destiny ...
> and our tremendous opportunity facing a world that
> cannot go on making poems unless we make good.
> It is amazing to me how the simple elements of the
> art are tacitly and erroneously assumed to be valid
> before they have been examined in their anatomic elements. Naturally you can't blame most students for
> accepting the purely adventitious phenomenon of English
> prosody (in a new language where it doesn't apply ...).
> (SL, 269.)

What he now calls the American idiom he used to call
the American language: an error of excess, but an error
that proved worth committing; just as Fenollosa's reduction of ideographs to etymological pictures – according to
the scholars, an error of simplification – was an error
worth committing. By looking at a foreign language

through Fenellosa's notes, Pound saw his way to a poetic
of the image, valid in the tongue he wrote but long mislaid. By looking at what he took to be a new language,
American (as strange to English poetry as Pound's Chinese),
Williams saw his way to a poetic of the variable foot,
valid in the tongue of Chaucer and Wyatt but long mislaid.
('The "new measure", ' he wrote in 1951, 'is much more
particular, much more related to the remote past than I,
for one, believed, It was a natural blunder....')
(SL, 299.)

Two remarkable letters, one to Kay Boyle in 1932 and
one to Jean Starr Untermeyer in 1948, set forth the program of metrical invention which for the last third of his
lifetime has been Williams's major preoccupation. 'I have
been watching speech in my own environment ... actively at
work watching how words match the act, especially how they
come together. The result has been a few patches of metrical coherence which I don't as yet see how to use.' Metric
grows between the words we have, not out of a scansion
chart: 'Prose can be a laboratory for metrics. It is lower
in the literary scale. But it throws up jewels which may
be cleaned and grouped. I don't think any poetry ever
originated in any other way. It must have been inherent in
the language, Greek, Latin, Italian, English, French or
Chinese. And this should blast that occasionally pushing
notion that the form of art is social in character. Such
an opinion is purest superficiality. The form of poetry is
that of language....' (SL, 130.)

'Free verse - if it ever existed - is out.... Whitman
to me is one broom stroke and that is all. Nature, the
Rousseauists who foreshadowed Whitman, the imitation of the
sounds of the sea per se, are a mistake. Poetry has nothing to do with that. It is not nature. It is poetry.'
(SL, 135.)

In 1946 he reports a polite heckler asking at a lecture
for evidence of 'the new way of measuring.' 'It was a fair
question but one I shall have to postpone answering indefinitely. I always think of Mendelejeff's table of atomic
weights in this connection. Years before an element was
discovered ... its presence had been predicated by a blank
in the table....' In 1954, in a letter to Richard Eberhart, he at last produces the demonstration. It bears out
fully the intuitions hazarded in the 1932 letter to Pound;
the progression of the words (which 'need only be taught to
keep as distinguished an order, as chosen a character ...
as in the best of prose') and the 'musical pace,' the progression of the measure, go on simultaneously without entangling one another; and he bears this out by scanning
some instances of his last-period three-ply line.

Or rather, not scanning - counting. What Williams has
been laboring to achieve since 1912, it turns out, is
simply this separation of the strict musical form from the
free pulse of the words. One doesn't apprehend the
measure by noting where the words bump, heave, or undulate,
and then placing scansion marks over these incidents, and
then attempting to group the scansion marks into symmetrical bunches. And for want of this principle, the termino-
logy of which remains to be developed, everyone supposed,
everyone including, presumably, Williams himself, that
Spring Strains or By the Road to the Contagious Hospital
was 'free verse.' To have firm grounds for knowing otherwise is a great liberation of the understanding.

If only for its passages on metric, the 'Selected
Letters' is an indispensable book for anyone interested in
locating and understanding the poetic activity of the
1950s. The poetry of the 1950s is Pound uncanorous;
Williams in his latest work (a fifth part of 'Paterson' is
now pending); the Creeley-Olson-Zukofsky nexus; Charles
Tomlinson writing Cambridge English cross-fertilized from
America; somewhat laggard owing to technical impatience,
the Layton-Dudek-Souster group in Canada; and Alan Neame
of the great Cocteau translation. The work in this list is
of varying nature and uneven quality; some of it is in the
laboratory stage. All of it answers to the Williams
account of an enlightened poetic. It is by no means all of
equal importance, or durability; all of it reflects honest
labor, directed at a metrical rationale. It is no longer
possible to say that the 'free' metres play tennis without
a net, nor that they flirt with traditional schemes always
in the offing, just unrealized. We can now say that they
approximate, more or less closely, more or less intelligently, to a new way of measuring and counting. The iambic
pentameter of the textbooks doesn't exist; but, like
Sievers' schemes of Anglo-Saxon metric, it had to be invented to explain, say, Shakespeare: who came along, not
counting on his fingers but making real what a Surrey or a
Dekker had intermittently heard without quite being able
to write it. So Williams looks forward to 'some infant
now' who will 'find the way we miss.' Unless we prepare
our ears by paying attention to the writers who are *at
work*, we shall perhaps be one day in the position of those
who carried on disputations concerning quantitative and
accentual verse, not knowing that they were contemporaries
of Shakespeare.

'I Wanted to Write a Poem'

Boston, April 1958

Sub-titled The Autobiography of the Works of a Poet, this is not strictly a work by Williams, but is rather a distillation of notes from a series of interviews over a period of five months. Providing, as it does, basic bibliographical information together with Williams' comments on each item, it is in effect an extension of his autobiography.

---

104. WINFIELD TOWNLEY SCOTT, SOME TALK ABOUT VERSE, 'NEW YORK TIMES BOOK REVIEW'

13 December 1958, 26

It is fitting that a poet who has always gone his own insistent, intelligent, bull-headed, sweet way should eventually have a bibliography of his work unlike any other. In essence, that is what 'I wanted to Write a Poem' is, a bibliography of Dr. Williams' books and pamphlets. But the bibliographical data serve, precisely as the dictionary says data should serve, 'as a basis for discussion and inference.' As each item is catalogued, there are also given the poet's own reminiscence of publication, writing methods, friends and foes or, indeed, whatever. Edith Heal, a novelist and journalist, made many visits to the Williams home in Rutherford, N.J., and took down the doctor's talk.

As bibliography, the book is undistinguished. 'Paterson, Book Two' is chronologically out of order. There is no listing of the first New Directions edition of 'In the American Grain.' There are, in Miss Heal's quotations from books, a few typographical errors without indication as to whether they are pious transcriptions, and so one assumes they are oversights in the present text.

Chiefly to be regretted is the slimness of the bibliographical information. When Miss Heal ventures beyond title, total pages, publisher, and date, she inclines to give us minor matters such as dedications and reprintings. The space would have been better used in brief physical descriptions of the various volumes.

There is nothing slim about Dr. Williams' conversation, and Miss Heal, who no doubt had to be a selective editor, has caught the charm of its directness and truthfulness. Some of it has been encountered before in the 'Selected Letters' or the 'Autobiography,' but it is here with a fresh slant, and most of the material is new.

Sometimes the reminiscence is a little startling: 'My first interest was the theatre. I was at home on the stage. I loved to act in college plays. I even contemplated giving up medicine to be a scene-shifter.'

Sometimes it goes to the very core of Dr. Williams' poetry: 'To get the line on paper. To make it euphonious. To fit the words so that they went smoothly and still said exactly what I wanted to say. That was what I struggled for.'

Everywhere it is the talk of the kind of old man Yeats longed to be: a 'foolish, passionate man.' And a wise and rewarding one, too.

105. HUGH KENNER, TO MEASURE IS ALL WE KNOW, 'POETRY'

Vol. XCIV, no. 2, May 1959, 127-32

What survives the death of the body at the end of 'Paterson (Book Four)' is the imagination

 (I have told you, this
is a fiction, pay attention);

hence this coda. Book Five is a poem of vigorous survivals: a play of Lorca's, a Breughel 'Nativity', a great French or Flemish tapestry displaying the hunt of the Unicorn, this latter 'the living fiction' in which you can identify

>   wild rose
> pink as a lady's ear-lobe when it shows
>   beneath the hair,

created by

[quotes P V, iii, 269, line 31, and 270, lines 1-5]

These things endure. It is a great achievement to have so presented them that they endure in the verse actively, emanating passion, not simply resisting decay with the aid of some museum's air-conditioning. Here is part of the account of the Breughel:

[quotes P V, iii, 263, lines 5-23]

Neither frozen nor arrested nor fabricated, this life simply goes on for ever. So, by implication, does the poet's imagination:

[quotes P V, i, 247, lines 9-15]

'The cavern of death' is a typical image, the merest denotative convenience, preserved from slackness only by pace. In Book V pace and drive propel a disquieting transparency of statement unknotted by Williams' characteristic musculature of diction. The angular, half-unassimilable word no longer juts; nothing impedes the rapidity of declaration.

Though functional, this facility is not unrelated to a certain unexpected susceptibility to paraphrase that seems inherent in the conception of the poem. In the summer of 1957 Dr. Williams told an interviewer, '"Paterson IV" ends with the protagonist breaking through the bushes, identifying himself with the land, with America. He finally will die but it can't be categorically stated that death ends *anything*. When you're through with sex, with ambition, what can an old man create? Art, of course, a piece of art that will go beyond him into the lives of young people, the people who haven't had time to create. The old man meets the young people and lives on.'

This explication, as banal and engaging as a twelfth grade valedictory, is to be found in 'I Wanted to Write a Poem', Edith Heal's transcription of a summer's interviews, a wonderfully interesting little book though yawning with missed opportunities. A running bibliography, printed in red, states the topics of the poet's reminiscences, which appear without quotation marks. Miss Heal is pleased with this device, and notes that her subject was pleased with it too. She also points out that 'paragraphing is accomplished by spacing between paragraphs to give the effect of a burst of speech because that is exactly the way the words came to me', and Dr. Williams for his part says concerning his early collection, 'Al Que Quiere', that 'the titles of the poems tell you how I looked around me and saw something that suggested a poem: Man with a Bad Heart, Child, The Old Man, Dedication for a Plot of Ground'.

They don't set up as a knowing pair, these two. 'I asked Dr. Williams if his poem Portrait of a Lady had been suggested by either Henry James or T. S. Eliot. Then I read the poem and we laughed and agreed that it could not have been suggested by the work of either gentleman. I include it so the reader will see why.' There is ample excuse for the reviewer who concluded from this volume that Dr. Williams was an agreeable man without talent, fiercely determined to experience the sensations of being a writer. Such a man would express himself no differently. 'This was automatic writing,' he says of one book. 'I sat and faced the paper and wrote.' Or again, of some short stories, 'I wrote it down, without technical tricks. I kept the literary thing to myself.' He sounds wonderfully naive, and we nearly conclude that Miss Heal simply wasn't talking to the man who wrote The Descent or 'The pure products of America/go crazy...'. She was encouraging a retired New Jersey doctor to leaf through his albums: 'Blizzard tells about me, the doctor. I had to go out in the snow to make a night call. I can remember the moment the last lines speak of....'

On the other hand, she wasn't talking to a litterateur. 'I wrote it down, without technical tricks': exactly so: his art was the art of seeing what to write. The casual social gusto of 'I Wanted to Write a Poem' is intimate with his creative depths. Reviewing Robert McAlmon in 1924, Williams wrote, 'Villon could not exist now if there were the faintest feeling about his writing that he had sought to be effective.... "Le mot juste" is the ready word, it has no other significance. This is fundamental. There cannot be in literature a seeking for words.... It is dangerous ground, but good writing is rare.' So for fifty years he has used the ready word, with results often remarkable. The ready cadence also: 'I was looking for a metric figure - a new measure. I couldn't find it and I couldn't wait for it. I was too impatient: I had to write.'

The energy, the activity, lie near the top of his mind, where the words are also. Hence they unite, words and energy, without involving that urge to be effective which has its springs a little deeper in the psyche, down in the regions where the Self becomes aware that it can cut a dramatic figure. The poems seem just dashed off, as indeed they were: 'By the road to the contagious hospital ...' was written in fifteen minutes or so. To write anything at all of the smallest interest by this means requires the rarest balance of literacy and impulse, a balance only possible to naiveté of a certain order. The naiveté makes the poems possible without itself (at best) getting shredded into them. Cellophane-thin, it protects from corrosion an exceedingly delicate mechanism of apprehension, ticking away in full view. The very air is polluted with knowingness: let a trace enter, and the poet would be ruined for ever, the poet who is determined to rely, in twentieth century America, neither on books nor on a literary tradition. Pound had virtually to invent the the books he relies on, Eliot the tradition. Miss Moore, whose late works show her moving quite as innocently close to the occasions of her poems as Williams, chose to invent symmetrical little jewelled watch movements, to serve for forms. Williams, who has written memorably of invention, invents nothing we can categorize, not forms, not traditions, merely the poem in hand, an improvisation and at the same time 'a machine made out of words'. 'It is dangerous ground, but good writing is rare.'

So much we can learn from the very transparence of 'I Wanted to Write a Poem', a transparence the habit of which made possible the strong verse of 'Paterson V', which like Villon 'could not exist if there were the faintest feeling about his writing that he wanted to be effective'. It is menaced by a dozen clichés of feeling: sentimentalities about old age and harlots, birds and flowers ('Flowers have always been his friends' - a laxative cadence that miraculously does not spoil one of the finest pages in the poem). It evades cliché by paying it no heed. It opens with a conventional eagle and conventional sentiments:

[quotes P V, i, 241, lines 1-10]

- yet the words seem to have written themselves, and guard, not having been put there by somebody for effect, what was in the sentiment before convention overtook it. This mysterious process suggests in turn to Williams, as it has suggested to other poets, the analogy of the dance, that ordered energy which posits without insisting; yet not bothering his head about the need to refurbish this worn image, he can end as strongly as he began:

[quotes P V, i, 277, line 22, and 278, lines 1-14]

'Patterson (Book Five)'

Norfolk, Conn., September 1958

106. M. L. ROSENTHAL ON 'THE TRANSFORMING AND SAVING
POWER OF THE IMAGINATION', 'NATION'

31 May 1958, 500

Rosenthal, then poetry editor of the 'Nation', marked the
occasion of Williams' seventy-fifth birthday with a selection and an essay, Salvo for William Carlos Williams, from
which this review is excerpted. Writing for the same
occasion, Kenneth Rexroth noted Williams' humility and
generosity towards young writers. 'You have always known
where the only kind of human power that matters was to be
found - in the creative act' ('Assays' (New York, 1961),
A Public Letter for William Carlos Williams' Seventy-fifth
Birthday, 204).

... Williams' remarkable alertness to the subtler life of
the senses - how it feels to be a growing thing of any
kind, or to come into birth; how the freshness of the
morning or the feel of a particular moment in a particular
season impresses itself upon us; what impact the people
glimpsed or encountered in a myriad transitory situations
make upon us at the moment of the event - gives him a
keener and more adventurous insight into the aesthetic
potentialities of that life. The general population's
insensitivity to those potentialities is one of his concerns. He links this problem to another: the absence of
a 'language' that will enable Americans to cultivate,
direct and shape their crude and, at present, suicidal
energies. 'The pure products of America,' he has written,

'go crazy.' They have lost contact with European tradition, and left to themselves they run to emptiness and depravity. His 'In the American Grain' is an attempt to sum up the materials of an informing American myth; it is one of the truly germinative American prose-works of this century, a perfect complement to his fiction with its close-ups of the splintering violences and innumerable undeveloped sources of strength in American culture. The waste of possibility - it is in dealing with this crucial theme in poems like To Elsie and The Raper from Passenack that Williams comes closest to despair.

His greatest effort to deal with it is in the 'Paterson' sequence. In this long poem he chose to base his structure on the movement of the river he has elsewhere called the 'filthy Passaic.' He sought an *open* structure like that of Pound's 'Cantos'. 'I decided there would be four books following the course of the river whose life seemed more and more to resemble my own ...: above the Falls, the catastrophe of the Falls itself, ... below the Falls and the entrance at the end to the great sea.' At the beginning the city of Paterson (an epitome of the American scene, with the poet - sometimes called 'Dr Paterson' - its unrecognized prophet) is seen as a sleeping stone-giant. The people, automatons whom he *might* give more vital existence to, walk 'unroused' and 'incommunicado.' They do not know the organic relatedness that gives unconscious meaning to every moment in the lives of primitive peoples. Grossness, destructiveness, daredevilry and divorce - and the constant dullness and blocking-off of self-discovery and communication - are the outward signs of of our condition. Everywhere the sexual life is thwarted and distorted; we are the victims of a sexual confusion inseparable from our cultural confusions - Williams shares this theme with Lawrence, but gives it a peculiarly American emphasis. The first four books of 'Paterson,' completed in 1951, were intended to be the whole work. They constitute a devastating comment on every phase of our life, though a comment relieved by momentary oases of perceived or envisioned beauty, and they 'end' modestly and familiarly, as they began, in the midst of things, in the midst of predicament.

Now, in his fifth book of 'Paterson,' Dr. Williams reopens the issues. Or rather, he refocuses them. The transforming and saving power of the aesthetic imagination is played like a brilliant light over old archetypal motifs and symbols - sexuality versus chaste love, reality versus the ideal, the Virgin and the Whore, the hunted-down Unicorn pictured in a famous tapestry now at The Cloisters in

New York, amid a setting both natural and courtly. Such themes and images do the refocusing, placing the poet's perspectives in sharper relation to the bedeviled perspectives of the culture at large.

The four passages from 'Paterson V' presented in this issue can each be viewed as a self-contained poem. I see no diminution of the characteristic skill and excitement of of their author's work in them, but rather a mellowing without loss of energy - Paterson's 'roar of the present' removed just enough to give the poem another, a much needed dimension....

107. W. D. SNODGRASS ON WILLIAMS' LATE CHANGE TOWARDS 'CONVENTIONAL ENGLISH POETRY', 'HUDSON REVIEW'

Vol. XII, no. 1, Spring 1959, 117-19

The Spring Verse Chronicle from which this review is taken includes comments on books of verse by Roethke, Cummings and I. A. Richards, and on a biography of Cummings.

Snodgrass (b. 1926) is an American poet and university teacher, whose most recent book is 'The Fuehrer Bunker' (1977).

Unlike Roethke, William Carlos Williams, in spite of his long involvement with the *avant garde*, has never been one to learn from literary movements and excitements, since the first forming of his mature style, changes have come about in that style chiefly because of the events in his life. He is perhaps chief of those (like Wallace Stevens and Marianne Moore) whom the prospect of old age and the awareness of death as a reality have shocked into a new poetic life.

This change, oddly enough, usually involved a shift toward conventional poetry - a shift away from experimental techniques and a concern with style as such, toward a more intense concern with subject. No one would deny, I think, the full success of the best poems in Williams' last volumes: The Descent, To Daphne and Virginia, The Host, and, especially, Of Asphodel. I hope that no one would deny, either, that a tremendous change in style has made these poems possible, and that this change has been toward conventional English poetry.

[quotes Asphodel, That Greeny Flower, PB, 153, lines 1-10]

I would not suggest that this comes about through any willingness on Williams' part - if you talk to him, he is as full of theories as ever. It is just that when he approached this poem, he found a subject, his love for his wife, which was so important to him and about which he had so many things which *had* to be said, that he stopped being a rather academic theorizer on the nature of poetic language and said what he had to get said, in whatever way he could get it said.

One can only be grateful for this late blossoming of Williams'; I would hardly maintain that 'Paterson (Book Five)' is a major part of this renaissance. It is, on the whole, a weaker performance. Still, it has real virtues: a firm translation from Sappho, an affectionate letter from Josephine Herbst, a good description and meditation upon the Unicorn tapestries, and many passages of clear, clean writing which anyone might envy:

[quotes P V, iii, 269, lines 6-23]

How much would you have? Again, Williams' style has always required a certain unevenness of performance. The liveliness of his mind and method have always demanded the freedom to be wrong, pigheaded, pompous, even loud-mouthed - anything but correct and half-dead. It has obviously paid off for him, both as a person and as a poet. His good work is so extremely powerful that it has made his weaker work worth reading, if only to know more, even the weaknesses, even the follies, of so generous a mind.

108. CHARLES OLSON ON 'PATERSON' AS PROCESS, 'EVERGREEN REVIEW'

No. 11, Summer 1959, 220-1

Charles Olson (1910-70) is a widely influential American poet, and author of 'The Maximus Poems' (1960, 1968, 1975), 'Archaeologist of Morning' (1970) and a remarkable book on Melville, 'Call Me Ishmael' (1966). Olson's important essay Projective Verse (1950) appears to have been influenced by, and in its turn to have influenced, Williams. Olson's theory of 'composition by field' is related to the central

tenet of Williams' essay The Poem as a field of Action
(1948, published in 1954 in 'Selected Essays', that 'The
only reality we can know is MEASURE' (283). Chapter 50 of
Williams' 'Autobiography' is titled Projective Verse and a
large part of the chapter is verbatim from Olson's essay.

Olson was, as a poet and in his general sense of world
culture, greatly influenced by Pound, even to the extent
of following Pound's epistolary manner, as is manifest in
the passage in his 'Mayan Letters' (1953; the letters are
addressed to Robert Creeley), where Olson refers to
'Paterson', comparing it with Pound's 'Cantos':

> the primary contrast, for our purposes is, BILL: his
> Pat is exact opposite of Ez's, that is Bill HAS an emo-
> tional system which is capable of extensions & compre-
> hensions the ego-system (the Old Deal, Ez as Cento Man,
> here dates) is not. Yet by making his substance his-
> torical of one city (the Joyce deal), Bill completely
> licks himself, lets time roll him under as Ez does not,
> and thus, so far as what is the more important, method-
> ology, contributes nothing, in fact, delays, deters,
> and hampers, by not having busted through the very
> problem which Ez has so brilliantly faced, & beat
> ('Selected Writings of Charles Olson', edited, with an
> Introduction, by Robert Creeley (New York, 1966), 82-3).

I didn't find the poem easy just where the poet would seem
to have put the weight: the passage of the Cloisters'
tapestry on the hunt of the Unicorn.

One is on familiar ground in the other long passage of
the poem: 'There is a woman in our town,' etc., an open
man-Sappho poem to a stranger woman seen quickly, and
once, on the city street.

There is no distance in the Cloisters passage, such as
there was in 'Paterson' generally and in this instance
here, of the woman. I liked that distance. It defined
the edge of anything, as well as Dr. Williams' own edge,
as he was the 'poet' of 'Paterson.' Here, he is Paterson
him-it self, he is up against the face as closely as the
Cloisters story. It was a point of the old poem, that the
poet was in it to seek a language to deliver men & women
from the lump their lives were without it. The poet was
the one to survive the river and lay the meaning beside
its water. My difficulty with the new poem was that the
tapestry, even if the poet called it 'the living fiction,'
was a tapestry - a sewn cloth of flowers, a white one-
horned beast, and the dogs which hunt it. It was not hard
to enjoy the story, or the poem itself as a poem of mot-
toes written from it: of the identity of virgin and whore,

of the married man carrying a two-in-one image in his
head - the virgin whom he has whored, of the beast itself
wounded, and lay down to rest. It was the zero distance
of the cloth.
 I left it to itself, and to Williams, when there it
was. Walked by syllables, flowerword to flowerword the
intention of the poet and the one thing life (or it is
actually death) he seems to be saying has taught him, is
what one finds out he has made you do. It is no longer a
matter of a thing. It is a track, a movement after the
collision, which he lays down - and you yield to the step
of it from nothing outside it, including yourself & himself, and take nothing from it but itself, away.
 There is an objectivity (which is there not other than
anti-matter) which forces you, by an unexampled subjectivity of (whom Williams calls) 'I, Paterson, the King-
self' to bring you to his line.
 This is what he is talking about, in caps, in the poem
when he says a world of art alone is what has survived
since he was young; and that the only thing which escaped
from the hole of death is 'the imagination,' which cannot
be fathomed, it is through this hole we escape, through
this hole the imagination escapes intact. What looks like
culture-talk, and that thinking the Doctor so long has
said was not where it was, Not in ideas etc. (NOT pro-
phecy, he exclaims here), isn't - by the experience of the
text of the poem in what would appear to be its fussiest,
or cutest (flowers & all that, and at the feet of the
beloved) and least replica passage. Actually and solely,
& quite exactly, the poem offers nothing but *the path* of
itself. 'Nothing else is real.'
 I append these passages which shook out then with that
meaning:

>   Anywhere is everywhere /
>   The moral
>   proclaimed by the whore-
>   house
>   [and to the virgin as
>   well]...
>   Throw it away! (as she
>   did)
>
> •   no woman is virtuous
>   who does not give herself to her lover
>   - forthwith   /
>   and backward
>   (and forward)
>   it tortures itself within me
>   until time has been washed finally
>   under:

                                    and 'I knew all (or enough)
                   it became me   • '
     Take it or leave it,
              if the hat fits -   /
                                   A choice among the
                                                measures

109. JOHN BERRYMAN ON AN 'ECSTATIC ADDENDUM' TO
'PATERSON', 'AMERICAN SCHOLAR'

Vol. XXVIII, no. 3, Summer 1959, 390

Part of a composite review in The Revolving Bookstand, the
essay also considers books by Roethke, Cummings and Karl
Shapiro. A review in 'Times Literary Supplement', 26 June
1969, 680, proposes Williams as a model for Berryman.
   Berryman (1914-72) is an American poet whose works
include 'Homage to Mistress Bradstreet' (1956), a biography of Stephen Crane (1950) and 'The Dream Songs'
(1969). Dream Song No. 324 is An Elegy for W.C.W., the
Lovely Man ('Henry in Ireland to Bill underground').

'Paterson (Book Five)' is a kind of ecstatic addendum to
Dr. Williams' long poem. I wish everyone would read it.
The Unicorn (in tapestries, which the old man, 'I, Paterson, the King-self,' goes to see - question of bus
schedules for getting to the Cloisters) and the virgin,
other women, satyrs, painters, flowers, letters from old
friends (verbatim), the process of age, are the themes and
materials -

            (I have told you, this
      is a fiction, pay attention).

Many rhythms remind one of Pound's in the later 'Cantos';
well, who has a better right to them than Dr. Williams?
The gaiety of this old man is adorable. Any reader will
find passages for himself. My own favourite is two pages
at the beginning of Section 2 (after a translation from
Sappho and a page of economic junk that must be Pound)
about a woman seen in the street whom he *certainly wishes
he had spoken to*!

'Yes, Mrs Williams'

New York, June 1959

110. JOHN C. THIRLWALL, PORTRAIT OF A POET AS HIS MOTHER'S SON, 'NEW YORK TIMES BOOK REVIEW'

28 June 1959, 4

John C. Thirlwall (b. 1904) was a friend of Williams, editor of 'The Selected Letters of William Carlos Williams' and one of the first Williams scholars. He edited The Lost Poems of William Carlos Williams for 'New Directions', no. 16, and contributed to 'New Directions', no. 17, one of the first extended studies of 'Paterson'. Thirlwall was at one time 'preparing a biography' of Williams (editorial note, 'New Directions', no. 17). He wrote an introductory note for Williams' 'Many Loves and Other Plays' (1961).

'Determined women have governed my fate,' is the opening sentence of William Carlos Williams' fortieth (give or take one or two) published book. The three most important women in his long and productive life (he is 75) have been his mother, Raquel Hélène Rose, his grandmother, Wellcome, and his wife, Florence - all most 'determined' women, judging by references to them in his poems and prose. His grandmother appears in several poems, his wife in three novels (beginning with 'White Mule'), but his mother figures in only one collected poem, Eve.

This apparent slight Williams has amply atoned for to the woman who dominated his mind and almost his will for sixty-six years in this record of his mother which he has been writing and rewriting for over thirty years (portions

have appeared in Dorothy Norman's periodical, 'Twice a
Year,' 1938, and in the introduction to Francisco de
Quevedo's 'The Dog and the Fever'). 'Forgive me/I have
been a fool - (and remain a fool),' he wrote to his mother
in Eve some twenty years before her death: 'if you are not
already too blind/too deaf, too lost in the past/to know
or to care - /I will write a book about you - /making you
live (in a book)/as you still desperately/want to live -
to live always - unforgiving.'

Mrs. Williams, who lived to the incredible age of 102,
stayed with her son and daughter-in-law from 1918 until her
death in 1949. A broken hip confined her to bed for twenty
years, and this mother who had lived almost exclusively in
and for her two sons was hard to entertain. Son Willie hit
upon the expedient of translating a Spanish novella, 'El
Perro Y la Calentura' ('The Dog and the Fever'). Between
translation bouts Mrs. Williams would ramble on about her
childhood and youth in Mayaguez, Puerto Rico, and in Paris,
where she had studied art. 'Yes, Mrs. Williams' is a compilation of the notes Dr. Williams smuggled out of his
mother's room.

Like most aged persons, Mrs. Williams was drawn irresis-
tibly to her own childhood and youth. The picture emerges
of a shy, uncertain girl, dominated by her adored doctor-
brother, by a stern father, and by an equally stern mother.
She married apparently to escape the strangulating environment of her island, bore two sons to her English husband
and then proceeded to dominate *their* lives.

This little book would be nothing more than a faded pas-
tiche of Verbena and caracoles did it not throw significant
light on the career as poet and physician of son Willie,
Dr. William Carlos Williams. 'Certainly her life had a
definite form and purpose - not by any means sentimental,'
he wrote in this book. 'It was based on somewhat rigid
loyalties to the idea.' The rest of this passage is quite
instructive and revealing. Writing to a young friend
shortly after his mother's death, Dr. Williams made explicit his feelings about the domineering mother: 'I would
have been enslaved by her if she had had her will. I
fought her because I was forced to fight her to preserve
myself.'

The ideal of Purity and Perfection which the mother in-
stilled in her two sons insured their success but it also
scarred their personalities. Carlos, taking his mother's
counsels literally, strove always to be perfect man, perfect poet and perfect physician. When his aim exceeded
his grasp, he sank into a misery of self-abasement. 'My
poor mother always taught me the highest ideals,' he told
me in 1953; 'to be an artist - to be pure - to be sexless -

and that almost tore me apart.'
  In these pages Dr. Williams reveals much of his true purpose and drive, hitherto hidden. 'What I believe to be the hidden core of my life will not be easily deciphered,' he wrote in the 'Autobiography.' The mother revealed here as consumed with a passion for perfection to be attained only by her two sons holds a clue to this 'hidden core.'

111. THOMAS PARKINSON, 'I WAS LISTENING WITH MY VERY EYES', 'SAN FRANCISCO CHRONICLE'

19 July 1959, 18

Parkinson (b. 1920), who teaches at the University of Cali-California, Berkeley, is a poet and critic. He has written two books on Yeats and edited 'A Casebook on the Beat' (1961).

One of William Carlos Williams' finest poems is The Horse Show, in which he talks to his mother 'intimately, a thing never heard of between us.' It is a very great poem, and Dr. Williams' 'Yes, Mrs. Williams: a Personal Record of My Mother' is its background. I mean that 'Yes, Mrs. Williams' records, without corrective intervention of censorious intellect, some fifteen years of discourse. It is seldom intimate, and there is very little 'I and Thou' in their conversation. If Mrs. Williams describes a dream, it seems as if it happened to someone else. Certainly Dr. Williams dismisses its personal reference quickly: 'You should not be so frightened. You must have been frightened sometimes in your life. It is primitive fear.'
  In place of intimacy, self-revelation, there is objectivity, surprisingly clear in both of them. Their sympathy is based on this, their mutual capacity for letting an object, a proverb, any event, come in clean. They talk without sentiment of past person and process that would, in people of less fundamental detachment, be blurred by the imposition of personal emotion. Little of the conversation was motivated by a desire to cut a figure, make an effect, gain a victory over interlocutor. In fact, only a subterfuge by Dr. Williams, an offer to help his mother translate Quevedo, made it possible for him to transcribe

her conversation as she spoke.

So she spoke without self-consciousness of what, in her very old age, remained wonderful - remarkable - in her past. She quotes proverbs. '*El Que se hace de miel, se lo comen las hormigas*: He who makes himself honey will be eaten by the ants.' She considers children: 'I think the older I get the more I enjoy little children. They're like little birds, jumping around that way. They're so light and springy you know.' As a child, a colored maid tells her of the Devil: 'I was listening with my very eyes.' Out of all this comes a revelation, but it is exposure of sensibility - a hard core of apprehension, accumulating precise memory of event, never crusted over or dulled by experience. There was, as Dr. Williams notes in summarizing her motives, little softness in her. And as his father warned him on his death bed, she was strange and difficult.

Dr. Williams saw her, finally, as a woman with a definite purpose, by no means sentimental or self-pitying, but with her purposes turned outward, to see realized in the accomplishments of her men the desires she could not herself fulfill. 'But such women are not soft, they drive, they do not comfort - they are too restless, too far gone into the destructive ideal - that is why they are afraid to die: For if their life could have been their end, then they have not lived as they desire.'

This book is something more than a supplement to Dr. Williams' autobiography, that brilliant work. It is a tribute and a recognition of indebtedness, a genuine memorial. Mrs. Williams appears in all her infirmities as a person, indestructible, alert, sensible. 'Don't you write about me, she would say - but I confess that I paid little attention to her.' We should be glad that he paid so little attention to her, and so much.

'The Farmers' Daughters'

Norfolk, Conn., September 1961

112. IRVING HOWE ON WILLIAMS' USE OF ORGANIC FORM AND
'PRECISE MINIATURES OF DAILY LIFE', 'NEW REPUBLIC'

13 November 1961, 18-19

Three other books are reviewed in this essay, Stories: New, Old, and Sometimes Good.
    Howe (b. 1920) is an American literary critic and writer on politics. His 'World of Our Fathers' (1976) won him the National Book Award.

William Carlos Williams is by now so deservedly honored an American writer, there can be little harm or impudence in suggesting that his poetry has been somewhat overrated. Except in a few great poems like The Yachts, he does not command a very interesting, certainly not very supple mind; and in lyric verse the quality of the writer's mind reveals itself more forcibly - since there is no mediating agent or fable - than in realistic fiction.
    Williams has a gift for carving miniatures of daily life with such sympathetic precision that they seem to take on an aura of value beyond the limits of what he says or shows. But let him try, as in his long poem 'Paterson,' to employ more complex structures, and the result is often a kind of sentimental incoherence. He can make the phenomenal world seem wonderfully fresh, as if the act of naming were renewed each day, but when he needs to relate that world to human consciousness he tends to become a romantic simplifier. He resorts to cries of delight and other 'elemental' responses which, like all willed simplicities, soon come to appear extremely contrived.

Now one might suppose that weaknesses of this kind would be especially glaring in his fiction, and indeed I remembered his stories as honest flat and grey, mere slabs of reportage about the miseries of life in northern New Jersey. But in reading this collection of 52 Williams stories I have found myself repeatedly surprised to discover how good they now seem. The book is too large, of course: had it been kept down to 15 or 18 stories it would have been truly first-rate. As it is, one must pick and choose, stumbling on such gems as The Use of Force, Jean Beicke, and Old Doc Rivers.

The stories weave into one another, not through a recurrence of theme, character and incident, but through the steadying presence of Dr. Williams himself, a figure notably different from and usually more interesting than William Carlos Williams the *avant garde* poet. Almost all the stories are set in the Paterson-Rutherford area, one of the bleakest in the country, but while Williams sees its ugliness and renders its outrage to eye, nose and ear, he does not shrink from it. Rough, busy and impatient, he moves through his world with the assurance of a man who knows he is of some *use*, and perhaps it is that knowledge which enables him to care genuinely for human beings. He has no illusions, he harries the malingerers - for there is another patient always waiting; but his heart remains open and unsullied, responsive to the wailings of a slum brat or the groans of an old lush.

Williams listens to people. Apparently he believes his responsibility as a doctor involves letting them talk themselves out; besides, he enjoys it, knowing how to appreciate a sudden encounter or conversation; and what they tell him often forms the matter, or at least the impetus, of his stories. His world is one of the few in modern literature where people still connect with one another, and if for no other reason that would make his stories notable. Believing in his work and aware that he does it well, Williams is proud, even pleased with himself. And precisely there, I think, lies the secret of his power as a story-teller: precisely in that innocent and unashamed vanity of his, which braces and tightens the stories, leading them back to such themes as the psychic content made possible by necessary work and the relaxed self made possible through immersion in a public role. How pleasant it is to move through these grim stories with a man who sees no reason to look upon his life with nausea or contempt, and whose readiness for experience opens him to the possibilities of affection. And in the stories all this comes through as it hardly can in the poetry, for what matters in Williams' fiction is not so much the narrowness of his private sensibility as the positive strength of his public role.

Most of the stories are loosely constructed, beginning at whatever point Williams' interest in a character happens to strike fire and ending when he turns away to other patients. Even when there is a plot, it is ramshackle, though not with the calculated artlessness of an Anderson or Hemingway, for most of the stories are episodes along the Williams way, segments of his time and experience. As Philip Rahv observed some time ago: 'What Williams tells us is much too close to him to lend itself to the alienation of design; none of his perceptions can be communicated through the agency of invented equivalents. The phenomena he observes and their meanings are so intimately involved with one another ... that formal means of expression would not only be superfluous but might actually nullify the incentive to creation.'

Yet the stories do have their own kind of aesthetic unity. If ever I have been persuaded of the validity of 'organic form' as a critical notion - the form that is said to proceed not from executive techniques but from an inner harmony or consistency of feeling - it is in reading these stories. What holds them together is the presence of Williams himself, not always a likeable man but usually vibrant with energy and purpose. Indifferent to the formulas of modern criticism, he has no concern to establish 'ironic distance' between himself and his world: he speaks out directly both to the readers and the characters within his stories, for in part his stories are versions of the conversations that have filled his life. And at times such passages of direct statement can be very moving, as in his reflections about getting up in the early hours of the morning to visit a patient:

> These are the great neglected hours of the day, the only time when the world is relatively perfect and at peace. But terror guards them. Once I am up, however, and out it's rather a delight, no matter what the weather, to be abroad in the thoughtful dawn.

What one feels at the end is the appropriateness of Williams himself, doctor listener and story-teller, a man who has found pleasure and fulfillment in useful work. For the present moment in American experience there could hardly be a more vital or disturbing image.

113. ARTHUR M. KAY ON 'A MATTER-OF-FACTNESS THAT RIVALS DEFOE'S', 'ARIZONA QUARTERLY'

Vol. XVII, no. 4, Winter 1962, 368-70

To the physician, the patient's living room had a curious excitement about it:

> There was nothing properly recognizable, nothing straight, nothing in what ordinarily might have been called the predictable relationships. Complete disorder. Tables, chairs, worn-out shoes piled in one corner. A range that didn't seem to be lighted. Every angle of the room jammed with something or other ill-assorted and of the rarest sort.

What intrigues, delights the doctor in Comedy Entombed: 1930 about such disorder and brokenness is that it has, after all, 'An unrecognizable order! - Actually - the new!' It is Williams' gambit in all these stories to play things exactly as they are, with an insistent, uncompromising artlessness that is above posturing and beyond objectivity. 'Life's nonsense,' as Wallace Stevens tells us, 'pierces us with strange relations.'

It is quite natural for critics to praise Williams' 'native freshness,' 'vitality,' 'immediacy,' as they do. Rarely do we find experience rendered in so unfiltered a way. As another patient, Emily, in Mind and Body, says, she once ate up knowledge out of books. But - 'Finally it turned me cold. Those men know nothing at all. It is life, what we see and decide for ourselves, that counts.'

The fifty-two stories in this collection, written over some twenty-five years, tell the truth, mainly. And the truest and best of them are drawn from the medical practice - stories like the devastating The Use of Force or Jean Beicke. Perhaps this is because such pieces, with their stark authenticity, open doors upon a special world of forceps, pain, diagnosis, and prognosis, whose priests and mysteries continually fascinate. Or because the physician must look on and know suffering, courage, and death as an actuality hidden from us behind screen and curtain. The view we get of Williams' people is a clinical one. As the body is bared, so is the soul stripped to reveal its petty embarrassments as well as its deepest despairs. Williams, to the advantage of both his arts, is the best of listeners, a man whose compassion and acceptance inspire confidences. The lid is lifted to expose

nearly every sort of neurosis and abnormality. In The
Knife of the Times a housewife is seduced by her childhood
girl friend. In The Sailor's Son Mrs. Cuthbertson's
maternalistic benevolence has led her to give a poor boy a
job on her farm; she discovers him lying in the hay with a
motorcycle rider. One would think these matters have lost
their power to shock. It is a testimony to Williams'
technique that they do shock. They are presented with a
matter-of-factness that rivals Defoe's.

There is no judging. Williams shares with Chaucer and
Whitman the philosophical inclusiveness that makes truth
bearable. In Danse Pseudo-macabre the doctor, who cannot
choose his time for philosophy, lies in bed musing at
three in the morning listening to the summons of the telephone.

> That which is possible is inevitable. I defend the
> normality of every distortion to which the flesh is
> susceptible, every disease, every amputation. I challenge anyone who thinks to discomfit my intelligence
> by limiting the import of what I say to the expounding
> of a shallow morbidity.

Truth is tempered, not only with compassion, but with
an affirmative affection. What Williams loves in his
people is the life in them, their stubborn vigor - the
dandelion thrusting up through the sidewalk. He is enchanted by the girl with the pimply face, 'A tough little
nut finding her own way in the world.' The doctor in The
Farmers' Daughters boasts of the phenomenal vitality of a
climbing rose in his garden; it thrives against overwhelming odds though the nurseryman was sure it would not
last a winter. Scrawny, misshapen little Jean Beicke, so
worthless a piece of humanity that 'somebody ought to
chuck her in the garbage chute' dies grasping for life;
yet even the details of a postmortem do not obscure the
doctor's deep involvement.

This is never the affectation of affection. Nor are
the objects of affection sentimentalized or prettified.
The heroines come with short, thick legs, 'bunches of
varicose veins about them like vines.' One hero is
'pasty, and covered with a macular eruption which was more
than likely luetic.' Another is 'one of those fresh
Jewish types you want to kill at sight.' Williams' healthiest and most attractive specimens are primitive, animal
types, placid and self-contained, like Mable Watts, in The
Colored Girls of Passenack - Old and New always independent and smiling, never in the least embarrassed or subservient in her manner. Such have, we are told,

'tremendous furnaces of emotional power ... unmatched in any white.'

The medium for that utter verisimilitude which is Williams' key signature is American vernacular, in high fidelity. Here and there an expression may be dated, but I think that no American writer from 'Huckleberry Finn' to 'The Catcher in the Rye,' not ever Lardner, does it better. Some of the short pieces are presented as 'verbal transcripts.' Almost never is the narrator's voice 'literary.' Here is the opening paragraph of An Old Time Raid:

> We were having an absinthe party over at the Franklin House. It was a regular thing with us in those days. We'd drink absinthe and shoot pool, then drift out around midnight wherever else we were going. Sometimes up to Paterson. You know.

Many of the stories are, in effect, dramatic monologues in this vein. 'Collected Stories,' actually, covers a multitude of forms: vignettes; plotless slices, pieces, and hunks of life; straightforward autobiography; essays and descriptive sketches illustrated with anecdote and dialogue.

William Carlos Williams is a major poet. Surely it would be unfair to compare him with the great short-story writers. There is nothing in this collection like The Dead or Flowering Judas or Babylon Revisited. The Farmers' Daughters, the last and longest, is surely not the 'great long story' it is called on the dust jacket. It is not even very long, except by contrast with the others. Old Doc Rivers avoids the sentimentality its title might suggest to some, but, with all its honesty, it is not much more than a reminiscence about an 'unforgettable character'. Long or short, the stories lack density, richness, dimension, design. It is as though many were born between patients and somewhat prematurely. This may be the price paid for immediacy and native freshness. Perhaps we have it all, the good and bad, from Dr. Williams himself when he tells us, 'When by chance we penetrate to some moving detail of life, there's always time to bang out a few pages.'

Still, if we do not have here a supreme fiction, we have something very good and very distinctive. We ought to be grateful for having the stories in this new volume. As for Williams' other prose works, only one novel, 'The Build-Up' of his 'White Mule' trilogy, is in print. It is to be hoped that something is being done about that.

'Many Loves and Other Plays'

Norfolk, Conn., September 1961

114. KENNETH REXROTH, MASTER OF THOSE WHO KNOW, 'NEW LEADER'

11 December 1961, 29-30

Rexroth's review concludes by considering, in general terms, 'The Farmers' Daughters'.

Obviously, some playwrights have been very great poets, but few poets who were not primarily dramatists have ever been good playwrights. Even fewer poets have ever written readable prose fiction. Longfellow wrote a novel; so did Swinburne. Ghastly productions, both of them, though for different reasons. Almost all the great nineteenth-century poets whose portraits decorate the corridors of grammar schools tried their hands at playwrighting. Their work is not only dull and undramatic; it was a failure with theatre audiences in their own day.

Curiously, only Swinburne and Shelley, neither of whom we consider as thinking dramatically at all, wrote plays that are still performable. We may think of the verse of 'Atalanta in Calydon' as on the level of the taste of the hero in 'This Side of Paradise,' but when staged it is a remarkably effective play and more convincingly Greek than Gilbert Murray's translation of Euripedes into pseudo-Swinburnian verse. Shelley's 'The Cenci' is always being reviewed somewhere and is a *tour de force* of deliberate archaism, a genuine Elizabethan tragedy of blood. Many people think it is the best thing Shelley ever wrote. Swinburne's cycle of plays on the career of Mary Stuart

also contains some of the finest dramatic writing of the
19th century and certainly could be put on successfully
today.
   The point is, however, these are archaistic, literary
plays, though not really closet drama. So are the Noh
plays of William Butler Yeats, the only truly radical
innovations in the English theater in our time. Properly
performed, they are gripping, practically hallucinatory in
their effect, but they are hardly about ordinary folk
encountered in the streets of 20th century Dublin. As for
W. H. Auden, except for his first playlet - the symbolic,
mythic 'Paid on Both Sides' - his work seems to have
failed as drama. And Thomas Hardy's 'The Dynasts' is not
really a play at all.
   William Carlos Williams is the only major poet I can
think of who has written effective, more or less realistic, plays about contemporary people. This is a strange
state of affairs. In France, not only Jean Cocteau and
Paul Claudel, but even people as unlikely as Francis
Jammes or Guillaume Apollinaire, wrote plays and saw them
performed. Ibsen, don't forget, always thought of himself
as a poet.
   This lack in the English-speaking stage can be laid
simply at the door of its arrant commercialism. It is
absurd that the doggerel of Christopher Fry or Maxwell
Anderson should see thousands of hours of successful production. T. S. Eliot managed to force his way into the
theater by virtue of his tremendous prestige - in Broadway
terms, a hot commodity. Of course, his plays are not
realistic and not about contemporary people; furthermore,
they are not very good.
   Williams has been fascinated with show business, the
real Broadway thing. He has tried to write in those
terms. To a Turkish student of contemporary American
literature, his plays might look like some of the deeper
excursions of the commercial theater. They undoubtedly
seem so to Williams, and he has never been able to understand why nobody else agrees with him.
   His plays have an absolutely veridical diction, a sweet
ingenuousness, a simple, country doctor kind of morality,
and considerable constructive skill. Properly performed,
they should knock an uncorrupted audience into the aisles.
Alas, point by point, these are precisely the virtues
Broadway does not want, and any possible commercial audience has been corrupted by decades of absorbing the opposite vices. Even so, when some off-Broadway or university
theater does perform a Williams play, it turns out to be
successful enough. 'Many Loves,' for example, has been
running in repertory for more than a year at the Living

Theater in New York.
Anyway, here are all of Williams' plays except the whimsical poetic one-acters of his youth. They're in print. Somewhere a few copies may survive the holocaust, and comes the Revolution, they may be a great success at the Kropotkin Theater on Luxemburg Avenue - or somewhere in some less naughty world than this. Meanwhile, let's hope the college drama groups take them up....

115. NORMAN HOLMES PEARSON, REVIEW, 'YALE REVIEW'

Vol. II, no. 2, December 1961, 331-2

The review opens with a consideration of 'The Farmers' Daughters'.
Pearson (1909-75) taught at Yale University, and besides being co-editor of the influential 'Oxford Anthology of American Literature' (1938) was an assiduous and important collector of American literary materials. He was the literary executor of H.D. (Hilda Doolittle), and in recent years edited a number of volumes of her work, for publication by New Directions.

... William Carlos Williams' interest in the theatre has been life-long, as John Thirlwall shows in the historical sketch of the author's work as a playwright, which comes as an appendix to 'Many Loves, and Other Plays.' The interest is not surprising. Williams' concern with conversation as the design of a novel or short story carries over easily into a medium where there can be nothing so primary as dialogue. As a poet, his struggle for a diction and a line which are natural and direct finds an appropriate challenge to meet in the limitations and possibilities of the spoken voice on the stage. His libretto for 'The First President,' an opera and ballet for which the music has been written but the chance for staging never given, derives (as a libretto) part of its interest from Williams' concept of a national hero. An even greater part comes from the diligently cut crystal of verse lines that take shape without reference to an inherited model. In plays like 'Many Loves' and 'A Dream of Love' his actors gain individuality through the same qualities which characterize the figures in 'The Farmers' Daughters.' At their best, they talk the same fresh language in both books, they have the same capacities for feeling, they have the same agonies of frustration.

Williams once described 'A Dream of Love' as being otherwise than 'the fully dramatic play as generally known.' The intelligent interest of the audience in the drama of this particular play lies, he said, 'not so much in conflict ... as in revelation, development of the Doctor's situation,' - as in his search for the beautiful and the dream of love which includes it the Doctor involves the mistress who says yes and the wife whom he loves. The jacket describes the play as 'a penetrating and poetic treatment of infidelity and marriage.' It is penetrating and poetic, but it could better be called a study in ultimate fidelity. Continued revision of the text, over the last decade, has tightened and intensified the design until now, no matter what Williams once thought, there are both a conflict and a revelation. It is his best play.

'Many Loves' has been his most successful venture into the theatre, and ran for nearly a year off-Broadway. It relies as many of his plays do, not on a tension within a single group of characters but on tension between groups, achieved contrapuntally. 'Many Loves' is a dialogue between four inner-plays which interact and become one. Williams is an artist to be read and reckoned with in any field or form.

116. BENJAMIN T. SPENCER, REVIEW, 'MODERN DRAMA'

Vol. VI, no. 1, May 1963, 97-8

Spencer (b. 1904) is an American teacher and critic.

'But one must be at the advancing edge of the art: that's the American tradition,' wrote William Carlos Williams in a letter nearly thirty years ago; and in these five pieces which have been recently issued as his 'Collected Plays' he constantly manifests the experimental impulse espoused in his dictum on American art. Like Whitman he looks beyond the present to the future development of the art form with which he is concerned; and he too might have written, as did Whitman in Poets to Come, that his plays are, above all, 'indicative words for the future.'

Each of the five plays has its own distinctive mode of experimentation, the most notable perhaps being the libretto for an American opera on George Washington, for which Theodore Harris has written the music. Convinced that grand opera 'must look to America for its rekindling, Dr. Williams has acutely reflected on the character of Washington and on the form of an opera that could properly reveal the 'flaming' essence of the man beneath the somewhat stolid image in which history and tradition have cast him. With a fresh insight into the inherent depth and dedication of the first President and with a feeling that he was the originator of 'the thing we [Americans] still labor to perfect,' the librettist has devised a unique kind of impressionistic opera in which time and place sequences are secondary and in which the music rather than the text liberates for the audience the real character of Washington from the mere events which, as Dr. Williams has said, have imprisoned him. In the stage directions for the various scenes - e.g., with Arnold, with his wife, or at Valley Forge - the librettist has added detailed directions on the lighting to give appropriate impressions of Washington's 'feeling spirit,' and he has suggested occasions in the production when the orchestra should even drown out what Washington is saying. Perhaps Dr. Williams' demands in this opera are too heavy, for thus far it has not been produced.

Quite different in mode of experimentation are the three prose playlets which constitute his Trial Horse No. 1, as he has subtitled 'Many Loves.' The unity of these playlets lies in their counterpoint: they illustrate varying textures of love - adolescent, deviant, familial - and thus illuminate one another by contrast. In addition, however, cutting through the substance of the prose playlets and frequently interrupting the main action with poetic dialogue, a counterplay involving the entrepreneur, the playwright, and the leading lady allows further comment not only on abnormal and possessive love but also on the future of American drama. Hubert, the playwright, must in many ways reflect Dr. Williams' own aspirations and and beliefs when he declares that his 'purpose is/to write for the stage such verse as never/has been written heretofore' - a verse which is not Shakespeare 'diluted down. A new con-/ception more suited to ourselves.' (pp. 14-15) Over the commercial objections of his 'backer,' Hubert insists that verse is the proper medium for the drama of the future, because only it can project 'what I am saying

beyond the words' (p. 32); only through poetry can the
audience be lifted 'to a world it never knew ... beyond
the/dirty boards into the empyrean.' (p. 33) But whatever
his hopeful vision of a poetic drama may indicate for the
future, Dr. Williams has done much to give body and reality to 'Many Loves' through the acuteness of his ear for
the tone and pace and diction of the colloquial idiom,
whether it be that of farmer, mill worker, or suburban
housewife. In 'Many Loves' one feels something of the
authentic simplicity with overtones of complexity that
the poet-playwright Hubert discusses and that are to be
found in Dr. Williams' short stories. This sensitive projection of American idiom has given the playlets the
flavor of life and, no doubt, is in large measure responsible for the year's run that 'Many Loves' has enjoyed in
repertory.

More nearly topical than the other plays, 'Tituba's
Children' skilfully conjoins through character and atmosphere the Salem witch trials and what Dr. Williams con-
strues as a similar witch hunt during the McCarthy era.
After dramatically showing the cruelty unleashed on such
dignified innocents as Giles Cory and the bewildered
Sarah Good by the hysterically malicious and hard-faced
little New England girls (Tituba's children) of the seventeenth century, the drama interweaves the parallel plights
of Mac and Stella, disguised respectively as Giles and
Sarah, in the Washington of 1950. Irresponsible colum-
nists become the latter-day witches, abetted by Senators
Pipeline, Yokell, Gasser, and Wise. But it is the less
topical and experimental 'A Dream of Love' that may well
prove to be the most durable of all the plays. Carefully
detailing the setting of furniture and paintings and the
appearance of the characters, Dr. Williams has drawn on
his own experience as a physician in characterizing Dr.
Thurber, who as also a poet has his 'dream of love' which
leads him into an enduring devotion to his wife but also
into casual affairs with other women; for the dream, as
Doctor Thurber's poem makes clear, (p. 122) is not only of
love but of desire as well. Or, in terms of the poem itself, love is not only 'All white!/a locust cluster/a shad
bush/blossoming' (p. 122) but also 'Yellow, yellow,
yellow/ .... a honey-thick stain/ ... spoiling the colors/
of the whole world - .' (p. 126) Yet the final dream of
love, as Dr. Williams has said, is realized by Dr.
Thurber's wife, Myra, after his death during an assigna-
tion in a hotel room. The play is thus finally Myra's
tragedy, with her ultimate recognition and acceptance of
her rival's role in her husband's life, with a clearer
definition of her own relationship to her dead husband,

and with an awareness, as the variations in his poem show, that love may also be 'a northern flower' or 'a wild/ magnolia bud - / ... on the black/sky.' (pp. 191, 193) Reappearing as a spirit after his death, Dr. Thurber discourses paradoxically on the nature of his fidelity and on the ties between woman and the creative imagination; and the presence of the colored maid Josephine and the milkman adds further dimensions to the dream of love in the most complex of Dr. Williams' plays.

Such complexity is virtually absent from the final play in the volume, 'The Cure,' which Dr. Williams first drafted after a stroke some ten years ago. Here the interrelationship of healing and love, which Dr. Williams has treated so sensitively elsewhere, is not controlled through form, and the lack of aesthetic distance permits exaggerated situations and abrupt and thinly motivated action to converge into unconvincing melodrama and sentimentality. But this failure cannot obscure the vitality of the collected plays as a whole; nor can it dim the probability that a viable and cogent American drama and poetry must take their cue from Dr. Williams rather than, say, from Mr Eliot.

'Pictures from Brueghel'

Norfolk, Conn., June 1962

The English edition was published in London, by MacGibbon & Kee, in October 1963. Both editions include 'The Desert Music' and 'Journey to Love'.

---

117. STANLEY KUNITZ, FROST, WILLIAMS, AND COMPANY, 'HARPER'S MAGAZINE'

October 1962, 100-1

Beginning with a consideration of Frost's 'In the Clearing', the review discusses 'Pictures from Brueghel' before going on to the work of a number of other poets.

Kunitz (b. 1905), an American poet, teacher and editor, won the Pulitzer Prize for his 'Selected Poems 1928-1958' (1958). His 'A Kind of Order: Essays and Conversations' appeared in 1975.

... No fireworks or testimonial dinners, so far as I know, greeted the publication of William Carlos Williams' 'Pictures from Brueghel and other poems' ... but that may be explained by the fact that Dr. Williams is a mere child short of eighty and still an incorrigible rascal. The collection embraces work of the past decade, containing more than fifty poems not previously available in book form, as well as the complete texts of 'The Desert Music' (1954) and 'Journey to Love' (1955), the latter including Asphodel, That Greeny Flower, a modern love poem that will stand comparison with the best in the language.

An extraordinary aspect of Dr. Williams' book is that

the reader is not tempted to make apologies for the most recent poems: they dance as smartly as anything he ever wrote. His responsiveness to experience is a kind of beauty in itself; he remains awake at the controls of his technique - what a joy it is to watch him tinkering with his 'variable foot'!; and he has never stopped tuning his ear to catch the true idiom of the living tongue. The image that he presents to us is not that of the wise ancient or of the poet-as-hero: the man who walks through his poems is the man of our time, fallible, vulnerable, full of marvels. In one of his latest poems, The Stone Crock, the style is characteristically open, almost casual, on the verge of flatness, yet at the same time exquisitely taut, partly as a result of the felt discipline of the mind in its motion, and partly because of the sensitive manipulation of the short fourth line of each stanza - a departure from Dr. Williams' habitual triads - culminating in the isolated power of the very last word of the poem after we have been led to expect it to be thrown away:

[quotes The Stone Crock, PB, 28-9]

118. ROBERT CREELEY, THE FACT OF HIS LIFE, 'NATION'

13 October 1962, 224

A leader of the Black Mountain movement and editor of 'Black Mountain Review', Creeley (b. 1926) is one of the most influential poets of his generation, and has also written short stories and a novel. Until 'Selected Poems' (1976), the most comprehensive collection of his poetry was 'Poems 1950-1965' (London, 1965). The present review is included in Creeley's 'A Quick Graph: Collected Notes and Essays', as are reviews of three other Williams books.

There is no simple way to speak of this book. When a man makes something so much the fact of his own life, then we are all of us involved because each life is first of all that singular.

[quotes The Yellow Flower, PB, 89, lines 1-9]

What we have been told too often to care for in our lives are the plans, tomorrow's solutions, what we can look forward to; no one speaks of what is here to be seen, right now. But that is what there is, to speak of. Against the confusions which come of a blindness to that fact, Dr. Williams puts the things he sees, feels, knows, in the life given him. He has said for a long time that there can be 'No ideas but in things,' and by that he means that no man or woman can hope to avoid what they literally are, or, equally, the reality of which they are a part. We live just as and where we are. As this man does here, for example:

[quotes The World Contracted to a Recognizable Image, PB, 42]

Whatever a poem uses for its means - the rhythms, the order of its words, etc. - all of these must come from what has provoked the writing to begin with. The mind and ear, in this sense, are stripped to hear and to organize what is given to them. The *dance* Williams has used as a metaphor for this recognition of life and its use is present to all:

[quotes lines 25-36 of The Dance, PB, 33]

In The Desert Music - the title poem of an earlier collection (1954) included, together with 'Journey to Love' (1955), in this present book - the music for this dance is 'a music of survival, subdued, distant, half heard....' As an answer to the superficial music of a 'nauseating prattle,' Williams gives 'the form of an old whore in/a cheap Mexican joint in Juarez her bare/can waggling crazily ...':

[quotes The Desert Music, PB, 115, lines 12-18]

And again, finding a form which is apparently human, but which has no simple identity, 'propped motionless - on the bridge/between Juarez and El Paso - unrecognizable/in the semi-dark ...':

[quotes The Desert Music, PB, 119, lines 16-20]

The *dance*, the acts of a life, move to that *music*, the force of the life itself. Anything a man does might well be in reverence of that fact. For the making of a poem it is essential:

[quotes The Desert Music, PB, 120, last 8 lines]

The most recent poems in this book have the same root.
I cannot pick and choose among them because they are all
true. Taste will always argue, but there must come a time
when each poem takes its place among the others in that
life which it works to value, to measure, to be the fact
of. What can one say more than this:

[quotes To Be Recited to Flossie on Her Birthday, PB, 35]

119. ALAN STEPHENS, DR. WILLIAMS AND TRADITION, 'POETRY'

Vol. CI, no. 5, January 1963, 360-2

Stephens (b. 1925) is an American poet and teacher.

Dr. Williams has continued to write in extreme old age
with a boyish eagerness of perception and with what seems
a lucid innocence that is in fact by no means defenseless
- it has maintained itself, decade after decade, by virtue of a solid technique managed with Horatian cunning.
His art is stable - between the earlier poems and these
latest there are no changes of the sort met with, for
example, in Eliot or Yeats; his earlier techniques are in
this book simply more efficiently established. In this
he resembles Thomas Hardy, and in certain other respects
as well. 'Unadjusted impressions have their value,'
Hardy wrote, adding that one may well give experience
its due by setting down 'diverse readings of its phenomena as they are forced upon us by chance and change' -
which defines nicely the central tone of Dr. Williams's
work. (There is something else to notice in Dr. Williams:
as a friend of mine said, he 'mops up - very workmanlike -
a good many loose perceptions that nobody else has bothered to want'.) The work of both men defines a locale;
though Hardy's language seems to take a more substantial
grasp on experience than Dr. Williams's, this is not
always easy to show in the particular case. The best
poems of each man are not obviously different from their
numerous inferiors; but to discern the best poems is to
find that each man at his best can be matched by only a
very few of his contemporaries.

 I have wanted to link myself up with a traditional

art, Dr. Williams explained in 'The Selected Letters', and
in this collection he calls attention to his new measure,
which uses 'the variable foot' and gives us 'the counted
poem, to an exact measure'. These phrases show his concern for the traditional, but I think they are misleading
– not so much descriptions as enthusiastic cries.

'Measure' calls for a unit of measurement, and in our
verse you can select your unit from only a few possibilities: you can count beats, or syllables, or feet constructed of definite and recurrent combinations of stressed and
unstressed syllables; the identity of the line is a matter
of simple arithmetic, and you will search in vain for such
a basis in Dr. Williams's line. The concept of the variable foot no doubt has for Dr. Williams a special analo-
gical value, just as the concept of the eye of the phoenix
had for Japanese painters when they sought to render the
shape of one kind of bamboo leaf; but to speak of the variable foot as a unit of measurement is like speaking of an
elastic inch. Although it is true that often in his verse
there is a more or less regular beat, and that many lines
take a more or less equal time, the attempt to find a
metric in these facts will be occupied as much with exceptions as with any rule.

I believe that the identity of Dr. Williams's line has
no metrical basis, but that nonetheless the line has a
definable identity. The general principle is this: a line
is a line because, *relative to neighboring lines*, it contains that which makes it in its own right a unit of the
attention; and it is as precisely various in its way as
are the shadings of accent that play about the abstract
norm of the metrical foot, for it too has a norm against
which it almost constantly varies, allowing for feats of
focusing on values that would be otherwise indistinguish-
able. The norm is the ordinary unit of the attention in
language – the formal architecture of the sentence. This
principle, it seems to me, also underlines verse with a
metrical basis – is indeed the ultimate principle of all
verse; if this is so, then audible rhythm, whether produced
by a formal metric or by improvisation, is not the supreme
fact of the verse line (though it is of course indispensable) and Dr. Williams will have been working in the tradition all along.

In 'Pictures from Brueghel' he continues to favor short
lines, over which he arranges relatively long sentences,
and this, along with his frequently intricate grammar,
makes for poems that go at top speed, and that require
plenty of freshly developing detail, in order to handle the
feeling, which is simple and very intense. It is verse
that cannot slow down for extended discursive or meditative

passages without beginning to move arbitrarily and grow
tedious in sense - as I think happens in the long piece,
Asphodel, That Greeny Flower, mainly because there is not
enough new activity coming on in any given passage. In
the title poems, on the other hand, there is a pleasant
spareness of language, in vivid movement; and in half a
dozen others there is Dr. Williams's characteristic clean
force, a magnificent firm rhetoric: The Lady Speaks is
as beautiful and moving as anything he has done. There
are others - A Negro Woman, To Daphne and Virginia, The
Sparrow, Shadows, The Orchestra, and the version of Theocritus - which make his later work, like his earlier,
irreplaceable in the tradition.

120. KEITH HARRISON, REVIEW, 'SPECTATOR'

29 May 1964, 731

Harrison (b. 1932) is an Australian poet and teacher.

Pound tells a story somewhere of Williams as a boy being
fascinated with detail, the tying of a shoe-lace could
hold his attention entirely. So it is interesting to see
Williams in his little poem to Pound saying:

> Your English
> is not specific enough
> As a writer of poems
> you show yourself to be inept not to say
> usurious

It is a sly, yet very warm tribute - and with Pound's
anecdote, is a key to Williams's poetics; his world is
almost completely visual, his images all 'specific.'
Williams's attraction for Breughel, then, is almost inevitable, and the first group in this book is a straight
description of some of the major canvases. I cannot see
much merit in them *as poems*. The clipped bare lines have
a certain neatness and charm, but to my ear - or should it
be my eye? - that's all. Elsewhere, though, the method is
highly successful, particularly in the poems where he is
dealing with personal circumstances. What emerges in

these is a vivid apprehension of the physical world and a
strong sense of attachment to people.

Two further things struck me in reading this book - one
is that Williams is a poet who must be taken in bulk; my
previous reading of him had been scanty and bewildering,
because I had missed the recurrent preoccupations, the
deliberate apparently unfinished quality of many of the
poems. The other is that he is in some ways a conventional and even a romantic poet: in Asphodel, That Greeny
Flower, the concepts and symbols are all old hat, yet
because of the delicate play of images the poem is fresh
and original. There are a number of excellent poems in
this book which anyone who cares for poetry will want to
read. Williams stuck with the Imagist techniques when
others had abandoned them, and he made them do surprising
things. One is grateful above all for a sense of pleasure.

121. DONALD DAVIE, TWO WAYS OUT OF WHITMAN, 'REVIEW'

No. 14, December 1964, 14-18

Reviewed also is Theodore Roethke's posthumous collection
'The Far Field' (1963).

Davie (b. 1922), a British poet and critic of note,
teaches at Vanderbilt University, and is the author of
'Purity of Diction in English Verse' (1952), 'Articulate
Energy' (1955) and 'Ezra Pound: Poet as Sculptor' (1964).
His 'Collected Poems' appeared in 1972. 'Pound', his
second study of the American poet, was published in 1976,
and 'The Poet in the Imaginary Museum: essays of two
decades' in 1978.

The case of William Carlos Williams remains the rock on
which Anglo-American literary opinion splits. And ready
as we may be to cry out on British taste for its confident
insularity, I do not find myself sorry or indignant that
British readers, by and large, hold on to their misgivings about what Williams's achievement amounts to.
This is no more than Williams himself seems to have expected: he was so sure that American poetry must break free
of British precedents, and applied himself so resolutely
to this end, that it is no surprise if the British reader
finds himself shut out from Williams's poetry. This makes

it sound as if Williams were an old-fashioned cultural
nationalist, parochially American all through, and the
poorer for it. And for many years, especially when
Williams the stay-at-home was set up against Pound the
cosmopolitan, it seemed that the case was indeed as simple
as that. But no one can think so any longer. Williams
was not simple-minded, though it was part of his rhetorical
strategy often to seem so; he was an elaborate and sophisticated theorist of poetry, though the affectations of his
prose conceal the fact; and in his way he was thoroughly
cosmopolitan, though his court of appeal was French
rather than British, and French painting more than French
poetry. And so younger Americans have been able to make a
programme for themselves out of what Williams and Pound
have in common. One may agree with the Black Mountain
poets that this programme or something like it, represents
indeed 'the tradition' in American poetry of the present
(more than, for instance, the currently fashionable poetics
of exhibitionism derived from Lowell's 'Life Studies'), and
yet one may still believe that Williams's intrinsic
achievement is altogether more precarious and perverse than
such poets will admit. One may admire Williams's disciples
(I think of Edward Dorn, of Robert Creeley), more than one
admires Williams.

Or rather, more than one admires Williams's poems. For
Williams himself was obviously an exceptionally amiable
man, upright and unswerving in his vocation. He earned
the windfall which undoubtedly came to him (and this is
touching) at the very end of his life, in three collections
all published when he was over seventy: 'The Desert Music
and other poems' (1954), 'Journey to Love' (1955), and
'Pictures from Brueghel' (1962). These now appear in
London, in a book confusingly entitled after the last of
them. They ought to be read in chronological order, which
is not how they are printed.

Some of Williams's best pieces are here: in 'Desert
Music', The Descent, To Daphne and Virginia and (less
certainly) The Host; in 'Journey to Love', The Ivy Crown
and (much less certainly) Asphodel, That Greeny Flower,
as well as a slighter piece, Address; and in 'Pictures
from Brueghel', The Polar Bear, The Dance, The High Bridge
above the Tagus River at Toledo, An Exercise, and The
Turtle.

The poems in 'Pictures from Brueghel' are mostly
slight, though deft and graceful at their best. Many pages
are both self-indulgent and self-regarding, and the pre-
tentiousness of, for instance, Some Simple Measures in the
American Idiom and the Variable Foot will raise the blood-
pressure of all but the most committed devotees. (I agree
with G. S. Fraser that British readers cannot *hear*
Williams's rhythms; I often doubt if Americans can hear

them either.) In this, his last collection, Williams is
much of the time writing as *chef d'école*, there are many
'exercises' or examples of how-to-do-it, and the poems
about Brueghel paintings, for instance, talk about 'art',
and therefore about themselves, in a way which in any
other writer would be stigmatized as the most constrictive
sort of aestheticism. On the other hand, there is a new
departure here: 'Pictures from Brueghel' experiments, as
the earlier poems do not, with suppression of punctuation-
stops, so as to achieve syntactical ambiguities of great
complexity, yet controlled.

Even in the more ambitious and impressive poems from
the other collections, Williams spends a lot of time
talking about what he is doing even as he does it. For
example, in Asphodel, That Greeny Flower,

[quotes PB, 154, lines 12-18]

Or, later in the same poem,

[quotes PB, 159, lines 16-28]

This is a poetics of ad-libbing; the poet starts at a
point very far from his subject, and talks his way ner-
vously nearer and nearer to it. Wherever we pick up the
poem we find Williams speaking with a blunt and vulnerable
directness which is peculiarly his, and very appealing;
but because of his doctrine of 'figures', the poem as a
whole is not direct at all, but extremely oblique and cir-
cuitous in the way it approaches the subject.

Among the 'figures' which Williams uses most often are
flowers. We think of him, on the basis of his earlier
anthology-pieces, as remarkable particularly for finding
his figures (or his 'images', as we tend more laxly to
call them) in unpoetical places - in the waste lot, the
rubbish heap, the suburban by-pass: and, sure enough, he
seems to admire Brueghel for finding figures that are unpoetical by Italian Renaissance standards. But in these
later pieces we are more often disconcerted by figures
such as flowers which by our standards are very poetical
indeed. Not only asphodel but daisies, mustard-flowers,
jonquils and violets, even, and indeed especially, roses -
flowers, or rather the names of flowers, are all over the
place. The device is at its lamest in The Pink Locust;

[quotes PB, 141, lines 13-25]

This is something worth saying. But the way of saying it!
From whatever standpoint this is surely wretched writing,

ad-libbing at its most poverty-stricken. In a slightly
better poem, Deep Religious Faith, or in one of the positively good ones, The Ivy Crown, flowers still have a
symbolic significance which is fixed and inert, imported
into the poem as a stock response, not created nor re-
created in language. (The same is true of the flowers in
Olson's 'Maximus Poems'.) And not only flowers get this
treatment. In The Desert Music the music which is
appealed to is as much of an inert talisman, as little
created or re-created, as near to the unsupported assertion, as in many of these poems flowers are. And under
the influence of this the valuable directness of utterance
degenerates into something stolid and glib, as at the end
of A Negro Woman:

>   holding the flowers upright
>   as a torch
>   so early in the morning.

To my ear the same tone sounds at the end of The Gift,
where none of the stock 'figures' are in play:

[quotes PB, 62, concluding lines]

One can admire the courage of this directness in confront-
ing a subject so awesome as Christ's Nativity, and it is
perhaps our nervousness with the subject which makes us
hear as mawkish what in fact is tender. But the flatu-
lence of this ending is another matter. It is, I suspect,
the very note of the *faux-naif*. And I suspect also that
no American ear can register this as off-key, simply
because so much of American literature from the first has
been committed to recovering Adam's innocence, a valuably
child-like naiveté of perception. If Williams, like other
devoted Americans, lapses into the *faux-naif*, this is the
price he cannot help but pay for what he sometimes triumphantly achieves, the tone of the true naif, piercing
and unforgettable. Almost certainly the British reader
values this less than he should: we are nervous at being
found so much in the open, unprotected by any armour of
wit. And so the poems we shall find it easiest to admire
are The Descent, where Eliot's Burnt Norton in the background (Williams triumphantly survives the comparison)
gives a sort of witty double perspective; and To Daphne
and Virginia, where the tone becomes momentarily, and un-
typically, sardonic:

>   We are not chickadees
>   on a bare limb

with a worm in the mouth.
The worm is in our brains....

122. THOM GUNN ON 'A VALID ALTERNATIVE OF STYLE AND ATTITUDE', 'ENCOUNTER'

Vol. XXV, no. 1, July 1965, 73-4

This is the concluding passage from an essay titled William Carlos Williams and a footnote lists a number of Williams' works, the earliest being 'In the American Grain' (1925) and the latest the English edition of 'The Collected Later Poems' (1965). Gunn has little to say about 'The Collected Later Poems', much more to say about 'Paterson I-V' (English edition, 1964), but his remarks about 'Pictures from Brueghel' are particularly illuminating because of his perception of the place 'disorder' plays in Williams' work. Hence, although it is slightly later in date, it seems appropriate to include this excerpt with reviews of 'Pictures from Brueghel'.

... The first book of his to be published over here was his most recently written, 'Pictures from Brueghel,' which contains his last three collections of poems. There is a bareness about it that I can imagine was at first disconcerting to readers unfamiliar with Williams. But the bareness is not a sign of tiredness, rather it is the translation into language of a new ease in his relationship with the external world. A result of the ease is seen in the much greater emphasis on the personal that we find in this volume. In Dog Injured in the Street and The Drunk and the Sailor, for example, poems which twenty years before would merely have implied Williams as onlooker, the subject is Williams himself so much involved in what he witnesses that he as good as participates in it. Another result of the ease is in the style, which is transparent to his intentions as never before. Statement emerges from Williams as both subject and author of the poem, not from him merely as author.

It is, however, from 'Paterson' that Williams consciously dates his final development in style. The passage from Book II that he here reprints as a separate poem

entitled The Descent contains many lines divided into
three parts, which he called 'variable feet.' I do not
find the name very clear: as Alan Stephens has pointed out
in a review, a variable foot is as meaningless a term as
an elastic inch; but if calling it so helped Williams to
write this last volume, then it is sufficiently justified.
Specifically, it gave him a rationale for the short lines
grouped in threes that he wanted to use, of which the
rhythms are as flexible and varied as in the best of his
earlier poetry. This poem is about old age and is expressed largely in abstract terms; in tone, even in sound, it
bears an astonishing - though we may hardly assume derivative - resemblance to some of the best passages of the
'Four Quartets'; it advances with a halting, exploratory
movement which is itself much of the poem's meaning. He is
speaking of the re-creation achieved by memory:

[quotes from The Descent, PB, 73, lines 14-22]

Memory is a means of renewal, and for Williams anything
that renews is an instrument for the exploration and definition of the new world, which he labours both to 'possess' and be part of. For possession of the details is
achieved not through the recording of them, but through the
the record's adherence to his feeling for them. The process is not of accumulation but of self-renewal.

>   The roar of the present, a speech
>   is, of necessity, my sole concern

he has said, in 'Paterson,' but he is agent for the present only through the fidelity of his love for it.
   The nature of the process is defined in this book with
a renewed confidence, also. If in 'Spring and All' the
poet is seen as the firm antagonist to disorder and in
'Paterson' as helplessly involved with that disorder, he
is seen in The Sparrow finally as in a world where perhaps
the words order and disorder are irrelevant. The sparrow
is to a certain degree helpless, but he can 'flutter his
wings/in the dust' and 'cry out lustily.' In this poem
the poet and his subject-matter share in the same activity, the essence of which is the expression of delight at
one's own vigour. Vigour and delight inform the style
itself, relating anecdote, description and statement
smoothly and easily. 'It is the poem/of his existence/
that triumphed/finally,' he says of the sparrow, and in
saying so might have been writing his own epitaph, for
poem and existence are seen here to be expressed in similar terms.

There is more than self-expression involved; and, clearly, if we wish to learn from Williams' achievement, we should mark the clarity of evocation, the sensitivity of movement, and the purity of language in his efforts to realise spontaneity. But at the same time we should remember that these qualities, easy as they are to localise, cannot be learned from him in isolation. They, and the self-discipline controlling them, derive from a habitual sympathy, by which he recognises his own energy in that of the young housewife, the boys at the street corner, the half-wit girl who helps in the house, the sparrow, or the buds alternating down a bough. His stylistic qualities are governed, moreover, by a tenderness and generosity of feeling which makes them fully humane. For it is a humane action to attempt the rendering of a thing, person, or experience in the exact terms of its existence.

Valedictories

123. DENISE LEVERTOV, WILLIAM CARLOS WILLIAMS, 'NATION'

16 March 1963, 16

Levertov (b. 1923), an American poet, was born in England and her earliest poetry was influenced by Herbert Read. Since 1947 she has lived in the United States and is a leading figure in the Black Mountain movement. More strongly perhaps than any other member of that movement, Levertov has been influenced by the poems and ideas of Williams, and this obituary is one of several pieces on him in her prose collection 'The Poet in the World' (1973).

William Carlos Williams has left more for us than we realize. Even those - an increasing number in recent years - who love his work are often curiously unfamiliar with it; not because they have not troubled to read it well, but because of its inner abundance and intrinsic freshness. One is forever coming across something new on pages one thought one had known long since. It is as if his poems were plants, changing with the seasons, budding and blossoming over and over.

 Of asphodel, that greeny
  flower ...

And this is timelessness.
 But he has given us also a great gift within time: that is to say, his historical importance is, above all, that more than anyone else he made available to use the whole range of the language, he showed us the rhythms of speech

as poetry - the rhythms and idioms not only of what we say aloud but of what we say in our thoughts. It is a mistake to suppose that Williams' insistence on 'the American idiom' even implied a reduction; on the contrary, it means the recognition of wide resources. Williams' poems, God knows, are not written in 'the speech of Polish mothers': but he demonstrated that the poem could (and in some sense must) encompass that speech. Only a poetry with its roots in the language *as it is used* can be free to explore and reclaim all those levels that otherwise become 'only literature.' Only a poetry freed from rhythmic patterns that had become habitual and inapt can discover the rhythms of our experience. He cleared ground, he gave us tools.

When I first met Dr. Williams about twelve years ago he had already had a serious stroke. Over the years I used to say to myself each time I went to Rutherford, 'He's old and frail; this may be the last time you will see him.' And each time he would astonish me again with his vitality, his shrewd humor, his undeviating, illuminating attention to what concerned him - the poem, the poem. This passionate concern flamed up out of his frailness and made one forget it. Always I left his house in a state of exhilaration. Except for the last time of all, a few weeks ago, when his tongue could no longer find the words he needed for the ideas one could see in his eyes, and he kept giving up in mid-sentence, sad and baffled. Yet even then, vague as he had become about many things, there remained that eagerness to hear a new poem, that acute, *distinguishing* listening. Concerning dates and events he was more confused that day than I had ever seen him, but poetry remained in pristine focus.

I have always felt that all of his works - the tremendous output of poems, plays, essays, stories, letters, novels - were to an unusual degree parts of a whole, complete though each was in itself. This is perhaps one of the marks of a great writer. The shorter poems in particular partake, in their multiplicity, of this unity that is meant by Arnold's term, 'criticism of life': when we see them in relation to one another, each separate poem, though it had given us of itself before, begins to release more levels of meaning than we realized when we read it in isolation.

Working always toward an order, a measure consonant with his time, it was in old age, with a body of work already done that would have appeased the demon of a lesser man, that he arrived at his greatest poems - those in 'The Desert Music' (1954) and 'Journey to Love' (1955)....

124. HAYDEN CARRUTH, WILLIAM CARLOS WILLIAMS AS ONE OF US, 'NEW REPUBLIC'

13 April 1963, 30-2

The death of William Carlos Williams on March 4 was expected and even longed for, in the pitiable way that human beings must adopt when they are touched and concerned, by those who knew him. He had been ill for a long, long time. We can be grateful, on his account and our own, that even during the last tortured years he was able to write some of the time. The work of the final decade contains some of his most beautiful writing, as full of life as ever. And that - his undeviating dedication to life and all it implied - was the key to everything he wrote, everything he did. It gave him, one fervently hopes, the satisfaction he deserved. Certainly it will continue to satisfy us and those who come after us, if there are any, as we turn to it again and again in his poems.

In paying tribute to Williams, I should like to quote a poem of his which has never appeared in any of his books. It was found last summer by Mrs. Williams when she was rummaging among family papers; somehow it had got mislaid. It is called Child and Vegetables, and was published in the magazine 'This Quarter' (Vol. II, No. 4, dated April-May-June 1930); probably it was written about a year earlier. Here it is:

> The fire of the seed is in her pose
> upon the clipped lawn, alone
>
> before the old white house
> framed in by great elms planted there
>
> symmetrically. Exactly in the centre
> of this gently sloping scene,
>
> behind her table of squash and green
> corn in a pile, facing the road
>
> she sits with feet one by the other
> straight and closely pressed
>
> and knees held close, her hands
> decorously folded in her lap. Precise

>   and mild before the vegetables,
>   the mouth poised in an even smile
>
>   of invitation - to come and buy,
>   the eyes alone appear - half wakened.
>
>   These are the lines of a flower-bud
>   tight petals, thoughtfully
>
>   designed, the vegetables, offering
>   in a rite. Mutely the smooth globes
>
>   of the squash, the cornucopias
>   of the corn, fresh green, so still
>
>   so aptly made, the whole so full
>   of peace and symmetry ...
>
>   resting contours of eagerness
>   and unrest -

No doubt the most famous statement Dr. Williams ever uttered is the theme recurrent in his poems, especially 'Paterson,' that there are 'no ideas but in things.' And no doubt it is also the least understood by his disciples and admirers (who today are many), even though Williams took trouble to amplify his meaning.

When they set aside everything in 'Paterson' beyond the statement that there are 'no ideas but in things,' when they say that the statement is literally true, when they claim it as a sanction for their anti-intellectual attitudes, and finally when they use it as a warrant for attempting to write poems without ideas, poems which (in their terms) will have the 'purity' of 'self-existent objects,' then they are doing Williams, themselves, and all poetry, a grave disservice.

On the face of it, the statement is literally not true. Williams, who was a physician as well as a poet and by all accounts a good one, did not believe it to be literally true; without sophistry, he couldn't do so. Take an idea of the order of 'a stitch in time saves nine.' It is a simplistic idea, coated with layers of sanctimony and unction. Nevertheless, it can be stripped of its offensive qualities and revealed at the center as a true idea, what is called a 'self-evident' idea. But it is not self-evident because it occurs objectively; on the contrary, no objects combined in nature could ever express it; it did not exist until a mind made it, and it could not exist now if there were no mind to recover it.

For a long time people have been trying to invent a truth of art which could supersede the truth of objective reality. At some rather indeterminate point in the history of culture it was seen that the work of art is a dynamic structure, and that like all dynamic structures it possesses a certain self-existent quality, or what we call autonomy. Then about a hundred years ago the concept was seized upon as a means of turning art into an anti-reality which would have its own laws and hence would be more interesting, beautiful, and durable than the whole objective world. At first the effort issued merely in art-for-art's sake dilettantism, soon discredited. But through the refinements of the symbolists, expressionists, futurists, surrealists, neo-metaphysicals, etc., the notion has gained wide currency among artists and intellectuals, and even among certain branches of philosophy. In essence it holds that language, through the 'revolution of the word,' has constituted itself a new reality with its own self-revealing authority, different from an fundamentally opposed to the old-fashioned reality, whatever that may have been. At the same time, however, the poem, being a structure of language, possesses its own solely objective validity.

Meanwhile, other people, including some artists and intellectuals, were being consumed in furnaces, intoxicated in gas chambers, afflicted by rapists and torturers, disinfected by brainwashers - all reality's old merry pranks.

Clearly, neither things nor ideas (nor poems, of course) have the kind of irrelative self-completeness (which the autonomists desire), and such self-completeness is only the dream-product of a deeply divisive mania. The truth is that things and ideas and poems are realities among many realities, conformable to the general laws, not opposable in any useful sense.

But reality (whatever it is) is intractable, and usually ugly and boring as well, with the result that some people will always try to escape it by one means or another. You can't blame the poets more than the rest. Beyond this, reality consists of Right and Wrong; and since Wrong is by nature ascendant, Right is continually tempted into sanctimony and unction (to say nothing of bigotry), and the effort to resist these temptations is difficult and tedious - another reason for escaping. It is all a misfortune, the whole business; so grave a misfortune indeed that people lately have taken to calling it an absurdity. But no degree of absurdity can extricate man from reality, or relieve him, so long as he is alive, from the necessity of thinking about it.

What does Williams say? 'When a man makes a poem, makes it, mind you, he takes words as he finds them interrelated about him and composes them - without distortion which would mar their exact significance - into an intense expression of his perceptions and ardors that they may constitute a revelation in the speech that he uses.' I was tempted to cut this statement in order to make it more readable, but I didn't; here it is in all its ambiguity and inclusiveness. Williams' fine instinct for style always deserts him when he comes face-to-face with an ultimate question of principle. Here his emphasis on *words*, *speech*, *expression*, etc., seems to put him squarely in the anti-realist camp, alongside Valèry and Gottfried Benn. But we know from his whole work that Williams devoted himself, perhaps more fervently than any other modern poet, to life as it is lived. He was drawn two ways at once, a deep ambivalence that runs through all his writing.

He speaks also of a *revelation* without saying what is revealed, though elsewhere he seems to imply that it is beauty in the Keatsian sense. Is it equal to truth, to morality? One can't possibly tell, because like other poetic radicals of his generation Williams distrusts these terms and seldom uses them except in disparagement. Nor can we learn much from observing that Williams connects revelation to perceptions and ardors, two imprecise terms which are interesting here chiefly because they denote the subjectivity of poetic materials. But if we go back to the verb in Williams' statement - *composes* - I think we can get at the active part of his view of poetry, and we can see how it works by looking once more at the rediscovered Child and Vegetables.

It isn't a great poem, but it is good enough and quite characteristic. Here are a number of objects - a child, a house, trees, a table, some vegetables, a road. With the great skill which was always his, Williams presents them in all their immediacy and self-proclaiming presence. Very good. But did these objects occur this way in reality? The answer is no. Can things collected objectively possess symmetry or any other mode of arrangement? No again. The arrangement was made by the poet. If you like, it was *seen* by the poet; to me the distinction is academic. The point is that another poet might have seen these objects quite differently- haphazardly or even brutally.

The arrangement, the composition, the disposition - it is everything and it is an idea; it is an idea in the mind, not in things. And can anyone doubt that it is also an idea which entails an act of judgment, *an act of*

morality? Even if the whole force and tone of the poem
did not assure this, Williams himself made it explicit by
his use of such loaded words as *peace* and *symmetry*. This
is as close as he ever came to sanctimony, but it is close
enough; the poem might be better if these words were
removed (though it is interesting to see that *symmetri-
cally* in the fifth line appears without distortion and
hence is properly poetical). The poem is an idea, it is
a specifically moral idea, and it lives because this is
so.

On a far broader scale and in a far more complex condition of control, 'Paterson' also is a moral idea. In
its substance it is, like all fine poems, a life-affirming
idea. It is a defense of the Right without sanctimony.
It is an acknowledgment of reality, and a confrontation as
well, with no feelings spared. It is, incidentally, an
explicit avowal that the poet's mind in all its faculties
is an indigenous component of reality; that is what is
meant by 'no ideas but in things.' Finally, it is not an
escape into any kind of anti-reality, linguistic or other,
but an assertion of ultimate human dignity; that is to
say, an assertion of the efficacy of ideas (especially
the procedural ideas of love and justice) in the face of
whatever is brought to bear against us.

Certainly it is time now to say these things loudly and
lovingly. William Carlos Williams was one of us; committed to our life, our reality, our enigma. He was a man
of courage who required neither escape nor mystification.
His poems will be our bulwark, I think, long after the
anti-realists have followed their inadequate doctrines
into the history books.

125. KENNETH BURKE, WILLIAM CARLOS WILLIAMS 1883-1963,
'NEW YORK REVIEW OF BOOKS'

Vol. I, no. 2, Spring-Summer 1963, 45-7

Burke, who was one of the earliest influential American
critics to recognize Williams' talent and who followed his
whole career, fittingly provides its most substantial
valedictory. (Burke's review of 'Sour Grapes' is No. 10,
above.) The essay is reprinted in Burke's 'Language as
Symbolic Action' (Berkeley, Calif., 1966), 382-91.

William Carlos Williams, poet and physician. Trained to
crises of sickness and parturition that often came at odd
hours. An ebullient man, sorely vexed in his last years,
and now at rest. But he had this exceptional good luck:
that his appeal as a person survives in his work. To
read his books is to find him warmly there, everywhere
you turn.

In some respects, the physician and the poet might be
viewed as opposites, as they certainly were at least in
the sense that time spent on his patients was necessarily
time denied to the writing of poetry. But that's a superficial view. In essence, this man was an imaginative
physician and a nosological poet. His great humaneness
was equally present in both roles, which contributed
essentially to the development of each other.

'There is no thing that with a twist of imagination
cannot be something else,' he said in an early work,
whereby he could both use flowers as an image of lovely
womanhood and speak of pathology as a 'flower garden.'
The principle made for great mobility, for constant
transformations that might affect a writer in late years
somewhat like trying to run a hundred yards in ten sec-
onds flat. At the same time, such shiftiness in the new
country of the poet's mind allowed for imaginal deflec-
tions that could be at once secretive and expressive.
Also (except that the simile fails to bring out the
strongly personal aspect of the work) his 'objectivism'
was like inquiring into baseball not in terms of the rule
book, but rather by noting the motions and designs which
the players in some one particular game might make with
reference to the trajectories of a sphere that, sometimes
thrown, sometimes struck, took various courses across a
demarcated field. Such constant attempts to see things
afresh, as 'facts,' gave him plenty to do. For he proceeded circumstantially, without intellectualistic short-
cuts - and with the combined conscientiousness of both
disciplines, as man of medicine and medicine man.

An anecdote might help indicate what I have in mind
about Williams. (For present purposes, I think, we should
refer to him thus, though the usage does greatly mis-
represent my personal attitude). Some years after
Williams had retired from his practice as a physician, and
ailments had begun to cripple him, we were walking slowly
on a beach in Florida. A neighbor's dog decided to accompany us, but was limping. I leaned down, aimlessly hoping
to help the dog (which became suddenly frightened, and
nearly bit me). Then Williams took the paw in his left
hand (the right was now less agile) and started probing
for the source of the trouble. It was a gesture at once

expert and imaginative, something in which to have perfect
confidence, as both the cur and I saw in a flash. Feeling
between the toes lightly, quickly, and above all *surely*,
he spotted a burr, removed it without the slightest cringe
on the dog's part – and the three of us were again on our
way along the beach.

I thought to myself (though not then clearly enough to
say so): 'And here I've learned one more thing about
Williams' doctrine of "contact."' It concerned the
'*tactus eruditus*,' and I quote words that he had tossed,
as a line all by itself, into a somewhat rough-and-tumble
outburst, This is My Platform, (1) he had written in the
twenties.

Some forty years earlier, when I had first haggled with
him about this slogan (which is as basic to an understanding of him as the statement of poetic policy he makes
several times in his writings, 'No ideas but in things'),
the talk of 'contact' had seemed most of all to imply that
an interest in local writing and language should replace
my absorption in Thomas Mann's German and André Gide's
French. Next, it suggested a cult of 'Amurricanism' just
at the time when many young writers, copying Pound and
Eliot, were on the way to self-exile in Europe while more
were soon to follow. (I mistakenly thought that I was to
be one of them.) Further, it seemed to imply the problem-
atical proposition that one should live in a small town
like Rutherford rather than in the very heart of Babylon
(or in some area that, if not central to the grass roots
of the nation, was at least close to the ragweed).

But over the years, as Williams persisted unstoppably
in his ways, the nature of his writings gradually made it
clear that the implications of 'contact' and its particular kind of 'anti-poetry' were quite different, and went
much deeper. I feel sure that, whatever may be our un-
certainties about the accidents of his doctrine, its
essence resides in the kind of physicality imposed upon
his poetry by the nature of his work as a physician.
Thus, as with the incident of the dog, my understanding of
his slogan took a notable step forward when, some time
after giving up his practice, he said explosively that he
missed the opportunity to get his hands on things (and he
made gestures to do with the delivering of a child). However, my thesis is not made any easier by the fact that,
while including Aaron Burr among his band because Burr
felt the need 'to touch, to hear, to see, to smell, to
taste' (thus being 'intact' in the ways of contact), at
the same time Williams disapproved of Franklin, 'the face
on the penny stamp,' and complained with regard to Franklin's perpetual tinkering: 'To want to touch, not to wish

anything to remain clean, aloof - comes always of a kind of timidity, from fear.'

The point is this: For Williams any natural or poetic concern with the body as a sexual object was reinforced and notably modified by a professional concern with the body as a suffering or diseased object. (Think how many of his stories testify to his sympathetic yet picturesquely entertaining encounters with wide areas of both physical and social morbidity.) The same relation to the human animal in terms of bodily disabilities led him to a kind of democracy quite unlike Whitman's, despite the obvious influence of Whitman upon him. 'After some years of varied experience with the bodies of the rich and the poor a man finds little to distinguish between them, bulks them as one and bases his working judgments on other matters.' (In any case, the political editorializing in Whitman's come-one-come-all attitude had lost its meaning, other than as a pleasant sentiment, in proportion as Congress erected legal barriers to the flow of immigrants by a quota system.)

The same stress upon the all-importance of the bodily element accounts also for the many cruel references to subsidence that are scattered through 'The Collected Later Poems.' (We shall later get to the earlier, more athletic stages.) Consider The Night Rider, for instance, that begins, 'scoured like a conch/or the moon's shell/I ride from my love/through the damp night,' and ends: 'the pulse a remembered pulse/of full-tide gone.' The theme naturally lends itself to other minds of imagery: 'The old horse dies slow'; the portrait of an old goat, 'listless in its assured sanctity'; a time of drought (The Words Lying Idle); the tree, stretched on the garage roof, after a hurricane; homage to the woodpecker, 'stabbing there with a barbed tongue which succeeds'; apostrophizing the self, 'why do you try/so hard to be a man? You are/a lover! Why adopt/the reprehensible absurdities of/an inferior attitude?'; with the mind like a tidal river, 'the tide will/change/and rise again, maybe'; there is the theme of The Thoughtful Lover who finds that 'today/the particulars of poetry' require his 'whole attention'; and of a Bare Tree he writes, 'chop it down/and use the wood/against this biting cold.' In this group, certainly, would belong The Injury, an account of the poet lying in a hospital bed; he hears 'an engine/breathing - somewhere/in the night: - soft coal, soft coal,/soft coal'; in terms of the laboring engine's sounds as he interprets them, he makes plans for the next phase, 'the slow way ... if you can find any way.' This expression of dispiritedness wells up so simply, so spontaneously, it is itself a

poignantly beautiful instance of spirit. And for a happy
and charming variation on such themes, there is Spring is
Here Again, Sir, ending:

[quotes concluding 8 lines of Spring is Here Again, Sir,
CLP, 198]

The sullen reference (already quoted) to using the 'bare
tree' as firewood reminds us that whereas in an early poem
fires came 'out of the bodies/Of all men that walk with
lust at heart,' in later poems the theme of fire could be
modified by merging with connotations of the purgative
Thus, there is the ecstatic section to do with fire in
'Paterson.' And his rightly well-known piece, Burning the
Christmas Greens, interweaves this elation of the purgative with the color that is always the best of omens in
Williams' work. I have at times got courage from the
thought that a poem of his, entitled At Kenneth Burke's
Place, has for its ending a reference to a greening apple,
'smudged with/a sooty life that clings, also,/with the
skin,' and despite a bit of rot 'still good even unusual
compared with the usual.'

But this moves us to a further step in his benignly
nosological approach to the subject-matter of poetry. I
refer to his interest in the sheer survival of things, so
that he would record the quality of an ungainly apple from
a gnarled old unpruned, unsprayed tree, 'as if a taste
long lost and regretted/had in the end, finally, been
brought to life again.' Thus it seems almost inevitable
that he should get around to writing a long poem, The
Desert Music. Along these lines, I have thought that an
ideal subject for a poem by him would be a gallant description of weeds, wildflowers, bushes and low trees
gradually carving out a lifelihood for themselves in the
slag piles around Scranton. This would be done without
sentimentality. (Poems of his like that can't be sentimental, for they say what's actually there in front of
him, as with his lines on the rat, surviving even infec-
tions deliberatly imposed by the hellish ingenuity of man-
made plagues, an animal 'well/suited to a world/condi-
tioned to such human "tropism/for order" at all cost.')
Here would belong his many poems that, by the very accuracy of their description, testify to his delight in scattered, improvised bits of beauty, as with things one can
see during that most dismal of transitions, Approach to a
City (tracks in dirty snow, 'snow/pencilled with the
stubble of old/weeds,' dried flowers in a bar-room window,
while 'The flags in the heavy/air move against a leaden/
ground.') In such observations, he says, he can 'refresh

himself. Cannot one easily see how his doctoring figured
here, teaching him never to overlook 'a mud/livid with
decay and life,' and where the doctor had found sheer
life, challenging the poet to go a step further and spontaneously find it beautiful, as a theologian might have
striven to find it good?

   See, on this point, The Hard Core of Beauty, describing
things on 'the/dead-end highway, abandoned/when the new
bridge went in finally.' Just stop for a while, go back
over that line, ponder on each moment – and I'm sure
you'll agree that, whatever its cruel, spare sharpness,
there's something softly nostalgic like a voice heard
through a mist. Within it there's the thought that never
left him, the beauty and cleanness of the river around the
falls at Paterson, before its rape by the drastic combination of raw politics, raw technics and raw business. (In
earlier years, he referred to the area as 'the origin
today of the vilest swillhole in christendom, the Passaic
river.') All the time the poet-doctor is pointing out,
again and again, what survives, there is also the poignancy of what is lost.   And in 'Paterson,' along with the
love, there is the tough, unanswerable, *legalistic documentation* of man's brutal errors, and their costliness to
man. As he put it in another book, 'Poised against the
Mayflower is the slave ship.' This too was *contact*. And
he has done for that damned botched area just west of the
Hudson (that hateful traffic-belching squandering of
industrial power atop the tidal swamps) something quite
incredible: he has made it poignantly songful. He went on
singing, singing, singing, while the rivers and the soil
and the air and the fires became progressively more polluted in the name of Progress, while more and more of the
natural beauties were ripped apart, singing while each
year there spread inexorably farther west a cancerous
growth of haphazard real-estating that came to enclose his
own fine old house in some measure of the general urban
sprawl. When the sun rises behind 'the moody/water-loving
giants of Manhattan,' eight miles to the east, they must
cast their shadows for a time on the houses west of the
Meadows. And in any case the troublous monsters at a distance, magical in the morning or evening mist, did unques-
tionably cast their shadows on his work.

   I have said that Williams was never 'sentimental.' But
I must say more on this point, in view of Wallace Stevens'
remark in his preface to Williams' 'Collected Poems 1921-
1931': 'The Cod Head is a bit of pure sentimentalization;
so is The Bull.' But, as you must expect of Stevens, the
word is used in a quite alembicated sense, to name 'what
vitalizes Williams,' and to serve as a proper

accompaniment to his 'anti-poetic' side. To see most
quickly how the two motives work together, one needs but
think of a gruffly beautiful line like 'the moon is in/
the oak tree's crotch.' Or 'Little frogs/with puffed out
throats,/ singing in the slime.'

I meant that Williams' typical use of imagery does not
involve *false* or *forced* sentiment. If I correctly inter-
pret Wallace Stevens' Nuances of a Theme by Williams (in
'Harmonium'), Stevens meant by sentiment any personal
identification with an object, as distinct from an appreciation of it in its pure singularity, without reference
to its possible imaginary role as a mirror of mankind.

In this sense, Williams is 'sentimental.' For all his
'objectivist' accuracy, Williams' details are not in essence descriptions of things but portraits of personalities. Typically in his poems the eye (like a laying on of
hands), by disguised rituals that are improvised constantly anew, inordinates us into the human nature of
things.

As regards the two poems that Stevens specifically mentions, the ending of The Cod Head ('a severed codhead
between two/green stones - lifting/falling') involves
associations that might ultimately fit better with a title
somehow combining 'severed godhead' and 'codpiece' - and
something similar is obviously afoot at the end of the
poem The Bull: 'Milkless/he nods the hair between his
horns/and eyes matted/with hyacinthine curls.' As with
Marianne Moore, Williams' observations about animals or
things are statements about notable traits in people.
Along with their ostensible nature, the sympathetic reader
gets this deeper dimension as a bonus, an earned incre-
ment. Let's be specific. I shall quote a brief item
that, if it doesn't seem almost like nonsense, must seem
like what it is, a marvel:

[quotes Poem, CEP, 340]

Here is the account of a consummate moment in the motions
of an unassuming cat, an alleycat, I like to think, that
just happened to have a home - plus the inanity of the
consummation, as hinted by the empty flowerpot. How differently a dog would have managed, barging in and doubtless bumping the flowerpot over! What trimness the poet
brings to his representation of trimness! And in its perfectly comic study of perfection, it is so final, I could
easily imagine it being used as the epilogue to something
long and arduous. Inevitably, he called the lines just
Poem.

Stevens' point led us away from our main point. But in

his own way he leads us back again, when he ends by observing that an alternative preface might have been written presenting Williams as 'a kind of Diogenes of contemporary poetry.' Diogenes wrote when Greek culture was decidedly in a valetudinarian condition; and though neither poet nor medico, in his proverbial downrightness he could properly be taken to stand for Williams' particular combination of the two.

There are many cases where Williams' diagnostic eye, modified by an urge towards encouragement, becomes the sheerly appreciative eye. Cf. Stevens: 'He writes of flowers exquisitely.' But it's also a fact, for instance, that whenever Williams bears down on the description of a flower, connotations of love and lovely woman are there implicitly, and quite often explicitly. Thus, in Stevens' sense, the poems are inherently 'sentimentalized.' Whatever the gestures of *haecceitas* (the sense of an object in its sheer thisness), with Williams lyric utterance is essentially a flash of drama, a fragment of narrative, a bit of personal history mirrored as well in talk of a think as in talk of a person.

And for this reason, given his initial medical slant, the tendency always is towards a matter of welfare. Dante said that the proper subjects for poetry are *venus*, *virtus* and *salus*. The 'anti poetic' strain in Williams' poetry gives us a medical variant of *salus*, nowhere more startlingly contrived than in this neat abruptness:

[quotes CEP, 328]

When the child, successfully clutching the ball, hits 'the old back yard,' by God he is home.

Stevens' use of imagery is more airy than Williams', quite as the world of a part-time insurance man differs from the world of a part-time medical doctor, though each of these poets in his way is strongly aware of the appetites. That great 'heavy' of Williams, The Clouds, is interesting in this regard. The deathly horses, in a 'charge from south to north' while a writhing black flag 'fights/to be free,' are racing in a gigantic turmoil (something like a visual analogue of Wagner's Valkyrs). It's a vision of such death as goes with fire, famine, plague and slaughter. That's how it starts. The second section is a kind of inventory, a quick sampling of the great dead, and done somewhat haphazardly, like glances at the scurrying clouds themselves. It brings the poet forcefully close to a vision of pure spirit despite himself: 'The intellect leads, leads still! Beyond the clouds.' Part three is a 'scherzo,' a kind of joke,

grisly in this context, about a 'holy man' who, while
'riding/the clouds of his belief' (that is, officiating at
a service) had 'turned and grinned' at him. And the final
stanza gets torn into unfinished uncertainty, quite like
'the disordered heavens, ragged, ripped by winds.' It is
a gorgeous poem, at times almost ferocious, and stopped
abruptly, in the middle of a sentence, as with the boy who
had conscientiously caught the ball.

Elsewhere Williams aims at less drastic kinds of
spirit, the most puzzling or puzzled contrivance being
perhaps at the end of the long late poem, Asphodel, That
Greeny Flower. To be sure, the flower is green, and
that's all to the good. But a few lines before the close
we are informed 'Asphodel/has no odor, save to the imagination.' Yet in an earlier poem we had been assured:
'Time without/odor is Time without me.' And one of
Williams' most amusing early poems was an itemized rebuke
to his nose for the 'ardors' of its smelling.

At this point, another personal anecdote occurs to me,
for its bearing upon Williams' character. On one occasion, when visiting us, he told me ruefully of misbehavior
on his part (an incident that also falls under the head of
'contact'). A little delegation of solemn admirers had
come to pay him homage. Naturally, he was grateful to
them. But as his poems overwhelmingly testify, he was
also mercurial. And in the very midst of their solemnity
at parting, since one of the little band happened to be a
pretty young woman he gave her a frank, good-natured smack
on the fanny. It was all part of the game, done on the
spur of the moment, and it had seemed quite reasonable.
It was the *tactus eruditus* in capricious relaxation. But
his visitors were horrified, and he realized that he had
spoiled the whole show. He confessed to me his gloom at
such unruly ways. But is it not a simple scientific fact
that the poet they had come to honor owed much of his
charm to precisely such whimsicality as this? One might
class it with another occasion when, in a talk at a girls'
school, he earnestly exhorted them, 'You must learn to be
a man.' Maybe some of them did - but all were furious.
How were they to be reminded precisely then that he was
also the man who has written: 'Anyone who has seen 2,000
infants born as I have and pulled them one way or another
into the world must know that man, as such, is doomed to
disappear in not too many thousand years. He just can't
go on. No woman will stand for it. Why should she?'

I wish that, to commemorate Williams, some publisher
would now reissue his 'Al Que Quiere,' just as it was in
the original 1917 edition. It shows with such winsomeness
this quirky aspect of his genius. Consider the crazy

Danse Russe, for instance, a poem delightfully alien to
the pomposities that Eliot did so much to encourage; yet
in their way the verse and prose of this 'Diogenes' have
been written into the very constitution of our country:

[quotes Danse Russe, CEP, 148]

   Here also was first published the well-known Tract, his
instructions to his 'townspeople,' on 'how to perform a
funeral,' lines that were read by the minister, as a final
goodbye, at the side of Williams' own grave. That was
exactly right. And at the end of the book there is a long
poem (The Wanderer, a Rococo Study) which, though it was
written before the poet had fully got his stride, and is a
kind of romantic allegorizing that he would later outlaw,
yet is in its way notable, particularly as a stage in
Williams' development. For after several preparatory
steps which it would require too much space to detail here,
it leads up to a ritualistic transformation involving an
imaginary baptism in the waters of the 'The Passaic, that
filthy river.' These lines should be enough to indicate
how the merger of poet and physician initially involved a
somewhat magical process thus:

[quotes The Wanderer, CEP, 11, lines 23-30]

Here, surely, was the essential ritualistic step by which
he began his 'contact' with 'anti-poetry' - and though
often, in later years, he turned to the sheerly beautiful,
even sheerly decorative, here we see the tubes and coils
and sluices of the powerhouse. Or am I but tricked by the
occasion into going back forty-plus years, and seeing him
too much as I saw him then? Yet recall (in 'Journey to
Love') that late poem, The Sparrow, dedicated to his
father, 'a poetic truth/more than a natural one,' and thus
a delightful contribution to the *comedie humaine*. As you
follow the great variety of *aperçus* that use as their
point of departure this busy mutt-bird, his ways of con-
gregation, his amours and family life you heartily agree
it's 'a pity/there are not more oats eaten now-a-days.'
Here is no less than Aesop singing.
   In the course of doing this piece, I found among my
notes a letter dated May 10, 1940. Presumably I had sent
Williams some pages which he had read with his usual mixture of friendliness and resistance. He writes (enclosing
a poem):

   If I hadn't been reading your essay and thinking my own
   thoughts against it - I shouldn't have stepped on the

word 'prebirth' and so the poem (completely independent
of the whole matter otherwise) might not have been
written.
   THEREFORE the poem belongs to you. I like it as
well as anything I have written –

Then, after some other matters, he returns to the subject
abruptly: 'All I wanted to do was to send you the poem.'
   At the time I assumed that he meant the gift figura-
tively. But after inquiring of John Thirlwall, who has
spent so much effort tracking down Williams' scattered
work, I think it possible that friendly Wm. C. Wms.,
strong man two-gun Bill, may have meant the gift literally, and I may possess the only copy of the poem. In any
case, I append it here, since it is a lovely thing to end
on. It has a kind of reversal which crops up somewhat
mystically, every now and then, among his poems, and which
is probably implicit in many other passages. In the light
of such forms, when he writes 'It is nearly pure luck that
gets the mind turned inside out in a work of art,' we may
take it that he had such reversals in mind:

>   CHERRY BLOSSOMS AT EVENING
>   *In the prebirth of the evening*
>   *the blue cherry blossoms*
>   *on the blue tree*
>   *from this yellow, ended room –*
>   *press to the windows*
>   *inside shall be out*
>   *the clustered faces of the flowers*
>   *straining to look in*
>   (Signed) William Carlos Williams –

Note

1 A section of Della Primavera Trasportata Alla Morale,
   See CEP, 63.

126. PETER WHIGHAM, WILLIAM CARLOS WILLIAMS, 'AGENDA'

Vol. III, no. 2, October-November 1963, 25-32

'Agenda' is a distinguished British magazine of modern poetry and poetics, the most important British forum for American modernist and post-modernist poetry. This essay is included in a William Carlos Williams special number of the magazine.

Whigham (b. 1925) is a British poet and translator and is editor of 'Agenda'.

To start with an apology (on behalf of British letters). William Carlos Williams was born in 1883. He was the author of some 35 collections of poems. He was also the author of 'Paterson', the most sustained effort in new poetry outside 'The Cantos'. His prose works include stories, plays, histories, novels & anti-novels, & autobiography. He received the Bollingen Award, The National Book Award, the $5,000 Award of The Fellowship of American Poets. He was an honorary graduate of Bard, Pennsylvania, Buffalo, & Rutgers. He was unquestionably the most influential modern American writer to remain in America. And he never received a British imprint. (1) This year, apart from the customary notice in 'The Times', & news bits illustrative of the President's enlightened comments on the occasion, his death passed unnoticed. (As did Cummings', and he only achieved his imprint last year.) Williams was never an anglophile; and in recognition of this we have bestowed on him the silence & neglect reserved specifically for our better writers. With Belloc, with Santayana, & with Ford, let his shade relish, ironically, the honour.

William Carlos Williams, poet, was also Dr Williams G.P. He practised all his adult life in his home-town of Rutherford, New Jersey, an area comparable to and far worse than the industrial waste-lands of Lanarkshire. The excreta of a grossly material society lie like a dishevelled strait-jacket across the land. It would need a vocation indeed to work there. That he did so directly influenced his poetry. In it there is an absorbing precision; a habit of treating every case as a fresh case, nothing assumed *a priori*; toughness (as a shell) blended with compassion; & a preoccupation with the psychology of appearances: all qualities one would expect from a scientific training and the hard practice which he had. Inheritance also contributed, here in part, and in other qualities almost entirely. Strangely little seems due to literary influence.

By blood Williams was Spanish, French, Danish & English. He was also, in Pound's amusing & exact phrase, the 200% American. The play between the two, the retarding effect which his European inheritance had on his Americanism,

forms the subject of much of Pound's excellent early
essay, Dr Williams' Position.(2) He saw the value, as yeast,
of the un-American slowness in Williams' nature. He has
a telling little vignette (in a separate essay) in which
he compares Williams, confronted with a given situation,
to a dog getting into its basket. The dog will turn
round on its own tail 3 or 4 times before deciding which
way it wants to lie. His refusal to take anything at all
for granted is frequently irritating. But it is nearly
always justified. At least, it lends the slightest of his
imagismes, a mode not given to philosophic overtones, a
weight - specifically, an ontological direction, they
would not normally bear. This is important because he is
the least philosophic of the moderns. It is perfectly
true to say, that because of his avowed instrumentalism
(aesthetically his nominalism) a poem of Williams' is a
living example of James's description of the creative process, something discovered in the act of creation. Are
not poems *modi*, the only calligraphy with which we can
report certain sorts of experience? And given Dewey's
instrumentalism such means can be seen as equatable with
Williams objects. 'My poems,' he used to say, 'are
things.' Williams discovers what he wants to say in the
process of saying it.

It may be that his social gentleness, allied to the
compassion in his poetry, stems from his Latin blood. It
may be that his northern ancestry is responsible for his
ethics. He wanted his poems to create their own hierar-
chic order. (There is no external or received moral
order; or if there is, it was necessary, for his purposes,
to ignore it.) This was also a part of his Americanism,
the America of Emerson & Thoreau. Together with his radicalism it often secured him the label 'primitive' - as
though he were a sort of intellectual Grandma Moses. But
he was too a-philosophical ever to fall for Rousseau's
Savage. There was a difference between Evenings ('The
Desert Music'), & Lawrence's 'Mornings', in Mexico.

As for his literary antecedents, his early collections
are similar in their wistful Edwardian romanticism to the
rejected poems in the 1st 'Personae', though even here his
attitude to the past differs fundamentally from Pound's -
a point I shall enlarge on in a minute. If Pound's forerunners are more to the forefront than Williams', that is
because of the sort of American writer Pound is. College
friends, sharing the same views about many things, sociological & economic as well as aesthetic, closely linked in
their belief that by renovating craft they would revit-
alise poetic vision, Williams & Pound nevertheless belong
to opposite traditions in U.S. letters. There are the
inward & outward looking Americans: the continentals &

the Europeans. Ezra Pound's lifelong dilemma, which has
among other things given such a remarkable tension to his
work, is that he is too balanced a blend of the two. He
is not Henry James's passionate pilgrim. Nor, in spite of
the London Gosses, was he ever the innocent abroad. Certainly, like Washington Irving, he made his polite pilgrimages; on the other hand he is against obscurantism &
all sorts of lip-service; he believes in the possibility
of quite radical social betterment; he is an optimist; he
believes in reason; in a chosen epitaph, he is the kid
from Idaho, irreverent, impatient, honest, & knowing
beyond his years. With all this he has spent his entire
adult life in Europe, mostly in the heart of Europe,
Italy, reassembling with immense pains, love, & discern-
ment, pieces of Europe's past, & of the past of civilisa-
tions ruined before American was invented. 'These fragments I have shored,' etc. The re-emergence of the neo-
Platonism of his early days, together with the craggy
American-ness (Grandma Moses) of his features in old age -
he is a 3rd Century American to Williams' 1st - and his
insistence in a recent interview on his quite ordinary, if
deep, American feelings underline this dilemma. Williams
has none of this complexity. Like the wagon master of
those prairie caravans, he moves daily through totally new
territory. His sole aim is to come to terms with his
surroundings. He examines object by object, stripping
each of its civilised accretions as he explores, verbally,
its inner nature. According to the manner in which this
mastery of the external world is pursued will come the
ordering of it. Order, as an end, is seen as the accident
of the means to order, which is knowledge. Here he seems
far from Pound, most American, like Dewey, where Pound is
most European, at home with the aesthetics of someone like
Arthur Symons. But in the sort of knowledge they are both
after, their positions are identical. They both believe
that the word creates the form and the form is (neo-
Platonically) the core of the object.

>   I stood still and was a tree amid the wood
>   Knowing the truth of things unseen before....
>   **EZRA POUND,** A Tree

There are 3 short prose quotations which may be useful
here.

> There is no poetry of distinction without formal inven-
> tion...*

> One doesn't seek beauty. All that an artist ... can do

is to drive towards his purpose, in the nature of his materials.†

Nothing is good save the new. If a think have novelty it stands intrinsically beside every other work of artistic excellence. If it have not that, no loveliness or heroic proportion will save it. It will not be saved above all by an attenuated intellectuality.‡

And there are the last lines of 'Paterson':

[quotes closing 15 lines of 'Paterson V', 277-8]

It was Vernon Lee who first touted the German word *Einfuhlung* around in English literary circles. She offered the alternative term, *empathy*. In recent years the word has become a part of critical jargon. The artist in his product becomes one with the object of his contemplation. Theories of any sort, especially fin-de-siècle, neo-Platonic ones such as this, were of course anathema to Williams. However, this particular theory happened to be his practice. More than this, it is plain from the 'Paterson' quotation that the type of knowledge thus acquired was the only type he considered worth having - or even possible, i.e. direct intuitive knowledge such as the schoolmen assure us is proper to the angelic hosts. It has nothing at all to do with the descriptive or ratiocinative processes we use in daily life. Here is where Williams most closely resembles Pound. For they both believe that the word, charged as in poetry (more broadly, the art medium, whatever it may happen to be), produces such knowledge. This is their nominalism. The word defines. Definition creates.§ And, in Williams, the process determines its own ethic or end. In a phrase, the poet intuits verbally. In his intuitions he experiences modes of being other than his own, so acquiring mastery his ambience and, implicitly, his own order. Here is the closing section of Book III of 'Paterson'. It contains one of the clearest & most complete of Williams' statements on the function of poetry. There is certainly primitivism, but not the false naiveté of the civilised modern. The base for Williams' aesthetic is no less than a re-statement of the primordial belief in the efficacy of sympathetic magic.

[quotes closing 31 lines of 'Paterson (Book Three)', 172-3]

Book III, introduced by an epigraph from Santayana's 'The

Last Puritan', is more specifically concerned with the search for a factive poetry than the others. The epigraph incidentally provides a succinct retort to European, particularly English, readers who are inclined to deprecate the 'jejeune' framework of 'Paterson'. They imply that only an American city, raw & impersonal, could be thought of in this way. An English or European town is itself too like a human to be compared to one. No European could possibly conceive of Oxford or Freiburg or Toulouse as an analogue of the human mind. Santayana, whose literary & philosophic eminence are presumably unquestioned, did not consider the notion in any way jejeune.

After what has been said it will be obvious that a poet with Williams' preoccupations would be, in everything he wrote, an innovator, a conscious craftsman, - each new poem an experiment. The same has been said of Pound & of Auden. It is true of Auden for different reasons. No magic enters here, no notions of empathy. Art is a game, & the skills are the rules. The idea of the game & its possible base as an aesthetic are outlined in pp. 421 & 422 of 'The Dyer's Hand'. It is a way in which Auden, as poet, can have his cake & eat it: the insiders can feel that the outsider in their midst is really like one of them, for his outsideness is 'only a game'; and if he likes to quibble about a funny meaning he attaches to the word 'game', well, that is a part of his outsideness, too. With Pound & Williams the same obsession with technique, different from Auden's, results in work quite unlike each other's. The reason is in the opposite ways they treat history. For Pound, history is a perspective on the present. 'What you depart from is not the way.' He is seldom so 'modern' as when camping out in Provence or ancient China. Eliot noted this in 1928. Williams, when he makes an excursus into the past, and March & History are good examples of this, sees it always from the standpoint of the present. The frescoes do not come alive: they remain frescoes. The present serves only to show the deadness of the past, the past the vitality of the present. Pound's perspective glass frequently finds the present wanting. The point to be made is, that literary historics such as sestinas & the ballade would clearly attract Pound more than Williams. Which leaves untouched the proposition that they are both first & foremost craftsmen & innovators at the deepest level, however dissimilar their finished *oeuvres*.

It used to be the fashion to say that Carlos Williams had got 'stuck in imagism'. To begin with, imagism is a school of considerably wider application than its denigrators would have one believe. An imagist poem is not just a picture poem. An image, in the original defition, is 'that which presents an intellectual & emotional complex in an instant of time'. Such an image must be capable of bearing the same emotional weight as a symbol. It operates as as one of Mr Eliot's 'objective correlatives'. The weakness of imagism lies in its kinetic element, or lack of it. This, of course, is also its strength. The whole poem is an image (technically); the parts may contain images (non-technical). The difficulty being to sustain the stasis, or bind a cluster of such - over time - in a hyperstasis. This is primarily a metrical problem. Metric - melopoeia - is, after all, one of the modes of charging the image. Pound solved this problem before he came to his long poem; Williams, by means of his, although he did not achieve a final solution until the last 4 volumes of his life, 'The Desert Music', 'The Journey to Love', 'Paterson (Book Five)', & 'Pictures from Brueghel'. His crown is not in 'Paterson', but here. In these works he evolved what he called the variable foot. Its origin stems from as far back as 'Paterson (Book Two)'. It was in the early twenties that he finally abandoned free verse & began his search for a measure which, in its variations within a pattern, would reflect the movement of modern life. The pattern he finally called the triadic stanza, the measure, the variable foot. The endeavour to perfect the American idiom in verse achieved fruition in the same works. It had been with him from the beginning.

It is just in this matter of kinetics, in his understanding of the exigencies of the breath, that his influence has been so strong on poets such as Charles Olson, Robert Duncan, & Robert Creeley. It is particularly strong in Olson's manifesto for projective verse (1950), a seminal work for those now learning to write. Williams himself thought so highly of it that he reprinted it in his autobiography. Currently, Williams' monument, outside his work, lies in the last 20 years of American poetry, from Olson onwards. It is an influence more like Pound's than Eliot's. Practising poets discharge their debt as they write. He is a gentle, pervasive exemplar, interested in all things, committed to none but his life craft. One who did not suffer the change of life that overtakes so many of our poets, but, like Yeats & Pound, went on writing better & better until he was unable to write at all. If, as H.D. has it, he sometimes shows a hairy chest, it is only a male shyness, and one he largely grew out of. Whether Faber's constant refusal to handle Williams has anything to do with the revulsion he felt, & said he felt, for all that has to be taken for granted in Eliot's poetry before one can actually get to the poetry, I do not know.

Literature as a continuing order, the ideas that went into Tradition and the Individual Talent drew from Williams the vitriolic description of Eliot as an 'archbishop of procurers to a lecherous antiquity'. From the same book, 'Kora in Hell', he has, 'There is nothing sacred about literature, it is damned from one end to the other. There is nothing in literature but change and change is mockery.' How could the author of 'The Sacred Wood' be expected to accede?... But Faber's censorship has gone. Williams is here - if only in some of the poetry printed in 'Agenda'. And MacGibbon & Kee announce publication next spring of 'Paterson' (entire) and 'Pictures from Brueghel' & other poems including Asphodel. The other day, I asked a boy about to go up to Oxford what he required from poetry. He paused, and then said, 'An absence of preconceived ideas.' One may want other things also. But such a statement points towards Williams (whom the boy had never read), and away from Yeats and Eliot. A time-lag of 60 years, & the poems to-day as relevant to immediate problems of technique & theory as when they were first written.

Despite all his exactitude of observation and his similar surface skills, he is not in his total effect like any epigrammatic poet, Martial, say, or Jonson. Nor, despite the lovely Portrait of a Lady, is he in the least like Herrick, who lacks mystery. Herrick's fascination with the enigma of surfaces is not the same thing. Williams, too, was a materialist in that sense, but with him one is always aware of something else: the mysterious and sad connection there is between the detail and the whole. A humane note. And that is Williams, a poet of warm, penetrating and, at his greatest, tragic humanity.

Notes

*Introduction to the 'Collected Later Poems': W.C.W. New Directions.
†ditto
‡The Prologue to 'Kora in Hell'
§Herein, of course, lies the whole mystery of the λογοδ.
1 Fifty years before this article Williams' 'The Tempers' was published in London by Elkin Mathews. In 1953 the London publisher Peter Owen issued an edition of 'Paterson Books 1 and 2' from the New Directions sheets. As Whigham notes, late in his essay, MacGibbon and Kee published several important volumes of Williams posthumously. News of their acceptance of 'Pictures from Brueghel' arrived in Rutherford two days after Williams' death on 4 March 1963.
2 Included in 'Literary Essays of Ezra Pound', edited by T. S. Eliot (London, 1954), 389-98.

127. EDWARD DAHLBERG, WORD-SICK AND PLACE-CRAZY, FROM
'ALMS FOR OBLIVION' (1)

1964, 20-7

Dahlberg (b. 1900) is an American essayist, poet, novelist, social critic and autobiographer. Two of his letters are incorporated into the text of Williams' 'Paterson', and others are included in Dahlberg's 'Epitaphs for Our Times' (1967). Williams' review of Dahlberg's 'The Flea of Sodom' was published, after Williams' death, in 'Edward Dahlberg: American Ishmael of Letters', edited by Harold Billings (1968). Among Dahlberg's publications are 'Bottom Dogs' (1929, with an Introduction by D. H. Lawrence), 'Truth is More Sacred' (1961, based on an exchange of letters with Herbert Read),'Because I was Flesh' (1964) and 'The Confessions of Edward Dahlberg' (1970).

Books are wild beasts or brackish water or dead ravines. It is hard now to find a book that one can depend upon, and in which branch is bough, bird is bird, and apple talks like apple. Books are more mixed and dirty than ever, and though there is rot and swinepen in every poet, the old Levitical differences between fungused places and unclean froggish things and the arbute and gillyflower are gone. There is so much lion and jackal mischief in our morals, and man at best, as Hamlet says, is indifferent honest, that the poet is no longer homely and plain about simple and plain things. He is like William Carlos Wil-Williams, the Paterson rock poet, who gives us skill and invention in the place of the Cana marriage wine. His original books are Medusa's, likely to turn the heads of a generation into stone, and 'Paterson' and 'The Later Collected Poems' are lawless art. 'Paterson', which he says is the pride of locality, is a word-manual for the journeyman poet, and its hard river words will yield much pleasure to the reader. Socrates once said that the misuse of words induces evil in the soul, and this remarkable observation is very close to the problem of the Paterson poem; Williams had a martial passion for the sentence - his phrases have the firing-power of an automatic revolver. Bleak mountain skill, or what we call poetic invention, can slay the spirit. Originality is often a stepmother Muse that gives her breast to the hawk and the mountain, and is the greatest curse in our literature;

there is a surfeit of originality in 'Paterson'.
   Williams was a congealed river-and-rock man who wrote a very remarkable hot book, 'In the American Grain'. But our most gifted writers have too much seawater in their heads, and all of them were cold men. Let it be enough here just to mention Thoreau's 'Walden' and 'A Week on the Concord and Merrimack Rivers', for the titles of these wonderful volumes are ample proof of their contents. Melville's 'Moby-Dick' is an astonishing but inhuman masterpiece. Shale and river books are not wisdom literature. Hawthorne, who had as polar a soul as Thoreau, cried out against his boreal nature. In The Christmas Banquet Hawthorne writes that to be cold is the most wretched plague of the heart; yet the debile, sinning husband of Hester Prynne in 'The Scarlet Letter' is Chillingworth.
   The early Greek thinkers believed that where there was too much moisture there was injustice, saying that man at first was a seagoing shark; correct science or not, this is an unusual truth about people. Take heed, then, of those wild, watery men in literature, and remember that Odysseus is miserable until his hapless water-journey is ended, and that he pines not so much for Penelope as for Ithaca, his swine, sheep and fruits.
   A poet ought to be one, to have a single deity that wills and purposes for his whole nature. We imagine a writer to be both Diogenes and Hercules, blunt speaking and a moral force. Without Hercules's lion's skin and club, philosophy and poetry and science are deceitful, profligate and willess. We look in vain for moral volition in 'Paterson' and 'The Later Poems', for the rocks that simulate fortitude are inhumanities and the water is death. Heraclitus said that too much moisture is death to the soul. It is true that poets have more unstable water in them than other thinkers; Plutarch is more reliable than Shakespeare. There is no mistaking the riggish vices of such caitiffs as Antony and Cleopatra in Plutarch, but there is enough anarchy in the great English poet to confuse the reader, and these wantons are plumaged peacocks with astonishing Asiatic lusts, which Shakespeare forces us to admire. However, Iago had one nature, reechy Goneril is single, and Timon is of one stuff.
   The American poet is double, his character chameleon, and he has double moral hands, unlike the philosopher Charles S. Peirce who wrote out his questions with one hand and answered them with the other. As for Williams, it is impossible to know what his affections or his morals are; he so constantly changes his shape that he is like that ever-changing debtor in the comedy of Epicharmos who

refuses to pay his creditor because he says he is no
longer the same person who borrowed the money. We cannot
be in moral debt to Williams because we do not know what
he owes us either in negations or in a straight honest
yes. In art, as Dostoyevsky has written, two plus two
equals five, and this provides for the underground nihilism in modern man; but in morals two and two are always
four. The distinction between art and ethics cannot be
so considerable as to make it almost impossible to know
the difference between the false and the true, between
Acheron and the tender, growing earth. Either we are to
get health from a poet or else all this sick water-verse
will drive us mad.

We cannot put upon a poet a creed or religion, but he
must have one character or we will have the most dreary
pluralistic morals, a moral for every new occasion. The
shabbiest cynics at Athens had a few lentil, lupin and
thyme rules by which they lived and were recognized. One
finds this hardy fare of customs and morals in Homer and
in those philosophical dogs who slept and cohabited in
the public porches and were as houseless, unblanketed and
unroofed as the Paterson poem, and one of whom offered the
following recipe for his pupils: 'Set aside ten minas for
a chef, a drachma for the doctor, five talents for a flatterer, a talent for a whore, three obols for a philosopher.' It is this kind of receipt that we call style or
form in a poet or thinker, and whether it is reckoned
good or not, it is clear. We blame man less for a principle we may not agree with, and reject, than for his
confusion, which we may not comprehend and accept; confusion is the begetter of the greatest evil in the soul.

It is impossible to know whether Williams is a man-hater or not, for though he employs a people's language,
the bare hummocks, the 'treeless knoll', and the waterworks in the poems are nomadic nihilism. 'The water
married to the stone' is not pioneer hardihood but supine
pessimism and dingy misanthropy. He is homeless and
parentless, begotten by January ravines, and always outside among 'humped roots', 'calcined husks', with 'rock,
bole and fangs'; his affections, moreover, are so *natured*
that he can neither house, kitchen, nor table man or
earth. The words 'stone' and 'rock' appear seventy-eight times, and 'falls' nineteen times; besides these,
'river' and 'stream' occur perhaps even more often than
the stones, and 'gorge', 'ledge', 'precipice' and 'cataract' are also reiterated. Toward the end of the long
poem divided into four parts, Williams gives us a log
which tells the amount of shale and red sandstone that
are at the various depths of a well. 'Fanged'toothed

rock', 'grasshopper of red basalt' and 'gulls upon the
ice-strewn river' look at first like force and stoicism -
we often mistake what is raw and primitive for innocence
and primal strength - but are really cold, wet verse.

It is the letters in 'Paterson' that are the sun and
the blood, the human cry and the conscience absent in the
shale and pickerel-weed. The most rancorous epistles are
written by an anonymous woman bitterly chiding this man
who has become place, for place can be a liar and devour
us. The woman writes that the poet has metamorphosed her
faculties into some 'impenetrable congealed substance',
'rough ice'. An Egyptian osier burial basket has more
human warmth than those feral, cold nature poems.

To use Platonic language, what is in the world must
have its counterpart in universals, that is, horse as a
particular of the world must be represented by universal
horseness, and a chair must have its ideal chairness. In
'Don Quixote' the barber's basin is also the helmet of
Mambrino; if the one is not also the other, we have
either common matter as it is precisely uttered by Williams, or inhuman abstractions, and one without the other
is confusion and madness. Melville writes in 'Moby-Dick',
'Be thou in the world, but not of it,' which counsels a
man to be familiar with Polonius and Hamlet, Christ and
Barabbas, and to be able to know one from the other.
Williams tells the reader of the 'Later Poems' to be
reconciled with the world, advice that is likely to beget
a charlatan, a busybody and a liar, and that is what the
world has been to every real poet, including Jesus who
cries out, 'O I have overcome the world!'

Both Thoreau and Williams relish a tawny sentence; 'The
Concord and Merrimack' and 'In the American Grain' are
American canonical geography; Williams has submitted to
Greenland and to savage territory as much as he dares. He
wrote with deep understanding of the pilgrims that came to
conquer a vast wilderness continent and were possessed by
it. Take the following phrases out of these two authors'
volumes and judge whether they belong to Thoreau or to Williams: 'eels and a moon', 'rock, bole and fangs', 'sweet-
barked sassafras', 'treeless knoll', 'pumice-covered',
'calcined husks', 'file-sharp grass', 'flint arrow head',
'old swale'. Do not think this American literary geology
is of trifling value, not to be remembered. Homer also
has his catalogues of ships, of names, and of towns, and
they are poems. There was a writer of Greek comedies by
the name of Mermippus who in 429 BC drew up a list of
imports which are edible verses, for the mind eats what it
perceives, and it must thrive and not sicken upon its food:
'Hides and vegetable relish from Cyprus; grains and meat

from Italy; pork and cheese from Syracuse; sails and papyrus from Egypt ...' One cannot feed too long on the bogs of Thoreau or on the ravished gravel and grubby river Paterson; those that fall in love with this wild malignant beauty will be sorely wounded by it. Thoreau and Williams are frontier minds, with an acute wind-and-bramble logic of the physical ground, but all earth is not suitable habitation for the imagination. I can't talk to rocks and trees, says Socrates.

Look at this poet William Carlos Williams: he is primitive and native, and his roots are in raw forest and violent places; he is word-sick and place-crazy. He admires strength, but for what? Violence! This is the cult of the frontier mind. 'The hungry animal underlying all other power.' He has succumbed to the frontier ground no less than Crêvecoeur, Fenimore Cooper, Twain and Parkman. But who wants to read these American anchorites on bleak ravines and desolate scrub-pines just to be more inhuman than one already is by nature? What Shakespeare truth or Jeremiah vision is there in these cankered mists and gulches?

Paterson is a homeless, desperado poem; it's all outdoors. 'Hypaethral' is the word Thoreau uses. The Paterson Falls is icy nihilism. The poet longs to leap from the ledge into the fatal ice flood, but he has the minister's wife and a tight-rope walker fall into the February river, and when it is dredged the bodies are found, ice-caked. 'Rather the ice than their way.' But this is fearful ice-sickness, which is the dread of human touch and being involved with people. That's all there is to those cataracts, the waterworks, and the rapids; he knows it but as animal skin has knowledge. Melville was also a lawless cold writer; he wrote 'Mardi' to heat his blood. 'In the American Grain' is Williams's one hot book, with tropical Aztec and Florida Indian names, and reptile and alligator sexuality, with 'sugar cane from the Canaries', 'the oil of walnuts ... drawn like olive oil', 'Chicaca ... stocked with maize' and 'loaves made of pulp of plums'. The jasper floor of Montezuma's palace is as asiatic as Menelaus's dwelling. There is a lovely chant to Raleigh where Williams writes, 'the true form escaped in the wind, sing O Muse ... of the pursuit of beauty and the husk that remains ... sing O Muse.' But Williams, understanding the tabu fear of touch of the American returns in 'Paterson' and in the 'Later Collected Poems' to the 'hard, repressive pioneer soil of the mind'. The poet desires to be place, 'the gap between touch and thing'. But can locality judge the heart, the liver and the affections? Like Melville who succumbed to the Pacific, Williams says

goodbye to Montezuma, Joppa, Nineveh and disappears in the
Paterson River. He is just homeless, without parent, or
man or woman to be near; a prey of the firecest elements.
There is no creative metamorphosis but brutish submission
and the cowering animal feeding upon its own paws.
   The writing Ishmael bothered Williams. He had a fine
imaginative faculty but distrusted books. He made some
observations about Dante, Isaiah and the Aztecans. Like
all pioneers Williams hated the old world, and took his
revenge upon the old European culture. He thought that
the ancient civilizations could not be seeded here, which
is a frontier perversion. Melville turned to Job and Lear,
Thoreau to the 'Bhagavad-Gita', and Charles S. Peirce used
Duns Scotus. Woe be to him who lets any of his higher
faculties remain unexplored, wrote Thoreau.
   No people require maxims so much as the American. The
reason is obvious: the country is so vast, the people
always going somewhere, from Oregon apple valley to boreal
New England, that we do not know whether to be temperate
orchards or sterile climate. Great cultures come out of
small Homeric or Hebraic lands; our bigness has given us
such humbug size that we are too big for pity or sorrow or
for others. Is a man given a talent to use it for himself
alone? What our genius lacks most is being simple. If
that is clear a poet won't reject his head, as Williams
did, because it will smell, according to the Upanishads,
like a raven's nest. He will not, like Williams, take up
violence in his arms as a bride.
   When a poet has some abiding morals in him he can make
whatever images he likes, for it will be clear to him that
books are the lilies and birds that are more than raiment
and meat.
   We must return to 'In the American Grain', the genius
of the wild and the savage flower in Williams. He tells
us a dark parable, and he was the first to gather up
American history as a fabulist. He relates how the discoverers came to plant the old European soul here, and
though they killed and subdued everything, it was they who
were enslaved by primitive river and mountain. The plan-
ters were fierce ice men, Red Eric, Hudson, LaSalle, Car-
tier, DeSoto, Raleigh. We think Christian non-resistance
archaic Asian wisdom, and do not understand how old in
lore was brave Montezuma, who submitted to Cortes and a
miserable small band, giving him rubies, gold, emeralds,
knowing what has always been Indian knowledge, that the
conqueror will be the slave. Even the Aztecan names -
Napateca, Caliquen, Paraxcoxi - are ancient volcanic gods
which enter us as we kill them.
   We are still discoverers, new-world logicians, mistaking

the Pharaoh cliffs of New Mexico and Arizona and that
Egyptian Nile peninsula, Florida, for the ancient epical
civilization. There is a terrible truth in this American
fable; every discoverer we have had has been a wild home-
steader among the seers of the world. Melville, Thoreau,
Parkman, Prescott and Williams are all river and sea and
plateau geniuses, ranging a continent for a house, and all
of them outdoors.

Note

1 'Alms for Oblivion' (Bloomington, Minn., 1964).

'The Collected Later Poems'

Norfolk, Conn., May 1963, new edition

This revised edition has minor modifications and an additional section beginning with An Editorial Note by John C. Thirlwall (see Wallace, 'Bibliography', 70). The English edition, with identical contents, was published in London by MacGibbon & Kee in June 1964.

---

128. JAMES DICKEY, FIRST AND LAST THINGS, 'POETRY'

Vol. CIII, no. 5, February 1964, 321-2

This is a section from a review of eleven books of poems. Dickey (b. 1923) is an American poet, novelist, reviewer and lecturer, and author of 'Poems 1957-1967' (1968) and 'Deliverance' (1970).

... William Carlos Williams is now dead, too, and that fact shakes one in quite a different way. Has any other poet in American history been so *actually* useful, usable and influential? How many beginning writers took Williams as their model: were encouraged to write because ..Well, if *that's* poetry, I believe I might be able to write it, too! Surely his practice has opened up many people to peotry - to the potential poetry in themselves and in their everyday world - in a wholly exemplary way, converting the commonplace, the trivial, the traditionally 'ugly' into poetry of a highly personal and a thoroughly public order: who, after all, has not *seen*

   ... a cylindrical tank, fresh silvered

upended on the sidewalk to advertise
some plumber's shop ...?

Williams' readers will know what to expect in this reissue of 'The Collected Later Poems', and will be glad to have the seventeen previously uncollected poems and good older poems like A Unison. Here is all of Williams' later work except for 'Paterson' and the poems gathered in 'Pictures from Brueghel'. One will find here, also, Williams' most discouraging qualities, monotony and arbitrariness, which proceed from what looks suspiciously like the notion that to *present* were sufficient - were *always* sufficient. If a man will attend Williams closely he will be taught to see, to fasten on the appearance and the meaning that is for him in the appearance, on the sensory apprehension and truth of an object or scene in a way that is perpetually open to him - to any of us - and has but to be used at any given moment, and he will write solid and usually short, unrhymed, near-prose poems about how the concrete particulars of the world look and feel to him. Whether or not that is enough, I suspect we must leave to later generations to decide. It is, however, a very great deal, and Williams as a kind of large-looming divine average, as a man writing out of his whole humanity with the sympathetic but unflinching scrutiny of a responsible doctor, is and will be the authentic hero of this approach. Surely no poet is more American, and in that there is reason to hope for us all ....

129. THOMAS CLARK, MOVING IMAGES, 'NEW STATESMAN'

23 July 1965, 126

One way of seeing Williams's achievement might be to consider Ezra Pound's statement of the defects of Imagism, from which Williams broke away in the Twenties and Thirties. Pound believed the Imagists thought only of a stationary focus and failed to include the 'moving image'. His phrase has been taken to mean 'moving' in the sense of emotional evocation, but it's at least as plausible to suppose Pound meant an image that would contain the actual movement of things toward appearance. Certainly the poetry of Aldington, Flint and HD was stationary as regards the 'object', from which it kept a safe distance. Their poems are examples of writing *about* what has been seen, from the remote vantage of a descriptive mode allowing objects to lie inert to the gaze of a separated 'subject'. Williams's work is distinguished by his ability to write from within the act of perception, making his poem a mark of the complex interaction between the manifested field and the mind's gesture to apprehend it.

He was concerned that poetry should be an instrument of perception, writing in his 'Autobiography' that 'the poet thinks with his poem, in that lies the thought, and that itself is the profundity'. This passage comes as elucidation of Williams's famous dictum 'no ideas but in things'. The 'ideas' of his poems are *in* things, *ideas* in the ancient sense of the occurring form, look or appearance of a thing, its transit from simple substance to an existence as the image of the mind. The poems in this book contain the form of developing awareness, and of the coequal movement of things coming to be known. In a small poem like The Banner Bearer, for instance, the pointing of the word 'intent' so as to carry an initial sense of observed *intention* over the line into an adverbial meaning which registers the continuation of motion, shows Williams's care for the particular fashion of a dog's appearance:

[quotes CLP, 81]

   Clearly the 'idea' of the dog's style is not help prior to the occasion but discovered therein. It should be obvious how Williams's method here differs from that of Eliot, say, or of Wallace Stevens. His distrust of those more speculative poetries shows in an essay written on the occasion of Stevens's death:

> Stevens seldom comes down on a statement of fact. It is always '13 ways of looking at a blackbird', which cannot but weaken any attack. His attack is cumulative, it is implicit in the final settlement as a whole which would be the lawyer's way.

The point here, for Williams, is that no 'final settlement' can, or rightly should, be forecast, and that the danger of such an effort is to deprive the poem of its proper integrity, an undivided attention to what is happen-*now* in the act of writing. Williams's own 'attack', in a poem like Burning the Christmas Greens, offers its terms ('green is a solace') not as parts of a meditative design but as turns of mind subject to the cancellations of the immediate encounter.

It's not, then, simply a metaphor to say that Williams does 'think with his poem', that its words are an actual opening allowing him to receive and articulate the placement of his body. His long insistence on 'The American Idiom' was directed, not to any preferred diction, but to a restoration to poetry of the integrated body as *speech* - with its direction impelled by an instant working of the mind at one with the action of respiratory, muscular and nervous systems. The Injury, in this book, bespeaks the way an awareness of physical urgencies effects the plotting of verse. The poignancy of this is the product of his sense of *utterance* and its disclosure of rhythms the grammatical forms of discourse disallow. The syntax of his poetry like that of speech is paratactic or sequential ('and it quiets and ...'), he employs conjunctions or dashes to mark the consecutive nature of occurrence, while eschewing the causal or logical connections we customarily use to establish a cumulative knowledge of situation. Williams's typical syntax reproduces in some degree the living procedure of perception, a linear, disjunctive, groping movement; the grammatical 'total view' can be gained only as hindsight.

In the poem The Crystal Maze (II), the accretion of clauses, syntactical paralleling of parts of the experience, disclose an immediate process prior to any logical sorting of contents. Valéry, in 'Tel Quel', wrote a syntax that it is 'a system of habits at hand that it is good to revive from time to time and to readjust in full consciousness'. Williams's readjustment, here, is a rejection of the grammatical circuit of the sentence in favour of a linear projection that more accurately registers the path of an increasing awareness. The order of words has the gestural order of utterance, the poet's sign of undivided being and his actual presence in the world.

'The William Carlos Williams Reader'

New York, September 1966; London, March 1967

130. PHILIP TOYNBEE, A POET OF HIS TIME, 'OBSERVER'

19 March 1967, 27

Toynbee (b. 1916) is a British journalist and fiction writer.

If a ballot were held mong cultivated Americans to choose the dozen best American poets of the century it is my guess that the following names would appear on the final list: T. S. Eliot, Ezra Pound, Robert Frost, Hart Crane, Edwin Arlington Robinson, Wallace Stevens, William Carlos Williams, Marianne Moore, John Crowe Ransom, Allen Tate, Theodore Roethke and Robert Lowell. Many might include John Berryman and leave out Roethke: some would prefer E. E. Cummings to Edwin Arlington Robinson; but I believe that my own list is the one most likely to emerge.

How many of these names are known at all to a majority of cultivate Englishmen? How many are well known? How many are known not only by their names but also by their poetry? I suspect that the only household names in England are those of Eliot, Pound, Frost and Robert Lowell. One might perhaps add Wallace Stevens and Marianne Moore to this shorter list, but it seems that all the other have fallen, until now, into the category of poets who do not travel; who seem to lose too much when they lose the compatriot readership for whom they wrote.

Williams, for example, has been known in England mainly for a single anthology piece, and it is a poem which has come in for at least as much ridicule as admiration. Here it is: -

[quotes The Red Wheelbarrow, CEP, 277]

   This is a poem which might well be taken more seriously in the immediate present than it has been in the past. It curiously resembles the dead-pan realism of a painter like Jasper Johns, and those other artists who believe that all that is required to produce a work of art is the artistic occasion. Put an old beer can on a stand in a gallery and it will become a work of art because it will be looked at with the intensity which is demanded by a work of art. But this is not a theory which I subscribe to, and I have never been impressed by Williams's famous verses. They seem to me to be *faux naïfs* and painfully self-conscious.
   But the serious claims for Williams have never been based on this sort of poem, but on certain of his longer lyrics and, above all, on his long poem 'Paterson'. 'Paterson' was published in England three years ago by the same publishers who have now given us Mr Rosenthal's WILLIAM CARLOS WILLIAMS READER. It is my impression that 'Paterson' fell like a hazel nut rather than a stone into the placid well of English cultural life - where I have been sitting, I won't deny, as placidly as most of my colleagues. It needed the new book to drive me back to the earlier one.
   Mr Rosenthal gives us a very persuasive and intelligent introduction, followed by 100 pages of verse, 30 pages of prose-poetry and nearly 300 pages of assorted prose. And this is surely a misconceived allocation. Judging by the selections from novels, the short stories, the fragments of autobiography, Williams was a lively and thoroughly competent prose writer, but in no way an extraordinary one.
   But there are many beautiful and striking poems in this anthology as well as three seductive passages from 'Paterson'. Williams was very much a poet of his own generation, which is the generation of Pound and Eliot. Pound was his life-long friend, and although they seem to have vociferously differed about what modern poetry should be and do, Williams was clearly influenced by Pound a good deal more than he knew.
   Like Pound he was once an Imagist; a follower, that's to say, of that pre-First-World-War group who believed that the sole proper function of the modern poet was to make simple and vivid statements about visual appearances. Like Pound, Williams uses a largely irregular metrical pattern: like Pound, he often falls into demotic American, but sometimes, too, into foreign languages and rather too

often into OK cultural references. Like Pound and Eliot, he uses quotations as integral parts of his own poem. Like Pound's 'Cantos' 'Paterson' is partly an assault on modern America and the financial vices of a capitalist system. As in the 'Cantos' so in too much of Williams's verse there is an obscurity which seems *voulu* and unnecessary.

My own impression is that Williams never quite succeeded in escaping from the general idiom of his time: he never quite forged the kind of quirky, individual and utterly original instrument which Frost so notable forged for himself, particularly in his longer poems. There is too much in 'Paterson' which reminds us of other books and writers. (His image of the Passaic River, which runs all through 'Paterson' - and very beautifully - reminded me both of Joyce's Anna Livia and of Virginia Woolf's 'Waves'.) And the one really original element in 'Paterson' - the interpolation of documentary fragments in the form of letters received by the poet, newspaper accounts of local episodes and so on - seems to me to be a disastrous mistake. (But another of those ancient mistakes which some very, very modern writers are making all over again, with an air of shattering originality: Williams was collecting 'found' poems at least 30 years ago.)

But beyond all the unconscious imitations in Williams's verse, beyond the mistakes, the affectations, the mannerisms of his age, one can't help hearing a real poet struggling to get out. 'Paterson' may not quite succeed in its immensely ambitious aim - which was both to celebrate and excoriate the whole of modern American by describing one man's life in one small town - but it is a poem which leaves image after image in the mind. Here is the Passaic River in its fallen state, disgustingly polluted in the lower reaches: -

> If it were only fertile. Rather a sort of muck, a
>   detritus,
> in this case - a pustular scum, a decay, a choking
> lifelessness - that leaves the soil clogged after it,
> that glues the sandy bottom and blackens stones - so
>   that
> they have to be scoured three times when, because of
> an attractive brokenness, we take them up for garden
>   uses.
> An acrid, a revolting stench comes out of them, almost
>   one
> might say a granular stench - fouls the mind.

It is the word 'granular' which settles the issue, and casts its horrid illumination backwards on the whole pas-

sage. But I cannot end without saying that Williams
knew - as all good poets have known - that his proper
function was to glorify the world; and every passage of
disgust in 'Paterson' is a contribution to that end.

131. UNSIGNED REVIEW, THE WILLIAMS GRAIN, 'TIMES LITERARY
SUPPLEMENT'

13 April 1967, 305

The American edition of this book, out last year, carried
on its jacket a photograph of Williams frowning into the
sun. Not at all the genial old man of the later pictures,
but, from the set of the head to the corrugations of the
unzipped windcheater, very much he who curtly replied to
the protesting European in 'The Great American Novel:" "As
far as I have gone it is accurate'. Williams was tough
and tender - more than a bit sentimental in fact. Or perhaps Lawrence takes his measure more justly in that review
of 'In the American Grain' where he speaks of the need
Williams intuited for 'a supreme sensuous delicacy and at
the same time an infinitely tempered resistance'. That
was the best Williams got for many a year in England. His
appearance in Pound's 'Active Anthology' brought from
Lawrence's principal defender the observation that all
this was fifteen years out of date, a too late reaction
against 'the wordy debility of Georgianism'. Of course,
that was a long time ago. But only the other day we were
being told by a front-line critic about 'Williams' poetry
of red brick houses, suburban wives, cheerful standardized
interiors'. Williams earned the right to that frown.

At this point, Williams is decidedly 'in' and, for good
or ill, has replaced Eliot in the affections of younger
readers. But one of the results of the long delay (the
news that a British publisher would take his poems came
two days after his death) seems to be the odd order in
which we have so far had his works. As yet, although
there is the 'Collected Later Poems', we have still to
wait for the 'Collected Early Poems', and the same goes
for his first substantial prose work, 'In the American
Grain'. Shall we ever see the whole of the even earlier
'Great American Novel' or the fascinating prose accompaniment to 'Spring and All'?

The tantalizing extracts from these printed by M. L.
Rosenthal will more than whet a reader's appetite and
exasperation. Professor Rosenthal has not had an easy

job: there is so much to choose from. The poems here are
justly representative. He has omitted the letters, but he
gives us a wide-ranging look at the fiction and 'other
prose'. Perhaps no choice could have been perfect. Here,
there are no 'Pictures from Brueghel' poems, only Book One
of 'Asphodel', no 'Desert Music', merely the first scene
of the first act from Williams's three-act play, 'A Dream
of Love'. This last - though the extract makes little
sense on its own - is no real loss, for Williams's plays
are among his more embarrassing productions. Perhaps the
scene could have been left out altogether and then we
could have had The Destruction of Tenchtitlan without which
no selection from 'In the American Grain' can be really
adequate. But one's perhapses must not be allowed to
cloud the fact that the appearance of a Williams reader is
a decidedly happy occasion.

132. CHARLES TOMLINSON, DR. WILLIAMS' PRACTICE, 'ENCOUNTER'

Vol. XXIX, no. 5, November 1967, 66-9

The concluding part of this review-essay considers the
work of Denise Levertov and Kenneth Rexroth. Notes are as
they appear in the original.
    Tomlinson (b. 1927) is a British poet and teacher,
whose work from its earliest stages has been influenced by
that of Marianne Moore and Williams. He is editor of the
Williams volume in the Penguin Critical Anthologies
Series (1972) and author of 'Selected Poems 1951-74' (1978).

Five years ago - nay, not so much - you would have been
hard put to find the merest handful of Williams' verse in
an English bookshop. We have had to wait long for the
appearance in England of his 'Collected Earlier Poems,'
but meanwhile there is a new Penguin Williams selection,*
M. L. Rosenthal's 'The W. C. Williams Reader,'† and a
volume of essays from various hands under the editorship
of J. Hillis Miller‡ who has already proved himself to be
brilliantly equipped to deal with - though I think he
overrates - the art of this poet. Among Miller's ablest
commentators are Kenneth Burke, Marianne Moore, Hugh
Kenner, and Thom Gunn, and the usefulness of his book is

greatly increased by his inclusion of Richard Macksey's excellent chronology and bibliography.

The Penguin selection is brief but judicious, Rosenthal's 'Reader' intelligent and packed: we are given large chunks of the prose in this latter and even a long scene from one of Williams' not very good plays. Undoubtedly many favourites are missing, but the reason for this is a clear one: Williams wrote a lot and, for so prolific and hurried a writer, a lot that was good. Perhaps one of the pieces that could be shed without much loss would be that rotten poem, Impromptu: The Suckers. It is Dr. Williams at his least inventive, dashing things off between patients. The doggedness, rather than the dash, repays in Williams: 'of a slow but accurate understanding' he says of himself. And he will return again and again to a theme or a term over the years to achieve that accuracy. Ian Hamilton complains recently of Williams' 'rambling Americanising' in an intemperate article that tries to sink Williams under the faults of his followers. Williams more than justified the right to his own faults by a quality of persistence, beautifully illustrated by Pound in the essay Mr. Miller reprints.

One of the terms to which Williams' persistence keeps returning him is Whitman's 'contact.' 'Contact' was the title of the magazine Williams edited in the 1920s, and the *tactus eruditus* he speaks of in one poem is his obstetrician's reappraisal of that term. 'I am mad for it to be in contact with me,' says Whitman of nature in 'Song of Myself.' So is Williams. The difference lies in that *eruditus* and the way it enters his poetry. 'A fact with him,' says Kenneth Burke, 'finds its justification in the trimness of the wording.' Whitman is a great poet, but he is never trim.

'The sharpened faculties which require exactness' (as Marianne Moore puts it) are what distinguishes the tone of Williams from that of his origins. When he speaks, in the prose section of 'Spring and All,' of Whitman, the company he puts him in is that of Gris and Cezanne, announcing that 'Whitman's proposals are of the same piece with the modern trend toward imaginative understanding of life.' At this point, the imagination for Williams was identified with the cubist re-structuring of reality, and after a rapid transition from Gris, Cezanne, and Whitman to Shakespeare, Williams tells us of the last named: 'He holds no mirror up to nature but with his imagination rivals nature's composition with his own.' Williams' cubist perspective dominates his inheritance. Kenneth Rexroth, in an excellent and too little known essay, The Influence of French Poetry on American, has commented on

Williams' cubist allegiances and he expresses the relation
between these and Williams' famous localism with great
perspicacity:

> ... Williams could be said to belong in the Cubist
> tradition - Imagism, Objectivism, the dissociation and
> rearrangement of the elements of concrete reality,
> rather than rhetoric or free association. But where
> Reverdy, Apollinaire, Salmon, Cendrars, Cocteau, and
> Jacob are all urban, even megalopolitan, poets of that
> Paris which is the international market of objects of
> *vertu*, vice and art, Williams has confined himself in
> single strictness to the life before his eyes - the
> life of a physician in a small town twenty miles from
> New York. In so doing, his localism has become inter-
> national and timeless. His long quest for a completely
> defenceless simplicity of personal speech produces an
> idiom identical with that which is the end product of
> centuries of polish, refinement, tradition, and revolu-
> tion.

On the face of it, the inheritance Williams brings to
cubism seems to be very close in spirit not only to Whitman
but also to Emerson and Thoreau. If 'contact' is re-
explored, so is Emerson's attachment to the vernacular:
'the speech of Polish mothers' was where Williams insisted
he got his English from. 'Colleges and books only copy the
language which the field and work-yard made,' said Emerson.
Williams' famous 'flatness' comes not from the field, but
from the urban 'work-yard' of New Jersey. As Hugh Kenner
writes of Williams' characteristic diction: 'That words set
in Jersey speech rhythms mean less but mean it with greater
finality, is Williams' great technical perception.'

Emerson seems to have prepared the ground for Williams'
other war-cry, 'No ideas but in things' with his 'Ask the
fact for the form.' Thoreau sounds yet closer with:
'The roots of letters are things.' Again Emerson tells
over things - 'The meal in the firkin; the milk in the
pan; the ballad in the street; the news of the boat ...' -
in the shape of a list very like Williams' 'rigmaroles' as
he calls his poems. 'Bare lists of words,' says Emerson,
'are found suggestive to an imaginative mind.' When
Williams, long after Emerson and after Whitman's application of this, constructed 'list' poems, he came in for
suspicion, as in the interview he prints as part of
'Paterson V' and which Mr. Rosenthal includes in his
selection:

[quotes P V, ii, 262, first 3 questions and answers]

And, of course, Emerson and Whitman had said it time and again before him, though Emerson could never quite get there in his own poetry and Whitman, as Williams complains, 'took his eyes off the words themselves which should have held him,' 'he forgot ... everything but his "message".'

'Paterson V' came out in 1958. Years before, Williams had formulated his kind of poem made out of anything and with a jagged pattern, in the 1920 preface to 'Kora in Hell,' when he wrote that a poem is 'tough by no quality it borrows from a logical recital of events nor from the events themselves but solely from the attenuated power which draws perhaps many broken things into a dance by giving them thus a full being.' He was to return to the idea of poem as dance. If, as with Emerson, Williams seems to 'ask the fact for the form,' the form, once it comes, is free of the fact, is a dance *above* the fact. After 'Kora in Hell' he had another shot at the formula in the prose of 'Spring and All' (1923) where he concludes of John of Gaunt's speech in 'Richard II' that 'his words are related not to their sense of objects adherent to his son's welfare or otherwise, but as a dance over the body of his condition accurately accompanying it.' This summary of Williams' own methods is hard to come by in its full context. Mr. Miller prints part of it and Mr. Rosenthal, with some overlaps, other parts. Mr. Miller, in his introduction, even goes so far as to say that, without the prose in 'Spring and All,' 'two of Williams' most famous poems, By the Road to the Contagious Hospital and The Red Wheelbarrow ... cannot be fully understood.' But he tantalisingly fails to relate these two poems to their surrounding prose. Mr. Macksey, one of the contributors to Miller's collection of essays, also remarks on the links, but doesn't specify what they are. All this is bound to frustrate the reader of a poet whose early works are often unobtainable - 'The Great American Novel' is a case in point - and whose early formulations often surpass his later ones. Mr. Rosenthal interestingly concludes his volume with Williams' latish essay, On Measure -Statement for Cid Corman (1953). Is it too much to hope that soon we shall see the text of Speech Rhythm?§ This is Williams' earliest piece (a first draft of it dated from 1913) on the same theme, where, as one researcher tells us,

> Williams never once refers to American Speech as distinct from English in this (his best) version of

Measure. Nor does he assume a specifically American
prosody. On the contrary, he relates his concept of
a flexible system - a structural method - to the current preoccupations of Imagism. (M. Weaver in 'Form,'
No. 2, p. 22).

One sees how the element of chauvinism - the American
fact at all costs! - crept into and often distorted
Williams' thinking: he had to pull against those famous
exiles Pound and Eliot, he had to prove the worth of that
native ground; but although, as Mr. Gunn's essay reminds
us, 'he insisted on the American idiom, we must,' says Mr.
Gunn, 'remember why: writing "thoroughly local in origin
has some chance of being universal in application"; that
idiom is part of a widely-used language, his enrichment of
which has a bearing on all of us who read and write it.'
So he of the conversations with Valery Larbaud, he who
wrote of Matisse and admired Juan Gris, he who was to
translate Soupault and Char, refused to be led away from
the dissonant roar of the Passaic River. It is only by
the time of 'Paterson,' Book IV, that he will bring Europe
into the documentation of the city, when the dissonances
of the local are measured against the funeral of the
Abbess Hildegard and the chorale she 'had enjoined them to
sing ... she had written for the occasion.' Within the
milieu of the Stieglitz group, Williams focused the cubist
tradition on locality, aligning cubist fragmentations with
those of modern photography (Stieglitz, Steichen). Then
in turn he was to face the local towards the universal.
By 'Paterson V' he had *earned* the right to address
Brueghel, Bosch, Dürer, Toulouse-Lautrec, and the artists
of the Unicorn Tapestries - they whose localism was also
now a universal affair.

Yet Williams' particularity certainly shortened the
temper of some of his formulations. Rexroth who now
shares a Penguin Modern Poets volume with him pays him
there a decidedly sentimental homage:

*The day will come
When a young woman will walk by the lucid
    Williams River,
Where it flows through an idyllic
News from nowhere sort of landscape ...*

He once had sharper things to say about a kind of Americanism that Williams more than occasionally seemed to be
promulgating: 'When today someone tells me that my Duty is
To Express What Is Native to America, i am just a little
afraid that tomorrow i shall be told to Go Back to Russia

Where i Came From.'

Perhaps it was something of this strain in Williams that caused Kenneth Burke to remark that often what calls for commendation is not 'in the excellence of his poetics, but in the excellence of his results.' As a 'way' for poetry 'bare lists of words' and their suggestiveness to 'an imaginative mind' could only mean anything in terms, of a practice far from naive and accompanied by great aural precision. Williams, in one of his last poems, specifies the elements of that precision if his often centrifugal forms are to succeed:

[quotes Song, PB, 15-16]

It is a quality of ear - the mind's ear - that marries the disparate elements in Williams' verse, a quickness to catch the beauties of asymmetrical arrangement and rigmarole, which, like the components of a mobile, seem to be moving out of the true, until we see that that 'true' was one of our 'reconceived mental ratios and the components relate to a whole after all ....

Notes

*'Penguin Modern Poets' 9. DENISE LEVERTOV, KENNETH REXROTH, W. C. WILLIAMS, 3s. 6d.
†'The W. C. Williams Reader.' Edited by M. L. ROSENTHAL. MacGibbon and Kee, 42s.
‡'William Carlos Williams: a Collection of Critical Essays.' Edited by J. HILLIS MILLER, Prentice-Hall, 16s.
§Not yet published.

Bibliography

This section lists primary bibliographical materials and primary sources.

WALLACE, EMILY MITCHELL, 'A Bibliography of William Carlos Williams' (Middletown, Conn., Wesleyan University Press, 1968).
HARDIE, JACK, 'A Celebration of Light': Selected Checklist of Writings about William Carlos Williams, 'Journal of Modern Literature', May 1971, 593-642.
HEAL, EDITH, ed., 'I Wanted to Write a Poem' (Boston, Mass., Beacon Press, 1958).
LAXON, MARTHA, The Criticism of Williams' 'Paterson': an Introduction and Bibliography, 'Thoth', vol. II, no. i, 1970, 40-8.
MARIANI, PAUL L., 'William Carlos Williams: The Poet and His Critics' (Chicago, American Library Association, 1975).
WAGNER, LINDA WELSHIMER, William Carlos Williams: a Review of Research and Criticism, 'Resources for American Literary Studies', vol. I, 1971, 17-29.
WAGNER, LINDA WELSHIMER, A Decade of Discovery, 1953-1963, 'Twentieth-Century Literature', January 1965, 216-27.
WHITE, WILLIAM, William Carlos Williams: Bibliography Review with Addenda, 'American Book Collector', vol. XIX, no. 7, 1969, 9-12.
[WILLIAMS] 'A Recognizable Image: William Carlos Williams on Art and Artists', ed. Bram Dijkstra (New York, New Directions, 1979).
WILLIAMS, WILLIAM CARLOS, 'The Embodiment of Knowledge', ed. Ron Loewinsohn (New York, New Directions, 1975).
WILLIAMS, WILLIAM CARLOS, 'Imaginations', ed. Webster Scholt (New York, New Directions, 1970).

Williams bibliographical materials appear regularly in the annual 'American Literary Scholarship' (since 1964) and the quarterly 'American Literature'. Also relevant are 'Autobiography', SE and SL.

This section lists reviews and published comments on Williams' work from 1909 to 1970 which have not been reprinted in the present collection

'Poems'
Ezra Pound, letter to W.C.W., 21 May 1909 ('The Letters of Ezra Pound 1907-1941', ed. D. D. Paige (New York, Harcourt Brace & World, 1950), 7-8).

'The Tempers'
Ezra Pound, Introduction to 'The Tempers' (first published in 'Poetry Review', London, vol. I, no. 10, October 1912, 481-4 with selection of the poems); W.C.W. to Harriet Monroe, 5 March 1913, SL, 23-5, and Monroe, 'A Poet's Life' (New York, Macmillan, 1938), 269-72.

'The Great American Novel'
Matthew Josephson, 'Broom', October 1923, np.

'In the American Grain'
Clifton Fadiman, 'Bookman', October 1928, 222.

'A Voyage to Pagany'
'Saturday Review of Literature', 22 September 1928, 159; 'Independent', 28 September 1928, 121, 309; 'New York Times Book Review', 30 September 1928, 2; 'Bookman', October 1928, 222; 'New York Evening Post', 20 October 1928, 8M; Ezra Pound, 'Dial', November 1928, 389-98 (reprinted in 'Literary Essays of Ezra Pound'); 'Boston Evening Transcript', 1 December 1928, 6.

'The Knife of the Times'
'Saturday Review', 7 May 1932, 719.

'Collected Poems 1921-1931'
Carl Rakosi, 'Symposium', October 1933, 332-4; Charles G. Poore, 'New York Times Book Review', 18 February 1934, 2; Conrad Aiken, 'New Republic', 18 April 1934 (reprinted in Aiken's 'A Reviewer's ABC').

'White Mule'
Fred R. Miller, 'New Republic', 7 July 1937, 257; Willard Maas, 'New York Herald Tribune Books', 11 July 1937, 4; William Carlos Williams, 'Writer', August 1937, 243-5; Isabel Thomas, 'Canadian Forum', October 1937, 254.

'Life Along the Passaic River'
Paul Rosenfeld, 'New York Herald Tribune Books', 27 February 1938, 6; Ezra Pound, 'Townsman', July 1938, 30.

'The Complete Collected Poems 1906-1938'
Babette Deutsch, 'Nation', 19 November 1938, 542; 'New Yorker', 19 November 1938, 92; J. G. Brunini, 'Commonweal',

3 February 1939, 415; Horace Gregory, 'New York Herald Tribune Books', vol. IX, no. 10, 5 February 1931; Louis Untermeyer, 'Yale Review', Spring 1939, 612-13; Mason Wade, 'New York Times Book Review', 23 July 1939, 2 and 12; Ruth Lechlitner, 'Poetry', September 1939, 426-35; R. P. Blackmur, unlocated source, reprinted in 'Language as Gesture', 347-50.

'In the Money'
Clifton Fadiman, 'New Yorker', 2 November 1940, 69; Richard Cordell, 'Saturday Review', 9 November 1940, 5; Ruth Lechlitner, 'New York Herald Tribune Books', 17 November 1940, 18; Fred T. Marsh, 'New York Times Book Review', 17 November 1940, 7; Eleanor Godfrey, 'Canadian Forum', December 1940, 290; 'Time', 2 December 1940, 83.

'The Wedge'
Horace Gregory, 'Saturday Review', 2 November 1944, 48, 50; R. P. Blackmur, review in 'Language as Gesture' dated 1945.

'Paterson (Book One)'
Ruth Lechlitner, 'Weekly Book Review', 22 September 1946, 601; Horace Gregory, 'Briarcliff Quarterly', October 1946, 186-8; Anne Fremantle, 'Commonweal', 4 October 1946, 601; 'New Yorker', 26 October 1946; George Snell, 'San Francisco Chronicle', 12 January 1947, 20.

'Paterson (Book Two)'
Richard Eberhart, 'New York Times Book Review', 20 June 1948, 4; Ruth Lechlitner, 'New York Herald Tribune Books', 27 June 1948, 3; Frederick W. Eckman, 'Golden Goose', Autumn 1948, 36-8; William Van O'Connor, 'Saturday Review', 25 September 1948, 30; Thomas Hornsby Ferril, 'San Francisco Chronicle', 7 November 1948, 83; Edwin Honig, 'Poetry', April 1949, 37-41.

'The Clouds'
Hubert Creekmore, 'Saturday Review', 9 October 1948, 33; David Daiches, 'New York Herald Tribune Books', 30 January 1949, 17; R. W. Flint, 'Kenyon Review', Summer 1950, 541-2.

'A Dream of Love'
'New Yorker', 29 January 1949, 72; David Daiches, 'New York Herald Tribune Books', 30 January 1949, 17.

'Selected Poems'
Thomas Hornsby Ferril, 'San Francisco Chronicle', 29 May 1949, 10; Harold Barrows, 'New York Times Book Review', 17 July 1949, 4; James R. Caldwell, 'Saturday Review',

20 August 1949, 27; Eugene Davidson, 'Yale Review', Summer 1949, 724-5; Richard Wilbur, 'Sewanee Review', January 1950, 130-43.

'Paterson (Book Three)'
Richard Eberhart, 'New York Times Book Review', 12 February 1950, 5; Selden Rodman, 'New York Herald Tribune Books', 5 March 1950, 5; Leo Kennedy, 'Chicago Sun', 20 March 1950; Thomas Hornsby Ferril, 'San Francisco Chronicle', 30 April 1950, 22; William Van O'Connor, 'Saturday Review', 20 May 1950, 41; 'New Yorker', 22 July 1950, 75; R. W. Flint, 'Kenyon Review', Summer 1950, 541-2.

'The Collected Later Poems'
Richard Eberhart, 'New York Times Book Review', 17 December 1950, 1; Hayden Carruth, 'Nation', 3 March 1951, 209-10; G. D. McDonald, 'Library Journal', 15 March 1951, 519; Ben Ray Redman, 'Saturday Review', 21 July 1951, 35.

'Make Light of It'
J. M. Scherr, 'Library Journal', 1 October 1950; 'Time', 4 December 1950, 79-80; 'New Yorker', 9 December 1950, 167; Richard Sullivan, 'Chicago Sunday Tribune', 17 December 1950, 4.

'Paterson (Book Four)'
Charles Olson in 'Mayan Letters', letter of 8 March 1951; Ruth Lechlitner, 'New York Herald Tribune Books', 1 July 1951, 3; 'Time', 16 July 1951, 94, 96; Paul Engle, 'Chicago Sunday Tribune', section 4, 22 July 1951, 3; Hugh Kenner, 'Poetry', August 1952, 276-90 (reprinted in his book 'Gnomon').

'Autobiography'
Paul Engle, 'Chicago Sunday Tribune', section 4, 16 September 1951, 3; Conrad Aiken, 'New York Herald Tribune Books', 16 September 1951, 1 (reprinted in 'A Reviewer's ABC'); Selden Rodman, 'New York Times Book Review', 16 September 1951, 6, 22; 'Time', 8 October 1951, 118, 120; 'Nation', 20 October 1951, 333; 'New Yorker', 20 October 1951, 134; 'Cleveland Open Shelf', November 1951, 27; Vivienne Koch, 'Poetry', May 1952, 89-95; Vivienne Koch, 'Kenyon Review', Summer 1952, 502-10; Irving Stone, 'Yale Review', Winter 1952, 316-18.

'The Collected Earlier Poems'
Lawrence Ferlinghetti,'San Francisco Chronicle', 6 January 1952, 18; 'Booklist', 1 February 1952, 183; G. D. McDonald, 'Library Journal', 15 March 1952, 533; Robert Beum,

'Poetry', August 1952, 291-4; Robert Beum and R. W. Emerson, 'Golden Goose', October 1952, 33-5, 38-40; Richard Eberhart, 'New Republic', 10 November 152, 20; Harvey Shapiro, 'American Mercury', December 1952, 111-12/

'The Build-Up'
H. C. Webster, 'Saturday Review', 18 October 1952, 18; Robert Gorham Davis, 'New York Times Book Review', 19 October 1952, 5; Warren Beck, 'Chicago Sunday Tribune', 26 October 1952, 6; 'Atlantic Monthly', November 1952, 112; T. E. Cassidy, 'Commonweal', 7 November 1952, 126-7; Richard Eberhart, 'New Republic', 10 November 1952, 20-1; Paul Pickrel, 'Yale Review', Winter 1953.

'The Desert Music'
Nicholas Joost, 'Chicago Sunday Tribune', 23 March 1954; Winfield Townley Scott, 'New York Herald Tribune Books', 28 March 1954; 'Booklist', 15 April 1954, 316; G. P. Meyer, 'Saturday Review', 5 June 1954, 21; G. D. McDonald, 'Library Journal', 15 June 1954; 'New Yorker', 10 July 1954, 68; Babette Deutsch, 'Poetry', March 1955, 351-5; John E. Palmer, 'Sewanee Review', Spring 1955, 295-6; Sister M. Bernetta Quinn, 'Imagi', vol. VI, 1955; Thomas Cole, 'Voices', January-April 1956, 35-7.

'Selected Essays'
Robert Creeley, 'Black Mountain Review', Winter 1954, 53-8. Selden Rodman, 'New York Times Book Review', 7 November 1954, 7, 44; Richard Eberhart, 'Saturday Review', 20 November 1954, 20, 38; Sidney Alexander, 'Commentary', January 1955, 96-8; Hugh Kenner, 'Hudson Review', vol. VIII, no. 1, 1955 (reprinted in 'Gnomon').

'Journey to Love'
Babette Deutsch, 'New York Herald Tribune Books', 13 November 1955, 4; Randall Jarrell, 'Yale Review', Spring 1956, 478.

'In the American Grain' (1956 edition)
Jean Garrigue, 'Poetry', August 1957, 315-20.

'The Selected Letters'
Phoebe Adams, 'Atlantic Monthly', September 1957, 84-5; Gene Baro, 'New York Herald Tribune Books', 1 September 1957, 1; Paul Engle, 'Chicago Sunday Tribune', 1 September 1957, 6; Morton Dauwen Zabel, 'New York Times Book Review', 1 September 1957, 3; Horace Reynolds, 'Christian Science Monitor', 5 September 1957, 7; 'New Yorker', 7 December 1957.

'Paterson (Book Five)'
Richard Eberhart, 'New York Times Book Review', 14 September 1958, 4; Babette Deutsch, 'New York Herald Tribune Books', 28 September 1958, 11; John Ciardi, 'Saturday Review', 11 October 1959, 37-9; Thom Gunn, 'Yale Review', December 1958, 297-9; 'New Yorker', 20 December 1958, 20; Henry Wells, 'Voices', Summer 1959, 49-52.

'I Wanted to Write a Poem'
G. D. McDonald, 'Library Journal', 1 Paril 1958, 1100; 'Christian Science Monitor', 10 April 1958, 7; 'Booklist', 15 April 1958, 471; Phoebe Adams, 'Atlantic Monthly', May 1958, 87; Paul Engle, 'Chicago Sunday Ribune', 5 July 1959, 5; Babette Deutsch, 'New York Herald Tribune Books', 6 July 1958, 9.

'Yes, Mrs Williams'
Babette Deutsch, 'New York Herald Tribune Books', 21 June 1959, 4; Phoebe Adams, 'Atlantic Monthly', July 1959, 80-1; Paul Engle, 'Chicago Sunday Tribune', 5 July 1959, 5; John Ciardi, 'Saturday Review', 11 July 1959, 32-3; Janet Fiscalini, 'Commonweal', 18 September 1959, 519-21.

'Many Loves'
Donald Malcolm, 'New Yorker', 24 January 1959, 68-9; Henry Hewes, 'Saturday Review', 31 January 1959, 24. (These are reviews of performances.)

'The Farmers' Daughters'
Van Wyck Brooks, 'Harpers', June 1961, 83-5 (this is the book's introduction); Raymond Walters, 'New York Times Book Review', 10 September 1961, 56; Curtis Harnack, 'Chicago Sunday Tribune', 29 October 1961, 3; Burton Robie, 'Library Journal', 1 December 1961, 4209; Cid Corman, 'Massachusetts Review', Winter 1962, 319-24.

'Pictures from Brueghel'
Phoebe Adams, 'Atlantic Monthly', August 1962, 145; P. N. Furbank, 'Listener', 16 April 1964, 645; Linda Welshimer Wagner, 'American Weave', Winter 1963-4, 37-9; Geoffrey Grigson, 'New Statesman', 1 May 1964, 691; Norman Talbot, 'Poetry Australia', December 1965, 31-8; 'Times Literary Supplement', 7 May 1964, 396.

Valedictories
Paul Trédant, 'Nouvelles littéraires', 14 March 1963, 6; John Ciardi, 'Saturday Review', 23 March 1963, 18-20; Frederick Eckman, 'Chicago Literary Times', April 1963, 1; Josephine Jacobsen, 'Commonweal', 10 May 1963, 191-2.

'The Collected Later Poems' (revised edition)
Donald Finkel, 'Prairie Schooner', Winter 1964-5, 367;
M. L. Rosenthal, 'Spectator', 25 June 1965, 822; John
Press, 'Punch', 7 July 1965, 29.

'White Mule' (new impression)
'New Statesman', 23 July 1965, 126-7; 'Times Literary
Supplement', 29 July 1965, 629; Denis Donoghue, 'Manchester Guardian Weekly', 29 July 1965, 11; 'Punch', 11 August
1965, 216; M. L. Rosenthal, 'Spectator', 20 August 1965,
241-2; 'Observer', 25 October 1970, 32.

'In the Money' (English edition)
Irving Wardle, 'Observer', 6 February 1966, 27; 'Times
Literary Supplement', 10 Feburary 1966, 97; Penelope Mortimer, 'New Statesman', 11 February 1966, 200; R. G.
Price, 'Punch', 16 February 1966, 250.

'The William Carlos Williams Reader'
Edmund Fuller, 'Wall Street Journal', 15 September 1966,
16; Sherman Paul, 'Nation', 10 October 1966, 356; T. L.
Vince, 'Library Journal', 15 October 1966, 4956; Alden
Whitman, 'New York Times', 25 October 1966, 47M; Webster
Schott, 'Life', 18 November 1966, 8; 'Choice', January
1967, 1019; Raymond Rosenthal, 'New Leader', 30 January
1967, 23; D. M. Davis, 'National Observer', 6 February
1967, 31; Louise Bogan, 'New Yorker', 4 March 1967, 162;
'Times Literary Supplement', 13 April 1967, 305; C. B.
Cox, 'Spectator', 14 April 1967, 425; S. P. Zitner,
'Poetry', October 1967, 41.

'The Collected Earlier Poems' (English issue, 1967)
Julian Symons, 'New Statesman', 16 June 1967, 849; 'Times
Literary Supplement', 22 June 1967, 556; Ian Hamilton,
'Punch', 19 July 1967.

'I Wanted to Write a Poem' (2nd impression)
Philip Toynbee, 'Observer', 17 December 1967, 21; 'Times
Literary Supplement', 18 January 1968, 62.

'In the American Grain' (revised edition)
Edmund Fuller, 'Wall Street Journal', 15 September 1966,
16; D. M. Davis, 'National Observer', 6 February 1967, 17;
Karl Shapiro, 'Book Week', 26 February 1967, 17; 'Choice',
June 1967, 424; 'Times Literary Supplement', 22 June 1967,
556; Ian Hamilton, 'Punch', 19 July 1967, 109.

'A Voyage to Pagany' (new edition)
Harry Levin, 'Yale Review', no. 59, 1970, 520-31 (the

book's introduction); 'Publisher's Weekly', 10 August
1970, 48; 'Saturday Review', 14 November 1970, 31;
'Nation', 14 December 1970, 635.

'Imaginations' (1970)
William Heyen, 'Saturday Review', 1 August 1970, 21-4;
'Atlantic Monthly', September 1970, 128; 'Time', 21 September 1970, 106; 'Christian Science Monitor', 14 November
1970, B1; 'Nation', 23 November 1970, 534; 'Choice',
December 1970, 1378.

This section lists books which are wholly, or centrally,
concerned with Williams. Listing is alphabetically, by
author or editor.

ANGOFF, CHARLES, ed., 'William Carlos Williams: Papers by
Kenneth Burke, Emily Mitchell Wallace, Norman Holmes
Pearson, A. M. Sullivan' (N.J., Fairleigh Dickinson University, 1974).
BRESLIN, JAMES E., 'William Carlos Williams: an American
Artist' (New York, Oxford University Press, 1970).
BRINNIN, JOHN MALCOLM, 'William Carlos Williams'
(Minneapolis, University of Minnesota Press, 1963).
CONARROE, JOEL, 'William Carlos Williams' "Paterson":
Language and Landscape' (Philadelphia, University of
Pennsylvania, 1970).
DIJKSTRA, BRAM, 'The Hieroglyphics of a New Speech:
Cubism, Stieglitz and the Early Poetry of William Carlos
Williams' (Princeton University Press, 1969).
DUPEYRON MARCHESSOU, HÉLÈNE, 'William Carlos Williams et
le renouveau du lyrisme' (Paris, Presses Universitaires
de France, 1967).
GUIMOND, JAMES, 'The Art of William Carlos Williams: a
Discovery and Possession of America' (Urbana, University
of Illinois, 1968).
MAZZARO, JEROME, ed., 'Profile of William Carlos Williams'
(Columbus, Ohio., Merrill, 1971).
MAZZARO, JEROME, 'William Carlos Williams: the Later
Poems' (Ithaca, N.Y., Cornell University Press, 1973).
MILLER, J. HILLIS, 'Poets of Reality' (Cambridge, Mass.,
The Belknap Press of Harvard University, 1966).
MILLER, J. HILLIS, 'William Carlos Williams: a Collection
of Critical Essays' (Englewood Cliffs, N. J., Prentice-
Hall, 1966).
OSTROM, ALAN, 'The Poetic World of William Carlos
Williams' (Carbondale, Southern Illinois University
Press, 1966).
PAUL, SHERMAN, 'The Music of Survival: a Biography of a

Poem by William Carlos Williams' (Urbana, University of
Illinois, 1968).
PETERSON, WALTER S., 'An Approach to "Paterson"' (New
Haven, Conn., Yale University Press, 1967).
RIDDEL, JOSEPH N., 'The Inverted Bell: Modernism and the
Counterpoetics of William Carlos Williams' (Baton Rouge,
Louisiana State University Press, 1974).
SANKEY, BENJAMIN, 'A Companion to William Carlos Williams'
Paterson' (Berkeley, University of California Press,
1971).
SIMPSON, LOUIS, 'Three on the Tower: The Lives and Works
of Ezra Pound, T. S. Eliot and William Carlos Williams'
(New York, Morrow, 1975).
TOMLINSON, CHARLES, ed., 'William Carlos Williams: a Critical Anthology' (Harmondsworth, Penguin Books, 1972).
TOWNLEY, ROD, 'The Early Poetry of William Carlos Williams' (Ithaca, N.Y., Cornell University Press, 1975).
WAGNER, LINDA WELSHIMER, 'The Poems of William Carlos
Williams: a Critical Study' (Middletown, Conn., Wesleyan
University Press, 1964).
WAGNER, LINDA WELSHIMER, 'The Prose of William Carlos
Williams' (Middletown, Conn., Wesleyan University Press,
1970).
WEATHERHEAD, A. KINGSLEY, 'The Edge of the Image: Marianne
Moore, William Carlos Williams, and Some Other Poets'
(Seattle and London, University of Washington Press,
1967).
WEAVER, MIKE, 'William Carlos Williams: the American Background' (London, Cambridge University Press, 1971).
WHITAKER, THOMAS R., 'William Carlos Williams' (New York,
Twayne Publishing Co., 1968).
WHITTEMORE, REED, 'William Carlos Williams, Poet from
Jersey' (Boston, Houghton Mifflin, 1975).
WILLARD, NANCY, 'Testimony of the Invisible Man: William
Carlos Williams, Francis Ponge, Rainer Marie Rilke, Pablo
Neruda' (Columbia, University of Missouri Press, 1970).

A select list of books with substantial material on
Williams.

CAMBON, GLAUCO, 'The Inclusive Flame: Studies in American
Poetry' (Bloomington, Indiana University Press, 1963).
DEMBO, L.S., 'Conceptions of Reality in Modern American
Poetry' (Berkeley, University of California Press, 1966).
DONOGHUE, DENIS, 'Connoisseurs of Chaos: Ideas of Order in
Modern American Poetry' (New York, Macmillan, 1965).
FRIEDMAN, MELVIN J., and VICKERY, JOHN B., eds, 'The
Shaken Realist: Essays in Modern Literature in Honor of

Frederick J. Hoffman' (Baton Rouge, Louisiana State University Press, 1970).
KENNER, HUGH, 'A Home-made World: The American Modernist Writers' (New York, Knopf, 1975).
MARTZ, LOUIS L., 'The Poem of the Mind' (New York, Oxford University Press, 1966).
PEARCE, ROY HARVEY, 'The Continuity of American Poetry' (Princeton University Press, 1961).
QUINN, SISTER M. BERNETTA, 'The Metamorphic Tradition in Modern Poetry' (New York, Gordian Press, 1955, 1966).
ROSENTHAL, M. L., 'The Modern Poets' (New York, Oxford University Press, 1960).

Appendix

**The printing of Williams' works 1909-67
A selected list**

The publications listed are those for which printing figures are available. See Emily Mitchell Wallace, 'A Bibliography of William Carlos Williams' (Middletown, Conn., 1968).

Title	Place of publication	Publisher	Date	Quantity	Price
'Poems'	Rutherford, N.J.	the author	1909	100	25c
'The Tempers'	London	Elkin Mathews	1913	1,000 (approx.)	1s. and 1s. 6d.
'Al Que Quiere!'	Boston	Four Seas Company	1917	1,000	$1.00
'Kora in Hell: Improvisations'	Boston	Four Seas Company	1920	1,000	$1.50
'Sour Grapes'	Boston	Four Seas Company	1921	1,000	$2.00
'The Great American Novel'	Paris	Three Mountains Press	1923	300	$2.50
'Spring and All'	Dijon, France	Contact Publishing Co.	1923	300 (approx.)	$2.00
'Go Go'	New York	Monroe Wheeler	1923	150	75c
'In the American Grain'	New York	Albert & Charles Boni	1925	unknown	$3.00 and $3.50
'A Voyage to Pagany'	New York	The Macaulay Company	1928	unknown	$2.50

Appendix

Title	Place of publication	Publisher	Date	Quantity	Price
'Last Nights of Paris'	New York	The Macaulay Company	1929	unknown	$2.50
'A Novelette & Other Prose'	Toulon, France	To Publishers	1932	500 (approx.)	$1.25
'The Knife of the Times and Other Stories'	Ithaca, N.Y.	Dragon Press	1932	500	$1.50
'The Cod Head'	Chapel Hill, N.C.	Harvest Press	1932	125	–
'Collected Poems 1921–1931'	New York	Objectivist Press	1934	500	$2.00
'An Early Martyr and Other Poems'	New York	Alcestis Press	1935	165	$7.50
'Adam & Eve & The City'	Peru, Vermont	Alcestis Press	1936	167	$5.00
'White Mule'	Norfolk, Conn.	New Directions	1937	1,100	$2.50
'Life Along the Passaic River'	Norfolk, Conn.	New Directions	1938	1,006	$1.75
'The Complete Collected Poems 1906–1938'	Norfolk, Conn.	New Directions	1938	1,500 (approx.)	$3.00
'In the American Grain'	Norfolk, Conn.	New Directions	1939	1,120	$1.00
'In the Money'	Norfolk, Conn.	New Directions	1940	1,500 (approx.)	$2.50

410 Appendix

Title	Place of publication	Publisher	Date	Quantity	Price
'The Broken Span'	Norfolk, Conn.	New Directions	1941	2,000	35c, 50c and $1.00
'The Wedge'	Cummington, Mass.	Cummington Press	1944	380	$3.50
'First Act'	Norfolk, Conn.	New Directions	1945	445	$3.50
'Paterson (Book One)'	Norfolk, Conn.	New Directions	1946	1,063	$2.50
'Paterson (Book Two)'	Norfolk, Conn.	New Directions	1948	1,009	$3.00
'The Clouds'	Cummington, Mass.	Wells College Press and Cummington Press	1948	60 250	$12.50 $ 5.00
'A Dream of Love'	Norfolk, Conn.	New Directions	1948	1,700	$1.50
'In the American Grain'	Norfolk, Conn.	New Directions	1948	2,200	$1.50
'Selected Poems'	Norfolk, Conn.	New Directions	1949	3,591	$1.50
'The Pink Church'	Columbus, O.	Golden Goose Press	1949	400	$1.00 and $2.00
'Paterson (Book Three)'	Norfolk, Conn.	New Directions	1949	999	$3.00
'Paterson (Books 1 & 2)'	Norfolk, Conn.	New Directions	1949	1,007	$1.50
'Paterson (Books 1, 2 & 3)'	Norfolk, Conn.	New Directions	1950	1,507 (sheets for 3,507)	$1.50

411 Appendix

Title	Place of publication	Publisher	Date	Quantity	Price
'The Collected Later Poems'	Norfolk, Conn.	New Directions	1950	4,700	$3.50
'Make Light of It'	New York	New Directions	1950	5,000	$3.50
'A Beginning on the Short Story'	New York	Alicat Bookshop Press	1950	1,000	$1.00
'Paterson (Book Four)'	Norfolk, Conn.	New Directions	1951	1,000	$3.00
'Autobiography'	New York	Random House	1951	5,000 5,000*	$3.75
'Paterson (Books 1, 2, 3 & 4)'	Norfolk, Conn.	New Directions	1951	2,000	$1.50
'The Collected Earlier Poems'	Norfolk, Conn.	New Directions	1951	5,000	$5.50
'The Build-Up'	New York	Random House	1952	6,000	$3.50
'Paterson (Books 1 and 2)'	London	Peter Owen Ltd	1953	500	8s. 6d.
'The Desert Music and Other Poems'	New York	Random House	1954	2,532 (signed 111)	$3.00 $10.00
'The Dog and the Fever'	Hamden, Conn.	The Shoe String Press	1954	1,000	$3.00
'Selected Essays'	New York	Random House	1954	3,350	$4.50
'Paterson (Books 1, 2, 3 & 4)'	Norfolk, Conn.	New Directions	1955	1,980	$1.50
'The Desert Music and Other Poems'	New York	Readers' Subscription Club	1955	1,000	$2.50

Title	Place of publication	Publisher	Date	Quantity	Price
'Journey to Love'	New York	Random House	1955	3,000	$3.00
'The Collected Later Poems'		Horace Mann School	1956	557	–
'In the American Grain'	New York	New Directions	1956	10,000	$1.25
'Kora in Hell: Improvisations'	San Francisco	City Lights Books	1957	1,500	$1.25
'The Selected Letters'	New York	McDowell-Obolensky	1957	2,000 (approx.)	$5.00
'I Wanted to Write a Poem'	Boston	Beacon Press	1958	3,543	$3.95
'Paterson (Book Five)'	Norfolk, Conn.	New Directions	1958	3,000	$3.00
'Kora in Hell: Improvisations'	San Francisco	City Lights Books	1958	1,500	$1.25
'Yes, Mrs Williams'	New York	McDowell-Obolensky	1959	–	$3.50
'Kora in Hell: Improvisations'	San Francisco	City Lights Books	1960	1,500	$1.25
'Paterson (Books 1, 2, 3 & 4)'	Norfolk, Conn.	New Directions	1960	2,000	probably $1.50
'The Farmers' Daughters'	Norfolk, Conn.	New Directions	1961	1,500	$4.50
'Many Loves and Other Plays'	Norfolk, Conn.	New Directions	1961	4,426	$6.50

Appendix

Title	Place of publication	Publisher	Date	Quantity	Price
'Pictures from Brueghel and Other Poems'	Norfolk, Conn.	New Directions	1962	7,500	$2.25
'Kora in Hell: Improvisations'	San Francisco	City Lights Books	1962	1,500	$1.25
'Selected Poems'	Norfolk, Conn.	New Directions	1963	6,751	$1.50
'The Collected Later Poems'	Norfolk, Conn.	New Directions	1963	2,904	$4.00
'Pictures from Brueghel and Other Poems'	London	MacGibbon & Kee	1963	1,500	30s.
'Paterson [Collected]'	New York	New Directions	1963	8,598	$1.85
'In the American Grain'	New York	New Directions	1964	5,169	$1.65
'Selected Poems'	New York	New Directions	1964	8,121	$1.50
'Kora in Hell: Improvisations'	San Francisco	City Lights Books	1964	2,000	$1.25
'The Collected Later Poems'	New York	New Directions	1964	2,032	$4.50
'Paterson (Collected)'	London	MacGibbon & Kee	1964	1,500	30s.
'Paterson (Collected)'	New York	New Directions	1964	7,493	$1.85

Appendix

Title	Place of publication	Publisher	Date	Quantity	Price
'Many Loves and Other Plays'	New York	New Directions	1965	2,443	$2.75
'The Collected Later Poems'	London	MacGibbon & Kee	1965	1,500	25s.
'White Mule'	London	MacGibbon & Kee	1965	2,000	30s.
'Selected Poems'	New York	New Directions	1965	7,803	$1.50
'Many Loves and Other Plays'	New York	New Directions	1966	3,770	$2.75
'In the Money'	London	MacGibbon & Kee	1966	2,000	30s.
'Pictures from Brueghel'	New York	New Directions	1966	5,134	$2.24
'The Collected Earlier Poems'	New York	New Directions	1966	2,475	$5.00
'Selected Poems'	New York	New Directions	1966	10,028	$1.50
'In the American Grain'	New York	New Directions	1966	5,043	$1.95
'Paterson (Collected)'	New York	New Directions	1966	8,593	$1.95
'The William Carlos Williams Reader'	New York	New Directions	1966	3,000	$7.50
'Kora in Hell: Improvisations'	San Francisco	City Lights Books	1967	3,000	$1.25
'The William Carlos Williams Reader'	London	MacGibbon & Kee	1967	2,000	42s.
'White Mule'	New York	New Directions	1967	cloth 1,490 paper 4,929	$4.95 $1.95

Appendix

Title	Place of publication	Publisher	Date	Quantity	Price
'In the American Grain'	London	MacGibbon & Kee	1967	2,000	30s.
'Autobiography'	New York	New Directions	1967	cloth 915 paper 4,029	$6.50 $1.95
'The Collected Earlier Poems'	London	MacGibbon & Kee	1967	1,500	42s.
'The William Carlos Williams Reader'	New York	New Directions	1967	5,000	$7.50
'Selected Poems'	New York	New Directions	1967	11,894	$1.50
'Pictures from Brueghel and Other Poems'	New York	New Directions	1967	1,013	$5.00
'I Wanted to Write a Poem'	Boston	Beacon Press	1967	5,500	$1.95
'In the Money'	New York	New Directions	1967	cloth 953 paper 5,094	$4.95 $2.75

*Denotes a second impression in the same year.

In the period 1968-74 New Directions Publishing Corporation, New York, has printed Williams' books as follows:

```
    CLOTHBOUND EDITIONS
12 titles reprinted              22,500 copies
 2 new titles                     7,000
                                 ──────
                                 29,500

    PAPERBACK EDITIONS
12 titled reprinted             299,500 copies
 1 new title                      9,500
                                ───────
                                309,000
```

City Lights Books, San Francisco, issued a further printing of 'Kora in Hell: Improvisations' in September 1974: 3,000 copies.

Index

The index is divided into four sections; I William Carlos Williams: writings; II Characteristics of Williams and aspects of his work and career; III Persons; IV Newspapers, periodicals, anthologies, and small publishers.

I WILLIAM CARLOS WILLIAMS: WRITINGS

A, B & C of It, The, 172, 206
'Adam & Eve & The City', 16, 409
All the Fancy Things, 125
'Al Que Quiere', 5, 54-8, 67, 68, 71, 95-7, 100, 101, 103, 259, 314, 367-8, 408
Arrival, 160
Asphodel, that Greeny Flower, 294-5, 300, 318-19, 340, 345, 346, 347, 348, 367, 376, 392
At Kenneth Burke's Place, 363
At the Ballgame, 161
Attic Which is Desire, The, 126
'Autobiography', 3, 5, 12, 18, 25, 31, 37, 43, 50, 57, 59, 89, 146, 241, 246-57, 261, 270-1, 272, 287, 302, 312, 320, 325, 326, 386, 401, 411, 415

Ballet Russe, 55
Banner Bearer, The, 386
Bare Tree, The, 362
Basis of Faith in Art, The, 283
'Beginning on the Short Story, A', 228, 411
Between Walls, 208
Birds and Flowers, 131
Birth of Venus, The, 259
Blizzard, 102, 314
Blueflags, 77
Botticellian Trees, The, 138
Brilliant Sad Sun, 125
'Broken Span, The', 169, 410
'Build-Up, The', 30-1, 272-4, 332, 402, 411
Bull, The, 125, 160, 261, 364, 365
Burning the Christmas Greens, 226, 363, 386
By the Road to the Contagious Hospital, 20, 161, 185, 310, 315, 395

Carl Sandburg's Complete
  Poems, 283
Catholic Bells, The, 34
Cherry Blossoms at Evening,
  369
Chicory and Daisies, 56
Child, 314
Child and Vegetables,
  355-6, 358-9
'Clouds, The', 199, 200,
  400, 410
Clouds, The, 266, 366
Cod Head, The, 125, 139,
  364, 365, 409
Cold Night, The, 81
Cold World, The, 153
'Collected Earlier Poems',
  4, 31, 41, 53, 55, 89,
  241, 258-61, 391, 392,
  401, 404, 411, 414, 415
'Collected Later Poems',
  24, 31, 33, 34, 146,
  172, 222-6, 241, 261,
  350, 376, 377-8, 380,
  381, 384-7, 391, 401,
  404, 411, 412, 413, 414
'Collected Poems 1921-
  1931', 7, 15, 16, 57,
  63, 124-39, 157, 277,
  364, 399, 409
Colored Girls of Passenack,
  The, 331
Comedy Entombed: 1930, 330
Complaint, 160
'Complete Collected Poems,
  1906-1938, The', 18, 19,
  38, 57, 156-64, 399, 409
Coronal, A, 160
Crude Lament, 53
Crystal Maze, The, 387
'Cure, The' (a play), 339
Cyclamen, 163

Dance, The, 342, 347
Danse Pseudo-macabre, 331
Danse Russe, 81, 368
Dark Day, The, 261
Dawn of Another Day, The,
  154

Death, 132, 134, 135
Dedication for a Plot of
  Ground, 314
Deep Religious Faith, 276,
  349
Della Primavera Trasportata
  Alla Morale, 14, 136, 369
Democratic Party Poem, 45
Descent, The, 281, 314, 318,
  347, 349, 351
Descent of Winter, The, 25,
  129, 160
Desert Music, The, 342, 349,
  363
'Desert Music and Other
  Poems, The', 32, 275-82,
  288, 293, 340, 347, 354,
  371, 375, 392, 402, 411
Destruction of Tenochtitlan,
  The, 20, 392
'Dog and the Fever, The',
  324, 411
'Dream of Love, A' (a
  play), 29, 199-201, 335,
  336, 392, 400, 410
Drunk and the Sailor, The,
  350
Dylan Thomas (review), 283

'Early Martyr and Other
  Poems, An', 16, 409
'Embodiment of Knowledge,
  The', 398
Eve, 163, 323, 324

Face of Stone, A, 152
Farmers' Daughters, The,
  331, 332, 336
'Farmers' Daughters and
  Other Stories, The', 38,
  327-32, 403, 412
'First Act', 410
'First President, The'
  (libretto), 29, 335, 337
Flowers by the Sea, 157
For a Low Voice, 226

George Antheil and the
  Cantilene Critics, 283
Gift, The, 349
'Go, Go', 75-6, 408
Good Night, A, 75, 163
'Great American Novel, The',
  12, 80, 102, 103, 105,
  146, 154, 391, 395, 399,
  408
Great Figure, The, 73, 101

Hard Core of Beauty, The,
  364
Hermaphroditic Telephones,
  The, 76
Hic Jacet, 53
High Bridge Above the Tagus
  River at Toledo, The,
  347
History, 374
Horse Show, The, 325
Host, The, 276, 318, 347
Hunter, The, 160

'Imaginations', 41, 98,
  398, 404
Immortal (*also called* The
  Immortal, *or* Proof of
  Immortality), 4, 132
Impromptu: The Suckers,
  259, 393
In Harbor, 97
Injury, The, 362, 387
'In the American Grain',
  6, 11, 12, 13, 20, 22,
  32, 35-6, 37, 84-108,
  109, 113, 114, 124, 144,
  147-8, 167, 287, 301,
  311, 317, 350, 378, 381,
  382, 391, 392, 399, 402,
  404, 408, 409, 410, 412,
  413, 414, 415
'In the Money', 21, 22, 23,
  165-8, 272, 400, 404,
  409, 414, 415
It is a Living Coral, 136
Ivy Crown, The, 347, 349

'I Wanted to Write a Poem',
  1, 7, 16, 37, 42, 48, 52,
  124, 156, 311-15, 403,
  404, 412, 415

January Morning, 55, 67, 72,
  97, 160, 203
Jean Beicke, 328, 330, 331
'Journey to Love', 29, 32,
  38, 294-300, 340, 342,
  347, 354, 368, 375, 402,
  412

Keller Gegen Dom, 56
'Knife of the Times, The',
  15, 118-20, 154, 228,
  399, 409
Knife of the Times, The,
  120, 331
'Kora in Hell: Improvisa-
  tions', 5, 7, 9, 10, 21,
  25, 37, 43, 59-69, 71,
  93, 97-9, 100, 103, 104,
  248, 376, 395, 408, 412,
  413, 414, 416

Lady Speaks, The, 345
'Last Nights of Paris', 409
Letter to an Australian
  Editor, 2
'Life Along the Passaic
  River', 15, 18, 19,
  150-5, 228, 399, 409
Locust Tree in Flower, The,
  157

'Make Light of It', 31,
  227-31, 255, 261,
  269-70, 401, 411
Man in a Room, 163
'Man Orchid', 153
Man with a Bad Heart, 314
Many Loves, 335, 336, 337,
  403

'Many Loves and Other Plays', 46, 323, 333-9, 412, 414
March, 14, 45, 78, 374
Marianne Moore (essay), 283
M.B., 56
Mental Hospital Garden, The, 276, 281-2
Metric Figure, 261

Nantucket, 130
Negro Woman, A, 345, 349
Nightingale, The, 80
Night in June, A, 154
Night Rider, The, 362
Notes from a Talk on Poetry, 12-13, 44
'Novelette and Other Prose, A', 409

Old Doc Rivers, 269, 328, 332
Old Man, The, 314
Old Time Raid, An, 269
On Gay Wallpaper, 128
On Measure-Statement for Cid Corman, 283, 395
Orchestra, The, 345
Ordeal, The, 53
Overture to a Dance of Locomotives, 102

Pastoral (CEP 121), 81, 95-6
Pastoral (CEP 124), 55
Pastoral (CEP 161), 56
'Paterson', 7, 8, 13, 21, 22, 24, 25, 26, 27-30, 31-2, 36, 37, 40, 44, 85, 159, 201, 250, 254, 256, 261, 264, 265-9, 271, 276, 287, 292, 302, 317, 320, 327, 350, 351, 356, 359, 363, 364, 370, 376, 377, 378, 379, 380, 381, 382, 385, 389, 390, 391, 413, 414; 'Paterson (Book One)', 92, 173-87, 213, 232, 238, 243, 400, 410; 'Paterson (Book Two)', 188-98, 218, 233, 238-40, 243, 311, 350, 400, 410; 'Paterson (Book Three)', 200, 210-22, 227, 232, 238-40, 243, 373, 400, 410; 'Paterson (Book Four)', 46, 213, 232-45, 312, 313, 396, 401; 'Paterson (Book Five)', 36, 38, 312-13, 315, 316-22, 373, 375, 395, 403, 412; 'Paterson (Books 1 & 2)', 32, 376, 410, 411; 'Paterson (Books 1, 2 & 3)', 410; 'Paterson (Books 1, 2, 3 & 4)', 411, 412
Perfection, 262
Philomena Andronico, 32
'Pictures from Brueghel and Other Poems', 32, 37, 340-52, 375, 376, 385, 392, 403, 413, 414, 415
Pink Locust, The, 300
Poem, 208, 290, 365
Poem as a Field of Action, The, 37, 283, 320
Poem for Norman McLeod, A, 159
'Poems', 3, 12, 49-51, 149, 284, 399, 408
Polar Bear, The, 347
Portrait of a Lady, 130, 160, 314
Portrait of the Author, 67, 155, 163
Postlude, 53
Pot of Flowers, The, 105
Pound's Eleven New Cantos, 283
Prelude, A (CEP 141), 55
Prologue to 'Kora in Hell', A, 283

Pure Products of America, The (To Elsie), 111, 130, 136, 139, 314, 316-17

Rain, 209
Raper from Passenack, The, 192, 317
'Recognizable Image: William Carlos Williams on Art and Artists, A', 398
Red Lily, The, 139
Red Wheelbarrow, The, 76, 160, 242, 256, 290, 302, 389, 395
Right Thing, The, 153
Riposte, 55
Rose, The, 75
Russia, 262

Sailor's Son, The, 331
Sample Critical Statement, 10
Sea-Elephant, The, 161
Second Marriage, 153
'Selected Essays', 13, 32, 37, 38, 44, 59, 62, 93, 98, 119, 146, 283-93, 398, 402, 411
'Selected Letters', 14, 16, 24, 25, 26, 30, 32, 37, 38, 43, 54, 146, 159, 172, 195, 301-10, 312, 323, 344, 398, 402, 412
'Selected Poems', 29, 30, 202-9, 292, 400, 410, 413, 414, 415
Shadows, 345
Simplicity of Disorder, The, 119
Some Simple Measures in the American Idiom and the Variable Foot, 347
Song (PB 15), 397
'Sour Grapes', 8, 70-4, 98, 101, 102, 103, 155, 359, 408

Sparrow, The, 297, 299-300, 345, 351, 368
Speech Rhythm, 395
'Spring and All', 12, 14, 25, 75-83, 103, 104, 109, 110, 111, 154, 161, 164, 351, 391, 393, 395, 408
Spring is Here Again, Sir, 363
Spring Song, 259
Spring Strains, 307, 310
Stone Crock, The, 341
Stop: Go (*from* Della Primavera), 131

'Tempers, The', 3, 4, 52-3, 69, 94, 95, 132, 149, 376, 399, 408
These Purists, 264
This Florida: 1924, 160
This is Just to Say, 16, 134, 139, 193, 217, 260
This is my Platform, 361
Thoughtful Lover, The, 362
'Tituba's Children' (play), 338
To, 366
To a Dog Injured in the Street, 276, 350
To a Solitary Disciple, 56
To Be Recited to Flossie on Her Birthday, 343
To Daphne and Virginia, 278, 281, 318, 345, 347, 349
To Elsie (The Pure Products of America), 111, 130, 136, 139, 314, 316-17
To Mark Anthony in Heaven, 160
To Waken an Old Lady, 160
Tract, 256, 259, 368
Trees, The, 161

Under the Greenwood Tree, 153
Unfrocked Priest, The, 268-9

Unison, A, 205, 385
Use of Force, The, 152, 328, 330

'Voyage to Pagany, A', 10, 11, 15, 30, 41, 109-17, 146, 154, 399, 404, 408

Waiting, 160
Waitress, The, 129
Wanderer, The, 368
'Wedge, The', 14, 23, 24, 25, 34, 46, 109, 169-72, 400, 410
'White Mule', 17-18, 140-9, 153, 165, 166, 167, 272, 323, 332, 399, 404, 409, 414
Widow's Lament in Springtime, The, 160, 164
Wild Orchard, 261
'William Carlos Williams Reader, The', 388-97, 404, 414, 415
Winds, The, 128, 138
Winter Trees, 261
Woman in Front of a Bank, A, 226
Words Lying Idle, The, 362
World Contracted to a Recognizable Image, The, 342
World Narrowed to a Point, The, 127
Writer's Prologue to a Play in Verse, 225

Yachts, The, 24-5, 46, 206-7, 242, 327
Yellow Flower, The, 341
'Yes, Mrs Williams', 323-6, 403
Young Sycamore, 126, 208
Young Woman at a Window, 157, 158
Youth and Beauty, 81, 164

CHARACTERISTICS OF WILLIAMS AND ASPECTS OF HIS WORK AND CAREER

aesthetics, aesthetic distance, 7, 8, 27-8, 67, 97, 100, 129, 144, 152, 183, 207-9, 210, 230, 231, 235, 329, 330
American idiom, language, 13, 19, 22, 24, 28, 34, 37, 80, 95-6, 137, 141, 151, 162, 166, 174-8, 181, 183, 186-7, 189, 194, 197-8, 201, 208, 210, 211-12, 214, 217, 219-20, 221, 222, 223, 224-5, 225, 228, 229, 234, 237, 242, 243, 251, 290-2, 298, 301-2, 308, 309, 316, 332, 338, 341, 353-4, 375, 379, 387, 394, 395-6; see also redeeming language
Americanism, 5, 8, 9, 10, 11, 15, 35, 60-1, 69, 82, 89-92, 95, 96, 99-100, 105-8, 112-14, 128-36, 137, 141-2, 145, 151, 153-4, 162-3, 166-8, 170, 178, 187, 189-90, 194, 234, 240, 241, 244-5, 248-9, 256, 258, 261, 272, 286, 287, 289, 303-4, 347, 361, 371, 393, 396
anti-poetic, presumed use of the, 15, 19, 21, 22, 31, 77, 124-7, 144, 156-8, 164, 201, 212, 229, 258, 305, 348, 361, 365, 366, 368, 384

beauty; rigor of beauty, 'Beautiful Thing', 185,

188-9, 193, 209, 214-16, 240, 358
British attitudes to WCW, 33, 114-16, 121-3, 148-9, 223-4, 225, 241-5, 322, 346-50, 388-9, 391-2, 395-6
brokenness of composition, 56, 59-69, 97-9, 104, 105, 108, 131, 221, 395, 397

collage method of 'Paterson', 26, 173, 174-8, 181, 183, 187, 194, 265-8; see also 'Paterson'
contact, 'tactus eruditus', 6, 8, 39, 72-3, 99, 100, 102, 244, 252, 290, 299, 328, 361, 364, 367, 368, 393, 394
cubism, 5, 40, 104, 393-4, 396

dance, 27, 182, 395
'divorce', separateness, alienation, 175, 180-7, 188-9, 211, 214, 219, 243
dramatist, 333-9, 392, 393

Europe, WCW's responses to, 10, 11, 103, 109-12, 112-14, 114-16, 187, 249, 254, 290, 317, 347, 382

fiction, 10, 11, 12, 15, 17, 18, 19, 20, 23, 30-1, 38, 41, 80, 102, 103, 105, 109-17, 118-20, 140-9, 150-5, 165-8, 227-31, 255, 261, 269-70, 272-4, 323, 327-32, 388-97, 400, 401, 402,
403, 404, 408, 409, 411, 412, 414, 415
flowers, flower poet, 82, 127, 157, 281, 294-5, 315, 321, 348-9, 360, 363, 366
free verse, 20, 95, 160-1, 171-2, 192, 203, 205, 209, 211, 256, 278, 284-5, 292, 308, 309, 375; see also poetics

imagination ('only the imagination is real'), 13, 63, 103-4, 295, 317-18, 321
Imagism, 20, 28, 34, 40, 41, 58, 118, 127-8, 145, 151, 157, 162, 171-2, 189, 192, 208, 242, 258, 261, 279, 284, 346, 371, 374-5, 385, 389, 394, 396
imitative form, 215, 239, 245
improvisation, 5, 7, 9, 10, 14, 97-9, 252; see also 'Kora in Hell'
incoherence, 29, 36, 98, 104, 105, 160, 182, 201, 234, 238-40, 292, 327
inner security, sense of, 7, 131, 133
interpenetration, metamorphosis, process, 7, 12, 24, 26, 37, 174-8, 181, 184, 208-9, 319-22, 378-9, 387
invention, 12, 24, 27, 315

localism, importance of the local, 5, 11, 20, 69, 89-92, 95-108, 153-4, 236-7, 242, 244, 253, 258, 287, 289, 301-2, 304, 327-32, 377, 381, 394, 396

machine, poem as, 23-4,
  169, 171, 206, 223, 225
macrocosm-microcosm, man-
  city, 26, 173-87, 188-
  98, 219, 267, 320; see
  also 'Paterson'
medical practice, and
  effect of, 1, 3, 15, 30,
  39, 78-9, 83, 95, 118-
  20, 128, 143, 146,
  150-1, 153, 154, 168,
  227, 236-7, 248-9,
  250-1, 252, 254, 277,
  284, 301, 302, 327-9,
  330-2, 356, 360-1, 364,
  366, 367, 370, 394
musical organization of
  'Paterson', 174-8

newness, the new, 9, 67,
  103-4, 105, 288, 330,
  373
'No ideas but in things!',
  7, 13, 21, 25, 39, 40,
  64, 73, 133, 159, 175,
  181, 185, 189, 193, 197,
  207, 219, 237, 241, 244,
  257, 279, 284, 292, 321,
  342, 352, 356-7, 361,
  371, 386, 394
nominalism, 41, 156
notation, 'unexpanded notation', 164, 209, 272-4,
  (unstructured realism)

objectivism, 9, 12, 13, 15,
  19, 21, 23, 24, 26, 39,
  78, 109, 112, 119-20,
  129, 139, 158, 165, 208,
  220, 276, 360, 365, 372,
  394
observation and definition,
  accuracy of, 9, 55,
  62-7, 71-2, 80, 96-7,
  130, 151, 152, 160, 162,
  164, 185, 208, 212, 222,
  234, 242, 244, 273, 316,
  327-32, 351-2, 358-9,
  385
opacity (Pound's term), 7,
  21, 57-8, 61, 97-8
organic form, 24, 37, 39,
  172, 329, 330-2

poetics: measure, prosody,
  the variable foot, 13,
  25, 27, 32, 33, 35, 37,
  38, 58, 66, 94-6, 136-7,
  162, 171, 174-5, 179,
  203, 220, 222, 223,
  225-6, 234, 238-9, 248,
  260, 276, 277, 278-9,
  279-80, 282, 285-6,
  286-7, 292, 295, 296-9,
  304, 305, 308-10, 312,
  314-15, 318, 320, 341,
  344-5, 347, 348, 351,
  354, 375, 389, 396;
  see also free verse
primitivism, 20, 85-6,
  102-3, 104, 105, 144,
  231, 251, 258, 371, 381
prose and poetry, melding,
  21, 25, 29, 103, 114,
  173, 177, 183, 188, 194,
  210, 211, 215, 234-5,
  239, 390, 395; see also
  collage; 'Paterson'

realism, 22, 97, 118-20,
  126, 139, 140-2, 143,
  143-5, 150-2, 152-3,
  157, 165-6, 166-8, 192,
  227-8, 229, 231, 269,
  272-3, 274, 327-32
redeeming language, a,
  173-83, 188-98, 210,
  212, 214, 219-21, 237
romanticism, 107, 124-7,
  132, 151, 159, 161, 191,
  258, 263-4, 327, 371

self-pity, alleged, 262,
  269

sentimentality, 14, 19, 20, 21, 28, 39, 97, 125-6, 151, 159-60, 161, 182, 185, 191-3, 195, 207, 230, 236, 264-5, 269, 327, 331, 332, 363, 364-5, 366, 391
simplicity and/or naïveté, 7, 40, 67-8, 69, 72, 75, 103, 130, 138-9, 162, 179, 315, 330-2, 334, 349, 389, 394
social consciousness and political involvement, 17-19, 21, 22, 24, 30-1, 118-20, 140-9, 151, 154, 165-6, 167-8, 177, 226, 233, 235, 237, 239, 254, 262, 276, 327-32, 338, 372, 390
spontaneity, 59-69, 71, 97-9, 104, 114, 131, 236, 242, 251, 252-3, 256, 270, 314, 327-32, 352
subject-object relations, 41, 70-3, 81, 86-8, 143, 208, 284, 289, 366, 386
surrealism, 255, 266, 269
symbolism, 9, 29, 107, 108, 151, 161, 174-8, 181-3, 185, 188, 197, 199, 210, 212, 214-16, 218, 219, 220, 230, 232, 237, 243; see also 'Paterson'

'things others never notice', perception of, 131-3, 164

urbanism, 169, 173-87, 191-5, 209, 243, 327-32

variable foot, see poetics
visual arts, 2, 5-7, 10, 14, 40, 44, 255, 258, 266, 269, 393-4, 396
'vividness', concreteness of rendering, 8, 13, 16, 96, 129, 193, 222, 327, 330, 346, 352

words, and words as things, 13, 14, 20, 22, 23-5, 26, 27, 34, 71, 81, 95-6, 112, 143, 156, 174-8, 201, 208, 225, 358, 372, 394-5, 397

III PERSONS

Abbott, Charles D., 32, 44, 46
Adams, Brooks, 2
Adams, Henry, 109, 110, 190
Adams, Phoebe, 402, 403
Aiken, Conrad, 57-8, 399, 401
Aldington, Richard, 3, 43, 122, 241, 385
Alexander, Sidney, 402
Anderson, Margaret, 61-2, 254
Anderson, Maxwell, 334
Anderson, Sherwood, 94, 120, 230, 253, 329
Angoff, Charles, 405

Antheil, George, 283
Apollinaire, Guillaume, 266, 334, 394
Arensberg, Walter, 6
Arnold, Matthew, 122, 161
Auden, W.H., 187, 224, 225, 334, 374
Ayscough, Florence, 298

Bandelier, Adolph, 91
Baro, Gene, 402
Barrows, Harold, 400
Bataille, Georges, 40
Baudelaire, Charles, 276
Beach, Sylvia, 146

Beck, Warren, 402
Belloc, Hilaire, 370
Benet, William Rose, 112
Benn, Gottfried, 358
Bennett, Joseph, 261-71, 292, 293
Berryman, John, 322, 388
Beum, Robert, 401, 402
Birch-Bartlett, Helen, 67
Bird, William, 12, 147, 154
Blackburn, Paul, 31
Blackmur, R.P., 21-2, 25, 163-4, 170-2, 206, 400
Blake, William, 137, 242
Blum, W.C., see under James Sibley Watson
Bodenheim, Maxwell, 5, 61
Bogan, Louise, 404
Boni, Albert and Charles, 12
Borrow, George, 135
Bosch, Hieronymus, 396
Bourne, Randolph, 288
Boyle, Kay, 24, 155, 159, 309
Brancusi, Constantin, 6
Breit, Harvey, 246-7
Breslin, James E., 40, 405
Bridges, Robert, 161
Brinnin, John Malcolm, 405
Brooks, Van Wyck, 69, 94, 403
Brown, Ashley, 288
Browning, Elizabeth Barrett, 264
Brueghel, Pieter (the Elder), 312, 396
Brunini, J.G., 399
Bryher (Annie Winifred Ellerman), 10, 44, 62
Bunting, Basil, 11, 134-8
Burke, Kenneth, 6, 8, 38-9, 63, 70-3, 86-8, 98, 121, 143, 290, 303, 359-69, 392, 393, 397, 405
Burt, Struthers, 122

Cain, James M., 192
Caldwell, James R., 400

Callaghan, Morley, 112-14
Cambon, Glauco, 406
Canby, Henry Seidel, 84-6, 89
Carman, Bliss, 1, 2
Carruth, Hayden, 218-21, 234-6, 355-9, 401
Carter, Thomas H., 288-93
Cassidy, T.E., 402
Cather, Willa, 122
Cendrars, Blaise, 394
Cézanne, Paul, 14, 393
Char, René, 10, 396
Chaucer, Geoffrey, 309, 331
Chekhov, Anton, 69, 227
Ciardi, John, 37, 277-9, 403
Clark, Thomas, 385-7
Claudel, Paul, 334
Coady, Robert J., 101
Cocteau, Jean, 249, 266, 334, 394
Cole, Thomas, 402
Collingwood, R.G., 217
Columbus, Christopher, 8, 22, 77, 87, 90, 91, 167
Conarroe, Joel, 405
Conrad, Joseph, 145, 147, 289
Cooper, James Fenimore, 381
Cordell, Richard, 400
Carmen, Cid, 31, 36, 38, 283, 395, 403
Cox, C.B., 404
Crane, Hart, 19, 20, 73-4, 89, 92-3, 130, 150, 187, 188, 190, 194, 232, 288, 388
Crane, Stephen, 145
Creekmore, Hubert, 400
Creeley, Robert, 31, 36, 310, 320, 341-3, 347, 375, 402
Crevecoeur, Hector St John de, 381
Cummings, E.E., 34, 135, 146, 157, 165, 204, 283, 298, 322, 370, 388
Cunard, Nancy, 254

Cunningham, J.V., 158
Curie, Pierre and Marie, 13, 268

Dahlberg, Edward, 14, 27, 146, 377-83
Daiches, David, 34, 224-6, 400
Dante Alighieri, 1, 288, 366, 382
Darwin, Charles, 1
Davidson, Eugene, 401
Davie, Donald, 35, 36, 47, 346-50
Davis, D.M., 404
Davis, Robert Gorham, 30-1, 230-1, 402
Davis, Stuart, 7
Dembo, L.S., 407
Defoe, Daniel, 331
Demuth, Charles, 105, 254
Derrida, Jacques, 40
Deutsch, Babette, 30, 130-1, 227-8, 399, 402, 403
De Voto, Bernard, 84
Dewey, John, 11, 371, 372
Diamant, Gertrude, 119
Dickey, James, 384-5
Dijkstra, Bram, 40, 43, 44, 57, 398, 405
Diogenes, 39, 127
Dobrée, Bonamy, 260
Donoghue, Denis, 35, 47, 404, 406
Dorn, Edward, 347
Dos Passos, John, 165
Dostoevsky, Fyodor, 379
Dreiser, Theodore, 94, 122, 253
Duchamp, Marcel, 5, 6, 9
Dudley, Dorothy, 54-8
Duncan, Robert, 375
Dupée, F.W., 165-6
Dürer, Albrecht, 396

Eberhart, Richard, 33, 37, 38, 46, 232-3, 279-80, 295, 309, 400, 401, 402, 403
Eckman, Frederick, W., 400, 403
Eliot, T.S., 10, 26, 29, 31, 32, 34, 79, 129, 130, 137, 161, 175, 179, 181, 187, 190, 194, 216-17, 218, 220, 237, 240-1, 242, 248, 251, 253, 266, 275, 287, 290, 292, 304, 314, 315, 334, 339, 343, 349, 361, 368, 374, 375, 376, 386, 388, 389-90, 391, 396
Ellis, Havelock, 26
Ellmann, Richard, 211-12, 255-7
Emerson, Ralph Waldo, 187, 190, 284, 287, 288, 371, 394, 395
Emerson, Richard Wirtz, 402
Empson, William, 202-6
Engle, Paul, 401, 403

Fadiman, Clifton, 21-2, 399, 400
Farge, Léon Paul, 10
Faulkner, William, 292
Fenollosa, Ernest, 193, 308-9
Ferlinghetti, Lawrence, 248-9, 401
Ferril, Thomas Hornsby, 400, 401
Fiedler, Leslie, 28, 191-5, 218
Finkel, Donald, 404
Fiscalini, Janet, 403
Fitts, Dudley, 26, 233-4
Fitzgerald, Robert, 202-6, 233
Flint, F.S., 2, 385
Flint, R.W., 29, 200-1, 400, 401
Ford, Charles Henri, 283
Ford, Ford Madox, (some-

times Maddox; originally
Ford Madox Hueffer), 2,
18, 145-8, 148-9, 246,
289, 290-1, 370
Fowlie, Wallace, 294-5
Francis, Thomas Edward, 46
Frank, Waldo, 6, 92-3, 94,
101, 287
Fraser, G.S., 259-61, 347
Fremantle, Ann, 400
Freytag-Loringhaven,
Baroness Elsa von, 252-3
Friedman, Melvin J., 407
Frost, Robert, 93, 187,
275, 340, 388, 390
Fry, Christopher, 334
Frye, Northrop, 293
Fuller, Edmund, 404
Funaroff, Sol, 17, 19
Furbank, P.N., 403

Galinsky, Hans, 39
Garrigue, Jean, 402
Garson, Greer, 268
Geismar, Maxwell, 253-5
Gide, André, 361
Ginsberg, Allen, 31, 46
Glasgow, Ellen, 122
Gleizes, Albert, 6
Godfrey, Eleanor, 400
Gogarty, Oliver St John, 260
Goll, Ivan, 10
Gompers, Samuel, 141
Goodman, Paul, 296-300
Gosse, Edmund, 247
Gourmont, Remy de, 60
Graham, Martha, 89
Gregory, Horace, 19, 22,
92, 124-5, 199, 400
Grigson, Geoffrey, 403
Gris, Juan, 10, 393, 396
Guimond, James, 405
Gunn, Thom, 36, 350-3, 392, 396, 403

Halsband, Robert, 228-30

Hamilton, Ian, 393, 404
Hammett, Dashiell, 191-2
Hardie, Jack, 398
Hardy, Thomas, 161, 334, 343
Harnack, Curtis, 403
Harris, Theodore, 337
Harrison, Keith, 345-6
Harte, Bret, 230
Hartley, Marsden, 6, 8, 99, 254
Hawthorne, Nathaniel, 34, 378
H.D. (Hilda Doolittle), 3,
14, 45, 62, 162, 171,
247, 254, 258, 335, 375, 385
Heal, Edith, 1, 16, 42, 92,
311-12, 313-15, 398
Heidegger, Martin, 40
Hemingway, Ernest, 12, 30,
38, 112, 118, 151, 230,
231, 244, 291-2, 329
Heraclitus, 378
Herbst, Josephine, 319
Herrick, Robert, 161, 276, 376
Hewes, Henry, 403
Heyen, William, 405
Honig, Edwin, 28-9, 180-4, 400
Hopkins, Gerard Manley, 245, 285
Horace, 276
Horan, Robert, 195
Horton, Philip, 19, 38, 156-8
Hoskins, Katherine, 303-5
Hovey, Richard, 2
Howe, Irving, 327-9
Howell, Reid, 12, 48
Hudson, W.H., 15, 147
Hulme, T.E., 242
Humphries, Rolfe, 206-7

Ibsen, Henrik, 334
Irvine, Maurice H., 199
Irving, Washington, 372

Index

Jacob, Max, 10, 394
Jacobsen, Josephine, 38-403
James, Henry, 34, 145, 147, 190, 248, 314, 371, 372
Jammes, Francis, 334
Jarrell, Randall, 25, 28, 29-30, 31, 169-70, 174-8, 184, 186, 195, 203, 206, 238-41, 402
Johns, Jasper, 389
Johns, Orrick, 3, 43
Johns, Richard, 18, 45
Jones, Ernest, 274
Jonson, Ben, 376
Joost, Nicholas, 283-6, 402
Jordan, Viola Baxter, 46
Josephson, Matthew, 37, 250-3, 399
Joyce, James, 116, 137, 141, 142, 178, 180, 181, 227, 228, 229, 247, 250, 266, 271, 290, 306, 320, 390

Kandinsky, Wassily, 6, 7, 43
Kay, Arthur M., 330-2
Kazin, Alfred, 140-2
Keats, John, 1, 135, 147, 190
Kennedy, Leo, 401
Kenner, Hugh, 36, 38, 41, 47, 306-10, 312-15, 392, 394, 401, 402, 407
Knopf, Alfred A., 18
Koch, Vivienne, 33, 200, 214, 215, 217, 218, 261, 271, 401
Korzybski, Alfred, 26
Kreymborg, Alfred, 5, 6, 69, 82-3, 118
Kunitz, Stanley, 340-1

Laforgue, Jules, 290
Lane, John, 148, 149
Larbaud, Valéry, 106, 396
Lardner, Ring, 166, 231, 332

Larsson, Raymond, 138-9
Latimer, Ronald Lane (James G. Leippert), 16
Laughlin, James, 17-18, 34, 46, 146, 148, 156, 305
Lawrence, D.H., 6, 9, 11, 19, 21, 35, 85, 89-92, 138, 207, 209, 290, 317, 371, 377, 391
Laxon, Martha, 398
Leavis, F.R., 10-11
Lechlitner, Ruth, 20, 23, 28, 29, 400, 401
Léger, Fernand, 23, 46
Leonard, William Ellery, 135
Levertov, Denise, 31, 36, 353-4, 392, 397
Levin, Harry, 41, 404
Lewis, H.H., 17, 18-19
Lewis, P. Wyndham, 145, 306
Lewis, Sinclair, 122, 231
Libby, Anthony, 40
Lilienthal, David E., 194
Lindsay, Vachel, 94, 101
Lippman, Walter, 26
Loewinsohn, Ron, 398
Longfellow, Henry Wadsworth, 333
Lorca, Federico Garcia, 244, 312
Lowell, Amy, 43, 122, 184, 192, 275
Lowell, Robert, 27, 28, 31, 184-7, 188-90, 224, 238, 283, 347, 388
Loy, Mina, 5, 6, 99
Lyle, David, 22, 26-7, 46
Lynd, R.S., 22-3, 45

Maas, Willard, 17, 399
McAlmon, Robert, 8, 12, 44, 46, 99, 121, 146, 147, 154-5, 254, 314
McDonald, G.D., 401, 402, 403
Macksey, Richard, 393, 395

Index

Macleod, Norman, 25, 159, 172, 307
Malcolm, Donald, 403
Mallarmé, Stephane, 179, 294
Mann, Thomas, 361
Mariani, Paul L., 42, 47, 153, 398
Marsh, Fred T., 400
Martial, 376
Martz, Louis L., 195-8, 281-2, 407
Masters, Edgar Lee, 94
Mathews, Elkin, 4, 52, 68, 69, 94, 149, 376
Matisse, Henri, 10, 396
Matthiessen, F.O., 24, 25, 46
Mazzaro, Jerome, 40, 47, 405
Melville, Herman, 378, 380, 381, 382, 383
Mencken, H.L., 18, 45, 94
Meyer, G.P., 402
Miller, Fred R., 17, 153-4, 399
Miller, J. Hillis, 7, 40, 41, 44, 159, 392, 393, 395, 397, 405
Milton, John, 190, 240, 244, 297
Monroe, Harriet, 4, 26, 60, 61, 241, 399
Moore, Marianne, 6, 7, 15, 16, 62-7, 83, 124, 131-3, 146, 155, 234, 254, 266, 283, 287, 289, 303, 305, 315, 318, 365, 388, 392, 393, 406
Morgan, Frederick, 218
Mortimer, Penelope, 404
Mumford, Lewis, 8
Munson, Gorham, 6, 9, 17, 43, 44, 73-4, 93-109, 121
Murray, Gilbert, 333

Nardi, Marcia, 27, 29, 264, 267

Neame, Alan, 310
Nietzsche, Friedrich, 40, 41
Nims, John Frederick, 222
Norman, Dorothy, 324

O'Connor, William Van, 28
Olson, Charles, 14, 36, 37, 42, 47, 310, 319-22, 349, 375, 401
Oppen, George, 23, 112, 124
Orage, A.R., 12
Ostrom, Alan, 405
Owen, Peter, 376

Palmer, John E., 402
Parkinson, Thomas, 325
Parkman, Francis, 381, 383
Patmore, Coventry, 286
Paul, Sherman, 404, 405
Pearce, Roy Harvey, 38, 407
Pearson, Norman Holmes, 14, 17, 112, 335-6, 405
Peirce, Charles Sanders, 378, 382
Peterson, Walter Scott, 406
Picabia, Francis, 6
Picasso, Pablo, 6
Pickrel, Paul, 402
Plato, 286
Poe, Edgar Allan, 11, 85, 93, 104, 127
Poore, Charles G., 399
Pound, Ezra, 1, 2, 3-4, 5, 6, 7, 9, 10, 11, 12, 13, 14-15, 17, 27, 28, 30, 33, 35, 36, 37, 38, 41, 42, 43, 45, 50-1, 52-3, 59-62, 69, 94, 95, 97, 116, 122, 124, 127, 130, 136, 137, 145, 146, 161, 162, 187, 190, 192, 193, 194, 195, 196-7, 220, 224, 237, 239, 241, 247, 248-9, 250, 251, 253, 254, 255, 256, 258, 266-8, 275, 283, 284,

287, 289, 290, 298, 302,
303, 304, 306, 308, 309,
310, 315, 317, 320, 322,
345, 346, 347, 361, 370,
371, 372, 373, 374, 375,
376, 385, 388, 389-90,
391, 393, 396, 399
Prescott, William Hickling,
  383
Press, John, 404
Price, R.G., 404

Quevedo, Francisco de, 324,
  325
Quinn, Sister M. Bernetta,
  402, 407

Rahv, Philip, 143-5, 329
Rajan, B., 34, 47
Rakosi, Carl, 399
Ransom, John Crowe, 34, 388
Ray, Man, 6
Read, Herbert, 353, 377
Redman, Ben Ray, 401
Reverdy, Pierre, 394
Reynolds, Horace, 402
Rexroth, Kenneth, 10, 37,
  44, 275-7, 316, 333-5,
  392, 393, 396
Rice, Philip Blair, 127-9
Riddel, Joseph N., 40, 41,
  45, 406
Rider, Albert Pinkham, 8
Riley, James Whitcomb, 1
Rilke, Rainer Maria, 240,
  299
Rimbaud, Arthur, 9, 59, 98,
  294
Riordan, John, 12-13, 44
Robie, Burton, 403
Robinson, Edwin Arlington,
  158, 388
Rodman, Selden, 37, 401,
  402
Roethke, Theodore, 318,
  322, 346, 388
Rosenfeld, Isaac, 173

Rosenfeld, Paul, 6, 8-9,
  19, 22, 44, 74, 76-82,
  162-3, 166-8, 399
Rosenthal, M.L., 236-7,
  316-18, 389, 391-2, 392,
  393, 394, 395, 397, 404,
  407
Rosenthal, Raymond, 404
Rothman, N.L., 142-3
Rourke, Constance, 89
Rousseau, Jean-Jacques, 85,
  86, 371

Salmon, André, 394
Salomon, I.L., 258-9
Sandburg, Carl, 60-1, 64,
  80, 94, 185, 192, 237,
  267, 275, 283
Sankey, Benjamin, 406
Santayana, George, 127,
  370, 373-4
Sappho, 319, 320, 322
Saroyan, William, 29, 242
Scherr, J.M., 401
Schott, Webster, 41, 398,
  404
Scott, Winfield Townley,
  272-3, 301-2, 311-12,
  402
Seldes, Gilbert, 11, 44
Sereni, Vittorio, 39
Shahn, Ben, 268
Shakespeare, William, 1,
  161, 337, 378, 381, 393
Shapiro, Harvey, 402
Shapiro, Karl, 32, 46, 283,
  322
Shayer, Michael, 31
Sheeler, Charles, 89, 283
Shelley, Percy Bysshe, 333
Simpson, Louis, 406
Sitwell, Edith, 211, 212,
  262
Slate, Joseph Evans, 92
Snell, George, 400
Snodgrass, W.D., 318-19
Socrates, 377, 381
Solt, Mary Ellen, 112

Soupault, Philippe, 10, 396
Spears, Monroe K., 213-17
Spector, Herman, 17
Spencer, Benjamin T., 336-9
Steichen, Edward, 396
Stein, Gertrude, 14, 30, 45, 116, 230, 231, 242, 251
Steinbeck, John, 166, 230
Steinmetz, Carl P., 12
Stendhal (Henri Beyle), 246
Stephens, Alan, 37, 343-5, 351
Stevens, Wallace, 15-16, 19, 19, 21, 34, 35, 38, 39, 93, 94, 124-7, 131, 132, 157, 161, 187, 192, 212, 220, 229, 287, 301-2, 305, 318, 330, 364-5, 366, 386, 388
Stieglitz, Alfred, 5-7, 40, 43, 89, 101, 254, 288, 396
Stone, Irving, 401
Strobel, Marion, 75-6
Sullivan, A.M., 405
Sullivan, Richard, 401
Swinburne, Algernon Charles, 51, 135, 180, 264, 333
Sykes Davies, Hugh, 10
Symonds, John Addington, 181
Symons, Arthur, 372
Symons, Julian, 404

Talbot, Norman, 403
Tarkington, Booth, 122
Tate, Allen, 34, 187, 268, 388
Taupin, René, 9-10
Tchelitchew, Pavel, 283
Thayer, Scofield, 11, 283
Theocritus, 276-7, 281
Thirlwall, John C., 29, 43, 46, 70, 83, 303, 323-5, 335, 369, 384
Thomas, Dylan, 244, 281, 283
Thomas, Isobel, 399

Thoreau, Henry David, 24, 371, 378, 380, 381, 382, 383, 394
Tomlinson, Charles, 33, 47, 392-7, 406
Toulouse-Lautrec, Henry de, 396
Townley, Rod, 406
Toynbee, Philip, 388-91, 404
Trédant, Paul, 39, 403
Tree, Iris, 254
Tu Fu, 298
Turnbull, Gael, 31
Twain, Mark, 245, 381

Untermeyer, Jean Starr, 309
Untermeyer, Louis, 21, 121, 400
Unwin, Stanley, 18, 148-9

Valéry, Paul, 170, 358, 387
Van Doren, Carl, 135
Van O'Connor, William, 400, 401
Vickery, John B., 407
Villon, François, 314-15
Vince, T.L., 404
Vogel, Joseph, 17

Wade, Mason, 400
Wagner, Linda Welshimer, 17, 45, 398, 403, 406
Wallace, Emily Mitchell ('A Bibliography of William Carlos Williams'), 5, 17, 39, 43, 48, 50, 75, 384, 398, 405
Walters, Raymond, 403
Walton, Eda Lou, 150-2
Wardle, Irving, 404
Warren, Austin, 121-3
Warren, Robert Penn, 34, 278-9
Watson, James Sibley (W.C. Blum), 11, 68-9

Weatherhead, Kingsley, 39, 406
Weaver, Mike, 13, 36, 43, 44, 45, 46, 89, 112, 396, 406
Webster, H.C., 402
Wells, Henry W., 25, 403
West, Nathanael, 121
West, Rebecca, 290
Whigham, Peter, 369-76
Whitaker, Thomas R., 89, 406
White, William, 398
Whitehead, A.N., 12, 13, 24, 44, 276
Whitman, Alden, 404
Whitman, Walt, 1, 5, 24, 43, 54, 72, 83, 136, 187, 190, 245, 248, 267, 284-5, 286-7, 288, 331, 336, 346, 362, 393, 394, 395
Whittemore, Reed, 42, 47, 305-6, 406
Wilbur, Richard, 207-9, 238, 401
Willard, Nancy, 406
Williams, Florence Herman, 323, 355
Williams, Raquel Helène Rose, 9, 83, 323-6
Willingham, John R., 286-8
Wilson, Edmund, 112
Wilson, T.C., 16
Winters, Yvor, 19-20, 158-62, 288
Woolf, Virginia, 390
Wordsworth, William, 137, 185
Wyat(t), Sir Thomas, 309

Yeats, William Butler, 51, 130, 137, 157, 158, 187, 218, 225, 247, 250, 277, 312, 325, 334, 343, 375, 376

Zabel, Morton Dauwen, 402
Zitner, S.P., 404
Zola, Emile, 22
Zukofsky, Louis, 11, 13, 14, 24, 25, 26, 42, 44-5, 46, 50, 109-17, 124, 136, 137, 169, 310

IV NEWSPAPERS, PERIODICALS, ANTHOLOGIES, AND SMALL PUBLISHERS

'Active Anthology' (Pound), 10
'Agenda', 36, 369-76
Alcestis Press, 11, 16, 409
Alicat Bookshop (press), 411
'American Book Collector', 398
'American Literature', 398
'American Literary Scholarship', 398
'American Mercury', 402
'American Scholar', 322
'American Weave', 403
'Arizona Quarterly', 330-2
'Atlantic Monthly', 246-7, 402, 403, 405

'Black Mountain Review' (Creeley), 146, 341, 402
'Blast' (England), 43
'Blast' (USA), 17, 24, 153
'Blues', 159, 162
'Booklist', 401, 402, 403
'Bookman', 399
'Book Week', 404
'Boston Evening Transcript', 399
'Briarcliff Quarterly', 25, 43, 178-80, 400
'Broom', 250, 399

'Cambridge Opinion', 36, 47
'Camera Work' (Stieglitz), 6, 43, 57

'Canadian Forum', 23, 399, 400
'Catholic Anthology' (Pound), 5
'Chicago Literary Times', 403
'Chicago Sun', 401
'Chicago Sunday Tribune Magazine of Books', 146, 222, 401, 402, 403
'Choice', 404, 405
'Christian Science Monitor', 402, 403, 405
'Cleveland Open Shelf', 401
'Commentary', 402
'Commonweal', 38, 138-9, 210, 399, 400, 402, 403
'Contact' (1920-3; Williams, McAlmon), 8, 10, 44, 62-7, 68, 98-9, 100, 108, 121, 154, 155, 250, 393
'Contact' (1931-2; Williams, McAlmon, Nathanael West), 10, 121-3
Contact Editions, 12, 99, 147, 154, 408
'Criterion' (Eliot), 10, 122
'Criticism', 40
Cummington Press, 23, 410

'Daedalus', 41
'Des Imagistes' (Pound), 5, 68
'Dial', 11, 15, 25, 44, 45, 63, 68-9, 70-3, 124, 283, 399
Dragon Press, 409
'Dynamo', 17

'Egoist' (Pound), 2, 5, 52, 68
'Encounter', 350-2, 392-7
'English Review', 145
'Essays in Criticism', 35, 47

'Focus Five: Modern American Poetry' (Rajan), 34, 47
'Form', 396
'Fortune', 140
'Forum' (USA), 18, 145-8
Four Seas Company (Boston), 68, 408
'Furioso', 305

'Glebe', 82
'Golden Goose', 400, 402, 410

'Harper's' (magazine), 403
Harvest Press, 409
Horace Mann School (publisher), 412
'Hudson Review', 261-71, 318-19, 402

'Imagi', 402

'Jahrbuch für Amerikastudien', 39
'Journal of the British Society of Aesthetics', 202
'Journal of Modern Literature', 398

'Kenyon Review', 29, 127, 158-62, 178, 200-1, 255-7, 400, 401

'Library Journal', 401, 402, 403, 404
'Life', 404
'Listener', 403
'Little Review', 23, 46, 59, 61, 68, 250
'Lyric', 30, 46

'Manchester Guardian
    Weekly', 404
'Manikin', 75-6
'Massachusetts Review',
    38, 46, 153, 403
'Mica', 46
'Migrant', 31, 36
'Modern Drama', 336-9

'Nation', 11, 28, 89-92,
    127-9, 143-5, 150-2,
    166-8, 173, 188-90,
    218-21, 234-6, 274,
    277-9, 286-8, 303-5,
    316-18, 341-3, 353-4,
    399, 401, 404, 405
'National Observer', 404
'New Caravan', 29
'New Democracy', 17, 93
'New Directions', 146, 250,
    323
'New English Weekly', 121-3
'New Freewoman' (Pound),
    52-3
'New Leader', 333-5, 404
'New Masses', 17, 18-19,
    24, 45
'New Republic', 17, 24, 28,
    46, 47, 140, 153-4,
    156-8, 165-6, 236-7,
    253-5, 327-9, 355-9,
    399, 402
'New Statesman', 259,
    385-7, 403, 404
'New Yorker', 21, 399, 400,
    401, 402, 403, 404
'New York Evening Post',
    399
'New York Herald Tribune
    Books', 17, 19, 23, 28,
    29, 112-14, 118-20,
    130-1, 227-8, 272-3,
    399, 400, 401, 402, 403
'New York Independent', 399
'New York Post', 119
'New York Review of Books',
    38, 359-69
'New York Times', 404

'New York Times Book
    Review', 30, 37, 46,
    140-2, 199, 230-1,
    232-3, 275-7, 294-5,
    311-12, 323-5, 399,
    400, 401, 402, 403
'Nouvelles Littéraires',
    39, 403

'Oberon' (Japan), 39
Objectivist Press, 109,
    124, 138, 409
'"Objectivists" Anthology,
    An' (Zukofsky), 14, 109
'Observer', 388-91, 404
'Origin' (Corman), 38
'Others' (Kreymborg), 6,
    82, 92, 250
'Oxford Anthology of
    American Literature',
    112

'Pagany', 18, 45, 121
'Partisan Review' (origin-
    ally 'Partisan Review
    and Anvil'), 17, 18-19,
    45, 143, 163-4, 165,
    169-70, 174-8, 186,
    191-5, 218, 238-41
'Pennsylvania Review', 43,
    50
'Poetry', 2, 4, 5, 16, 18,
    20, 28, 44, 46, 54-8,
    67-8, 75-6, 131-3,
    180-4, 283, 284, 296-
    300, 306-10, 312-15,
    343-5, 384-5, 400, 401,
    402, 404
'Poetry Australia', 403
'Poetry New York', 47, 195
'Poetry Review', 2, 4, 399
'Prairie Schooner', 39, 404
'Psychology', 93
'Publisher's Weekly', 405
'Punch', 404

'Review', 36, 346-50
'Rutherford American', 49

'San Francisco Chronicle', 248-9, 400, 401
'Saturday Review', 28, 37, 152-3, 162, 228-30, 233-4, 250-3, 258-9, 295, 301-2, 399, 400, 401, 402, 403, 405
'Saturday Review of Literature' (later 'Saturday Review'), 84-6, 116-17, 142-3, 399
'Scrutiny', 10, 44
'Secession', 70, 93, 250
'Seven Arts', 101, 287
'Sewanee Review', 31, 146, 184-7, 207-9, 218, 401, 402
'S4N' (Munson), 43
'Shenandoah', 288-93
Shoe String Press, 411
'Soil', 101
'Spectator', 345-6, 404
'Spectrum', 47
'Symposium', 14, 44, 399

'Tel Quel', 387
'Texas Studies in Language and Literature', 92
'This Quarter', 112, 355-6
'Thoth', 398
Three Mountains Press, 12, 147, 154, 408
'Time', 20, 22, 400, 401, 405
'Times', 370
'Times Literary Supplement', 10, 33, 34, 114-16, 147, 223-4, 241-5, 322, 403, 404
To Publishers, 147, 409
'Townsman', 45, 399
'Transatlantic Review', 145
'transition', 112, 116, 118, 119, 250
'Twentieth Century', 47
'Twice a Year', 324
'291' (magazine), 6

'Voices', 402, 403

'Wall Street Journal', 404
'Weekly Book Review', 400
Wells College Press, 410
'Westminster Magazine', 11, 134-8
'William Carlos Williams Newsletter', 42, 47
'Writer', 399

'Yale Review', 21, 29, 34, 36, 195-8, 211-12, 224-6, 305-6, 400, 401, 402, 403, 404

For Product Safety Concerns and Information please contact our EU representative GPSR@taylorandfrancis.com
Taylor & Francis Verlag GmbH, Kaufingerstraße 24, 80331 München, Germany

www.ingramcontent.com/pod-product-compliance
Lightning Source LLC
Chambersburg PA
CBHW051622230426
43669CB00013B/2153